Peter Norton's
PC Problem Solver

Second Edition

Peter Norton

Robert Jourdain

Brady Books

New York London Toronto Sydney Tokyo Singapore

Brady Books

A Division of Prentice Hall Computer Publishing
15 Columbus Circle
New York, NY 10023

ISBN: 1-56686-012-1

Printing Code: The rightmost double-digit number is the year of the book's printing; the rightmost single-digit number is the number of the book's printing. For example, 92-1 shows that the first printing of the book occurred in 1992.

95 94 93 92   4 3 2 1

Manufactured in the United States of America

Credits

Publisher
Michael Violano

Managing Editor
Kelly Dobbs

Editor
Susan Hunt

Production Editor
Kristin Juba

Book Designer
Scott Cook

Cover Designer
HUB Graphics

Editorial Assistant
Lisa Rose

Production Team
Howard Jones
John Kain

This book was typeset using Aldus PageMaker 4.2 on a Macintosh IIci computer with a Radius Color Pivot monitor. Screen reproductions in this book were created by means of the program Collage Plus from Inner Media, Inc. (Hollis, NH).

Contents

Part I. Using Dos Commands

Part II. Making Everything Work Together

Part III. Managing the System

Introduction

In the two years since this book first appeared, the computer industry has barreled along at full steam, leaving in its wake ever more hardware standards, ever more software complexities, and ever more confusion. DOS has acquired many new features, and its Shell program has been completely revamped. Microsoft Windows has flowered into a powerful, but extremely complicated, working environment. And, most software has branched into DOS and Windows versions, each making different demands on computers and their users.

Progress has its price. Today at least four generations of hardware and software coexist, each generation more complex and diverse than the last. We've moved from PCs to ATs to PS/2 machines and on to a vast menagerie of clones and laptops. To install and configure software, you may need to deal with five categories of memory, any of a dozen video standards, several varieties of printers (each with several standards of its own), disk drives and tape units of every imaginable form and capacity, and an endless parade of mice, modems, scanners, and more.

A decade of wild progress is all well and good, but what if you just want to be left alone to get your work done? After all, a Ph.D. in computer science is not for everybody. A lot of people cope with today's complexity by keeping to the straight and narrow. They confine themselves to a handful of DOS commands and largely shun the myriad utility programs available. In essence, they're pretending that it's still 1981, the years PCs first appeared. But, applications software is becoming much more complicated, and to use its advanced features (indeed, to use it at all) you must come to terms with the changing hardware and operating system in which it runs in. Besides, doing things in the supposedly easy way is actually doing them the hard way since a decade's improvements are being ignored.

Peter Norton's PC Problem Solver was written to help you through today's blooming confusion without sitting down to memorize a thousand concepts and ten thousand facts. The book consists of nearly 200 discussions, each describing a task that needs doing and the best ways to get it done. We think you'll find this thematic organization very useful. When a task or problem arises, you can look it up in the detailed table of contents and turn directly to a solution. There's no need to hunt through manuals and books organized by technical terminology.

This volume is intended for computer users at all levels of sophistication. It's been sectionalized so that beginners can avoid the heavy stuff and advanced users can jump directly to what they need to know. The book is heavily cross-referenced so that you can turn elsewhere if you need more information and so you won't be swamped with unneeded material (throughout, you'll find numbers like 12.3 that refer to a chapter and section where related material resides). We assume that you are familiar with the contents of the first third of an introductory DOS book, such as the *Peter Norton's DOS Guide.*

If your background on a specific topic is a little shaky, you can turn to one of the minitutorials found at the beginning of each chapter. They're good for a quick review of essentials or as a crash course in new subjects. You'll also find a long plain-English glossary in back and a detailed index. The motto of our book is: Look it up and get it done!

This is a computer user's book, not a computer buyer's book. We discuss hardware only in so far as you may need to physically reconfigure it to accomplish your goals. Otherwise, we've kept hardware complexities out of the way. We also discuss application software only from the point of view of configuring it to hardware, DOS, or Windows. Utility software, however, is mentioned again and again since it often solves problems better—or at least more efficiently—than DOS.

Peter Norton's PC Problem Solver is divided into three parts. Part I, "Using DOS Commands," presents basic DOS commands in terms of the tasks they perform. We've limited the discussions to the features you really need to know. The arcane and the highly technical have been omitted. In many cases, we've emphasized what can go wrong with DOS commands since DOS is not very helpful when you make mistakes. And, we've added many useful tips and tricks to make your work easier. In parallel, we've shown how each task is performed in the DOS 5.0 Shell program and in Windows 3.1.

Part II, "Making Everything Work Together," tackles the complex problems of making hardware, software, and DOS get along. We show

how to configure each and how to prepare the machine for operation. We've also included chapters about configuring and using modems and printers. New material has been added on memory management and laser printers.

Finally, Part III, "Managing the System," introduces the skills required to run a modern PC system well. The aim is efficiency and high productivity. We explain the wonders of Windows 3.1 and the basics of using Windows to share resources with other computers on a network. We tell how to optimize hard disk performance and manage large numbers of files. Last, but hardly least, we've included three chapters on how to avoid computer disasters and how to recover from disasters when they occur.

We hope *Peter Norton's PC Problem Solver* will find a place beside your computer and that with time your copy will become tattered from heavy use. Further revisions will appear as new developments (and new problems) arise. Happy computing!

Peter Norton
Robert Jourdain

Part I

Using DOS Commands

Chapter 1

Review of DOS Basics

- MINITUTORIAL: How DOS works
- Understanding a DOS manual
- Entering DOS commands
- Using global file name characters
- Dealing with DOS error messages
- Running programs in DOS
- An overview of the DOS Shell
- The DOS Shell file system
- Selecting files in the DOS Shell
- Running programs from the DOS Shell

MINITUTORIAL:
How DOS works

DOS (Disk Operating System) is a collection of programs that make an IBM personal computer work. There are actually two forms of DOS: MS-DOS and IBM-DOS (or PC-DOS). The first is sold by the company that originally developed DOS, Microsoft; most PC clones are sold with MS-DOS. IBM-DOS comes from IBM and is shipped with IBM-brand machines. The two are nearly identical, with MS-DOS tending to offer a few more features than IBM-DOS.

DOS has gone through years of development in which it has acquired more and more capability. Each version is released with a number that identifies it. The first DOS version was 1.0. Over the years, major improvements have brought versions 2.0, 3.0, 4.0, and 5.0. Between these major introductions, other versions have been brought out that include minor improvements (and occasionally important ones). These interim versions are given numbers like 3.1, 3.2, and 3.3. Some versions do nothing more than fix errors and are given a number like 4.01 (a corrected version of DOS 4.0).

The one main DOS program is called COMMAND.COM. When the computer is switched on, it automatically reads COMMAND.COM from a disk drive and puts it in charge of the machine. COMMAND.COM takes care of essential tasks like reading data from disk drives. Once COMMAND.COM is in control, you can run application programs like word processors and databases.

Besides doing the basic work of managing the computer, DOS provides a number of commands by which you can manage the files on the computer's disk drives, as well as exert certain kinds of control over the machine's printer, video display, and so on. For example, you can use the COPY command to copy a file from one disk drive to another. Or you can use the DIR command to see a listing of file names.

In the simplest case, when DOS takes charge of the machine at start-up, it places a symbol that looks like A> or C> on the left edge of the screen. This is called the DOS prompt. It is where you type in DOS commands. The cursor (flashing bar) on the screen appears next to this prompt. Once you type in a DOS command, like DIR, you press the ⏎ key, and DOS carries out the command; in this case, displaying a listing of files. Because commands are entered in this way, the line on the screen started by the DOS prompt is called the DOS command line.

After you have typed in a DOS command and pressed ⏎, DOS carries out (executes) the command. Once the command is finished, a new DOS prompt appears on the screen below the one just used. One command after another may be entered; the screen scrolls upward to make room for more.

When there has been an error in the way you typed a command, or there is some problem in completing a command, DOS displays an error message. Even when a command goes well, DOS may display some kind of message on the screen, perhaps to elicit further input from you. This book helps you to understand many of the error messages you may encounter; do not, however, neglect the complete alphabetical listing of error messages found in the back of your DOS manual.

Running software   When you want to start up an application program, say, a word processor, you just type its name on the DOS command line and then press ⏎. A program's name is the same as the name of the disk file that holds the program. For instance, if you're using the WordPerfect word processor, you would learn from its documentation that the name of the program is WP, so you would type WP ⏎ on the command line. The program would then be read from a disk and transferred to the computer's internal memory, after which it would appear on the screen.

Some application software allows you to place additional information on the command line, such as the name of the first document (data file) you want to work with. Thus, a command like WP MYFILE.TXT ⏎ would not only start up the word processor, but would also cause the word processor to load the document named MYFILE.TXT so that you could work with it. Generally speaking, it does not matter whether you use upper- or lowercase letters when you type in commands, but some software may be less flexible.

When a program is running, the DOS prompt (A>, B>, C>, etc.) disappears from the screen. You are then in the program, not in DOS. When you have finished work in a program, you quit (exit, terminate) and return to DOS, and the DOS prompt reappears to await your next command. If you need to use one of the DOS commands while inside an application program, perhaps to move a file from one place to another, you usually must quit first. In some applications, however, you can use some DOS commands without quitting (the application program's documentation will explain how).

Internal and external DOS commands   The main DOS program, COMMAND.COM, stays in the computer's memory at all times. It performs many of the most common DOS commands, like COPY, ERASE, RENAME, and DIR. However, some DOS commands are carried out by software that is not part of COMMAND.COM (CHKDSK and XCOPY, for example). The software for these commands is held in separate files, one file for each command. A file must be loaded into memory before the command can be executed. For this reason, these are called external commands, just as the commands performed by COMMAND.COM are called internal commands (DOS manuals indicate whether a command is internal or external). The files holding the external commands are found on the DOS diskettes and may be transferred to your hard disk.

If you enter an external command on the DOS command line and DOS responds with the error message, "Bad command or file name," it may be that DOS has not been able to find the file that holds the command. The required file may be in some other subdirectory on your hard disk drive. You'll need to tell DOS where to find it—this chapter and the minitutorials that introduce Chapters 5 and 6 will teach you how.

1.1 Understanding a DOS manual

DOS comes to you with a number of programs distributed on two or more diskettes, plus a manual to explain how these programs work. The manual is essentially a reference that also tries to be a tutorial. The tutorial aspects have improved with every DOS version, but many newcomers still find the manual forbidding. To the beginner, it is one page of gobbledygook after another, so the manual goes on a shelf and stays there. This is unfortunate: A DOS manual is not nearly so incomprehensible as it first seems and is packed with information that will get you out of trouble, save you time, and make your computer work much better. Although books like this one can largely stand in for a DOS manual, there may still be occasions when you'll need to consult a manual about obscure DOS features.

DOS manuals differ, depending on the DOS version and whether the manual accompanies MS-DOS or IBM-DOS. However, all have basically the same contents and presentation. You'll find:

- A general discussion of how DOS works, including discussions on the DOS command line, directories and directory trees, and basic rules for forming DOS commands and file names.

- In DOS 4.0 and 5.0, a discussion of the DOS Shell—a program that makes many DOS commands easier through a tree diagram, menuing system, and pull-down menus.

- A section on formatting diskettes and hard disks.

- A section explaining how to configure DOS so that it works properly with your computer equipment and software.

- A listing of all DOS commands, such as DIR and COPY. These listings take up about half of most DOS manuals.

- A section explaining how to make batch files, which are a special kind of file in which you store a number of DOS commands that may then be carried out automatically by just running the file.

- A listing of all messages that DOS writes on the screen, including many error messages that appear when something goes wrong. Recent DOS manuals tend to integrate these messages with the discussions of individual commands instead of lumping them together at the end of the manual.

■ A miscellany of short sections concerning foreign language alphabets and keyboard layouts.

Two sections in the manual are consulted most often: the listings of commands and messages. The commands section is divided into individual sections for each command, which are listed alphabetically from APPEND to XCOPY. Each section has several headings, starting with the command's purpose. These definitions are often far from comprehensible, even to people who are adept at using personal computers. Generally speaking, you're better off learning about DOS capabilities from a good book about DOS and then turning to the manual when you already understand a command's basic purpose.

Next comes a description of the command's format. The format tells the precise way in which the parts of the command must be entered on the DOS command line. The format is also sometimes called the command's syntax. When a DOS command won't work properly, the problem often is that you haven't entered it in the proper format. A quick look in the DOS manual can set things right. Unfortunately, a DOS manual may describe a command's format in a way that can sometimes appear like high mathematics. In fact, the system is not very complicated, as section 1.2 explains.

The format contains a number of words written in italics, such as *path* or *file name*. These words refer to the information you must enter in their place, such as the directory path to a file or a file's name. Such words are called parameters. Most manuals provide a list of parameters after presenting a command's syntax, giving details for each.

The command reference also tells the command type, marking it as internal or external. When it is internal, the command is performed by the main DOS program, COMMAND.COM. Since this file is always in memory, the command is always at your disposal. When the command is external, it is held in a separate file that bears the same name as the command. This file will have either a .COM or .EXE extension. Thus, the TREE command is found in the file TREE.COM. When the required file is not on hand, DOS issues a "Bad command or file name" message.

Most manuals also present a series of remarks that explain the meaning of the terms given for the command's format. Many of these are the same from command to command. But sometimes the only way to understand a command's format is to consult these remarks. Remarks are sometimes followed by notes, which often contain important information about a command's limitations and sometimes contain warnings against misapplication of the command.

Finally, all documentation gives examples of how a command is used. These tend to show the command in a simple application; they won't necessarily work properly if you just type them in without making adjustments for your computer's characteristics.

If you type in a command and receive an error message you cannot understand, turn to the alphabetical listing of DOS messages contained in the back of any DOS manual. You'll find an explanation of each message and an action that should be taken in response. These explanations are often quite clear, but you won't be able to comprehend them if you don't really understand the commands you are using. In the end, you'll save a lot of time by learning how to use DOS properly, rather than constantly dealing with error messages.

▮1.2▮ Entering DOS commands

DOS manuals contain an alphabetical listing of all DOS commands. Each entry gives a format for the command, telling how to construct the command so that it will work in a particular way. Even for a simple command like DIR, the format is cryptic:

```
DIR [d:][path][filename[.ext]][/P][/W]
```

As intimidating as this line may appear at first glance, such formats are really quite simple, and it is well worth your while to understand how they work. (Incidentally, IBM-DOS 4.0 manuals—but not those for MS-DOS 4.0—have dispensed with this notation and teach by example instead). Here are the steps to analyze a command.

The command name   A command begins with the command name, such as DIR, BACKUP, ERASE, RENAME, and so on. You always begin by typing in this name (well, almost always—see the discussion of external commands below). A few commands have both long and abbreviated forms. For example, CHDIR (Change Directory) can also be written as CD. The only point in this is to save you a little typing. Some commands are used so much that it really does save you time to learn to use the short, more cryptic forms.

Required parameters   The command name is followed by a number of other words that direct the action of the command to a particular disk or directory or that modify the command in some way. These are called parameters. For example:

```
RENAME filename filename
```

tells you that the command RENAME is always followed by two parameters, each a file name (the remarks section of the command's documentation explains that the first file name is the current file name and that the second is the new name you want assigned to the file).

Optional parameters   Parameters enclosed in brackets, [and], are optional—the command can work without them. The options give you greater control over the command. For instance:

```
DIR [filename]
```

tells you that a file name is optional; typing DIR ⏎ alone gives a directory listing of all files in the current directory. When you follow

DIR with a file name, the command behaves differently, listing just the one file and information about its size and date. Thus, the DIR command can search for individual files as well as list a group of them. Such features are explained in the DOS manual under the remarks or comments given for each command.

When brackets are placed within other brackets, as in [filename[.ext]], the inner brackets are an option available when the option given by the outer brackets is taken, but not otherwise. So, in this case, if you choose to list a file name, it may or may not have an extension. But you cannot include an extension in the command without choosing to include a file name.

Specifying files   Whenever a file name is specified in a DOS command, three options are always allowed. These options let you specify the location of the file. The options are:

1. You may precede the name of the file with a drive specifier, such as A:, B:, or C:, to name the disk drive where the file resides. For example, if you are seeking the directory listing for a file called MYFILE, and the current drive is drive C (making the DOS prompt look like C>), then you can specify that the file is found on drive A by typing:

    `DIR A:MYFILE` ⏎

2. Similarly, when a disk uses a directory tree to divide its files among many directories, you can specify the path to the file's subdirectory by writing it before the file name in standard DOS format (we cover this in the minitutorial in Chapter 5). If the file MYFILE is found in the subdirectory CATS, and this subdirectory is found along the path \ANIMALS\MAMMALS\CATS, then you can have the DIR command list the file by writing:

    `DIR \ANIMALS\MAMMALS\CATS\MYFILE` ⏎

    If you wish to use the drive specifier option as well, it must precede the directory path:

    `DIR C:\ANIMALS\MAMMALS\CATS\MYFILE` ⏎

3. Finally, any file name you include in a DOS command may be followed by a file name extension. The file name MYFILE.TXT, for example, has a .TXT extension. Whenever a command oper-

ates on a file whose name includes an extension, you must include the extension in the command. To DOS, the file MYFILE.TXT, with an extension, is considered an entirely different file than MYFILE. To see its directory listing, you would need to enter:

```
DIR MYFILE.TXT ⏎
```

In DOS manuals, the options for file names, extensions, drive specifiers, and directory paths clutter the formats given for the various commands. You'll see:

```
[d:][path]filename[.ext]
```

when a file name is required or:

```
[d:][path][filename][.ext]
```

when a file name is optional. The formats of DOS commands will not seem so complicated once you learn to see through this familiar pattern.

Switches   Many DOS commands end with one or more optional switches. A switch is just that, a means of turning a feature on (and sometimes off). Switches always begin with a slash character, / (not to be confused with the backslash, \), followed by a single letter. Again using the DIR command as an example, the /W switch causes the directory to be displayed in a compressed, five-column format:

```
DIR /W ⏎
```

In the DOS manual, when you see one or more switches listed in a command's format, look in the remarks or comments section to find out what each does. Note that sometimes a switch requires a value. The command format might contain an option like:

```
[/B:buffsiz]
```

meaning, in this case, that you may optionally instruct the command to create a buffer (a holding place in memory) of a specified size. If the desired size were to be 1,000 bytes, you would write the switch into the command this way:

```
/B:1000
```

Punctuation   A few DOS commands use a series of numbers or characters separated by commas. For example, a MODE command could look like this:

```
MODE lpt1:132,6,P
```

This command for setting up a printer is complicated and there is no need to be concerned about it here. But there is one point you should understand: When one of the values on the line is optional, and you want to omit it, you must include its comma anyway. If you didn't want to specify the value 6 in this particular command, you would type:

```
MODE lpt1:132,,P
```

External commands   Not all DOS commands are performed by the main DOS program that is loaded into memory when the computer starts up. Many commands are carried out by software stored in individual files found on the DOS diskettes and transferred to a hard disk during DOS installation. These external commands, including CHKDSK, BACKUP, and RECOVER, are actually individual utility programs. Like any other piece of software, they are run by typing the command name on the command line and pressing ⏎. The various options you choose for the command are then passed to the program the same way a file name is passed to an application program when it starts up.

Because these commands are actually stand-alone programs, DOS needs to know how to find the program file when it is not in the current drive and directory. This is done by typing in a path to the file that holds the command, then the command name, and then the rest of the command and its options. Let's say, for example, that you are working at drive A and you want to use CHKDSK, with the CHKDSK program file located along the path \UTILITY\DOS on drive C. If you only typed:

```
CHKDSK ⏎
```

at the A> prompt, DOS would simply look in drive A for the file. Instead, you must enter:

```
C:\UTILITY\DOS\CHKDSK ⏎
```

to specify for DOS the drive and the path of the CHKDSK utility. Options allowed with CHKDSK, such as a drive specifier and the /V switch, are used in the usual way:

```
C:\UTILITY\DOS\CHKDSK A: /V ⏎
```

In this example, DOS looks for the CHKDSK file in the \UTILITY\DOS subdirectory of drive C, directs CHKDSK to operate on drive A, and, by the /V switch, asks CHKDSK to list files as it examines them.

Recalling prior commands in DOS 5.0　　The DOSKEY program introduced with DOS 5.0 lets you view recent DOS commands, edit them, and reuse them. This memory-resident program is started by just typing DOSKEY ⏎. Once it is loaded, you can use the ⬆ and ⬇ keys to view earlier commands. Pressing ⬆ shows the prior command, and pressing it again shows the command before that one. Conversely, pressing ⬇ displays the command that followed the one currently displayed. You can see the oldest command used in your current work session by pressing PgUp and the most recent by pressing PgDn.

DOSKEY lets you edit the command line, regardless of whether the command line holds a command you've just typed in or an earlier command you've recalled. The ⬅ and ➡ keys move the cursor across the command line. Alternatively, you can use Ctrl-⬅ and Ctrl-➡ to shift the cursor by whole words or Home and End to jump the cursor to the beginning or end of the command. Once editing is complete, press ⏎ as always to put the command into effect.

1.3 Using global file name characters

Many DOS commands can act on groups of files. For example, several files could be copied from one disk to another with only one COPY command, rather than by several individual commands. You can erase groups of files in similar fashion or rename them. These group operations are performed by means of global file name characters (sometimes called wild-card characters), of which there are only two: the asterisk and question mark. (Because of this special use, these characters may not be used in file names.) Let's begin with the question mark.

The question mark   The question mark stands for unspecified individual characters in a file name. Consider the command:

        COPY MYFILE.TXT B: ⏎

This command copies the file MYFILE.TXT to drive B. If instead you enter:

        COPY MYFILE.TX? B: ⏎

DOS copies all files in which the file name is MYFILE and the extension is TX followed by any character to drive B. If there were a series of files named MYFILE.TX1, MYFILE.TX2, MYFILE.TX3, and so on, then all would be copied. Similarly, the expression:

        COPY MYFILE.??? B: ⏎

copies all files with the name MYFILE and any extension. The files MYFILE.TXT, MYFILE.OVL, and MYFILE.DOC would all be copied. The question mark can as easily appear in the file name itself:

        COPY MYFILE?.TXT B: ⏎

In this case, files named MYFILE1.TXT, MYFILE2.TXT, MYFILE3.TXT, and the like, would be copied. Question marks could replace every character in a file name. The command:

        COPY ????????.??? B: ⏎

copies all files to drive B.

The asterisk   The second global file name character, the asterisk, takes the place of sequences of question marks. For example:

```
COPY MYFILE.* B: [←]    is the same as  COPY MYFILE.??? B: [←]
COPY *.TXT B: [←]       is the same as  COPY ????????.TXT B: [←]
COPY *.* B: [←]         is the same as  COPY ????????.??? B: [←]
```

The asterisk may replace just part of a file name or extension. For instance:

```
COPY MY*.TXT [←]
```

copies MYFILE.TXT, MYPOEM.TXT, and MYREPORT.TXT (but not MYFILE.DOC since the extension differs). The asterisk represents any number of characters (up to the eight allowed) following the initial MY.

The use of the asterisk and question mark is not quite so straight-forward as it first appears, however. Reconsider the example:

```
COPY MYFILE.TX? B: [←]
```

This command would not only copy over files with names like MYFILE.TX1 and MYFILE.TX2, but also the file MYFILE.TX. This means that the question mark can even represent no character at all. Similarly:

```
COPY MY*.TXT B: [←]
```

would copy to drive B not only the files MYFILE.TXT and MY-REPORT.TXT, but also just MY.TXT. Note that the command:

```
COPY MY??????.TXT B: [←]
```

would do the same, copying files with varying length file names even though the question marks demarcate six characters.

Pitfalls in using asterisks   Beware of leading asterisks. They may not behave as you would guess. The command:

```
COPY MY*.TXT B: [←]
```

copies files with names like MYSTORY.TXT and MYPOEM.TXT to drive B. By extension, you might think that:

```
COPY *FILE.TXT B: [←]
```

would copy all files that have FILE as the last four characters of the file name. But the asterisk takes precedence over any characters that follow it up to the period separating the file name from its extension. Hence, this command is identical to:

```
COPY *.TXT B: [←]
```

The same is true within a file name extension. The command:

```
COPY MYFILE.*T B: [←]
```

is equivalent to:

```
COPY MYFILE.* B: [←]
```

Dangers of using global file name characters   Using global file name characters in erase commands is risky since an error can result in massive data loss. In fact, when DOS encounters the ERASE *.* (or DEL *.*) command, it issues a message asking whether you really want everything erased. But, in any other case, DOS immediately carries out the command and erases the files.

Although global file name characters can play greatest havoc through a faulty ERASE command, they also do their share of mischief in other ways. When making a mass COPY, be extra careful that the files are directed to the proper disk and directory. Otherwise, you'll end up wasting a lot of time hunting down and removing file copies that have ended up in the wrong place. Follow this rule: When you use an asterisk or question mark, pause before pressing the [←] key and reread what you have typed. If you're unsure that the proper files are selected, request a directory listing using the same specification.

These dangers can be avoided by using a DOS Shell like the Norton Commander. They eliminate the need for—or, at least, greatly ease the burden of using—global shorthand.

Commands that can't use global file name characters   Some DOS commands can't use global file name characters. For example, the TYPE command, which displays a file, expects the name of a single file. If you enter:

```
TYPE *.DOC [←]
```

you'll encounter an error message because TYPE cannot display a sequence of files. However, you can use the FOR command to achieve the desired effect. This command is normally used in batch files (section 9.1), but it also works from the DOS command line in a slightly modified form. To make TYPE display all files ending with .DOC, use:

```
FOR %F IN (*.DOC) DO TYPE %F [←]
```

You don't need to understand how this command works to use it (see section 9.5 for an explanation). Simply type the file name, complete with global file name characters, within the parentheses, and insert the DOS command name between the words DO and %F.

1.4 Dealing with DOS error messages

When you type in a DOS command and press ⏎, DOS tries to make sense of what you've typed. When it can't, it issues an error message. You'll find a listing of all error messages in the back of any DOS manual. There are hundreds of these messages, most of which you'll never see. Many are stored inside the main DOS file, COMMAND.COM, where they take up a good deal of memory. To conserve space, the messages are kept as short as possible, and this often makes them cryptic even to experienced PC users. In addition, DOS makes only a limited analysis of what has gone wrong, so it may issue an ambiguous message (like "Bad command or file name") that isn't much help in determining where you have gone wrong.

Three kinds of error messages appear on the screen:

- Start-up error messages: These are not actually DOS error messages, but rather those contained in a small part of the operating system that is built right into the machine. As the machine starts up, it performs a number of tests on itself. A very short message appears on the screen when a hardware error occurs; often the message is nothing more than a reference number. For example, a number ending in 03 points to a keyboard error; 06 to a disk drive error. The message "PARITY CHECK 1" indicates a faulty memory chip. Sometimes the problem can be remedied by replacing the malfunctioning component, but usually only a skilled technician can make the actual repairs. Chapter 24 contains advice for interpreting and dealing with start-up error messages. DOS manuals do not list these errors.

- Command error messages: Most messages that DOS displays on the screen result from interactions with DOS commands. Not all are error messages—some tell you that things have gone successfully or what to do next. And, when the messages do convey an error, they report a problem that can be solved by using DOS properly. Generally, you can remedy the problem by entering the command again, this time with its errors corrected. Sometimes a command will not work because DOS cannot find a file, and you must modify the command to include a directory path to the file.

Occasionally, you must reconfigure the machine to get the command working. For example, you might need to deinstall memory-resident programs when DOS reports that memory is insufficient.

■ Device error messages: These messages occur only after you have successfully booted the computer and typed in a DOS command. Like start-up error messages, device error messages report that something has gone wrong with your computer hardware. This is to say that you have correctly typed in a DOS command, but DOS cannot make the computer carry it out. These messages may indicate that your hardware—particularly a disk drive—is in need of repair or that a diskette has gone bad. But sometimes the problem is trivial. For example, the message "Drive not ready error" occurs when you've failed to close the door to a diskette drive that the machine is attempting to use.

Many device errors result from an improperly functioning disk drive. Disk drives can go out of alignment (especially much-used disk drives in machines without a hard disk). As we explain in the minitutorial in Chapter 24, hard disks can also fail in a multitude of ways. Many kinds of disk drive failures occur gradually. When the drive fails to read or write data, DOS tries again and again. If the drive still won't come around, DOS issues a message like:

```
General Failure error reading drive A
Abort, Retry, Ignore, Fail?
```

In response to this message, you must enter Ⓐ, Ⓡ, Ⓘ, or Ⓕ, corresponding to one of the four choices offered. Their meaning is as follows:

■ Abort: This choice quits the program and returns to the DOS prompt. This is the last of the four options you should try since you are likely to lose work that wasn't saved before the error occurred (well-crafted software can sometimes avoid such data loss).

■ Retry: This option makes DOS go back for another round of trying to write or read data to or from a disk. When a disk drive is having problems, but isn't completely out of whack, you may be able to complete the disk operation by requesting a retry one or more times. This action only takes a second or two and is always worth trying at least once.

■ Ignore or Fail: These two responses are similar. They cause the software that is accessing the disk to continue working, despite the failure to store or read data. Fail is superior to Ignore in that it helps the software realize that something has gone wrong and what the problem may be, so that the software's own error-recovery facilities may come into play (in fact, sometimes the Ignore option is not offered). In either case, the software may become confused, and it may be dangerous to go on working as though everything is all right. It's a good idea to quit the program and then restart it. If you have data you want to save before quitting, try saving it under a different file name or to a different diskette or subdirectory so that the original data file won't be ruined should the data be corrupted.

If you're lucky enough to get past the error by selecting Retry, count your blessings and respond to the problem at once. Otherwise, it is sure to recur. Often, one of the disk sectors holding the file has gone bad. Make a copy of the file, if you can, and then run a disk repair utility, such as the Norton Disk Doctor program found in the Norton Utilities. The utility will see to it that the bad disk sector won't be used again. When the error message occurs with a diskette, you can copy all files on the diskette over to an empty diskette and discard the one giving you trouble (you can try reformatting the faulty diskette and using it again, but it's risky to trust your data to it even if it formats successfully).

When a disk drive causes the "Abort, Retry, Ignore, Fail?" error message for many files, the problem is probably in the drive mechanics and not in disk sectors. On hard disk drives, this is an extremely serious condition that must not be ignored. Make backups of as much data as you can and then run the Norton Disk Doctor or some other diagnostic utility for an indication of what has gone wrong. Repairs or replacement of the drive may be inevitable. (We discuss hard disk drive malfunctions in section 24.4). On diskette drives, the problem is sometimes attributable to dust and grime inside the drive. Purchase a diskette drive cleaning kit (they're available in any software shop), read the instructions, and clean the drive. No improvement probably means that the drive is going out of alignment and needs to be taken to a repair shop for maintenance.

1.5 Running programs in DOS

To start an application program running in DOS, just type the program's name at the DOS prompt and press the ⏎ (the Enter key). The program's name, however, often is an abbreviated form of the name by which the program is sold. For example, the popular WordPerfect program is started up by typing WP, not WORDPERFECT:

    C>WP ⏎

A program's documentation will tell you the name you should type at the DOS prompt. It doesn't matter whether you use upper- or lowercase letters. Usually, the program is held in a file that has this name and that ends with either an .EXE or .COM extension (these extensions always indicate that a file is a program file). However, programs can also be launched from a batch file (section 9.1), which means that the file bearing the program name—the name you need to type to run the program—will end with a .BAT extension.

In the example above, the DOS prompt is C>, meaning that drive C (a hard disk drive) is the current drive. DOS expects to find the WordPerfect program file on this drive, under the name WP.EXE (or WP.COM or WP.BAT). If the program file was on a diskette in drive A, you could start up the program in the same way:

    A>WP ⏎

However, if drive C is the current drive, and not A, you must make A current by entering:

    C>A: ⏎

Alternatively, you can start up the program while drive C remains current by placing a drive specifier before the name of the file:

    C>A:WP ⏎

Be aware that DOS looks first for the .COM extension, then the .EXE extension, and then the .BAT extension. Should the file WP.BAT be in the same directory as WP.EXE, the command WP ⏎ will load WP.EXE.

Running programs located outside the current directory   Everything becomes much more complicated if the program resides on a disk that uses a directory tree. Such disks have their files divided among many directories that are arranged in a hierarchy. The tree starts with a root directory; various subdirectories branch from the root directory, more subdirectories branch from these first-level subdirectories, and so on. Read the minitutorial at the beginning of Chapter 5 for an overview of directory trees.

If WordPerfect were held somewhere in the directory tree of drive C, the directory that contains the program must be the current directory to load it by the command WP ⏎. Were WordPerfect to reside in a subdirectory named TEXTEDIT, and TEXTEDIT were not the current directory, you would have two choices for loading the program. You would either need to use the CHDIR command (section 6.3) to make TEXTEDIT the current directory and then load the program:

```
C>CHDIR \SUBDIR1\SUBDIR2\TEXTEDIT ⏎
C>WP ⏎
```

or you could load the program directly by typing in its directory path along with the program name:

```
C>SUBDIR1\SUBDIR2\TEXTEDIT\WP ⏎
```

DOS also provides a way of finding program files automatically without typing in directory paths. This is done by the PATH command (section 8.1), which lets you specify directories that are to be searched when a program file is not found in the current directory.

Command line parameters   Many programs take command line parameters. These are words that follow the program name when you type it in. The most common parameter is the name of the file that should be loaded as the program starts up. For example, in:

```
C>WP BIGFILE.DOC ⏎
```

the file BIGFILE.DOC is loaded by WP and immediately presented on screen. When BIGFILE.DOC is not in the same directory as the WP program, you'll need to specify a path to it, as in:

```
C>WP B:BIGFILE.DOC ⏎
```

or:

```
C>WP \SUBDIR1\SUBDIR2\BIGFILE.DOC ⏎
```

In fact, both the program name and its parameters can take a directory path or drive specifier:

```
C>\SOFTWARE\WP C:\SUBDIR1\SUBDIR2\BIGFILE.DOC ⏎
```

Auxiliary program files   Many programs constantly access a number of files that they create and maintain for their own purposes. Often such files are shipped with the program and must be installed on the disk from which you run the program. It's essential that the files are properly installed so that the program can find them. Otherwise, you'll encounter error messages (usually when the program starts up) reporting that the program is unable to find files you may have never heard of. Read section 12.2 to learn about software installation.

1.6 An overview of the DOS Shell

Starting with version 4.0, DOS includes a shell program. A shell is a kind of software that wraps around the operating system to present an easier-to-use interface between user and machine. Besides simplifying many DOS commands, the shell adds several important features, such as the ability to apply single DOS commands to a group of files selected manually from directory listings.

Many other DOS shells are available from independent software companies, most offering more features than the shell packaged with DOS. DOS 5.0 introduced an improved version of the shell that is closer in design to Microsoft Windows. It is this version that is used in examples throughout this book.

Unlike plain DOS, the DOS Shell lets you use a mouse. If you're not familiar with mice, see section 10.8. A mouse is especially useful in the DOS Shell for moving the cursor to any position in a directory listing to select a file for some action (such as COPY, ERASE, or RENAME). It also lets you choose options from menus without remembering keyboard codes. The DOS Shell does not require a mouse for its use, however. The cursor can still be controlled by the cursor keys on the keyboard.

Starting up the DOS Shell   The Shell is nothing more than a utility program that runs under DOS. It is divided among several files and is started up from the file DOSSHELL.BAT by entering:

    DOSSHELL ⏎

You must use the installation program that accompanies DOS to coordinate the DOS Shell files properly. To invoke the DOS Shell automatically when the computer is turned on, make DOSSHELL the last line in your AUTOEXEC.BAT file (section 11.1).

The screen layout   When you start the DOS Shell, it initially displays a screen labeled *MS-DOS Shell*, as shown in figure 1.1. The screen is divided horizontally, with the upper half holding a directory tree diagram on the left and a directory listing on the right. Just above are symbols representing each disk drive. This is the file system that is discussed in detail in the next section.

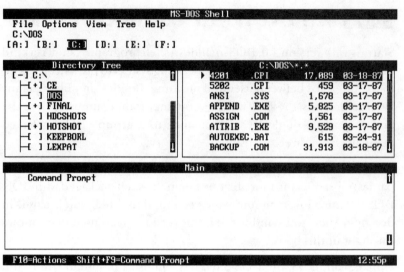

```
                            MS-DOS Shell
   File  Options  View  Tree  Help
   C:\DOS
   [A:]  [B:]  [C:]  [D:]  [E:]  [F:]

  ┌──────── Directory Tree ────────┐┌──────── C:\DOS\*.* ────────┐
  [-] C:\                          ↑│▶ 4201     .CPI    17,089  03-18-87 ↑│
   ─[+] CE                          │  5202     .CPI       459  03-17-87  │
   ─[ ] DOS                         │  ANSI     .SYS     1,678  03-17-87  │
   ─[+] FINAL                       │  APPEND   .EXE     5,825  03-17-87  │
   ─[ ] HDCSHOTS                    │  ASSIGN   .COM     1,561  03-17-87  │
   ─[+] HOTSHOT                     │  ATTRIB   .EXE     9,529  03-17-87  │
   ─[ ] KEEPBORL                    │  AUTOEXEC .BAT       615  03-24-91  │
   ─[ ] LEXPAT                     ↓│  BACKUP   .COM    31,913  03-18-87 ↓│
  └────────────────────────────────┘└─────────────────────────────┘

  ┌──────────────────────────── Main ────────────────────────────┐
  │  Command Prompt                                              ↑│
  │                                                               │
  │                                                               │
  │                                                               │
  │                                                              ↓│
  └───────────────────────────────────────────────────────────────┘

  F10=Actions   Shift+F9=Command Prompt                    12:55p
```

Figure 1.1

The lower half of the screen is labeled *Main*. It holds a list of individual programs or groups of programs. These programs can be started up just by choosing them from the menu. The list includes programs that accompany the DOS Shell as well as any programs that have been installed in the listing. A bar cursor (highlighted line) may be moved up and down the list of choices offered using the cursor keys or the mouse. Once the bar cursor is over the desired selection, you need merely press ⏎ (or click a mouse button) to start up the desired function. Initially four choices are offered:

- If you select Command Prompt, you're given an ordinary DOS prompt (such as A>) for entering ordinary DOS commands. This feature is necessary because some DOS commands, particularly configuration commands, are not available through the Shell. Once you've finished work on the command line, type exit ⏎ to return to the Shell.

- When you choose Editor, you start up a general-purpose text editor included with DOS 5.0. An editor is a simple word processor that is useful for tasks like editing your CONFIG.SYS and AUTOEXEC.BAT files. It cannot handle type styles like italics and boldface or fancy text formatting of any kind. It is unlikely that this program can read files created by your word processor.

■ Choosing MS-DOS QBasic starts up the BASIC programming language, which is mostly used for writing short utility programs. It takes special training to use this program.

■ Selecting Disk Utilities takes you to a submenu of utility programs for formatting, copying, comparing, and backing up disks. Each of these choices is discussed under its related heading in this book.

In addition to programs (or the DOS Prompt option) listed in the Main window, there are also a number of facilities available through the pull-down menus at the top of the screen. These are as follows:

■ File: This menu lists options for managing files, such as Copy, Search, and Rename. See the next section for details.

■ Options: This menu offers a potpourri of features for specifying how the Shell should work. For example, you can set screen colors or the display mode. In this book, you'll find discussions of these options along with the commands to which they are related.

■ View: This menu determines what information is displayed by the Shell. Instead of the split screen the Shell displays the first time you start it up, you can choose to have only the Program List, only a File List (directory tree and directory listings), or Dual File Lists to show directory trees for two disk drives at once. You can change views as you need to. Whichever view was in force when you quit the DOS Shell will be the view in which the Shell next starts up.

■ Help: This menu gives access to a number of on-line help files.

It's easiest to use the menus with a mouse. Although they're called pull-down menus, the Shell is designed so that a menu opens with a click of the mouse and stays open. You then click again on a menu choice or click outside the menu to close it without making a choice.

Menus can also be opened from the keyboard by typing [Alt] and the first letter of the menu name, such as [Alt]-[V] for the View menu. Then do the same for the menu selection, using whatever character is highlighted in the menu listing. For example, the Rename command highlights the letter *n*, so you would invoke the command by typing [Alt]-[N] after pulling down the File menu by typing [Alt]-[F].

█1.7█ The DOS Shell file system

The heart of the DOS Shell is the file system, facilities for managing files by directly accessing them in directory listings and directory tree diagrams. The file system is usually in view when the Shell starts up. If it's not, it can be brought into view by choosing Single File List from the View menu.

The file system screen is divided into several parts, as figure 1.2 shows. At the top, just below the pull-down menus, the DOS path for the current directory is displayed. Beneath the path is a bar of symbols, one for each disk drive. And below that, the screen is divided between a directory tree diagram on the left and a directory listing on the right.

```
                        MS-DOS Shell
  File  Options  View  Tree  Help
  C:\DOS
 [A:] [B:]  [C:]  [D:] [E:] [F:]

┌─────Directory Tree─────┐        C:\DOS\*.*
 [-] C:\                  ↑  → ► 4201    .CPI    17,089  03-18-87 ↑
  ┤+] CE                        5202    .CPI       459  03-17-87
  ┤ ] DOS                       ANSI    .SYS     1,678  03-17-87
  ┤+] FINAL                     APPEND  .EXE     5,825  03-17-87
  ┤ ] HDCSHOTS                  ASSIGN  .COM     1,561  03-17-87
  ┤+] HOTSHOT                   ATTRIB  .EXE     9,529  03-17-87
  ┤ ] KEEPBORL                  AUTOEXEC.BAT       615  03-24-91
  ┤ ] LEXPAT                    BACKUP  .COM    31,913  03-18-87
  ┤+] MACLINK                   BASIC   .COM     1,063  03-17-87
  ┤ ] NBACKUP                   BASIC   .PIF       369  03-17-87
  ┤ ] SAMPLES                   BASICA  .COM    36,403  03-17-87
  ┤ ] SHOTCOPY                  BASICA  .PIF       369  03-17-87
  ┤ ] TREES                     CHKDSK  .COM     9,850  03-18-87
  ┤ ] TROA                      COMMAND .COM    25,307  03-17-87
  ┤+] UTIL                      COMP    .COM     4,214  03-17-87
  ┤+] WINDOWS                   CONFIG  .SYS       249  04-14-91
  ┤ ] WP                 ↓      COUNTRY .SYS    11,285  03-17-87 ↓

 F10=Actions  Shift+F9=Command Prompt                    12:56p
```

Figure 1.2

Moving the cursor   Within the listings, there is always a bar cursor over one of the drive symbols, one of the tree directories, and one of the file listings. However, only one of these cursors will be current in the sense that it can be moved by the cursor keys. In trees and listings, a small arrow marks the cursor if it has been selected either by a click of the mouse or by pressing [Tab] repeatedly to cycle the arrow between screen areas. Only then can you use cursor keys to move a bar cursor over a drive symbol, directory, or file.

Changing drives   The tree diagram always shows the directory tree of the currently selected drive. To change to a different drive, click on that drive's symbol or move the bar cursor over the symbol and press ⏎. A few moments will pass as information is read from the drive, and then its directory tree will be displayed. Disks that have no subdirectories display a tree diagram consisting of just the root directory, such as A:\ or B:\. An arrowhead symbol appears in the tree diagram at the left edge of the current directory. By moving the bar cursor within the tree and then pressing ⏎, a new current directory is chosen. The arrowhead shifts to that position in the tree, and a file listing for the new active directory appears in the right window on the screen.

Expanding and collapsing tree diagrams   Tree diagram subdirectories may have a plus sign (+) to their left. This symbol means that the subdirectory holds other subdirectories that are not currently in view. To expand this branch of the tree so that these directories are in view, just click on the plus sign or move the bar cursor to this position and press the ⊞ key. To extend the expansion to all subdirectories in a branch, press ✳ instead. Once expanded, the symbol changes to a minus sign. Clicking on a minus sign (or pressing the ⊟ key) causes a branch to collapse back to the way it was. These choices are also available through the Tree menu at the top of the screen.

Directory listing contents   At the top of a file listing you'll find a line specifying which files in the directory are shown. Global file name characters (explained in section 1.3) are employed in this specification. Normally, this line is set to *.* to include all files. You can change it to, say, *.BAT to list only batch files (that is, only files with .BAT extensions). This is done by pulling down the Options menu, selecting File Display Options, and editing the specification shown.

Keep in mind that whatever specification you choose—whether to show all files, only batch files, or whatever—will be applied to all directory listings the Shell displays until you change the specification again. If you change the file specification and then change to a different subdirectory, don't be alarmed if all your files have disappeared. Just change the file specification back to *.* to display all files—or whatever specification you wish—and everything will be back to normal.

Using file management commands   Once you've brought into view the desired directory tree and file listings, you can apply commands listed in the File menu, such as Copy or Rename. In most cases, you must select one or more files from a directory listing before pulling down the File menu. For example, to rename a file, you begin by selecting the file you want to work with and only then do you pull down the menu and choose the Rename command. The Shell always automatically selects the first file in the listing when you first bring that listing into view. If you fail to select a file before choosing a command, the command will be applied to this file. See the next section to learn about different ways of selecting files.

1.8 Selecting files in the DOS Shell

Perhaps the most useful feature in any DOS shell is the ability to select or tag files. This is a very efficient way of operating on many files with a single command. Files can be selected by manually tagging each or by applying global file name characters to whole directories. You may combine the two approaches, for example, to select all files with a particular extension and then deselect a few of those chosen. Much time can be saved through intelligent application of this feature. For instance, instead of typing in one COPY command after another and waiting for each to do its work, you can quickly specify dozens of files that are to be copied and then leave the computer to do the work unattended. Figure 1.3 shows a directory listing in which several files have been selected.

Selecting files with a mouse   Files are selected with a mouse just by clicking on the file name. Clicking on another file causes that file to be selected and the previous file to be deselected. To select multiple files, hold down the Ctrl key as you click on the file names. Each file will be highlighted as it is selected. Alternatively, you can select a continuous series of files in a listing by selecting a file at one end of the series and then pressing the Shift key while clicking on the file at the other end; those two files and all files between them will be selected and highlighted.

Selecting files from the keyboard   To select a single file from the keyboard, just use the cursor keys to move the bar cursor to the file's listing. Selecting multiple files is a little harder. When the files are listed in series, move the cursor to one end of the series, hold down the Shift key, and then move the cursor to the other end of the series; all files between these points will be selected. When the files are not listed in sequence, select the first, and then press Shift-F8. You'll see the word ADD at the bottom right corner of the screen telling you that you have entered a special selection mode. Move the cursor to the next file you want to select and press the space bar. The file will then be selected without deselecting the first one. Proceed in this manner until you're done, then press Shift-F8 again to exit ADD mode.

Selecting all files or most files

Sometimes you'll want to select all files in a directory or most of them. Rather than select them individually, pull down the Files menu and choose Select all. All files in the directory listing, including those out of view, will be selected and highlighted.

When you want to select most files in a menu, select all files in this way and then deselect those you do not want. To deselect files with a mouse, hold down the Ctrl key while clicking on the file names. Unfortunately, this can't be done from the keyboard.

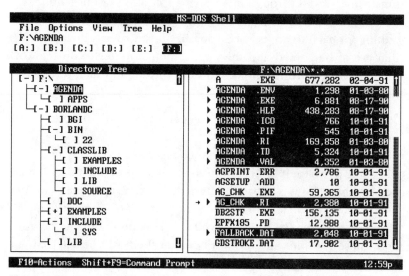

Figure 1.3

Selecting files by global file name characters

The DOS Shell also lets you use global file name characters (discussed in section 1.3) to select files. Pull down the Options menu and choose File Display Options. The dialog box shown in figure 1.4 appears. You can enter a global file name specification at the top of the box. The initial setting is *.* to cause all files to be displayed. Changing it to, say, *.COM would reduce the listing to .COM files alone. This specification applies to all directories and remains in force until you enter another or change it back to *.*. Once it is made, you can pull down the Files menu and choose Select all to tag the files. Only the files currently appearing in the directory listing are selected.

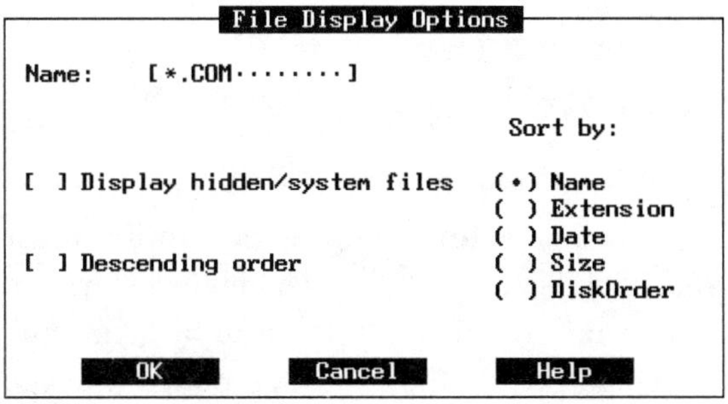

```
┌──────────── File Display Options ────────────┐
│                                              │
│ Name:     [ *.COM········]                   │
│                                              │
│                              Sort by:        │
│                                              │
│ [ ] Display hidden/system files   (•) Name      │
│                                   ( ) Extension  │
│                                   ( ) Date       │
│ [ ] Descending order              ( ) Size       │
│                                   ( ) DiskOrder  │
│                                              │
│                                              │
│       OK           Cancel         Help       │
└──────────────────────────────────────────────┘
```

Figure 1.4

1.9 Running programs from the DOS Shell

You can start up a program in the DOS Shell by moving the bar cursor to its directory listing and pressing [←] or by moving the mouse cursor over the listing and double-clicking the mouse (pressing the left mouse button twice quickly). You can also start up a program by taking the same action with the bar cursor over a file you want loaded into the program. This is done by associating the file's extension with the program that runs it. For example, if your word processor adds .DOC to all data files it creates, you could associate the .DOC extension to your word processor program file.

Say that the word processor program file is named MYWORD.EXE. Find it in a directory listing and move the bar cursor to it, selecting it with a click of the mouse button or a strike on the space bar. Then pull down the File menu and select Associate. A dialog box will appear to ask you to enter the associated extension. In this case, you'd type in DOC [←]. Notice that the period that separates file names and extensions is not entered. Then you'll be asked whether to prompt for options. Usually, it's best to choose not to. Otherwise, when the DOS Shell starts up a program, it will prompt you to type in codes for special options. Most programs don't require these options, which are explained in the DOS Shell manual.

Once the association has been made, pressing [←] when a data file has been selected (or double-clicking on the file name) will start up its associated program and then load the file into it. It doesn't matter what drive or directory the data file resides in because the DOS Shell will remember the location of the program file.

You may specify more than one extension that will invoke a particular program. The reverse, however, is not possible. Once you specify that files with .DOC endings belong to MYWORD.DOC, it's not possible to automatically load .DOC files into other programs. But you can always start up a program directly and then load any file you like into it. If your programs don't dictate particular file name extensions, make up your own.

The task swapper   The DOS Shell in DOS 5.0 includes a task swapper that lets you run several programs at once and move between them relatively quickly, all the while leaving the programs and their data files open. This feature should not be confused with true multitasking in which more than one program can run at the same time so that, for example, a spreadsheet could carry out a lengthy recalculation in the background at the same time that you edit text in a word processor. In the task swapper, only one program runs at any given moment. The swapper also does not offer any features for passing data between programs. The swapper is disk rather than memory based, meaning that you need to wait for programs to reload from disk when you switch to them.

To use the task swapper, you first must enable it by choosing Enable Task Swapper from the Options menu. Doing so causes the Main window to divide into two parts with the usual program list on the left and the Active Task List on the right. The latter lists all programs currently managed by the task swapper. Once the swapper has been enabled, all programs will be added to this list as they are started or they can be added by double-clicking on the program name while holding down a Shift key.

When a program has been loaded under the swapper, you can leave it and return to the Shell by typing Ctrl-Break or you can cycle from program to program without returning to the Shell by pressing the Tab key with Alt held down. To remove a program from the list, just exit the program using its usual exit command. If the program locks up, you may be able to recover by returning to the Shell by typing Ctrl-Break, selecting the program in the Active Task List, and then pressing Del. Then you can load the program anew. You should save data frequently when using the task swapper since an unrecoverable crash of one program may cause you to lose data in others.

Chapter 2

Directory Listings

- MINITUTORIAL: Files and directories
- Viewing a directory listing
- Listing groups of files
- Sorting directory listings
- Searching a directory for a file
- Printing directory listings
- Viewing a file's contents

MINITUTORIAL:
Files and directories

Computers process data, and data can be just about anything—a letter, columns of statistics, an architectural drawing, or financial records. Data is stored on either removable diskettes or hard disks. A lot of data from a lot of projects can fit onto one disk; for example, you might store several hundred business letters on a single diskette. Each letter is stored in its own place; in a sense, it is filed on the disk, so each letter constitutes a file. One file holds a letter to Mr. Jones, another file holds a letter to Mr. Smith, and so on. As more and more files are added to a disk, or as already existing files grow, the disk gradually fills.

To keep track of which file is which, we give them short descriptive names. The file holding the letter to Mr. Jones could be called JONES; the file to Mr. Smith, SMITH. It's you who decides on the names for files. Every file name in a directory must be unique so that one file cannot be confused with another. When you start a new letter with your word processing program, you'll need to make up a name for the new file that will be created on the disk to hold the letter. And, when you later want to edit the letter, you'll need to remember the file name so you can instruct your word processing program to fetch it from the disk.

The names of many files are gathered into a directory, which keeps track of the files. You can ask DOS to show you a directory listing. It will display not only the names of the files in a directory, but also the size of each file in bytes (1 byte = 1 character) and the date and time the file was last worked on. Figure 2.1 shows a typical listing. As you can see, the file names and their extensions are shown separately without a period between them. The *p* or *a* after the time refers to p.m. or a.m.

```
Volume in drive C has no label
Directory of  C:\NBACKUP

.                <DIR>       3-20-91   11:19a
..               <DIR>       3-20-91   11:19a
DEFAULT  SAV         64      7-09-90    2:23a
NBACKUP  HLP     178841      4-30-90    9:00a
NBCONFIG HLP      36013      4-30-90    9:00a
NB_FLP_R OVL     118989      4-30-90    9:00a
NB_FLP_B OVL     109195      4-30-90    9:00a
NBACKUP  EXE       3849      4-30-90    9:00a
NBACKUP  OVL     214485      4-30-90    9:00a
NBCONFIG OVL      73065      4-30-90    9:00a
NBINFO   OVL     108962      4-30-90    9:00a
NBACKUP  CFG       1494      7-09-90    2:16a
DEFAULT  SET       4884      5-12-91   12:09p
NBACKUP  LOG      39337      5-12-91   12:09p
DEFAULT  BAK       4884      7-09-90    2:23a
NBACKUP  TMP       2828      5-12-91   12:09p
DEFAULT  SLT         64      5-12-91   12:09p
NEWBAKUP         <DIR>      12-30-92   11:18a
      18 File(s)    698368 bytes free
```

Figure 2.1

Diskettes, particularly low-capacity diskettes, usually have only one directory. But high-capacity disks, like hard disks holding many millions of bytes of data, contain so many files that it's useful to organize them into a number of directories on the same disk. When a disk has more than one directory, it's said to have a directory tree, and the individual directories are called subdirectories. The term tree is used because the directories, starting from the disk's main directory, the root directory, are linked together in a pattern resembling the branches of a tree. Directory trees are discussed in a separate minitutorial in Chapter 5. They make DOS commands more complicated, but without them it would be next to impossible to organize lots of files.

Every directory listing begins with two lines telling which disk and which directory the listing is for. Disks can have a volume label—a word up to eleven characters long that identifies the disk. Volume labels are usually added to disks when they are formatted. The label may also be added or changed by the DOS LABEL command (which we discuss in section 16.7) or through utility software like the VL (Volume Label) program in The Norton Utilities. If a disk has a volume label, you'll see it displayed on the first line of a directory listing:

```
Volume in drive A is BACKUP12
```

or, if no label was created when the disk was formatted:

```
Volume in drive A has no label
```

(Here, Volume is synonymous with disk.) The second line of a directory listing gives the path to the directory listed (you'll need to understand directory trees—explained in the minitutorial at the beginning of Chapter 5—to follow this). For example, it might say:

```
Directory of C:\ANIMALS\CANINES
```

Or, for a root directory:

```
Directory of A:\
```

A general listing of any directory other than a disk's root directory always begins with the same two entries: one named . (a single period) and the other named .. (two periods). It is not clear why the designers of DOS decided to show these lines in directory listings since the entries display no useful information. The two symbols refer to certain information stored in the directory that DOS uses to find its way around the directory tree. The single dot refers to the directory itself, and the double-dot refers to the directory containing it (that is, the parent directory).

What follows is a listing of the files and subdirectories listed in the directory (subdirectories are tagged <DIR> and lack file sizes). These are displayed in the order in which they were created or copied to the subdirectory. When a file is erased, or a subdirectory removed, the directory slot that holds it is freed up. As new files and subdirectories are added, the vacant slots are reused before DOS adds new entries to the end of the listing. Because of this, you have practically no control over the order in which files appear in listings. Related files can't be grouped. However, listings can be sorted alphabetically or by some other criterion, such as by date or time. Directory sorting is discussed in sections 2.3 and 21.5.

All listings end with a tally of how many files were shown. Except in root directories, this number includes the . and .. entries. The tally also includes any subdirectories listed in the directory, for these are themselves files of a special kind. Be aware that certain kinds of files can be excluded from listings even when present in a directory. These include system files and hidden files that are used exclusively by DOS. You can learn more about these files in the minitutorial in Chapter 4.

2.1　Viewing a directory listing

The simplest way to view a directory is to type:

```
DIR ⏎
```

to display a list of file names, sizes, and dates. The listing represents files in the current directory of the current drive (see the Chapter 6 minitutorial). One way to obtain a file listing for some other directory is to change the current drive and directory to make the directory you wish to see the current directory. For example:

```
A>C: ⏎            make drive C the current drive
C>CHDIR \FISH\TROPICAL ⏎  make TROPICAL the current directory
C>DIR ⏎           view the directory
```

There's no need to change the current drive or directory when you have no other reason to do so. Just include a drive specifier (such as C:) and/or a directory path (such as \FISH\TROPICAL) within the DIR statement. To view the current directory of drive C when drive A is current, type:

```
DIR C: ⏎
```

To view the TROPICAL directory of drive C when C is the current drive, type:

```
DIR \FISH\TROPICAL ⏎
```

To view the TROPICAL directory when drive C is not current, type:

```
DIR C:\FISH\TROPICAL ⏎
```

Listing individual files　　When you want to find a particular file in a directory, add its name to the DIR command. For example, to find WIGGLE.DOC in the current directory, type:

```
DIR WIGGLE.DOC ⏎
```

You would be shown only a listing for WIGGLE.DOC if it's present in the current directory, saving you the trouble of scanning a complete directory listing for the one file. When a drive specifier or directory path is used in the command, place the file name at the end:

```
DIR A:WIGGLE.DOC ⏎
```

or:

```
DIR \FISH\ARCTIC\WIGGLE.DOC ⏎
```

or:

```
DIR C:\FISH\ARCTIC\WIGGLE.DOC ⏎
```

You can also list multiple files that are related by their extensions or some other characteristic. This is done using global file name characters, which are discussed in general in the Chapter 4 minitutorial, and specifically in regard to directory listings in section 2.2. Also, in section 20.5, we talk about how DOS and various utilities like the Norton Utilities FF (Find File) program can search an entire disk in seconds for a specific file or files.

Controlling scrolling   The listing of a directory that holds many files can quickly scroll out of view. On slower computers, you may have time to strike Pause (or Ctrl - Num Lock on early keyboards) to temporarily halt the listing, then press any key to continue. A far better method of controlling the display is to add the /P (for pause) switch at the end of the DIR command. For example:

```
DIR C:\FISH\ARCTIC /P ⏎
```

or just:

```
DIR /P ⏎
```

The directory is listed one screen at a time when you use the /P switch. Pressing any key takes you to the next screen; Ctrl -Break terminates the listing before it is finished. Incidentally, the same effect can be achieved by entering the vertical bar character and the word MORE after the DIR command:

```
DIR ¦ MORE ⏎
```

Fitting more listings on the screen   Another way of dealing with lots of files is to use the /W (for wide) switch to have DIR list only file names, and not the file sizes and dates:

```
DIR C:\FISH\TROPICAL /W ⏎
```

The file names are listed in several columns, so usually the entire directory can be listed on one screen. When you still have too many files, you can add the /P switch as well.

The DOS 5.0 Shell   The DOS shell can display file listings, program listings, or a combination of both. The View menu offers five choices. Single File List presents a screen with a directory tree on the left and file listings on the right, as shown in figure 2.2. Dual File List presents two such screens, one above the other. All Files presents just a file listing for the current directory with detailed information about the currently selected file. Program List presents a menu of programs that you have set up, and Program/File Lists creates a composite screen. Whichever option was chosen when you last exited the shell will be the one initally used when the shell is loaded again. Directory listings default to the root directory of the drive from which the shell started.

It may take a few seconds to assemble the directory tree information the first time you select a drive while using the shell. After that, directory listings appear instantly when you change between directories and disk drives.

```
================================ MS-DOS Shell ================================
  File  Options  View  Tree  Help
  F:\AGENDA
 [A:] [B:] [C:] [D:] [E:]  F:

┌───────── Directory Tree ─────────┐┌────────── F:\AGENDA\*.* ──────────┐
│[-] F:\                         ↑ ││  A        .EXE    677,282  02-04-91│
│ ├─[-] AGENDA                     ││  AGENDA   .ENV      1,298  01-03-80│
│ │ └─[ ] APPS                     ││  AGENDA   .EXE      6,881  08-17-90│
│ └─[-] BORLANDC                   ││  AGENDA   .HLP    438,283  08-17-90│
│   ├─[ ] BGI                      ││  AGENDA   .ICO        766  10-01-91│
│   ├─[-] BIN                      ││  AGENDA   .PIF        545  10-01-91│
│   │ └─[ ] 22                     ││ →▶ AGENDA .RI     169,858  01-03-80│
│   ├─[-] CLASSLIB                 ││  AGENDA   .TD       5,324  10-01-91│
│   │ ├─[ ] EXAMPLES               ││  AGENDA   .VAL      4,352  01-03-80│
│   │ ├─[ ] INCLUDE                ││  AGPRINT  .ERR      2,786  10-01-91│
│   │ ├─[ ] LIB                    ││  AGSETUP  .ADD         10  10-01-91│
│   │ └─[ ] SOURCE                 ││  AG_CHK   .EXE     59,365  10-01-91│
│   ├─[ ] DOC                      ││  AG_CHK   .RI       2,380  10-01-91│
│   ├─[+] EXAMPLES                 ││  DB2STF   .EXE    156,135  10-01-91│
│   ├─[-] INCLUDE                  ││  EPFX185  .PD      12,988  10-01-91│
│   │ └─[ ] SYS                    ││  FALLBACK .DAT      2,048  10-01-91│
│   └─[ ] LIB                    ↓ ││  GDSTROKE .DAT     17,902  10-01-91↓│
└──────────────────────────────────┘└───────────────────────────────────┘
 F10=Actions  Shift+F9=Command Prompt                              11:56a
```

Figure 2.2

At the top of every listing is a file specifier, normally *.*. The two asterisks are global file name characters, indicating that all files in a directory are shown (global file name characters are discussed in section 1.3). You can obtain a partial, specialized directory listing by altering this specification. This is done by pulling down the Options menu and selecting Display Options. A dialog box (shown in figure 2.3) opens to reveal the current file specifier. Edit the specifier, changing it to *.TXT or returning it to *.*, and then click on OK or press ⏎.

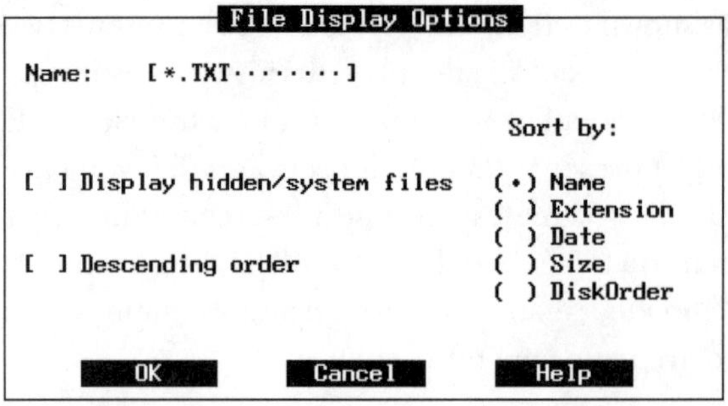

```
┌──────────────── File Display Options ────────────────┐
│                                                      │
│  Name:    [ *.TXT········]                           │
│                                                      │
│                                  Sort by:            │
│                                                      │
│  [ ] Display hidden/system files (•) Name            │
│                                  ( ) Extension       │
│                                  ( ) Date            │
│  [ ] Descending order            ( ) Size            │
│                                  ( ) DiskOrder       │
│                                                      │
│                                                      │
│     ███ OK ███     ███ Cancel ███   ███ Help ███     │
└──────────────────────────────────────────────────────┘
```

Figure 2.3

Windows 3.1   In Windows, when you enter the File Manager, you'll encounter a tree diagram of the selected drive. To view a directory listing of any subdirectory in the diagram, use the cursor keys to move the bar cursor to a subdirectory name or click on the subdirectory's icon. The currently displayed directory is marked by an open file folder icon; all other directories show closed file folders. (If the desired subdirectory is not in view, you can expand the tree by double-clicking on file folders or by moving the bar cursor to a file folder and pressing ⏎).

A subdirectory window like the one shown in figure 2.4 will open to display the file listing. By default, listings show only file names with an icon to the side indicating the file type. Subdirectories also appear in the listings using the familiar file folder icons. If you like, you can choose Tree Only or Directory Only to restrict the listing to one or the other. The window is initially divided evenly between tree and listings. To make more room for listings, choose Split from the View menu. A vertical bar will appear and will follow lateral motions of the mouse. When you click the mouse, a new boundary between tree and listings will be drawn at the bar position.

If you prefer to view DOS-style listings without icons, pull down the View menu and choose All File Details. A listing like the one shown in figure 2.5 will appear. If you want a simpler listing, choose Partial Details from the View menu. You'll be shown the dialog box in figure 2.6, where you can select the directory features you want to see. When a check box contains an *X*, the item marked will appear in directory listings. You can change the settings by clicking on the boxes with a mouse, or by using the ⬆ and ⬇ keys to move the cursor to a box and then pressing the space bar. The resulting listing still appears in one column, so you'll get information for only as many files as appear in a full listing.

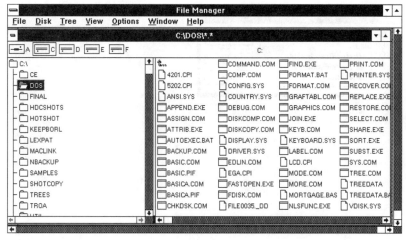

Figure 2.4

Windows will readily display any number of tree diagrams and listings, each in its own window. Just double-click on any of the drive symbols found at the top of a file manager window. A new window will open to display the tree for that drive, and you can then choose any subdirectory for a listing. To close one of these windows, choose Close from the Control Menu at the top left corner of the window or type Ctrl-F4 (you can't close the first window opened by the file manager; it's closed by exiting the File Manager).

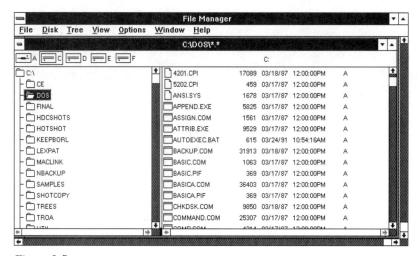

Figure 2.5

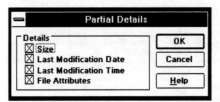

Figure 2.6

2.2   Listing groups of files

The simple command DIR ⏎ is the first DOS command learned by
many computer novices. Unfortunately, many people never go on to
learn to use the DIR command with more skill. The command can easily
be made to give you partial directory listings so that you can view only
certain files. This ability is particularly important when directories grow
large and listings quickly scroll out of view. The correct DIR command
can bring together just the files you want listed.

Partial directory listings are achieved by using global file name characters. These consist of two characters, the asterisk and question mark,
that DOS interprets in a special way when it encounters them in file
names and extensions. Their application can be a little complicated,
but the basic rules are simple. Refer to section 1.3 for more detail than
you'll find here.

The asterisk   The DIR command can be used to check for an
individual file by name. For example:

    DIR TURTLES.DOC ⏎

would display a one-line directory listing for the file TURTLES.DOC if
the file is present (otherwise, DOS would display the message "File not
found"). If you were to substitute an asterisk for the word TURTLES in
this command, DOS would interpret the asterisk as meaning "any file
name," and it would produce a directory listing of all files of any name
that have the extension .DOC. Hence:

    DIR *.DOC ⏎

would list TURTLES.DOC, LIZARDS.DOC, SNAKES.DOC, and so
forth. Similarly, you could instead replace the file name extension with
an asterisk, as in:

    DIR TURTLES.* ⏎

and DOS would list all files with the name TURTLES and any extension.
You might see TURTLES.DOC, TURTLES.TXT, TURTLES.BAT, and
so on.

These two cases may be combined into the statement:

    DIR *.* ⏎

This command would list all files with any file name and any extension—that is, all files in the directory. Thus, the command does exactly the same thing as a simple DIR ⏎ command.

The question mark   The second global file name character, the question mark, is more specific than the asterisk. It replaces particular characters within a file name or extension. Consider the command

        DIR CHAPTER?.DOC ⏎

The question mark would match to any character, and so the listing could include files named CHAPTER1.DOC, CHAPTER2.DOC, CHAPTERX. DOC, and so forth. Similarly, the command:

        DIR CHAPTER1.B?? ⏎

would list CHAPTER1.BAT and CHAPTER1.BAK, but would not list CHAPTER1. DOC.

Organizing file extensions   Many users don't use file extensions. As you can see, there's considerable power to be had in doing so if it's possible. However, many programs impose their own extensions, which must not be changed. The global file name characters may be applied to COPY, ERASE, and RENAME operations as well. A carefully devised scheme of file naming conventions provides a way of cataloging files and manipulating them easily. See section 20.7 for a discussion of how to develop such a system.

Sorting group listings   Section 2.3 explains how to make DOS sort directory listings alphabetically by file name or extension, or numerically by file size, time, or date. This feature may be combined with a partial listing to give you an orderly readout. Using the example of files named CHAPTER1, CHAPTER2, and so on, you could view an alphabetized listing by typing:

        DIR CHAPTER?.DOC ¦ SORT ⏎

You can print out the listing by adding >LPT1 (line printer 1) to the command:

        DIR CHAPTER?.DOC ¦ SORT >LPT1 ⏎

The DOS 5.0 Shell   In the DOS Shell, you can use global file name characters to specify the content of directory listings. Begin by pulling down the Options menu to choose Display Options. At the top of the resulting dialog box you'll find *.* displayed. This dialog box also lets you sort files, as section 2.3 explains. The two asterisks indicate that directory listings are set to show all files in a directory, and indeed at the top of every directory listing you'll find such a file specifier. You may edit the line to any other specification, such as *.BAT (as shown in figure 2.7) or CHAPTER?.DOC.

Once you've finished, click on OK or press ⏎. The dialog box will disappear, and the current directory listing will instantly change to reflect the new specification. You'll need to repeat this process, returning the specification to *.* to get full listings again. Otherwise, all subsequent listings for all directories on all disk drives will follow the new specification.

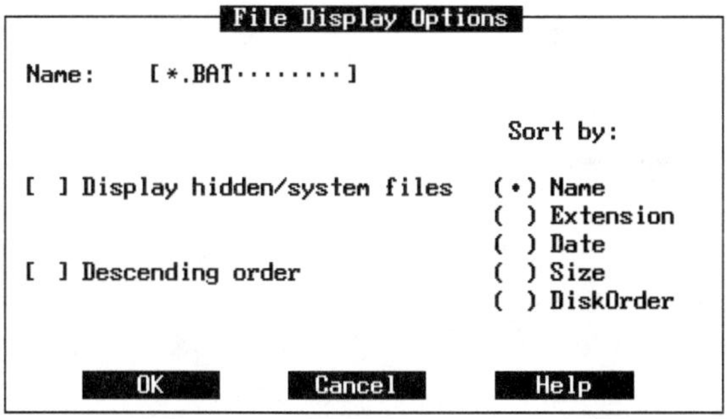

```
┌──────File Display Options──────┐
│ Name:    [*.BAT········]        │
│                                 │
│                    Sort by:     │
│                                 │
│ [ ] Display hidden/system files (•) Name     │
│                                ( ) Extension  │
│                                ( ) Date       │
│ [ ] Descending order           ( ) Size       │
│                                ( ) DiskOrder   │
│                                 │
│    ▐ OK ▌      ▐ Cancel ▌   ▐ Help ▌    │
└─────────────────────────────────┘
```

Figure 2.7

Windows 3.1   In Windows, once a file listing is in view, pull down the View menu and select By File Type. The dialog box shown in figure 2.8 will appear. At the top of the box is an area containing a global file name character specification for the files that should be listed. Initially, it is set to *.* so that all files will be shown. Change the specification to that of the files you want to view. For example, typing

    *.TXT ⏎

will reduce a directory listing to only files with a .TXT extension. As you can see, the dialog box offers additional options, letting you exclude directories, program files, and so on. When an *X* appears in the box to the left of a specification, the specification is enabled and the corresponding files appear in listings. Normally all are enabled.

The alterations you make through the View menu apply to all directory listings in the current window. Other File Manager windows may use a different specification. Note, however, that a window will initially use the specification of the window from which it was started. If you fail to keep track of the current specification, directories may appear empty when they are not. For this reason, it's a good idea to return the setting to *.* as soon as possible. These settings are not saved when you quit Windows, and all return to *.*.

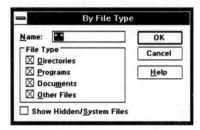

Figure 2.8

2.3 Sorting directory listings

It's hard to view directory listings when directories contain many files, particularly because DOS won't let you scroll a listing up and down. One way of bringing order to a crowded directory is to search it for particular groups of files (section 2.4). Another way is to sort the directory listing. This can be done alphabetically, by the files' names or extensions, or by the files' times, dates, or sizes.

Sorting is performed by using the SORT filter, which is combined with the DIR command. A special vertical bar character (|) separates the two—you'll find it as an uppercase character on the keyboard (its exact placement depends on which IBM keyboard design you are using). SORT is called a filter and not a command because it only works with other commands, filtering their output. To see a directory listing sorted alphabetically by file name, type in:

```
DIR ¦ SORT ↵
```

You can sort a directory listing based on other things—file extension, file date or time, or file size—by telling DOS the column of the first letter of the item on which you want to base your sort. For example, in the following line from a directory listing:

```
MYDATA    .DOC  2387   5-04-90  6:01p
```

the first letter of each file extension begins in the tenth column from the left, the file size in the thirteenth column, and so on. To sort by file name extension, type:

```
DIR ¦ SORT /+10 ↵
```
Sorts by file's extension

Similarly:

```
DIR ¦ SORT /+13 ↵      Sorts by file's size
DIR ¦ SORT /+24 ↵      Sorts by file's date
DIR ¦ SORT /+33 ↵      Sorts by file's time
```

As you can see, a sort made on the file name does not require the addition of /+ and a number. This is because when DOS does not find /+, it assumes that the sorting column is 1, which is the position of the first character of file names. You could also enter DIR | SORT /+1 ↵.

Problems of sorting files by date

Because of the American way of writing dates by month, then day, and then year, a listing sorted by date will start by giving you all files with a January date, then a February date, and so on. To avoid this pitfall, you can convert the date format to the one used in Sweden, which is by year, then month, and then day. To do this, place the following line in your CONFIG.SYS file (section 11.2):

```
COUNTRY=046
```

When the DOS file COUNTRY.SYS does not reside in the root directory of your boot disk, you'll need to specify a directory path to it in the command. If the file is in the directory \DOS, for example, on drive C, then you'd type:

```
COUNTRY=046,,C:\DOS\COUNTRY.SYS
```

The Swedish format also lists times using a 24-hour format. You'll find more information about the COUNTRY command in section 11.10. Be aware that changing the time and date format can have unwanted side effects in other DOS commands. So it's a good idea to change back the COUNTRY setting once you're finished. (You'll need to reboot the computer again.)

Sorting in reverse   You can make DOS reverse the sort by adding /R to the end of the command. For an alphabetical sort of file extensions made from *Z* to *A*, type:

```
DIR ¦ SORT /+10 /R ⏎
```

When /R is applied to numbers, such as file sizes, the listing starts with the largest file, instead of the smallest.

Permanent directory sorting   The SORT filter sorts a directory listing, not the directory itself. No change is made to the directory data held on disk. The next time you use an ordinary DIR command without the SORT feature, you'll find the listing in its usual haphazard order. Directories can be permanently sorted using special utility software like the DS (Directory Sort) program in The Norton Utilities. In addition to sorting whole directories, DS has an interactive mode in which you select individual files, or groups of files, and move them to arbitary locations in the directory listing. Utilities like DS can help DOS find files more quickly by listing important files, including subdirectory's files, at the top of directory listings. See section 21.6 to learn how to use directory sorting to improve hard disk performance.

The DOS 5.0 Shell   The DOS Shell normally sorts directory listings alphabetically by name. You can change the criterion for sorting by choosing Display Options from the Options menu. The resulting dialog box offers five sorting methods, as figure 2.9 shows. The last choice, Disk order, stands for the unsorted ordering found in normal DOS directory listings. Select a sorting method by clicking on it; or use the tab key to move the cursor to the Sort by part of the dialog box and the cursor keys to shift the check box marker to the desired position. Then click on OK (or press ⏎) to have the directory resorted. The selected sorting method will apply to all directory listings.

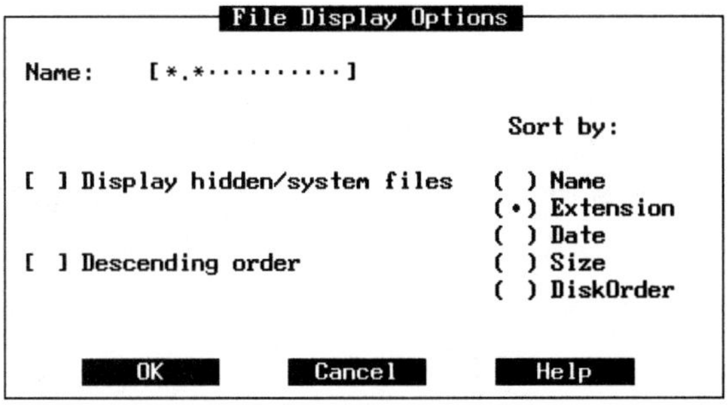

```
┌──────■File Display Options■──────┐
│                                  │
│ Name:    [*.*··········]         │
│                                  │
│                      Sort by:    │
│                                  │
│ [ ] Display hidden/system files  ( ) Name
│                                  ( •) Extension
│                                  ( ) Date
│ [ ] Descending order             ( ) Size
│                                  ( ) DiskOrder
│                                  │
│      ■ OK ■      Cancel      ■ Help ■
└──────────────────────────────────┘
```

Figure 2.9

Windows 3.1   In Windows, once a directory listing is in view, pull down the View menu and choose Sort by Name, Sort by Type, Sort by Size, or Sort by Date. The listing will instantly be reordered to your specification. Entries of the same type, size, or date are listed alphabetically. When multiple windows give listings, each can be sorted in its own way. Note that a window's initial sorting method follows that of the window from which it was opened.

▪ 2.4 ▪ Searching a directory for a file

To find out if a particular file is present in a directory, don't ask for a general directory listing and then scan it for the file. Instead, specify the file name in the DIR command. To look for the file MYFILE.TXT, type:

```
DIR MYFILE.TXT ⏎
```

If the file is present, DOS displays its directory entry alone:

```
MYFILE TXT 12603 11-07-89 10:07p
```

Otherwise, DOS reports:

```
File not found
```

To look for groups of related files, use the global file name characters discussed in section 1.3. For instance, if your word processor adds a .DOC extension to every file it creates, you can view a listing of all such files by typing:

```
DIR *.DOC ⏎
```

You might get something that looks like:

```
REPORT88  DOC  24558  10-14-88  12:06p
OUTLINE   DOC   5930  11-12-88  08.45p
REPORT89  DOC  79460  03-02-89  11:03a
```

Sometimes you may want to search for one or more files by the time or date it was created, or even by its size. The DOS DIR command can't give listings based on these characteristics. But you can ask DOS to give a full directory listing sorted by time, date, or size. Then it's easy to track down the file you're looking for. See the previous section to learn how.

■ 2.5 ■ Printing directory listings

You can print a copy of any directory listing simply by adding >LPT1 (line printer 1) to the DIR command. For example:

```
DIR >LPT1  ⏎
```

causes the directory to be printed. As with any directory command, you may specify a drive when you want a listing from a drive other than the current (default) drive:

```
DIR A: >LPT1  ⏎
```

and a directory path for a non-current directory:

```
DIR \MAMMALS\DOGS >LPT1  ⏎
```

and possibly both:

```
DIR C:\MAMMALS\DOGS >LPT1  ⏎
```

If the machine is properly configured, LPT1 will correspond to the printer in use. Substitute LPT2 for LPT1 if you have a second printer to which you want to direct the output. Alternatively, when working with a serial printer, direct the output to COM1 or COM2.

When the printer is not turned on, or it is offline, DOS will appear to do nothing at all for a while and then will display the message:

```
Write fault error writing device LPT1
Abort, Retry, Ignore, Fail?
```

Turn on the printer and, once it has initialized, type Ⓡ (for retry) to start it printing.

You also can output a directory listing to a file on disk. Just substitute the file name you want to use for LPT1. To write the directory \MAM-MALS\DOGS into the file DIRLIST, enter:

```
DIR \MAMMALS\DOGS >DIRLIST  ⏎
```

2.6 Viewing a file's contents

Sometimes it's useful to view a text file quickly without going through the trouble of loading it into a word processor. The TYPE command displays a file, continuously scrolling it upwards. It won't let you scroll the file up and down, and it provides no way of altering the file. To view the file NEWT.TXT, type:

    TYPE NEWT.TXT ⏎

This example assumes that NEWT.TXT is in the current directory. When the file is on another disk, or in another directory on the same disk, you can either move to the disk or directory where the file resides and then use the command, or you can modify the command to tell DOS where to find the file that you want to display. For example, if the DOS prompt is A> and you want to view a file in the subdirectory \REPTILES on drive C, you may either type:

    C: ⏎   move to drive C
    CHDIR \REPTILES ⏎   move to REPTILES subdirectory
    TYPE NEWTS.TXT ⏎   display the file
    A: ⏎   if required, move back to drive A

or you can just type:

    TYPE C:\REPTILE\NEWTS.TXT ⏎

Viewing a file page by page   By adding the expression | MORE to the end of a TYPE command (you'll find a key on the keyboard with a | character), TYPE will fill the screen and then stop and wait for you to press any keystroke before going on to the next screen. You cannot move back to screens already shown. Here is an example:

    TYPE DOCUMENT.TXT ¦ MORE ⏎

or:

    TYPE B:\LEVEL1\DOCUMENT.TXT ¦ MORE ⏎

Alternatively, you can temporarily stop the file display by pressing Pause (or Ctrl-Num Lock on older keyboards). Pressing any key starts the file scrolling again. This method is awkward, however. It's hard to view the continuously scrolling text, and harder still to strike Pause in time to stop the text you want to view. If the scrolling goes too far, there's no going back, and you have to start the command over again (press Ctrl-Break to return to the DOS command line). Characters are displayed as fast as the computer can draw them, so on very fast machines the screen is reduced to a blur.

Nonsense on the screen   The TYPE command displays utter gobbledygook if you ask to look inside non-text files, such as program files bearing the familiar .COM or .EXE file name extensions. A seemingly random assortment of alphabetic and graphic characters appears on the screen. These are codes used by the computer's microprocessor; they are meaningful only to computer programmers.

Some of these codes are interpreted by DOS in special ways. One code causes the computer to beep, and often the computer beeps repeatedly if TYPE is used to view a non-text file. With large files, the beeping may go on for a long time, but it can be stopped with Ctrl-Break. Another code acts as an end-of-file marker in text files. Even when encountered in a non-text file, this code brings the TYPE command to a sudden halt; because of it, sometimes you can view only a small portion of a large non-text file. However, some text editors and word processors won't be stopped by the end-of-file character.

Utility software   The DOS TYPE command has become less useful as software has grown more complex. Today, few major programs keep their data in simple text files. Normally, to track down a missing file, you must start up the program that created it and load one file after another until you find the one you're seeking. Utility software can do the job much more quickly by providing a library of viewers for viewing particular kinds of data files. The Norton Desktop for Windows, for example, has viewers for all major word processors, databases, and spreadsheet programs. It can display their data files just as the data appears in the programs themselves: spreadsheet files look like spread- sheets, and so on. Graphics can be expanded or reduced to fit into a window, and you can zoom in on sections of a graphic. The program also contains a facility for searching for files by looking for a specified string of text within the file. In this way, you can quickly peek into many related files, such as all letters addressed to Mr. Rumpelstiltskin, until you find the one desired.

The DOS 5.0 Shell   To view a file in the DOS Shell, begin by finding the file in a directory listing and selecting it (only one file can be viewed at a time). Then pull down the File menu and select View. A window opens to display the file, as figure 2.10 shows. You can scroll the file up and down using cursor keys (a mouse won't work). By pressing [F9], the text may be displayed in an alternate form in which the characters are represented by code numbers. This feature is useful for computer programmers. In either case, the text can't be edited. Press [Esc] (or click on the [Esc] symbol) to return to the File System.

```
                      MS-DOS Shell - PROSE.DOC
  Display  View  Help
  ┌  To view file's content use PgUp or PgDn or ↑ or ↓.                        ┐

When spring drew round, and with it the cold weather, during an icy Lent and the
 hailstorms of Holy Week, as Mme. Swann began to find it cold in the house, I us
ed often to see her entertaining her guests in her furs, her shivering hands and
 shoulders hidden beneath the gleaming white carpet of an immense rectangular mu
ff and a cape, both of ermine, which she had not taken off on coming in from her
 drive, and which suggested the last patches of the snows of winter, more persis
tent than the rest, which neither the heat of the fire nor the advancing season
had succeeded in melting.  And the whole truth about these glacial but already f
lowering weeks was suggested to me in this drawing-room, which soon I should be
entering no more, by other more intoxicating forms of whiteness, that for exampl
e of the guelder-roses clustering, at the summits of their tall bare stalks, like
 the rectilinear tress in pre-raphaelite paintings, their balls of blossom, divi
ded yet composite, white as annunciating angels and breathing a fragrance as of
lemons.  For the mistress of Tansonville knew that April, even an ice-bound Apri
l was not barren of flowers, that winter, spring, summer are not held apart by b
arriers as hermetic as might be supposed by the town-dweller who, until the firs
t hot day, imagines the world as containing nothing but houses that stand naked
in the rain.  That Mme. Swann was content with the consignments furnished by her
 Combray gardener, that she did not, by the intervention of her own "special" fl
orist, fill up the gaps left by an insufficiently powerful magic with subsidies
  ←┘=PageDown  Esc=Cancel  F9=Hex/ASCII                              12:12p
```

Figure 2.10

Windows 3.1   Windows does not provide a simple equivalent to the DOS TYPE command. You won't find a Type command in one of the File Manager windows, although most common DOS commands are found there. Instead, Windows includes a complete text editor by which you can edit plain text files, as well as view them. The editor is found outside the File Manager. Access it by opening the Accessories icon displayed by the Program Manager (the window that normally appears when Windows starts up). Choose Notepad from among the accessories, pull down the File menu, and select Open.

You'll encounter a dialog box like the one shown in figure 2.11. Begin by selecting the file's directory in the window marked Directories. The directory tree shown there works just as in a File Manager directory listing. You can change drives by pulling down the window below marked Drives. Once you've selected a folder, the files it contains are listed to the right. Only files matching the specification entered above in the File Name field appear in the listing. This specification defaults to *.TXT; change it to *.* to view all files. Then click OK to bring the file into view. You can have Windows word-wrap the file by selecting Word Wrap from the Edit menu, as figure 2.11 shows.

If you already have a good word processor at your disposal, you probably won't want to use the Notepad for much more than viewing files. It's a complicated piece of software. You can learn its editing codes from the Windows manual, or from the extensive on-line Help system that Notepad provides (just pull down the Help menu and select the kind of assistance you need).

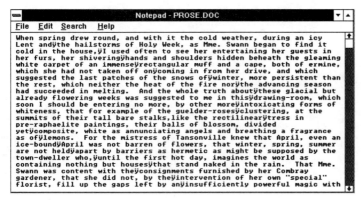

Figure 2.11

Chapter 3
Erasing Files

- MINITUTORIAL: How files are erased and unerased
- Erasing individual files
- Erasing groups of files
- Making files unerasable

MINITUTORIAL:

How files are erased and unerased

When DOS erases a file, it does not actually obliterate the data the file contains. Instead, it obscures the file name in the directory in which the file was listed. DOS also makes changes in the disk's file allocation table—a table of numbers that keeps track of which disk sectors are occupied by each file. By doing so, the disk space used by the erased file is freed for use by other files.

The file's directory entry is mostly left intact. Only the first letter of the file name is changed, replacing it with a special character indicating that the directory slot is free to receive the name of another file. Thus, in the simplest case, all that is required to unerase a file is to restore the first character of the file name and to reallocate the disk sectors belonging to the file.

Unfortunately, restoring erased files is not always that easy. After a file is erased, if other files have been added to the disk, or existing files have been modified, two things can happen that make it harder, or simply impossible, to perform an unerase:

■ Disk sectors that held information from the erased file may be incorporated into other files as they expand or used by new files. The data that had been held in those sectors is completely destroyed, but sometimes only parts of the erased file are lost. If it is a simple text file, the remains can be strung together into a new document with missing pages. But if the file is a program file, or a complex data file, a partial recovery will be useless, and the file is effectively lost.

■ Another file—perhaps one newly created by software, or one copied from elsewhere—can be listed in the directory slot that was used by the erased file. In this case, the entire prior directory entry is obliterated. Not only is the file name lost, but so are two pieces of information crucial to recovering the file: its size, and its starting position on the disk. Yet the file's sectors may remain intact even when the directory listing is lost. Utility software can help you track down the sectors and reassemble them into a new file (these utilities are discussed in Chapter 23).

Because of these two factors, it is essential that an accidentally erased file be unerased as soon as possible after it has been deleted. The odds of a successful recovery are greatly diminished if much work has been done with the computer since the erasure.

Disk sector allocation   The method by which DOS allocates empty sectors to a file depends partly on the DOS version. Generally, it uses free sectors closest to the outer edge of the disk. If an erased file happened to entirely reside toward the center of the disk, its deallocated sectors may survive for quite a while, especially if other erasures have left abundant open sectors elsewhere. Similarly, if a file's directory entry was near the end of a directory listing, and other erasures have freed up directory slots above, a file's directory entry may survive in spite of the addition of new files to the directory. For these reasons, if you are lucky you may be able to completely recover a file long after it has been erased.

Maximizing unerasability   Files are not necessarily laid out on the disk in contiguous sectors. A file may be scattered all over the surface of the disk, especially on disks that have been in use for a long time. This situation makes the disk drive operate inefficiently. As section 21.3 explains, there are special utility programs, like The Norton Utilities SD program, that can defragment files so that file sectors lay end to end. One benefit of keeping a disk defragmented is that, should a file need to be unerased, it is much easier to find the sectors belonging to it. Defragmenting also makes it less likely that you'll lose part of a file when the file is not unerased immediately.

Another good reason to keep your disks unfragmented is that when a number of files are erased at once, numerous unrelated disk sectors are freed. If the files were heavily fragmented—their sectors dispersed across the disk surface—it may be extremely difficult to determine which sector belongs to which file.

Data security   It's worth noting that the very conditions that make files unerasable also make the ERASE and DEL commands useless for purposes of data security. Anyone can use an unerase utility to see what has been erased from a disk and to recover desired information. Keep this in mind when you send out files on a previously erased diskette.

If you need to completely obliterate confidential information from a disk, acquire a utility that clears a file's disk sectors at the time it erases the file, or a utility that can go back and clear the contents of all unused disk sectors. These features are found in disk maintenance toolkits, such as in the WIPEINFO program in The Norton Utilities or the Shredder program in The Norton Desktop for Windows. These programs can clean up whole drives in one shot, and can even clean up the unused parts of sectors that hold the ends of files and may still bear data from deleted files.

Be aware that even after having used one of these utilities, it is sometimes possible to recover erased data using sophisticated equipment. This is because traces of the old data may continue to reside at track edges. Multiple wipes serve to overcome this problem. Of course, most users do not have to worry about this sort of high-tech snooping. In fact, the usual problem is just the opposite: After using one of these utilities, files cannot be recovered by unerase utilities—they really are gone for good.

A word of warning   Many newcomers to computers operate under the impression that because they own an unerase utility, they may be nonchalant in their use of the DOS ERASE or DEL command. As you can see from the discussion here, nothing could be farther from the truth. When you type in an ERASE command, you should always stop and think before pressing ←. Even when you manage to completely recover a mistakenly erased file, the confusion and anxiety involved may make you wish you had been in a little less of a hurry.

3.1 Erasing individual files

To erase a file, simply type in the word ERASE followed by the file's name and, if it has one, its extension:

    ERASE CHAPTER1 [↵]

or:

    ERASE CHAPTER1.DOC [↵]

Instead of ERASE, you may use DEL or DELETE—they work in exactly the same way:

    DEL CHAPTER1 [↵]

or:

    DELETE CHAPTER1 [↵]

As with any DOS command, when you want to change or in some way affect a file on a drive other than the current drive (the one specified by the DOS prompt) you must preceed the file name with a drive specifier. For instance, if the current drive is C and the file you want to erase is on drive A, then type:

    ERASE A:CHAPTER1 [↵]

Similarly, when the file is not in the current directory, you must specify its location with a directory path. If the file to be erased is in the subdirectory MICE, which in turn is listed in the subdirectory RODENTS, then to delete FILENAME.DOC you would type:

    ERASE \RODENTS\MICE\FILENAME.DOC [↵]

These two cases may be combined. When the file is found in the subdirectory \RODENTS\MICE on drive C, and some other drive is the current drive, type:

    ERASE C:\RODENTS\MICE\FILENAME.DOC [↵]

Erasing subdirectories   The ERASE, DELETE, and DEL commands can't erase subdirectories. Subdirectories are special files that appear like this in directory listings:

    ACCOUNTS <DIR> 7-08-88 11:05p

Still, DOS won't let you delete the subdirectory using ERASE. Instead, use the RMDIR command, which is explained in section 5.4.

Trying to use ERASE to delete a subdirectory can lead to massive data loss. If the subdirectory ACCOUNTS is listed in the current directory and you attempt to delete it by the command:

ERASE ACCOUNTS ⏎

DOS will assume that you are trying to erase not the subdirectory, but rather all files held in that subdirectory. It responds with the message:

Are you sure (Y/N)?

You can stop DOS from going on by striking the Ⓝ key and then ⏎. If instead you typed Ⓨ, DOS would delete every file in ACCOUNTS (however, subdirectories listed in the ACCOUNTS directory would go unscathed). Since the backslash character represents the root directory, the command:

ERASE \ ⏎

would erase all files in the root directory. This application of the ERASE command has victimized unsuspecting users. Keep it in mind.

Erasing special files   Files may be given special attributes (as explained in the minitutorial at the beginning of Chapter 4) so that the ERASE (or DEL or DELETE) commands will treat them differently. One attribute gives a file read-only status (section 3.3 tells how this is done). When a file is made read-only, application software can read it, but DOS won't let the software change the file. Further, read-only files can't be erased. If you want to delete a read-only file, you must change its attributes so that it is no longer read-only, and then you can delete it normally.

There are other special attributes that endow a file with system status or hidden status. These attributes are generally only used with special system files (files used by DOS) normally found only in a disk's root directory. Such files are omitted from directory listings, and only special software like the Norton Commander can inform you of their presence. If you have reached the level of sophistication in DOS that you have tracked down such files and want to delete them, you should know that the DOS ERASE command cannot do this either. You'll need utility software specially designed for the job, such as the Norton Utilities.

PITFALL | Chapter 8 describes a number of special DOS commands that let you temporarily modify the names of disk drives and subdirectories. These commands include ASSIGN, JOIN, and SUBST. They may be used in a number of situations, and sometimes their operation is unreliable. It's not a good idea to use ERASE while one of these commands is in use. If something goes wrong, files could be deleted from the wrong subdirectory or the wrong disk drive.

The DOS 5.0 Shell   To erase a file using the DOS Shell, first obtain a listing of the directory that holds the file, then select the file you want to delete (section 1.8 provides a full discussion of how to do this by either keyboard or mouse). Next, pull down the Files menu and select Delete.

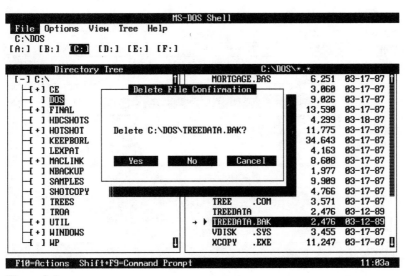

Figure 3.1

Before it actually erases a file, the DOS Shell displays a dialog box showing the name of the file and asking you to confirm that you want the file erased. Click on OK or press ⏎ to make the deletion.

For additional protection, you can have the shell prompt you for a second verification using a confirmation box. This feature is toggled on and off by pulling down the Options menu and choosing File Options.

You'll encounter a dialog box that includes the selection Confirm on delete. The option is selected when the accompanying check box contains an *X*. Make the selection by clicking within the check box or by pressing the tab key until the cursor moves to the check box and then pressing the space bar.

Windows 3.1   In Windows, begin by entering the file system and selecting the file you want to erase. Then pull down the File menu and select Delete. A dialog box, like the one shown in figure 3.2, will appear showing the name of the selected file. Then click on the Delete button. This safety feature ought to be adequate, but you may optionally have Windows prompt you for further confirmation with yet another dialog box. This feature is enabled or disabled by pulling down the Options menu and selecting Confirmation. The resulting dialog box offers a check box named File Delete. Once selected, Windows will prompt you for an additional confirmation whenever you delete a file.

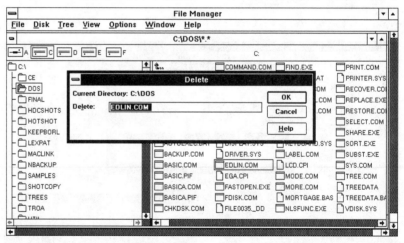

Figure 3.2

3.2 Erasing groups of files

Like some other DOS commands, single ERASE (or DEL or DELETE) commands can operate on groups of files by employing global file name characters. These are discussed in detail in section 1.3. There are two such characters, the asterisk and question mark. Using them, you can erase all files in a directory, or all files with a particular name or extension, or all files with particular characters in their names or extensions.

In DOS commands, the asterisk can take the place of an entire file name or extension, indicating that any name or extension may match in its place. Thus, to erase all files with the extension .DOC, you would type:

    ERASE *.DOC ⏎

Because the asterisk matches with any file name, files like TURTLES. DOC, LIZARDS.DOC, and SNAKES.DOC would all be erased by the command. To erase all files that share the name TURTLES but have any extension (such as TURTLES.DOC, TURTLES.OL, TURTLES.BAT, and just plain TURTLES), you would type:

    ERASE TURTLES.* ⏎

And to erase all files of any name and any extension, that is, all files in the current directory, type:

    ERASE *.* ⏎

As usual, any of these commands could take a drive specifier when the file is not found on the current drive, and a directory path when the drive is not in the current directory:

    ERASE C:*.DOC ⏎
    ERASE \ANIMALS\REPTILES\TURTLES.* ⏎
    ERASE C:\ANIMALS\REPTILES*.* ⏎

The second global file name character, the question mark, can also be used for mass erasures. A question mark matches a single character in a file name or extension. For example:

    ERASE TURTLES.DO? ⏎

erases all files named TURTLE that have a .DO extension ending in any character. The files TURTLES.DOC, TURTLES.DOS, and TURTLES.DOA would all be erased, and so would TURTLES.DO (in this case, the question mark matches when there is no character at all). You can use multiple question marks. For instance:

ERASE TURTLES.D?? `←`

would erase TURTLES.DOC, TURTLES.DZZ, TURTLES.DX, and TURTLES.D. While:

ERASE ?URTLE?.DOC `←`

would erase TURTLES.DOC, TURTLE.DOC, MURTLES.DOC, and MURTLE.DOC.

Accidental erasures   Mass erasures are dangerous. One false step, like a faulty directory path, and scores of files can be obliterated. When many files are erased at once, it may be especially difficult to successfully recover them with an unerase utility (see section 23.4). Always double- and triple-check that the typing of your ERASE command is correct and that you actually typed what you want the computer to do. When an ERASE *.* command attempts to erase all files in a directory, DOS displays the prompt:

Are you sure (Y/N)?

In response, you type either `Y` or `N`. But no message is issued in any other case, even when numerous files are to be deleted. If you aren't certain that the syntax of the ERASE command is correct, first try out a DIR command to get a listing of the files that will be affected:

DIR *.DOC `←`

and then, if the listed files really are the ones you want to erase:

ERASE *.DOC `←`

PITFALLS | Normally, you write a file name—with or without a drive specifier or directory path—in an ERASE command:

ERASE C:\PLANTS\TREES\WILLOWS.DOC `←`

If a directory path is given with no file name at its end, DOS will interpret the command to mean that all files in the subdirectory at the end of the path are to be deleted. For instance, the command:

ERASE \PLANTS\TREES `←`

causes DOS to delete all files in the TREES subdirectory. The effect is the same as if you had entered:

```
ERASE \PLANTS\TREES\*.* ⏎
```

In this regard, recall that the directory path for the root directory is a lone backslash. So, the command:

```
ERASE \ ⏎
```

would cause DOS to erase all files in the root directory.

It's easy to type in such a command by mistake. Fortunately, DOS guards against its unhappy effects by displaying the message:

```
Are you sure (Y/N)?
```

exactly as it does for the ERASE *.* command. But there is still room for accidents. Be aware that this message appears only when all files will be erased in a directory.

The DOS 5.0 Shell   The DOS Shell provides an added measure of both versatility and safety in making mass file erasures. Besides letting you select files using global file name characters, you can move through a directory listing and select multiple files that are not related by the way they are named. For example, the files ELEPHANT, GORILLA, and CHIPMUNK could not be specified as a group using global file name characters (unless a directory held only these three files). Three separate ERASE commands would be required from the DOS command line. But the DOS Shell lets you tag the three files from within a listing of many files and then erase them with a single command.

Section 1.9 explains how multiple files are tagged. Basically, you click the mouse over file names while the Ctrl key is held down, or you move the bar cursor to file names and press the space bar. Once all of the files you want to erase have been chosen, pull down the Files menu and select Delete, exactly as if you were erasing a single file. A dialog box will display a horizontally scrollable list of all selected files, as figure 3.3 shows. This list can be edited. Choose OK (or press ⏎) to delete the file.

You can add one more line of defense against errors by enabling confirmation boxes. This feature is selected by pulling down the Options menu, choosing File Options, and selecting the check box marked Confirm on delete. Thereafter, you'll encounter an additional dialog box for every file included in a mass deletion, telling you the file's name and asking for permission to proceed.

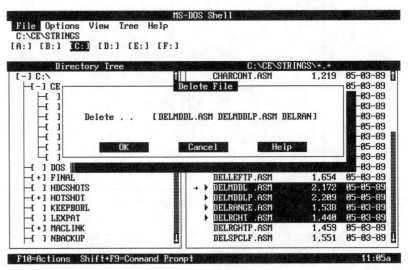

Figure 3.3

Windows 3.1   In Windows, begin by entering the File Manager and selecting the files you want to erase. Multiple files can be selected by holding down the Ctrl key while clicking the file icons (see section 18.4 to learn other methods). Then pull down the File menu and select Delete. A dialog box like the one shown in figure 3.4 will appear to show the names of the selected files. These are listed on a line one after another with a space between. When many files are selected, their names won't all fit into the box. But you can use the cursor keys to scroll back and forth along this horizontal listing, editing it as required. Alternatively, you may write a specification into the box using global file name characters, as though you were working from the DOS command line.

Then click on the Delete button. For safety's sake, you can have Windows prompt you for further confirmation with yet another dialog box. You'll need to specify Yes or No for each file as it comes up for deletion, or choose Yes to All to have all remaining files erased. This feature is enabled or disabled by pulling down the Options menu and selecting Confirmation. The resulting dialog box includes a Confirm on delete check box. Selecting this check box enables the confirmation figure. Otherwise, all files will be deleted in one action.

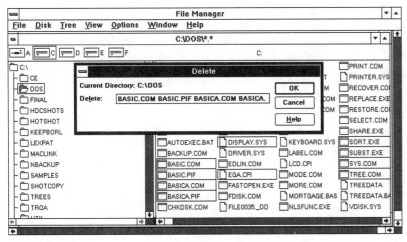

Figure 3.4

3.3 ▋ Making files unerasable

Unfortunately, DOS does not offer a way of making a file unerasable while keeping it normal in every other way. Unerasability would be a desirable feature, because it could help prevent mistakes. The only option currently available is to give a file read-only status, which makes it unerasable, but also prevents application software from changing the file (the file can still be opened for viewing). Read-only status is not usually desirable for data files, but it can be used to protect program files and system files (such as batch files) from inexperienced users who might devastate an entire directory with a single miscalculated ERASE command.

Be aware that you can use the COPY command to make a copy of a read-only file (the copy is not read-only), but it cannot be used to overwrite a read-only file. For example, when the file YOURFILE.TXT has been made read-only, then:

```
COPY MYFILE.TXT YOURFILE.TXT ⏎
```

will result in an error message, since MYFILE.TXT would obliterate the prior contents of YOURFILE.TXT.

Making erasable files unerasable   To give a file read-only status, type:

```
ATTRIB +R FILENAME.EXT ⏎
```

You can use a directory path when the file is not in the current directory, and a drive specifier if it is not on the current drive:

```
ATTRIB +R A:\LEVEL1\LEVEL2\FILENAME.EXT ⏎
```

The ATTRIB command is an external DOS command, meaning that it relies on a DOS file named ATTRIB.EXE. If this file is not in the current directory, or accessible via the PATH command (explained in section 8.1), then you must supply a directory path along with the file name:

```
C:\DOS\ATTRIB +R \LEVEL1\LEVEL2\FILENAME.EXT ⏎
```

Making unerasable files erasable   To undo the read-only status of a file, use the ATTRIB command in exactly the same way, but specify -R instead of +R. You can find out the current status of a file by omitting the -R or +R altogether, as in

```
ATTRIB FILENAME.EXT ⏎
```

DOS responds by displaying the file name and placing an *R* to the left of it if the file bears the read-only attribute. (You may also see an *A*, which indicates that the file needs backing up, as the minitutorial in Chapter 22 explains).

Making a file unerasable does not mean that the file becomes indestructable. If the disk is damaged, the file may be lost. Both hard disks and floppy diskettes can fail in many ways, some of which we discuss in Chapter 24. Unerasable files can also be destroyed by malfunctioning software, accidental disk reformatting, and other mishaps. So, be sure that these files are included in your backups.

The DOS 5.0 Shell   In the DOS Shell program, begin by selecting one or more files for which you want to change the read-only attribute. Then pull down the File menu and choose Change attributes. A dialog box will offer these choices:

1. Change selected files one at a time

2. Change all selected files at once

The first choice results in a succession of dialog boxes when multiple files are chosen, requiring you to specify the read-only attribute for each file in turn. The second choice lets you specify the read-only attribute just once no matter the number of files. In either case, you'll be shown the dialog box in figure 3.5.

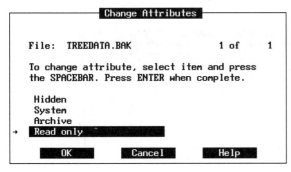

Figure 3.5

To select the read-only attribute, either click over the attribute name, or move the bar cursor over the name and press the space bar. An arrowhead appears to the left of the name when it is selected. Repeating this action deselects the attribute. Then click on OK (or press ⏎) and the read-only attribute will be changed.

You can find out the current status of a file's read-only attribute by selecting Show Information from the Options menu once a file has been selected. The second line of the displayed information reports the file's attribute, listing *r* when it is a read-only file.

Windows 3.1   In Windows, begin by entering the File Manager and selecting the file or files you wish to modify. Pull down the File menu and select Properties. You'll be shown a dialog box like the one in figure 3.6. If the Read Only check box is selected (contains an *X*), the file is already read-only. Otherwise, click on the box and then the OK button to make the file read-only. Reverse the process to return the file to normal erasable status.

You should be aware that, unlike the DOS Delete statement, the File menu's Delete command can erase read-only files. But it will first warn you with a dialog box that announces, "This is a system, hidden, or read-only file," and then lets you specify Yes or No as to whether the deletion should continue. This dialog box appears whether or not you have asked for such confirmation boxes through the Confirmation option in the Options menu.

```
┌──────────────────────────────────────────────────┐
│ ▬          Properties for PROSE.DOC               │
│ ┌──────────────────────────────┐  ┌────────────┐  │
│ │ File Name:   PROSE.DOC        │  │    OK      │  │
│ │ Size:        1,859 bytes      │  └────────────┘  │
│ │ Last Change: 06/05/90 01:18:10PM  ┌────────────┐ │
│ │ Path:        C:\SAMPLES       │  │  Cancel    │  │
│ │                               │  └────────────┘  │
│ │ ┌Attributes──────────────────┐  ┌────────────┐  │
│ │ │ ☐ Read Only   ☐ Hidden     │  │   Help     │  │
│ │ │ ☒ Archive     ☐ System     │  └────────────┘  │
│ │ └────────────────────────────┘                  │
│ └──────────────────────────────┘                  │
└──────────────────────────────────────────────────┘
```

Figure 3.6

TIP

Windows lets you select multiple files and change all of their read-only attributes at once. Just select the files in the normal way (such as by clicking on file icons while holding down the ⎡Ctrl⎤ key), select Properties from the File menu, click the read-only check box so that it shows an *X*, and press ⎡←⎤.

Even when multiple files have been selected, Windows displays only one dialog box with one set of check boxes to provide composite information on file attributes. In this case, a check box is empty when no files have a particular attribute, or a check box holds the usual *X* when all selected files possess the attribute. Should an attribute belong to only some of the selected files, the box is shaded instead of crossed.

When you choose OK to begin making changes, attributes marked by a shaded box instead of an *X* will not be assigned to all listed files, but will remain in force in files that already bear the attribute. To make an initially shaded attribute apply to all files, click the box until an *X* appears and then choose OK. Thus, if you select ten files and at least one already has its read-only attribute selected, the read-only check box will appear shaded and must be clicked until it contains an *X* to set the read-only attribute in the other files.

File names may be from one to eight characters long. It doesn't matter whether you type them in lowercase or uppercase letters. ACCOUNTS, taxes, and Hijinks are all acceptable file names. You can use any keyboard character in file names except those that have special uses in DOS. There are 14 of these:

    .   "   /   \   [   ]   :   ¦   <   >   +   =   ;   ,

It's difficult to remember all of these exceptions. To prevent mistakes, try to avoid using punctuation marks in your file names. Numerals, however, are useful. BACKUP37 and 15XYZ16 are both proper file names. Sometimes you may want to insert a space character into a file name, as in TAXES 90. DOS won't let you input file names like this, but some software does, and DOS can list them in directory entries; but it's not a good idea to put spaces in file names even when it's possible to do so. Instead, use a hyphen or the underscore character to substitute for a space: TAXES-90 or TAXES_90.

You can add an extension to the end of any file name. An extension begins with a period and is followed by up to three characters (again, you must avoid the 14 characters in the list above). Instead of calling a file ACCOUNTS, you might name it ACCOUNTS.DOC with the .DOC extension (for document) to indicate that the file holds a word processing document. Another file might be named TAXES.DOC, and a third could be FINANCES.DOC. It's a few more keystrokes to type an extension along with a file name, but the extension can tell you at a glance which of your programs the file belongs to.

Often, programs automatically add their own extensions to the files they create so that they can later identify the file as belonging to them. Some programs are unable to read data files if the user changes or removes the extension the program supplies. When software does not dictate an extension, you may devise your own system of extensions to classify files. File name extensions can be used to operate on groups of related files. This is done with global file name characters (or wild-card characters), which are discussed in section 1.4. Using them, you could request a directory listing of all files that end with .DOC, or could erase all files with the extension .TXT, and so on. Beginners might neglect file name extensions, but as the number of files you've created increases, you'll be glad to have taken the trouble to classify them with extensions.

Finally, you should be aware that all files may be given one or more attributes. These are markers that tell DOS to treat a file in special ways. One attribute can make the file a read-only file that can be read but not changed. Another attribute hides the file from directory listings. You'll find a full discussion of file attributes and how they can be set and changed at the end of this chapter (section 4.5).

4.1 Suggestions for naming files

By following the suggestions presented here when you name a new file, or rename an old one, you can avoid confusion and mistakes, and can apply DOS commands more powerfully.

Avoid acronyms   When a file's contents could be described as "The Great Train Robbery," you might be tempted to reduce the expression to an acronym, calling the file TGTR. You are very likely to forget the meaning of the acronym with time, and it will give no indication to others about what the file holds. It's also much harder to scan directory listings when they are full of acronyms. A name like TRAINROB is far better since it suggests the content. Similarly, TAXPRB92 is better than LIRSP92T, for "Letter to IRS about Problems in 1992 Taxes."

Use file name extensions   Newcomers to DOS frequently omit extensions when they name files. As you become more experienced with DOS, you will learn many ways to save time by handling groups of files with single DOS commands. But groups of files can usually only be specified if there is a common characteristic in their file names. When every file containing business correspondence is given a distinctive extension to its file name, such as .CSP, you can easily backup all of your correspondence with a single command, or view an alphabetized directory listing of just those files. But when no extensions are given to the file names, all sorts of unrelated files will interfere with such commands.

It is important to start naming files properly from the beginning. Otherwise, as you learn to handle files efficiently, you'll find that you may need to examine and rename hundreds of files to put your knowledge to work. Since at any one moment it may be much easier to perform a DOS command the hard way than to stop to reorganize all your files, you may be trapped into never organizing your files properly once you've gotten off to a bad start.

Relate files with file name characters as well as extensions
When files form a related group or series, you can use the last few characters of the eight-character file name to distinguish them. For example, if you were writing a long report, you might name the text files for each section as PART1.RPT, PART2.RPT, PART3.RPT, and so on (use two digits if the numbers exceed 9: PART01, PART02, and so on).

Each of these files might be associated with an outline created by another program, and named PART1.OL, PART2.OL, and PART3.OL. Using this scheme, you could ask DOS to list, copy, or print out various combinations of the files. For instance, to make backups, you could use the command:

```
COPY PART?.RPT A: ⏎
```

to copy the text files for all sections of the report (1, 2, 3...) to drive A, or:

```
COPY PART1.* A: ⏎
```

to copy over the text and outline files for just section 1, and:

```
COPY PART?.* A: ⏎
```

to copy over both text and outline files for all sections. (The use of the global file name characters ? and * is explained in section 1.3.)

Don't give a file the same name as the subdirectory in which it resides   DOS permits files to have the same names as subdirectories, but the behavior of some DOS commands can be confusing when this is the case. Let's say that the current directory contains both a file named PARROTS and a subdirectory named PARROTS. If you type DIR PARROTS ⏎, wanting to see the directory listing for the file PARROTS, DOS instead gives a complete directory listing of the files in the subdirectory PARROTS. There are a number of such complications, and they are easily avoided by carefully naming files and subdirectories.

Don't start file names with non-alphabetic characters   DOS allows you to begin file names with numerals or any of a number of punctuation marks and special characters, including:

```
'  ~  !  @  #  $  %  ^  &  (  )  {  }  _  -
```

but not:

```
.  "  /  \  [  ]  :  |  <  >  +  =  ;  ,
```

Generally speaking, these characters can make file names hard to read and type. More importantly, DOS does not alphabetize these symbols in a commonly understood way, as it does for the letters *A* through *Z*. If you begin file names with unusual characters, you won't be able to sort directory listings in a useful—or, at least, predictable—way, using the techniques shown in section 2.3.

4.2 Renaming a file

The command:

```
RENAME OLDNAME.TXT NEWNAME.TXT ⏎
```

renames the file OLDNAME.TXT to NEWNAME.TXT. This example assumes that the file you want to rename—in this case, OLD-NAME.TXT—is in the current directory. When the file is on another disk, or in another directory on the same disk, you can either move to the disk or directory where the file resides and then use the command, or you can modify the command to tell DOS where to find the file that is to be renamed. For example, if the DOS prompt is A> and you want to rename a file in the subdirectory \BIRDS\PARROTS on drive C, you can either type:

```
C: ⏎
CHDIR \BIRDS\PARROTS ⏎
RENAME OLDFILE.TXT NEWFILE.TXT ⏎
A: ⏎
```

or you can simply type:

```
RENAME C:\BIRDS\PARROTS\OLDFILE.TXT NEWFILE.TXT ⏎
```

TIP

DOS won't let you move a file between directories or drives by adding a directory path to the new file name. For example, the command:

```
RENAME C:\PARROTS\OLD.TXT C:\TOUCANS\NEW.TXT ⏎
```

won't move the file OLD.TXT from the PARROTS subdirectory to the TOUCANS subdirectory while renaming it as NEW.TXT. You'd just encounter an "Invalid parameter" error message if you tried.

The DOS 5.0 Shell   In the DOS Shell, bring a directory listing to the screen and select one or more files you want to rename. Then pull down the File menu and choose Rename. The dialog box shown in figure 4.1 will ask you to enter the new file name. Then click on OK or press ⏎ to change the file name. When multiple files have been selected, a succession of dialog boxes will appear so that you can rename each file in turn.

Figure 4.1

Windows 3.1

In Windows, begin by entering the File Manager and selecting the file you want to rename. Then pull down the File menu and select Rename. A dialog box like the one shown in figure 4.2 will appear to prompt you for the new file name. Type in the new name and press ⏎. The file will be renamed and the directory listing will immediately reflect the change.

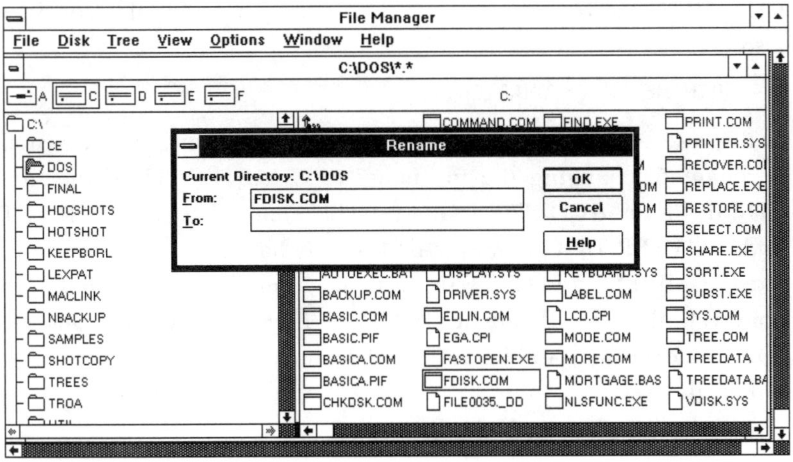

Figure 4.2

4.3 Renaming groups of files

You can rename several files with similar file names by using a single RENAME command (see section 4.2 to learn the basics of renaming files.) Let's say that your software creates four files with the same name, but different extensions, such as CHIMP, CHIMP.LST, CHIMP.TXT, and CHIMP.OL. To rename all four files as GORILLA (while keeping their extensions intact), use the command:

    RENAME CHIMP.* GORILLA.* ⏎

The asterisk, a global file name character (see section 1.3), tells DOS to rename files named CHIMP—with any or no file name extension—changing CHIMP to GORILLA, but leaving the extensions as they are. The four resulting files would be named GORILLA, GORILLA.LST, GORILLA.TXT, and GORILLA .OL. Note that the conversion is made for the file named CHIMP even though it has no file name extension. Of course, the command could include a DOS path:

    RENAME C:\PRIMATES\CHIMP.* GORILLA.* ⏎

Other group renamings of files are possible. Simply substitute an asterisk or question mark character in the file name itself, rather than the extension. For example:

    RENAME CH?MP.* CHUMP.* ⏎

Here, the question mark changes to a *U*, resulting in the file names CHUMP, CHUMP.LST, CHUMP.TXT, and CHUMP.OL. Consider also:

    RENAME CH*.* CHAPTER.* ⏎

In this case, any file name beginning with *CH* and having any extension is renamed, changing the file name to CHAPTER. Thus, the files CHIMP.TXT and CHEESE.DOC would be renamed to CHAPTER.TXT and CHAPTER. DOC. However, if file names have identical extensions, like CHIMP.TXT and CHEESE.TXT, the command would attempt to convert both files to the name CHAPTER.TXT, and the error message "Duplicate file name or File not found" would result (without renaming either file).

4.4 Changing a file's time or date

When organizing and archiving files, it's sometimes useful to be able to change the time and date given in a file's directory listing. This is referred to as the file's time stamp. The time stamp records the last time a file was changed, that is, the last time the file (or part of the file) was written to the disk. If you load a file and then save it, its time stamp will be changed even if you haven't altered the file. Conversely, closing a file without saving it leaves the time stamp unchanged, even when the file has been altered (keep in mind, however, that some software automatically saves changed files).

DOS provides no simple way of changing a file's time stamp. But there is a roundabout, three-step method that does the job.

Step 1   Change the current time or date held in the system clock to the values you want assigned to the file. (The system clock is given the current time and date when the computer starts up, either by typing it in, or, on many computers, by automatically reading it from a real time clock that keeps proper time even when the machine is turned off. See section 17.4 for details).

Say that the date held in the system clock is currently 6-21-90 and you want the time stamp for a particular file changed to the date 3-12-90. Change the system clock date by entering at the DOS prompt:

        DATE 3-12-90 ⏎

Step 2   Load the file into the software that created it (text files may be loaded into any text editor that can handle them). Once loaded, just save the file by whatever command the software uses, and then quit the program and return to the DOS prompt.

Step 3   Reset the system clock to the proper date. In this example:

        DATE 6-21-90 ⏎

TIP

By far the easiest way to change a file's time or date is to use utility software. Many DOS shells can perform this service, as can individual utilities like the FD (File Date) program that is part of The Norton Utilities. For example:

```
FD OLDFILE.DOC /D06-21-92 ⏎
```

This command changes the date of the file OLDFILE.DOC to June 21, 1992. FD can use global file name characters (section 1.3) to operate on groups of files, and a single FD command can extend its actions across multiple subdirectories.

4.5 Changing file attributes

Attributes are special markers that DOS attaches to files to classify them. There are five attributes that may be given:

- The read-only attribute changes a file so that it can be read, moved, or copied, but not changed or erased.

- The archive attribute marks a file as having been changed since it was last backed up. File backups are often made by special backup software, such as the BACKUP program that accompanies DOS or the Norton Backup. When the software finishes backing up a file, it turns off the file's archive attribute. When other software subsequently writes to the file, DOS turns the attribute back on. The next time the backup program is run, it can use the attribute to tell which files have been changed or created and need to be copied. In this way, files that have not been changed are not backed up needlessly.

- The subdirectory attribute marks a file as holding a subdirectory. All directories in a directory tree except the root directory are held in files.

- The hidden attribute causes DOS to not display a file in directory listings even though it is present in a directory. Most DOS commands, including COPY and DEL cannot operate on hidden files (however, the TYPE command will display a hidden file if you can somehow find out the file's name).

- The system attribute marks a file as belonging to the operating system (to DOS). Files marked with this attribute are also not shown in directory listings.

A file that does not have read-only, subdirectory, hidden, or system attributes is called a normal file. Because the archive attribute changes back and forth and does not actually categorize a file, a file is still a normal file whether its archive attribute is set or not.

Ordinarily, there are only two kinds of attributes that you might need to change, the read-only attribute and the archive attribute. DOS lets you alter these two attributes and also the system and hidden attributes. This is done with the ATTRIB command. The attributes are variously represented by the symbols *R, A, S,* and *H.* Placing a plus sign before the symbol specifies that the attribute should be switched on; a minus sign does the opposite. For example, to set the read-only attribute, type:

```
ATTRIB +R FILENAME.EXT ⏎
```

Of course, a directory path is used when the file is not in the current directory:

```
ATTRIB +R C:\LEVEL1\LEVEL2\FILENAME.EXT ⏎
```

To turn off the attribute:

```
ATTRIB -R FILENAME.EXT ⏎
```

Note that ATTRIB is an external DOS command, meaning that it is not kept permanently in memory, but rather requires a separate file named ATTRIB.EXE. If this file is not in the current directory, you must specify a directory path to it:

```
C:\DOS\ATTRIB -A FILENAME.EXT ⏎
```

Alternatively, use the DOS PATH command to keep all DOS files accessible from any directory. Section 8.2 explains how this is done.

Changing the attributes of many files with a single command
Use global file name characters (discussed in section 1.3) to alter attributes in groups of files. For example, to change all files with a .BAT extension to read-only, type:

```
ATTRIB +R *.BAT ⏎
```

This command would apply only to files in the current directory. Add /S at the end of the command to make it apply also to all .BAT files in all subdirectories beyond the current directory. When a tree's root directory is the current directory, every directory in the tree is affected. Thus, to turn on the archive attribute in every file on a disk, type:

```
ATTRIB +A \*.* /S ⏎
```

Finding out the current attributes of a file   If you type:

```
ATTRIB FILENAME.EXT ⏎
```

DOS responds by displaying the file name with an *R* to the left if the file is read-only and an *A* if the archive attribute is turned on. Both are turned on in this example:

```
A R C:\REPTILES\TOADS\SLIME.DOC
```

PITFALLS | If you acquire utility software that can change the subdirectory attribute, you should never apply this feature. A non-subdirectory file that is marked with the subdirectory attribute will cause the machine to crash when DOS tries to read it. Conversely, a subdirectory file that has its subdirectory attribute turned off will cause the directory and all subdirectories below to disappear from view, along with access to all files they contain. If the file is subsequently erased, much data will be lost.

The DOS 5.0 Shell   In the DOS Shell program (DOS 4.0 and later), begin by selecting one or more files for which you want to change the read-only, archive, system, or hidden attributes. Then pull down the File menu and choose Change attribute. A dialog box will offer two choices:

1. Change selected files one at a time

2. Change all selected files at once

The first choice results in a succession of dialog boxes, requiring you to confirm each file in turn before its attributes are changed. In either case, you'll be shown the screen in figure 4.3. The four attributes are selected in the same way as files are in directory listings. Either click the mouse over the attribute name, or move the bar cursor over the name and press the space bar. An arrowhead appears to the left of the name when it is selected. Repeating this action deselects the attribute. When the proper attribute combination is set, click on OK or press ⏎, and the attributes will be changed.

You can find out the current attributes of a file simply by following this procedure to the last step, but then choosing Cancel instead of OK. Arrows will mark the current attributes. More conveniently, select Show Information from the Options menu once a file has been selected. The second line of the displayed information reports the file's attribute, listing *r* for read-only, *a* for archive, *s* for system, and *h* for hidden.

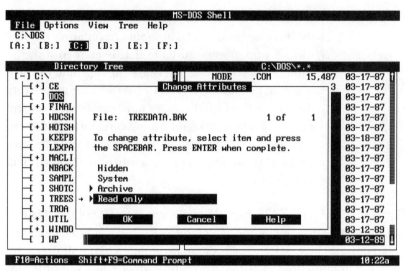

Figure 4.3

Windows 3.1   In Windows, enter the File Manager and select one or more files for which to change attributes. Then choose Properties from the File menu. You'll encounter a dialog box like the one in figure 4.4 that presents check boxes marked Read Only, Archive, Hidden, and System. Click on a check box to mark it with an *X* and then click the OK button to bring about the change in attribute.

You can determine the current attributes of a file by calling up the Properties dialog box in the same way. Then view the check boxes to see which attributes are currently selected. Exit the dialog box by clicking on Cancel.

When multiple files have been selected, check boxes are shaded instead of crossed for attributes that pertain to some but not all of the files. An *X* appears only when all files share the attribute. The box is empty when none have the attribute.

When you choose OK to begin making changes, attributes marked by a shaded box instead of an *X* will not be assigned to all listed files, but will remain in force in files that already bear the attribute. To make an initially shaded attribute apply to all files, click the box until an *X* appears and then choose OK. Thus, if you select several files and at least one already has its archive attribute selected, the archive check box will appear shaded and must be clicked until it contains an *X* to set the archive attribute in the other files.

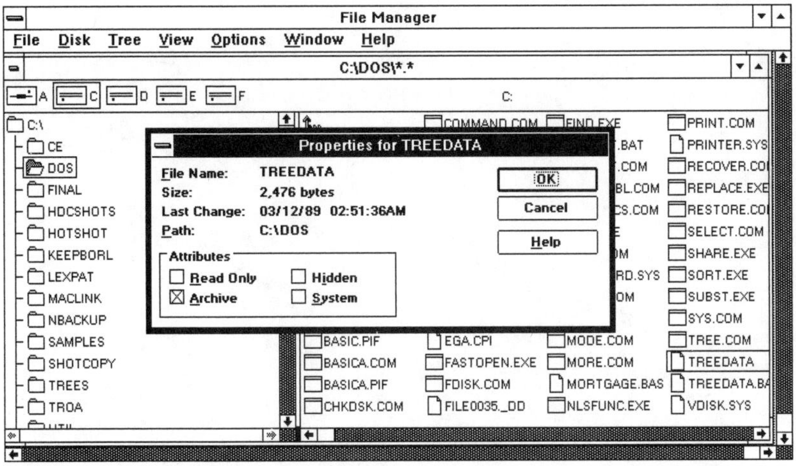

Figure 4.4

Chapter 5

Directory Trees

- MINITUTORIAL: All about directory trees
- Suggestions for designing directory trees
- Creating a new subdirectory
- Renaming and relocating subdirectories
- Removing a subdirectory
- Viewing and printing a directory tree

MINITUTORIAL:

All about directory trees

Directory trees are a way of organizing multiple directories on a single disk. Just like real trees, they start out with a basic trunk—usually called the root directory—from which branches, or subdirectories, grow. Directory trees are usually used on hard disks, but diskettes can have them too. On a hard disk, the number of files stored can easily reach into the thousands, and throwing that number of files into one huge directory listing would be like storing an entire library's collection of books in a huge pile.

When a disk is freshly formatted, it has only one directory, and the others are added by us as the need arises. With time, a hard disk may come to have hundreds of directories. One directory might hold tax information; another, personal correspondence. To indicate the purpose of each directory, you can give it a name of up to eight characters, like TAXES or LETTERS, just like a file name. Also like file names, a three-character extension may be added (TAXES.KGB).

When a disk has only one directory, you can tell DOS about a file without worrying about where the file is located—it's in the one and only directory. But once files are divided among many directories, you often need to specify a file's directory as well as its name when you ask a program to load it, or ask DOS to do something with the file, like copy it. For example, if a file named DOCUMENT.TXT is held in the directory named TAXES, as shown in figure 5.1 you could refer to the file with the expression \TAXES\DOCUMENT.TXT. To copy the file over to another disk (say, to drive A), instead of just typing:

```
COPY DOCUMENT.TXT A:  [←]
```

you'd type:

```
COPY \TAXES\DOCUMENT.TXT A:  [←]
```

Later when your word processor asked for the name of the file you want to work on, you could type:

```
\TAXES\DOCUMENT.TXT  [←]
```

Without the addition of \TAXES\, DOS wouldn't know which directory to look in to find DOCUMENT.TXT. It's important to note that the slash character used here is a backslash. It's not the usual slash found on typewriter keyboards (/). If you use an ordinary slash, DOS will issue an error message.

DOS lets you link a disk into a hierarchy, where several related directories are contained in a higher-level directory. For example, in figure 5.1 the directory named TAXES contains directories named IRS88, IRS89, IRS90, each containing files related to taxes of that year.

A system like this is sometimes used in filing cabinets, where several related file folders are kept in yet another folder. But in a computer, the system can be extended to directories within directories within directories, and so on. The directory named IRS88 could itself contain directories named RECEIPTS, DEDUCT, INCOME, each holding relevant files. And the related directories IRS89 and IRS90 could hold similar directories. These are also shown in figure 5.1.

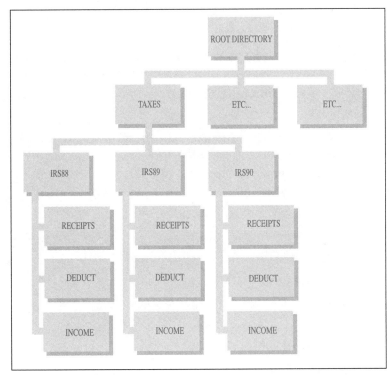

Figure 5.1

It's easy to see why this system is called a directory tree. The network of your directories grows outward like a tree, from trunk to branch to twig.

The directories are created in this order, starting (in this example) with TAXES, then IRS88, and then RECEIPTS. As the diagram shows, the TAXES directory, and others at the same level, are also contained in a directory. That directory is the main directory for the whole disk. It is called the root directory.

The root directory is the one directory that already exists on a disk when it is new—that is, after it has been formatted. When you hear about the directory on a diskette, usually the directory talked about is the disk's root directory. On both hard disks and diskettes, you can at any time create directories within the root directory (such as TAXES and LETTERS), and, if you need them, you can create additional directories within those directories (such as IRS88, IRS89, and IRS90), and so on. In a sense, all directories are subordinate to the root directory in this hierarchy, and for this reason all directories except the root directory are usually called subdirectories.

In the tree shown here, TAXES is a level 1 subdirectory, IRS88, IRS89, and IRS90 are level 2 subdirectories, and RECEIPTS, DEDUCT, and INCOME are level 3 subdirectories. DOS will let you create as many levels as you like.

It is important to understand that any directory, including the root directory, can contain files as well as other directories. At the start of this minitutorial we saw how the file DOCUMENT.TXT, residing in the subdirectory TAXES, was referred to with the expression:

```
\TAXES\DOCUMENT.TXT
```

What if DOCUMENT.TXT was instead located in the IRS88 subdirectory held by TAXES? Then the file would be referred to as:

```
\TAXES\IRS88\DOCUMENT.TXT
```

And if the file was in the RECEIPTS subdirectory held in IRS88, it would be referred to as:

```
\TAXES\IRS88\RECEIPTS\DOCUMENT.TXT
```

In the latter case, if your word processor asked for the file to work with, you would need to type in the entire sequence \TAXES\IRS88\RE-CEIPTS\DOCUMENT.TXT ↵. You can see that, although DOS will allow you to create as many levels of subdirectories as you like, there are some practical considerations to keep in mind when you're trying to decide on how many levels you want to use. Typing the chain of directories to a file nestled within 34 subdirectories could easily become an annoyance. In any case, this entire sequence is called a directory path, or sometimes a file path or just a path. It is the path from the root directory (which is represented by the first backslash in the sequence) to the file named DOCUMENT.TXT.

There are times when a directory path doesn't end with a file name. Instead, it just names a particular directory that you want to get to. For instance, say that DOCUMENT.TXT resides in the IRS88 subdirectory and you want to place a copy of it in IRS89. Then you'd have to type:

```
COPY \TAXES\IRS88\DOCUMENT.TXT \TAXES\IRS89 ←
```

This command seems much more complicated than the command COPY DOCUMENT.TXT B: ←, which copies a file between drives, but it is similar. Instead of copying the file to another drive, it copies it to another subdirectory on the same disk. Rather than specify only a file name, you have to type out the directory path leading to the file. And, instead of just specifying another drive, you have to write out the directory path to the directory where the file copy is to be deposited. Notice that there is no final backslash.

Consider, also, the following examples. To use the TYPE command to display the file BANKLIST.TXT kept in \TAXES\IRS88 (that is, in the subdirectory named IRS88) you'd type:

```
TYPE \TAXES\IRS88\BANKLIST.TXT ←
```

To erase the file CASHOUT.LST in the directory \TAXES\IRS90\ RECEIPTS, type:

```
ERASE \TAXES\IRS90\RECEIPTS\CASHOUT.LST ←
```

And, to request a directory listing for the subdirectory \TAXES, type:

```
DIR \TAXES ←
```

The root directory is indicated by the initial backslash. This symbol can be used alone. To ask for a listing of the root directory type:

```
DIR \ ←
```

Directories are created by the DOS MKDIR command and deleted by the RMDIR command. These commands aren't used every day, but a third command, CHDIR, is one of the most heavily used DOS commands. It sets the current directory, which is the directory to which DOS directs its operations by default—that is, when no directory is specified by a directory path. For instance, when IRS89 is the current directory in the tree shown in figure 5.1, then the command:

    DIR ⏎

has the same effect as:

    DIR \TAXES\IRS89 ⏎

These two commands are equivalent while IRS89 is current because, in the first case, DOS automatically directs the DIR command toward IRS89. Similarly, the command:

    TYPE MYFILE.TXT ⏎

would be equivalent in this case to:

    TYPE \TAXES\IRS89\MYFILE.TXT ⏎

Should you want to load MYFILE.TXT into your word processor, you could simply type:

    MYFILE.TXT ⏎

when the software asks for a file name—again, providing IRS89 is current. If not, you'd need to tell the word processor not just the name of the file, but the entire directory path up to it:

    \TAXES\IRS89\MYFILE.TXT ⏎

As you can see, directory trees make DOS harder to use. Much more typing is required, with greater chances of errors. You need to keep a mental map of the whole tree and to remember directory paths, sometimes long ones. Also, you must keep track of which directory is the current directory and constantly change the current directory to reduce the amount of typing necessary. However, DOS offers many features to help overcome these complexities, as the sections of this chapter and Chapters 6 and 8 explain.

Utility software can make working in directory trees much easier by displaying a visual image of the tree (a tree diagram). You can refer to a particular subdirectory simply by moving a cursor to it, or by clicking on it with a mouse. Individual subdirectories can be opened to display listings of the files they contain, and you can select a program you want to run, or files that are to be copied, erased, or renamed. All of this is done without typing in DOS paths like those explained in this section. These services are performed by DOS shells like the Norton Commander or the shell that comes with DOS 4.0, and by operating environments like Microsoft Windows or DesqView (see the minitutorial in Chapter 18 to learn about these kinds of software). Utility programs like the NCD (Norton Change Directory) program in the Norton Utilities also can make directory trees easier to use.

5.1 Suggestions for designing directory trees

A great shortcoming of DOS is its inability to easily modify a directory tree's structure. There are no DOS commands for moving branches of the tree from one position to another, or for renaming individual subdirectories (however, the DOS 4.0 Shell program can do the latter, as can Windows and the Norton Commander). While you can make such modifications in roundabout ways (section 5.3), you'll be much better off if you design your tree with a clear plan right from the start. The time invested will be repaid many times over, for a rational design compliments many labor-saving techniques presented elsewhere in this book. As you tailor the design to your needs, follow these suggestions.

Reserve the root directory for subdirectories   The root directory should serve as a table of contents for your hard disk. Unfortunately, many people use it as a convenient dumping ground for miscellaneous files (in fact, some beginners try to place all files in the root directory, a mistake that lasts only until the directory's available slots are filled). The root directory is not a good place to keep utilities, DOS files, batch files, program files, or data files. Generally speaking, it should contain only subdirectories and the files necessary for booting: COMMAND.COM, CONFIG.SYS, and AUTOEXEC.BAT (the first is discussed in section 17.1, the latter two in section 11.1). A newly formatted hard disk already has COMMAND. COM at the top of the otherwise empty root directory. Immediately add the other two files so that they will be listed next (DOS 4.0 users will have this done for them automatically by the installation program). Then create the subdirectories for the first layer of your directory tree. If you have fewer than 20 subdirectories at this level, you'll be able to type DIR \ ↵ to have DOS display a nonscrolling overview of the disk, with all level 1 subdirectories listed in a row. (A directory-sorting utility like the DS (Directory Sort) program in the Norton Utilities can move all subdirectories to the top of longer directory listings).

You may be tempted to load the root directory with device drivers (section 11.11) loaded by CONFIG.SYS, or memory-resident programs (section 15.4) loaded by AUTOEXEC.BAT. But these files can be accessed by directory paths. Instead of placing the line:

```
SKPLUS
```

in AUTOEXEC.BAT, which would load Borland's SideKickPlus utility from the root directory, write:

```
\UTILITY\SKPLUS
```

and place utilities like SKPLUS in a subdirectory named \UTILITY.

Keep subdirectories small   You'll have better control over your disk when subdirectories hold fewer files, just as you would have better control over a library by using a finer indexing scheme. Small directories make for faster directory searches and shorter directory listings. Shoot for single-screen directory listings; these are particularly useful if you haven't a DOS shell on hand for scrolling listings up and down. Ignore this rule, however, when classifying a group of strongly related files. For example, all program files for a particular application generally should go in the same directory. But data files should constantly be reorganized into finer subdivisions—that is, into more parallel subdirectories.

Keep the tree broad and shallow   It is tedious typing long directory paths again and again. You can avoid wasting time by keeping all frequently accessed files within the first two layers of the tree above the root directory so that they can be accessed with a two-word path, such as \UTILITY\RECOVERY. To achieve this organization, first-level subdirectories should largely be confined to holding the names of second-level subdirectories. Reserve the third level (and beyond) for archives and other seldom-used files.

Organize subdirectories around data, not application programs
Many people organize their hard disk's directory tree with most first-level subdirectories holding program files and second-level subdirectories holding data used by the respective programs, as figure 5.2 shows.

With the tree constructed in this way, the user typically moves to the subdirectory holding the program he or she wishes to use, starts it up, and then types in directory paths for the data files required. Thanks to the DOS PATH and APPEND commands (sections 8.1 and 8.2) there is no need to work this way. These commands let DOS find and start up a program no matter which subdirectory is current. The commands can be included in your AUTOEXEC.BAT file so that they are always at your disposal. Once this is done, you can banish all program files off to one branch of the directory tree that you'll seldom need to access. With the program files pushed aside, you may organize your level 1 subdirectories around projects, keeping related data sets in level 2 subdirectories. Figure 5.3 illustrates this scheme. When the directory tree is arranged this way, you can start up a program with the current directory set to the subdirectory that contains the files you'll be working on, thus saving you the trouble of typing in directory paths to load files, and avoiding the error of writing new files to the wrong subdirectory.

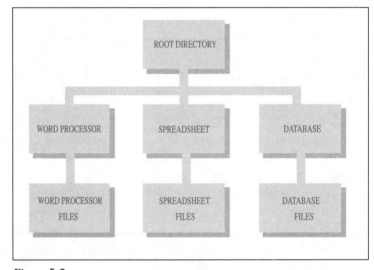

Figure 5.2

Give subdirectories short names   This rule is an obvious one, for many directory names will be typed thousands of times. It's usually best to shorten names rather than condense them. For example, a subdirectory containing utility software could, in eight characters, be called UTILITY, but UTIL would do just as well. However, dropping the vowels to make UTLTY is both hard to read and slow to type. Similarly, try to avoid condensing an expression like "Mexican Debt Crisis" to something like MXDBCRS—MEXDEBT would be much better.

Avoid extensions to subdirectory names   Few people are in danger of breaking this rule, since most are not aware that subdirectory names may be given a three-character extension just like file names. The subdirectory BIGDEAL could as well be named BIGDEAL.PT1. Not only are these extensions more work to type, but they make directory paths hard to read.

Avoid giving subdirectories the same names as files   DOS commands can yield confusing results when a subdirectory contains both a subdirectory named WP (for Word Perfect) and a program file named WP.EXE. The expression DIR WP ⏎ leads to a complete directory listing of the WP subdirectory rather than a search for the WP.EXE file. DOS itself does not become confused in such a situation (if you were to just enter WP ⏎, Word Perfect would be loaded and run) but you might become confused, and that is no better.

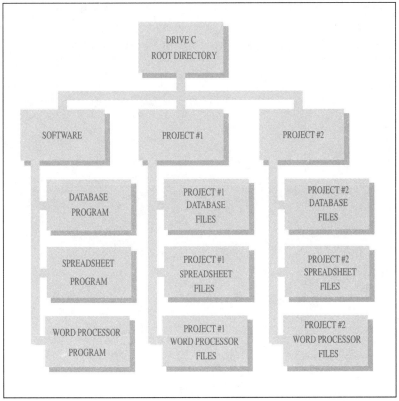

Figure 5.3

Create a subdirectory for DOS files   DOS files deserve a subdirectory of their own that is shared with no others. Don't install DOS files into the root directory. Only the main DOS program, COMMAND. COM, needs to be there, just as it is installed when the disk is formatted. Instead, place all DOS files in a subdirectory named DOS held in the root directory. Then add this subdirectory to your PATH command (section 8.1) so that all DOS facilities are available at any time, no matter what the current directory is. By keeping these files in one place you can easily upgrade to a new version of DOS. On the other hand, if multiple copies of various DOS utilities become scattered about the directory tree, you'll have an awful time finding and replacing them all when you upgrade.

Keep all (or most) batch files in the same subdirectory   Like DOS files, batch files also deserve their own directory listed in the PATH command. That way, any file will be available no matter what the current directory is. This approach lets you create batch files that can steer you from one part of the tree to another with only a few keystrokes; you can even set up a primitive menu system, which we discuss in section 9.10.

5.2 Creating a new subdirectory

The easiest way to create a new subdirectory is to first move to the subdirectory in which it will reside. Say that you want to create a subdirectory named PERSIAN in the subdirectory CATS shown in figure 5.4.

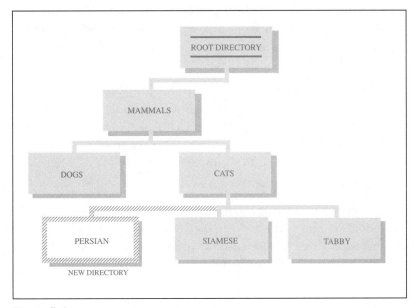

Figure 5.4

Use the CHDIR command (section 6.3) to move to the CATS Directory, making it the current directory:

```
CHDIR \MAMMALS\CATS ⏎
```

Then create the PERSIAN subdirectory by typing MKDIR (Make Directory) and then the directory name:

```
MKDIR PERSIAN ⏎
```

An abbreviated version of the command, MD, works in exactly the same way:

```
MD PERSIAN ⏎
```

DOS responds with an error message if the directory already exists:

```
Unable to create directory
```

If you ask for a directory listing of the newly created subdirectory, you'll find that it already contains two entries. In place of a file name, one has only a single period, and the next a double-period. These entries hold information DOS requires to navigate around the directory tree. (The single dot stands for the directory itself and the double-dot represents the directory that contains it.) These symbols may be used as a shortcut when moving around the tree or copying files, as sections 6.4 and 7.4 explain.

Creating directories outside the current directory   A new directory may be created without first moving to the directory that will contain it. In this case, you must supply a full path to the directory. For instance, if DOGS were the current directory in the tree shown in figure 5.4, you could create PERSIAN without first moving to CATS by typing:

```
MKDIR \MAMMALS\CATS\PERSIAN ⏎
```

It's almost as easy to create a new subdirectory on a drive other than the current drive. Just add a drive specifier, such as A: or C: to the command. If drive A were current, you would add PERSIAN to the directory tree of drive C by typing:

```
MKDIR C:\MAMMALS\CATS\PERSIAN ⏎
```

The DOS 5.0 Shell   In the DOS Shell, begin by selecting the directory in which the new subdirectory will be created. Select the single backslash at the top of the tree if you want the directory created in the root directory. Then pull down the File menu and choose Create directory. The dialog box shown in figure 5.5 will appear to accept the name of the new directory. Then click on OK (or press ⏎). The new directory will immediately appear in the tree diagram.

Windows 3.1   In Windows, enter the File Manager and select the directory in which the new directory will be created. Then choose Create Directory from the File menu. The dialog box shown in figure 5.6 appears, prompting you to enter the name of the new directory. Then click the OK button and the new directory will be created and shown in the tree diagram.

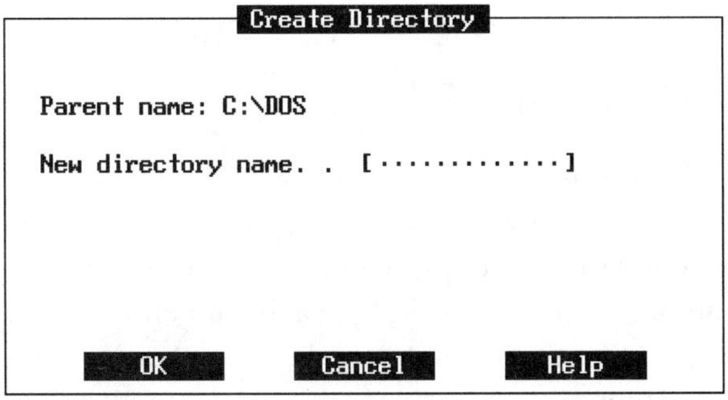

```
┌──────────────■ Create Directory ■──────────────────┐
│                                                     │
│  Parent name: C:\DOS                                │
│                                                     │
│  New directory name. .  [············]              │
│                                                     │
│                                                     │
│                                                     │
│   ▄▄▄▄▄▄▄▄▄         ▄▄▄▄▄▄▄▄▄▄         ▄▄▄▄▄▄▄▄▄▄    │
│      OK               Cancel            Help        │
└─────────────────────────────────────────────────────┘
```

Figure 5.5

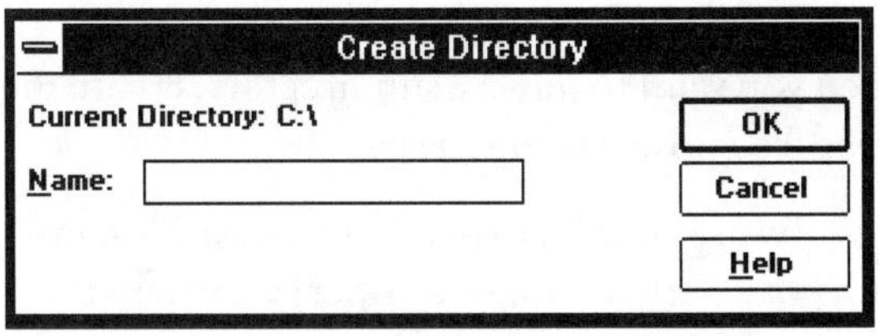

```
┌─────────────────────────────────────────────┐
│ ▬           Create Directory                 │
├─────────────────────────────────────────────┤
│ Current Directory: C:\              ┌──────┐ │
│                                     │  OK  │ │
│ Name:   [                    ]      └──────┘ │
│                                     ┌──────┐ │
│                                     │Cancel│ │
│                                     └──────┘ │
│                                     ┌──────┐ │
│                                     │ Help │ │
│                                     └──────┘ │
└─────────────────────────────────────────────┘
```

Figure 5.6

5.3 Renaming and relocating subdirectories

DOS offers no simple way of changing the name of a subdirectory. Once you've set the name with **MKDIR**, you're stuck with it. Similarly, you can't move a subdirectory to another place in the tree. It's possible to rename or move subdirectories, however, by making an entirely new subdirectory, copying all files to it from the subdirectory that you want renamed or moved, and then erasing the files in the original subdirectory and deleting it. When you want to rename a subdirectory without changing its position in the directory tree, you should create the new directory in the same subdirectory that the subdirectory that will be renamed is located. When you want to move a subdirectory, create the new directory at whatever tree position you desire.

Keep in mind that your software may be expecting its own files, even data files, in a subdirectory of a particular name, especially when it uses subdirectories automatically created during installation. Similarly, batch files, including AUTOEXEC.BAT, and DOS commands such as PATH and APPEND, may be tailored to a specific directory tree design. Don't change the tree structure without understanding the implications of every alteration.

In the example here, we'll rename a subdirectory named SIAMESE to, PERSIAN as shown in figure 5.7.

Step 1   First, create the PERSIAN subdirectory:

    MKDIR \MAMMALS\CATS\PERSIAN ⏎

Now there are three subdirectories—PERSIAN, SIAMESE, and TI-BETAN.

Step 2   Copy all files from SIAMESE to PERSIAN:

    COPY \MAMMALS\CATS\SIAMESE*.* \MAMMALS\CATS\PERSIAN ⏎

Step 3   Verify that the files have been properly transferred. First, find out how many files are in the PERSIAN subdirectory, either by moving to the subdirectory and typing DIR ⏎, or by the command:

    DIR \MAMMALS\CATS\PERSIAN ⏎

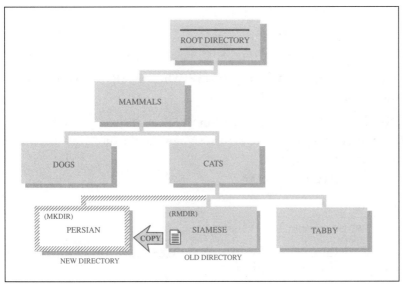

Figure 5.7

The number of files in the directory is displayed at the end of the directory listing. (Note that this number is two greater than the actual number of files because of the dot and double-dot entries at the top of each subdirectory.) Now do a directory listing of the SIAMESE subdirectory and see that the number of files matches. If it doesn't, something went wrong during the COPY operation, and it must be corrected. Perhaps one of the files could not be copied or there was too little disk space.

Step 4   Now that copies exist in the PERSIAN subdirectory, erase all files in the SIAMESE subdirectory. Mass erasures are always risky, and you must be very careful that the operation is performed on the SIAMESE subdirectory, and no other. It would be best to make SIAMESE the current subdirectory first:

```
CHDIR \MAMMALS\CATS\SIAMESE ←
```

If you have not set the DOS prompt to display the current directory name (section 11.2), then double-check that SIAMESE is current by entering DIR ← and looking for the directory name at the top of the directory listing. Once you are certain that you are in the SIAMESE subdirectory, type:

```
ERASE *.* ←
```

This command eliminates all files in the current directory. When used, the message appears:

```
Are you sure (Y/N)?
```

Type [Y] [↵] to begin the mass erasure. When the DOS prompt returns, the files are gone.

Step 5   Finally, remove the SIAMESE subdirectory. To do this, it must not be the current directory, so move to the directory that holds it:

```
CHDIR \MAMMALS\CATS  [↵]
```

Then type:

```
RMDIR \MAMMALS\CATS\SIAMESE  [↵]
```

You're finished. The subdirectory SIAMESE has, for all intents and purposes, been renamed as PERSIAN.

These same steps could as easily be used to move the SIAMESE subdirectory to another place in the tree. In this case, the new directory would also be named SIAMESE (any number of subdirectories may share the same name but the same name must not appear twice in the same directory). Of course, subdirectories contained in a directory cannot be copied over to another directory. If you wish to move a whole branch of the directory tree, you'll need to replicate it directory by directory and then copy files directory by directory. The XCOPY command can help you do this efficiently, since it can duplicate a whole branch of a tree and then copy all files between matching subdirectories. This command must be used carefully, lest it create the new branch in the wrong position in the directory tree. See section 7.8 for a discussion of XCOPY.

PITFALLS | This approach to renaming or moving a subdirectory can cause trouble when a disk is almost full. If the duplicated files take up more space than available, a "Disk full" message appears and the COPY *.* command stops before all files are copied. At that point you could erase the originals of the successfully copied files, making space for a file-by-file copy of the remainder. If your disk is nearly full, you should take action to head off running out of disk space (see section 20.2).

The DOS 5.0 Shell   The DOS Shell renames subdirectories but cannot move them. Begin by entering the File Manager. In the tree diagram, select the subdirectory you want to rename. Then pull down the File menu and choose Rename. You'll be shown the dialog box in figure 5.8. Type in the new subdirectory name and click on OK (or press ⏎). The new directory name will appear in the tree diagram.

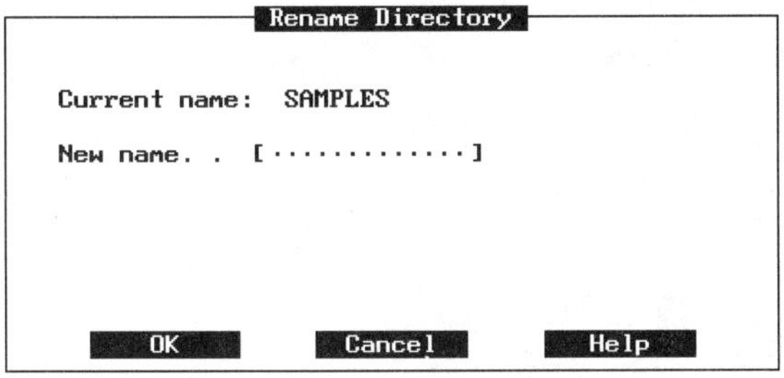

Figure 5.8

Windows 3.1   Windows lets you directly rename subdirectories. Just enter the File Manager and select the subdirectory you want renamed. Then pull down the File menu and choose Rename. You'll see a dialog box like the one shown in figure 5.9. Type in the new name (just the name, without a directory path or leading backslash) and click over the Rename button. The subdirectory will then be renamed. Note that you can't use this feature to move subdirectories by typing in a new directory path for the renamed directory.

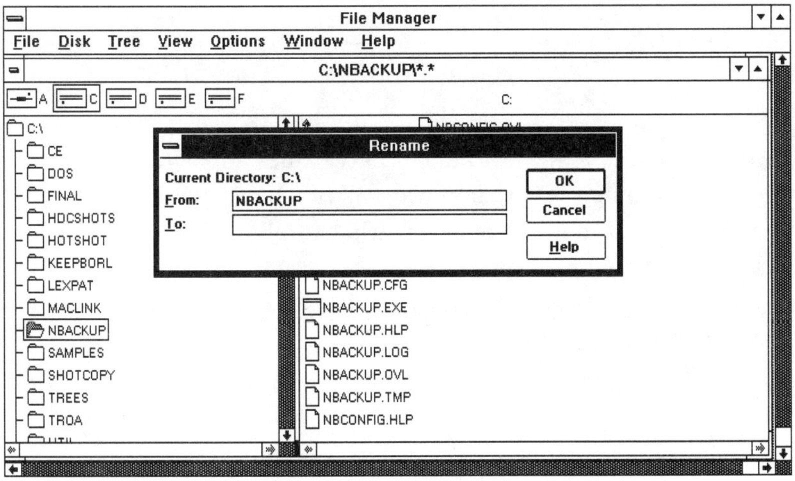

Figure 5.9

5.4 Removing a subdirectory

The RMDIR command removes subdirectories from a directory tree. It can't be applied to the disk's root directory, which is permanent. To remove the directory POODLES along the path \MAMMALS\DOGS\ POODLES, as shown in figure 5.10, you would type:

```
RMDIR \MAMMALS\DOGS\POODLES ⏎
```

You could also use an abbreviated version of the command, RD:

```
RD \MAMMALS\DOGS\POODLES ⏎
```

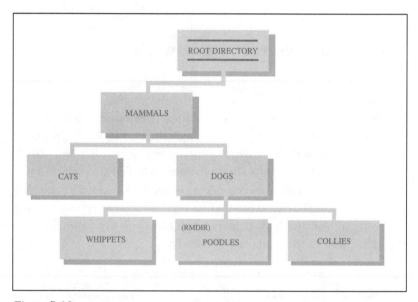

Figure 5.10

Restrictions on using RMDIR   Three rules apply to the directory that is eliminated. First, it must not be the current directory. If POODLES were current and you tried to eliminate it, DOS would respond with the error message:

```
Invalid path, not directory,
or directory not empty.
```

in which case you should move to the directory that contains POODLES:

```
CHDIR \MAMMALS\DOGS ⏎
```

and then apply the command. Because POODLES would then be found in the current directory, you could dispense with the path leading up to POODLES:

```
RMDIR POODLES ⏎
```

(Notice in this command that the word POODLES is not written with a leading backslash as \POODLES. DOS would understand the backslash as referring to the root directory and would try to eliminate a directory named POODLES listed there.)

The second restriction in the use of RMDIR is that the subdirectory to be removed must contain no subdirectories of its own. For example, you couldn't remove the subdirectory DOGS without first removing the subdirectories POODLES, WHIPPETS, and COLLIES one by one. This restriction prevents you from accidentally erasing a whole branch of the directory tree and all the files its subdirectories hold.

Finally, the subdirectory to be removed must contain no files. All files must be erased in advance. A single command can remove them all:

```
ERASE \MAMMALS\DOGS\POODLES\*.* ⏎
```

Some files are immune from erasure, however. These include read-only files, which you'll see in a directory listing, and hidden files, which are completely hidden from view. Files are made read-only or hidden either by the action of software you use, or purposely by the DOS ATTRIB command or various utility programs. To remove the subdirectory, you'll need to change such files into normal files (section 4.5 explains how) and then delete them. When DOS responds to a RMDIR command with the message:

```
Invalid path, not directory,
or directory not empty
```

even when no files or subdirectories appear in a directory listing of the subdirectory you are trying to delete, hidden files are probably the culprit.

The DOS 5.0 Shell   In the DOS Shell, begin by erasing all files in the directory that will be removed. If you fail to do this, you'll subsequently encounter an "Access Denied" message. Then, having selected the directory that will be deleted, pull down the File menu and choose Delete—the same command used for erasing files. The dialog box shown in figure 5.11 is then displayed, requiring you to confirm that you want the directory deleted.

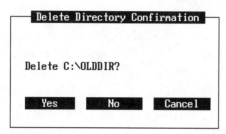

┌─ **Delete Directory Confirmation** ─┐

Delete C:\OLDDIR?

[**Yes**] [**No**] [**Cancel**]

Figure 5.11

Windows 3.1   Subdirectories are deleted in Windows just like files. Enter the File Manager and select the subdirectory. Then pull down the File menu and choose Delete. You'll be shown a dialog box like the one shown in figure 5.12 Click the OK button and the subdirectory will be removed.

Unlike DOS, Windows can delete a subdirectory even when it holds files, or when it holds other subdirectories, which may in turn hold files. It does this by converting the delete operation into a sequence of deletions of files and subdirectories. This feature is useful, but it can be extremely dangerous to your data because a wrong move can delete a whole branch of the directory tree and every file in it.

For added protection, you can have Windows display a confirmation box for each subdirectory and file to be deleted. This is just another dialog box in which you specify Yes or No, or Yes to All if you want to dispense with confirmation boxes for remaining deletions.

Confirmation boxes appear only if they have been expressly enabled. This is done by choosing Confirmation in the Options menu. The resulting dialog box displays a number of check boxes, the top two of which are labeled File Delete and Directory Delete. By selecting one or both of these check boxes, a confirmation box will appear with every deletion of a file, of a directory, or of both. This state of affairs continues until the Confirmation option is chosen again and the settings are changed.

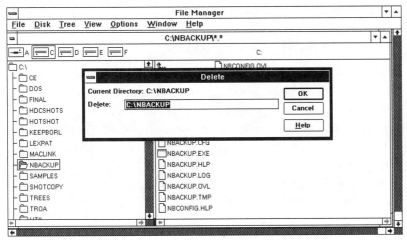

Figure 5.12

5.5 Viewing and printing a directory tree

Without the aid of a DOS shell, keeping track of the directory tree structure can be a nightmare. You can waste much time trying to find a particular subdirectory in a large tree, or worse, trying to find a particular file whose subdirectory you've forgotten. DOS shells can solve many problems by displaying a tree diagram and letting you obtain a file listing for each directory in turn with only a keystroke or two. But even without a shell program, there are some clumsy techniques for viewing directory trees.

DOS includes the TREE command for obtaining a comprehensive listing of every subdirectory on a disk drive. Starting with DOS 4.0, a graphical tree diagram, like the one shown in figure 5.13, is displayed by the command. But in earlier DOS versions, TREE only displays the path to each subdirectory and a listing of all subdirectories it contains. For example:

```
Path: \MAMMALS\FELINES
Subdirectories: LIONS
                TIGERS
                CHEETAHS
```

Such listings are displayed in succession, starting from the root directory. All subdirectories of a branch of the tree are shown before going on to subdirectories in the next branch. Thus, after the root directory, you are shown the first subdirectory listed in the root directory, the first subdirectory listed in that subdirectory, and so on. If you want to view a tree diagram in DOS 3.3 or earlier, you need to use a DOS shell or a utility like the NCD (Norton Change Directory) program found in the Norton Utilities.

TREE is an external DOS command, meaning that it resides in its own file named TREE.COM. When that file is in the current directory, or is made available via a PATH command (section 8.2), all you need to type to have the tree for drive C displayed is type:

```
TREE C: ⏎
```

This command works with DOS versions 3.3 and earlier. They always display data for an entire tree and thus require nothing more than a drive specifier. Beginning with DOS 4.0, however, you should include a directory path. Since a lone backslash represents the root directory, you can display an entire tree with the command:

    TREE C:\ ⏎

Specifying a subdirectory, as in:

    TREE C:\AQUATIC\MAMMALS ⏎

results in a partial tree display consisting of only the directory MAMMALS and all subdirectories beyond it.

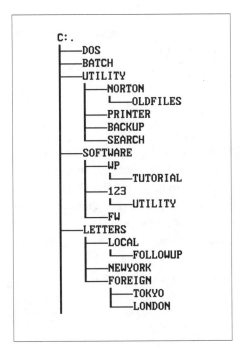

Figure 5.13

Listing files   In any DOS version, TREE can also list the files contained in each subdirectory. Add the /F switch to the end of the command:

    TREE C: /F ⏎

or, in DOS 4.0:

    TREE C:\ /F ⏎

The name of each file is displayed on its own line, with no information about size and date as in an ordinary directory listing. This feature makes the TREE listing much longer.

Printing tree listing   It's often convenient to print out the tree listing, since the displayed data can't be scrolled up and down on the screen. To do this, just append >LPT1 (line printer 1) to the command:

        TREE C: >LPT1 ↵

or, in DOS 4.0:

        TREE C:\ >LPT1 ↵

In DOS 4.0 and later, the diagram is drawn on the screen using graphic characters to form lines and corners. Most printers will substitute unrelated characters when the diagram is printed. You can have TREE replace the graphic characters with more presentable ones by adding /A to the command:

        TREE C:\ /A >LPT1 ↵

Modifying and annotating the tree data   It's possible to set up the tree data so that you can scroll back and forth in the listing and even add descriptive labels. This is done by making the TREE command write the tree data to a disk file instead of to the screen. Thereafter, you can load the file into your word processor and view it as you would any document. The tree data is sent to a file by appending the greater than (>) symbol to the command, followed by the name of the file that will hold the data. For example, to place the tree data for drive C in a file named TREEDATA, type:

        TREE C: >TREEDATA ↵

or, in DOS 4.0:

        TREE C:\ >TREEDATA ↵

As always, you can add a path to the directory where you want the file saved (a necessity if that directory is not the current directory):

        TREE C: >\DOS\TREEDATA ↵

or, in DOS 4.0:

        TREE C:\ >\DOS\TREEDATA ↵

Once the tree data is in a file, it can be loaded into any text editor or word processor and scrolled up and down. Be aware that many word processors won't display the graphic characters used by the DOS versions 4.0 and 5.0 of TREE, so it may be a good idea to use the /A switch mentioned earlier.

TIP

You can use a word processor to pare down and modify a pre-DOS 4.0 file so that it resembles a true tree diagram. Use whatever features your word processor offers. Most let you delete an entire line with a single keystroke. Keeping one hand over that key and the other over the ⬇ key, you can quickly eliminate the unwanted lines from the file. Then print it out as you would any document. The diagram will also be on hand for a quick look via the DOS TYPE command (section 2.6):

```
TYPE \DOS\TREEDATA ⏎
```

Of course, later changes in your directory tree won't be reflected in this diagram. If you use the TREE command to create an updated file, earlier annotations in the file will be wiped out. Happily, most trees don't change very much once they are well established. Just get in the habit of modifying the tree diagram file with your word processor whenever you use MKDIR or RMDIR to alter the tree.

Chapter 6
Moving between Directories

MINITUTORIAL:
The current drive and directory

DOS normally works in a world of multiple disk drives. When you tell DOS to do something—say, to display a directory listing—it has to decide which disk drive it will access. Similarly, if you ask DOS to start up a program, it needs to know on which disk it will find the file that contains the program.

DOS deals with this problem by always considering one disk drive to be the current drive. When you give DOS a simple command, it automatically applies the command to that drive. If the command won't work (say, the program file is not found) DOS displays an error message and redisplays the DOS prompt to await your next instruction. (The DOS prompt is the marker on the left edge of the screen, such as A> or C>, at which you type in commands for DOS to carry out.) Unless it's been specially configured to do so—we tell how in section 8.1—DOS does not automatically search for files on drives other than the current drive; you must specifically instruct it to do so.

When the computer is turned on, the current drive is whatever drive the machine booted from (see section 17.1). If the machine started off drive A, the current drive will be A. If, instead, the machine booted off hard disk drive C (with no diskette in drive A), the current drive will be C. You can always tell the current drive because it is the one written in the DOS prompt. The DOS prompt looks like A> when drive A is current, B> when B is current, and so on. (Be aware that the form of the DOS prompt can be altered so that it won't look like this, as section 11.2 explains. Also, you should know that by using a file called AUTOEXEC.BAT (section 11.1) you can change the current drive during booting. So, at start-up, the DOS prompt does not necessarily indicate the boot drive).

Changing the current drive   You can change the current drive by typing in the drive letter followed by a colon. If drive C is current and you want to make A current instead, enter:

    A: ⏎

The DOS prompt will change to A>. To move back to drive C, type:

    C: ⏎

Alternatively, you can make DOS direct its efforts to a drive other than the current drive by including one of these symbols in a DOS command. For example, the command:

DIR `←`

always shows a directory from the current drive. But:

DIR A: `←`

will make DOS display a directory of drive A, whether or not A is the current drive. This symbol, A: (or B: or C: or D:) is called a drive specifier. This is a term worth remembering because you'll encounter it again and again in the DOS world. Drive specifiers are often placed before file names to tell DOS that a file will be found on a drive other than the current one. For example, with drive C current, you could load a program named FW on drive A by entering:

A:FW `←`

Even as the program runs, drive C will remain the current drive. The current drive is also called the default drive, meaning that it is the drive upon which DOS works by default (when no drive specifier tells it to do otherwise.)

It is very important that you understand that application software usually will direct its actions to the default drive (the current drive) when you ask it to do something, such as save a newly created file. Within application software you may add a drive specifier to a file name to tell the software to access a different drive than the default drive. For instance, when the software asks you for the name of a data file to open, and the file is not on the current drive, you would need to add a drive specifier to the file name, just as in the DOS command above. If drive C is current and the software prompts you for the "Name of file to load:," then to load the file REPORT12.DOC found on drive A you would type:

A:REPORT12.DOC `←`

Directory trees   Unfortunately, DOS commands become much more complicated when you work with disks that have directory trees. Hard disk drives can hold thousands of files—far more than can practically be placed in a single directory. So the files are distributed among many directories that are arranged in a hierarchy originating from the disk's main directory (the root directory), with several sub-directories branching from the main directory, further subdirectories branching from those, and so on. The system splays out like a tree, and that is why it is called a directory tree. Generally speaking, a disk has only one tree, and it is up to you to create it, customizing the pattern and names of subdirectories to your needs. See the minitutorial in Chapter 5 for more information about directory trees.

(Be aware that diskettes can be given directory trees as readily as hard disks. Even if you don't have a hard disk, you may encounter trees on the diskettes on which software is distributed. So you need to understand them. Hard disk users must learn about and use directory trees or the hard disk quickly becomes unmanageable.)

As you might imagine, directory trees make matters more complicated for DOS. DOS needs to know not only the current drive (the default drive), but also the current directory (the default directory). A current directory is analogous to a current drive; it is the directory (out of all directories in a tree) to which DOS automatically directs its operations. When the current directory is not the one you need to access, you must tell DOS the name of the desired directory, just like you need to tell DOS the name of another disk drive when the current drive does not contain the files you want to access.

Directory paths   Directories are named by directory paths. A path describes a route through the directory tree to a particular subdirectory. It consists of nothing more than a sequence of directory names that lead up to the directory in question, with each directory name on the path separated by a backslash (\). For instance, here is the directory path to an imaginary subdirectory named LIZARDS:

```
\ANIMALS\REPTILES\LIZARDS
```

The details of directory paths are explained in the minitutorial in Chapter 5. For now, what you need to remember is that directory paths play an analogous role to the drive specifiers discussed above. When DOS needs to get at files in a particular directory, you must either make that directory the current directory (just as you can change the current drive), or you must specify the name of the directory in DOS commands so that DOS can temporarily find its way (just as you add a drive specifier to the DOS DIR command shown above.)

Changing the current directory   You can change the current directory by the CHDIR command. If the current directory were \ANIMALS\REPTILES\LIZARDS and you wanted to make \ANIMALS\REPTILES\TURTLES the current directory, you would type:

```
CHDIR \ANIMALS\REPTILES\TURTLES [←]
```

If you needed a directory listing of TURTLES, but wanted LIZARDS to remain the default directory, you would add the directory path of TURTLES to the DIR command:

```
DIR \ANIMALS\REPTILES\TURTLES [←]
```

Similarly, within software, if you needed to get at a file that is not in the default directory, you would preceed the file name by the directory path. If a program were to ask for the file you want to load, and you wanted to use the file REPORT7.DOC in the LIZARDS subdirectory, you would type:

```
\ANIMALS\REPTILES\LIZARDS\REPORT7.DOC [←]
```

The final complication in this system is that sometimes you need to specify both a drive and a subdirectory when naming files. If the current drive is drive A and you want to get to the file REPORT12.DOC on drive C, you would type:

```
C:\ANIMALS\REPTILES\LIZARDS\REPORT12.DOC [←]
```

Multiple directory trees   Matters can be even more confusing when more than one disk has a directory tree. Say that drive C is the default drive and that its subdirectory TURTLES is the default directory. If you change the default drive to, say, drive D, which also has a directory tree, then the new default directory will be whatever directory was last made the default directory for that drive. If that directory was \PLANTS\TREES\WILLOWS, then when you switch to drive D by entering D: [←], WILLOWS will become the default directory. If you again make drive C the default drive (C: [←]), TURTLES will be the default directory again.

If all of this is a bit confusing, don't worry—everyone gets confused at first. The worst part of it, dealing with two directory trees at once, is not difficult once you understand the basics. And utility software and DOS shells can simplify many aspects of working in directory trees. Still, it is important to thoroughly understand directories, directory paths, and directory trees. These concepts are the key to fluency in DOS.

6.1 ■ Finding the current directory

It's very important to always keep in mind which directory is the current directory. DOS directs its activities, such as COPY and ERASE commands, to this directory by default, and files can be damaged if you believe one directory is current when in fact another is. The best way to keep track of the current directory is to acquire a DOS shell like The Norton Commander or to use a tree-diagram utility like the NCD program in The Norton Utilities. Lacking these tools, there are three ways of finding out the current directory in DOS.

Method 1   By far the best way of keeping track of your location in a directory tree is to make the DOS prompt display the current directory at all times. You can do this with the PROMPT command. Type:

```
PROMPT $P--- ⏎
```

and DOS will then display the name of the current directory on the DOS command line, followed by three dashes. If the subdirectory\REPTILES\TURTLES on drive C is current, the DOS prompt will look like:

```
C:\REPTILES\TURTLES---
```

The symbol $P represents the entire directory path from the root directory to the current directory. You can substitute any characters you prefer in place of the three dashes, including spaces, to get a format that pleases you. The line:

```
PROMPT $P$G ⏎
```

produces the DOS prompt:

```
C:\REPTILES\TURTLES>
```

Here, the symbol $G represents the greater than (>) character. (The > character can't be used in a PROMPT command because > has a special meaning in DOS commands, and DOS would interpret it the wrong way.) Be sure to follow $P with at least one nonalphabetic character to separate your typing from the prompt. Otherwise the command line becomes hard to read, as in:

```
C:\REPTILES\TURTLESCOPY GALAPAGO.* B: ⏎
```

Once you've decided on a style you like, you can include the PROMPT command in your AUTOEXEC.BAT file (section 11.1) so that it will be automatically activated each time the machine is booted.

Method 2   Enter the CHDIR command without naming a directory to move to. Just type:

    CHDIR ⏎

or, using the abbreviated form of the command:

    CD ⏎

and DOS will display the name of the current directory, such as C:\MAMMALS\APES\GIBBONS, on the line below. You can find out the current directory on a drive other than the current drive by including a drive specifier. If you are working at drive A and enter:

    CHDIR C: ⏎

DOS would display:

    C:\MAMMALS\APES\GIBBONS

while drive A remains the current drive.

Method 3   Look at a directory listing. Simply type:

    DIR ⏎

and DOS will display the name of the current directory on the second line of the listing, such as:

    C:\MAMMALS\APES\GIBBONS

for a subdirectory, or:

    C:\

for the root directory (a single backslash with no directory names following it represents the root directory).

The DOS 5.0 Shell   The current directory is always evident in the DOS Shell. Most of your work in the shell is done within the File Manager, which displays a tree diagram for the current drive. The current directory is indicated by an arrow symbol to the left of one of the subdirectory names, as figure 6.1 shows. In addition, a complete DOS path for the current directory is displayed at the top of the screen just beneath the pull-down menus.

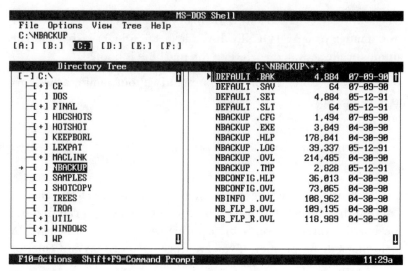

Figure 6.1

Windows 3.1   Within the Windows File Manager, at the top of any directory listing you'll find the path to the currently selected directory, as figure 6.2 shows.

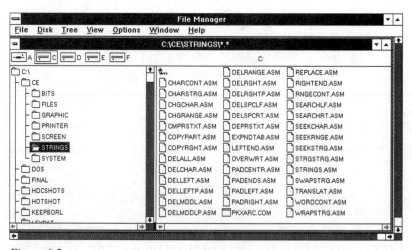

Figure 6.2

6.2 Moving between disk drives

To move between drives, type the drive name and a colon. For example:

A: ⏎

or:

C: ⏎

This action makes the drive you specify the current drive. It is the drive that DOS directs its activities toward by default if you specify no other; for this reason, it is also called the default drive.

When a disk has a directory tree (see the minitutorial at the beginning of Chapter 5 for a complete explanation), there also is a current directory, which is the one directory (out of many on the disk) that DOS acts on by default. Because virtually all hard disks have a directory tree, when you move to a hard disk drive (say, from drive A to drive C), you must consider what the current directory on drive C will be. DOS will always move to the directory that was current when drive C was last the current drive (before the current drive was changed).

PITFALLS DOS won't let you change the current drive and the current directory at the same time. For example, say that you want to move over to the POODLES subdirectory on hard drive C, starting from diskette drive A, as shown in figure 6.3. Assume that a few minutes before, drive C had been the current drive, and that the DOGS subdirectory had been the current directory when you shifted over to drive A. If you just type:

C: ⏎

you'll be returned to DOGS, even though you want to go to POODLES. You may be tempted to try this instead:

C:\MAMMALS\DOGS\POODLES ⏎

But it won't work. You must make the transition in two steps, first:

C: ⏎

and then:

CHDIR \MAMMALS\DOGS\POODLES ⏎

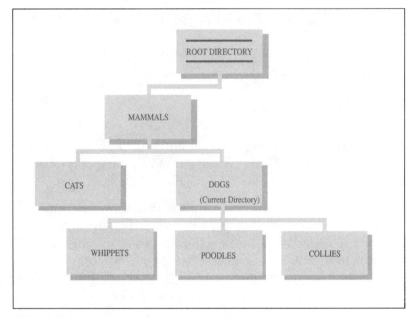

Figure 6.3

The DOS 5.0 Shell   In the DOS Shell, the File Manager displays a line of symbols at the top of the screen to represent each disk drive (drive B may be shown even when there is only one diskette drive, in which case it acts as a second symbol for drive A). You can move to any drive by clicking on its symbol. Alternatively, use the tab key to cycle the highlight cursor to the series of drive symbols. Then press ⬅ or ➡ to move the cursor to the desired drive. Pressing ⬅ selects the drive so that its directory tree, if any, is displayed below.

When you select a drive for the first time in a work session in the shell, you may have to wait a few seconds before the tree appears. The DOS Shell needs this time to scan the disk and assemble the tree. Thereafter, it keeps the disk information in memory even after switching to other drives. However, the information is discarded when memory is required for other purposes, and so you may have to wait for it to be reloaded any number of times.

Windows 3.1   To change drives in Windows, enter the File Manager by selecting its icon. You'll encounter an icon for each disk drive (figure 6.5) which may then be selected with the click of a mouse. A

keyboard shortcut is to hold down the Ctrl key while you type the drive
letter. Note that Windows, unlike DOS, does not have a default drive to
which activity is automatically directed.

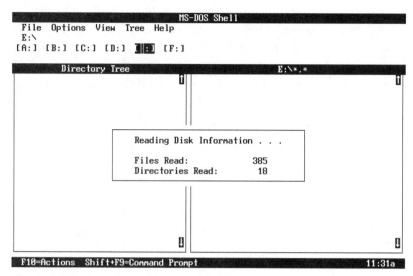

Figure 6.4

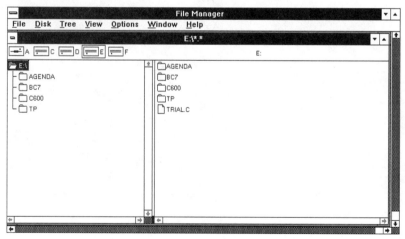

Figure 6.5

6.3 Moving between subdirectories

To make another subdirectory the current directory—the one to which DOS directs its actions when no other directory is specified—simply type CHDIR (change directory) followed by the path to the directory. For example, to move to the directory GIBBONS (shown in figure 6.6) when it is located in the directory tree at \ANIMALS\PRIMATES\GIBBONS, type:

```
CHDIR \ANIMALS\PRIMATES\GIBBONS ⏎
```

An abbreviated form of the command, CD, works just the same:

```
CD \ANIMALS\PRIMATES\GIBBONS ⏎
```

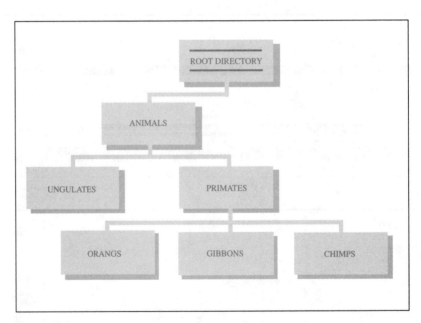

Figure 6.6

You can't use CHDIR to move to a directory on a different drive. If drive A is current (the DOS prompt is A>), and you want to move to the GIBBONS subdirectory on drive C, then type:

```
C: ⏎
CHDIR \ANIMALS\PRIMATES\GIBBONS ⏎
```

Of course, the second line would be necessary only if GIBBONS is not already the current directory on drive C. (As the minitutorial at the start of this chapter explains, each drive has its own current directory, and DOS commands directed to a drive always operate on that directory when no other directory has been specified.) If CHIMPS were current instead, you could make GIBBONS the current directory of drive C without changing the current drive from A to C. Instead of typing:

```
C: ⏎
CHDIR \ANIMALS\PRIMATES\GIBBONS ⏎
A: ⏎
```

you could type:

```
CHDIR C:\ANIMALS\PRIMATES\GIBBONS ⏎
```

This statement would leave A as the current drive while changing the current directory of drive C. It would be useful, say, if you were copying many files from drive A to several subdirectories on drive C. Instead of typing directory paths again and again for each COPY command, as in:

```
COPY FILE1.DOC C:\ANIMALS\PRIMATES\GIBBONS ⏎
```

you'd just change the current directory on drive C and then make the copies with the shorter command:

```
COPY FILE1.DOC C: ⏎
```

Role of the leading backslash   In all of these examples, the directory path is typed beginning from the root directory, which is specified by the first backslash in the path. For instance, in the expression:

```
\ANIMALS\PRIMATES\GIBBONS
```

The \ preceeding the *A* in ANIMALS represents the root directory. For this reason, when you want to move to the root directory of a disk, the proper command is:

```
CHDIR \ ⏎
```

or:

```
CD \ ⏎
```

When you omit the leading backslash, DOS assumes that the path you are specifying begins at whatever directory is the current directory on the disk. For instance, say that \ANIMALS\PRIMATES is the current directory and that you want to move to GIBBONS. Then you could type:

CHDIR GIBBONS [←]

DOS would understand this to mean, "move to a subdirectory named GIBBONS that is listed in the current directory." This method is useful for moving to subdirectories farther from the root directory. See section 6.4 to learn shortcuts for moving to subdirectories closer to the root directory or to subdirectories at the same level.

Utility software   The Norton Utilities contains a program that makes moving between directories a breeze. The NCD utility works in two modes. In the first mode, you just type NCD dirname [←] on the DOS command line and NCD finds the dirname directory and makes it the current directory. If more than one directory in a tree has the same name and NCD finds the wrong one, you can repeat the command to move on to the desired directory. Not only does NCD save you the trouble of typing the path to the directory, but you can even type only part of the directory name—just enough to identify it uniquely. For instance, if there is a directory named POTATOES, entering NCD PO [←] would find that directory so long as no other directory name begins with the letters *PO*. In its second mode of operation, NCD is loaded as a full-screen program that displays a scrollable tree diagram in which you can select the current directory with a highlight bar to it and pressing [←].

The DOS 5.0 Shell   In the DOS Shell, a tree diagram for the current drive is shown when you enter the File Manager, as figure 6.7 shows.

Using a mouse, you can switch between directories simply by clicking on the tree diagram. From the keyboard, use the tab key to move the bar cursor to the tree diagram, then the [↑] and [↓] keys to move the bar cursor over the target directory. Press [←] to make the directory current.

Windows 3.1   In Windows, moving between subdirectories is as easy as moving a bar cursor across a tree diagram. This is done by clicking the mouse on top of a directory name or icon. The currently selected directory is marked by an icon resembling an open file folder; others appear as closed folders. To expand a directory to show the directories it contains, just double-click on its icon. Collapse branches of the tree by double-clicking on directories farther to the left (closer to the root directory). Figure 6.8 shows a partially expanded directory tree.

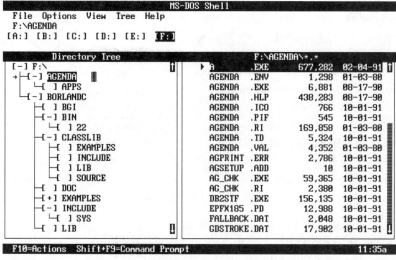

Figure 6.7

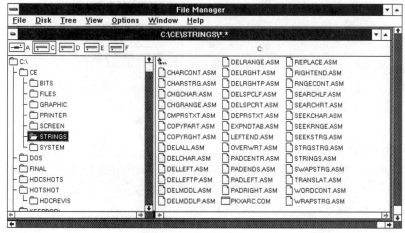

Figure 6.8

6.4 Moving to an adjacent subdirectory

DOS provides special symbols that can be used to move quickly between adjacent directories without typing in long paths. These symbols are the dot and double-dot, which are simply one period (.) and two periods (..). The dot refers to the current directory, and the double-dot to the parent directory of the current directory (that is, the directory that holds the current directory). Using these symbols, you can quickly move to a subdirectory above or below the current directory, or can shunt between parallel subdirectories that share the same parent directory.

Moving to the parent directory   Say that you are working in the directory tree shown in figure 6.9, in which SIAMESE is the current directory, and that you want to move to the parent directory, which is CATS. Instead of typing:

        CHDIR \FELINES\CATS ↵

you could accomplish the task simply by typing:

        CHDIR .. ↵

The double-period in this command represents \FELINES\CATS— that is, the whole DOS path up to, but not including, the current directory.

Moving to a directory above   Again using the directory tree shown in figure 6.9, say that CATS is now the current directory, and that you want to move to SIAMESE. Instead of:

        CHDIR \FELINES\CATS\SIAMESE ↵

just type:

        CHDIR SIAMESE ↵

Because no backslash is placed before the word SIAMESE, DOS assumes that the directory is held in the current directory, CATS. and so it understands that the path to the directory is \FELINES\CATS\SIAMESE.

Moving to parallel subdirectories   The double-dot symbol can help you move to parallel subdirectories, such as between SIAMESE and PERSIAN in figure 6.9. If SIAMESE were current, you could move to PERSIAN by typing:

```
CHDIR ..\PERSIAN ⏎
```

Again, the double-dot represents the directory path up to but not including the current directory. Thus, this statement is equivalent to:

```
CHDIR \FELINES\CATS\PERSIAN ⏎
```

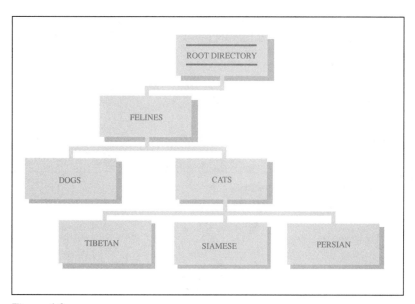

Figure 6.9

Advanced usage   Double-dots may be chained together to refer to subdirectories closer to the root directory. In figure 6-9, when SIAMESE is the current directory, the expression:

```
CHDIR ..\.. ⏎
```

moves you to the FELINES subdirectory, and:

```
CHDIR ..\..\.. ⏎
```

moves you to the root directory. If you take this formula too far by referring to an imaginary directory beyond the root directory, DOS issues an "Invalid directory" error message.

6.5 Moving to the root directory

The root directory can be made the current directory in the same way as any other subdirectory. Type CHDIR and then the path to the directory. For the root directory, that path is a single backslash:

    CHDIR \ ↵

or, using the abbreviated form of the command:

    CD \ ↵

You can tell that the root directory has been made the current directory by typing:

    CHDIR ↵

Used this way, CHDIR reports the current directory. When it is the root directory of drive C, you'll see:

    C:\

If you haven't moved to the root directory, you'll see the name of a subdirectory instead, such as:

    C:\ACCOUNTS

6.6 Moving to a subdirectory without typing a directory path

When you frequently shuttle between certain subdirectories, it may be worth a few moments to create simple batch files that will let you change directories without typing long directory paths. Batch files are nothing more than files that contain DOS commands (see the minitutorial at the beginning of Chapter 9). A batch file may be given any file name, but its extension must be .BAT. Say that you often move to a subdirectory named BALEEN, and that its full DOS path is MAMMALS\CETACEAN\WHALES\BALEEN. To move to that directory you'd have to enter:

```
CHDIR \MAMMALS\CETACEAN\WHALES\BALEEN  ⏎
```

This entire line could be placed in a batch file named BALEEN.BAT. As a batch file, when you type:

```
BALEEN  ⏎
```

DOS executes all the commands it finds in the file. In this case there is only one command, a CHDIR command that makes BALEEN the current directory. You can save yourself many repetitive keystrokes by making one of these batch files for each frequently used subdirectory change.

Step 1   If you have not already, begin by making a subdirectory (section 5.2) in drive C named BATCH to hold your batch files:

```
MKDIR C:\BATCH  ⏎
```

Step 2   Next, create the batch files. As section 9.1 explains, this can be done in several ways. The easiest approach is to just type:

```
COPY CON: C:\BATCH\BALEEN.BAT  ⏎
@C:  ⏎
@CHDIR \MAMMALS\CETACEANS\WHALES\BALEEN  ⏎
Ctrl - z  ⏎
```

The first line tells DOS to create a text file named BALEEN.BAT in the BATCH subdirectory. The second line makes drive C the default drive in case it is not already (the leading @ stops the command from being displayed when it is executed, as section 9.2 explains). The third line is the CHDIR command that you want to automate. The final keystroke, Ctrl - z , makes DOS write the file to the disk drive.

Step 3   Use the PATH command to make DOS look for the files in the BATCH subdirectory no matter what the current directory is. If you don't, DOS would only look for the files in the current directory, and you'd have to type the directory path to your batch files, thus losing as much time typing the path name as the batch files would have saved you. The PATH command is explained in section 8.2. In this case, simply typing:

```
PATH C:\BATCH  ←
```

does the job. Better still, place this line inside your AUTOEXEC.BAT file (section 11.1) so that the PATH command is automatically executed every time you boot up the machine (load the file into your text editor or word processor, add the PATH command, then save the file in plain-text (ASCII) form). Otherwise, you'll have to type in PATH C:\BATCH ← each time you boot.

PITFALLS   Setting up the PATH command may not be this easy for you. Check inside your AUTOEXEC.BAT file to see if a PATH command is already present. (AUTOEXEC.BAT is always located in the root directory of the boot disk (see the minitutorial in Chapter 17) and can be viewed by entering TYPE \AUTOEXEC.BAT ←.) There may be a PATH command in your AUTOEXEC.BAT file without your knowing it, for software installation programs sometimes insert one, or alter the existing PATH command. If you're using DOS 4.0, the installation program will have written one in.

A single PATH command can specify several directories for DOS to search in, and when a new PATH command is executed, the first is nullified. Thus, if you type in PATH\BATCH ←, as above, DOS will successfully find your batch files, but other files required by your application software may be placed out of reach. If a PATH command already exists in AUTOEXEC.BAT, load AUTOEXEC.BAT into a text editor and append the expression ;C:\BATCH to the command (don't leave any spaces between the end of the old command and the addition).

Utility software   Probably the easiest way of moving between subdirectories is to click a mouse over the desired directory in a tree diagram, a feature offered by numerous DOS shells, including the DOS 4.0 DOS Shell program, and Microsoft Windows. Those whose lack a mouse may find cursor movements across a tree diagram time consuming. In fact, sometimes typing a directory path on the DOS command line is quicker.

An alternate approach is to acquire a utility like the NCD (Norton Change Directory) program in the Norton Utilities. This program works much the same way as the batch file system presented above. You need only type the name of the subdirectory and the utility finds it and makes it the current directory. In fact, it is enough to type the first few characters of the subdirectory name—however many are required to distinguish it from all other subdirectories. As with other such schemes, confusion may arise when two or more subdirectories in the tree have the same name.

6.7 Searching for a subdirectory

When a directory tree becomes large, with many branches extending through several layers of subdirectories, it can be quite difficult to find a subdirectory if you've forgotten its exact location. You are reduced to typing one DIR command after another until the desired subdirectory turns up. It's hard to keep track of your progress through the tree, and you can easily overlook the subdirectory even during a supposedly exhaustive search.

The easiest way to find a missing subdirectory is to examine a directory tree diagram like those displayed by any DOS shell, including the shell shipped with DOS 4.0 and later. Unfortunately, earlier DOS versions do not offer this facility. Another possibility is to employ a utility like the NCD (Norton Change Directory) program found in the Norton Utilities. Using it, you can locate a subdirectory simply by typing its name without a directory path. For example, entering NCD SPIDERS ⏎ locates the SPIDERS subdirectory and makes it the current directory. If you can't remember the exact name of a subdirectory, typing just the first few characters of the directory name may bring it into view. When you don't have some other utility software on hand, you must resort to more time-consuming techniques.

You also can track down directories using the same software that searches for files (from DOS's point of view, a subdirectory is only a special kind of file). The Microsoft Windows Search command can do this, as can the FILEFIND program in the Norton Utilities. See section 20.4 for details.

The best way to proceed when you have only plain DOS to work with is to use the DOS TREE command to generate a tree diagram (in DOS 4.0 and later) or a listing of the directory tree contents (in earlier DOS versions), place the listing in a file, and then open the file with a word processor and use the program's search command to locate the directory. The tree listing gives the complete directory path up to the subdirectory, so you can then easily navigate your way to it.

To create such a file for drive C in DOS versions prior to 4.0, type:

```
TREE C: >C:\TREELIST ⏎
```

In DOS 4.0, enter:

```
TREE C:\ >C:\TREELIST ⏎
```

The expression >C:\TREELIST tells DOS to write the tree information for drive C into a file named TREELIST, placing the file in that drive's root directory (specified by preceeding the file name with a backslash.)

If you're using DOS version 3.3 or earlier, you can use the DOS FIND command (section 20.5) instead of a word processor to look for the subdirectory. To locate the directory IGUANA type:

```
FIND "IGUANA" C:\TREELIST ⏎
```

Be sure to capitalize the directory name.

Note that the TREE command is an external DOS command (FIND is also). It is held in a separate file, TREE.COM (or FIND.COM), apart from the main DOS file COMMAND.COM. So you may need a directory path to use it:

```
C:\DOS\TREE C: >C:\TREELIST ⏎
```

for DOS versions prior to 4.0, and:

```
C:\DOS\TREE C:\ >C:\TREELIST ⏎
```

in DOS 4.0 and later.

Chapter 7

Copying and Moving Files

- MINITUTORIAL:
  An overview of the
  COPY command

- Copying files between disk drives

- Copying files between subdirectories

- Copying files to and from a root
  directory

- Copying files between adjacent subdirectories

- Copying files between directory trees

- Copying groups of files

- Copying groups of files to multiple diskettes

- Copying files between multiple subdirectories

- Copying files by date

- Making a copy of a file in the same directory as
  the original

- Replacing one version of a file with another

- Duplicating diskettes

- Verifying that file copies are accurate

- Moving files

MINITUTORIAL:

An overview of the COPY command

The DOS COPY command can do a lot more than most PC users think. Here's a summary of the things it can do.

Function 1   COPY can copy files from one disk to another:

```
COPY A:FILENAME.EXE C: ⏎
```

from one directory to another in the same directory tree:

```
COPY \NOTES\OLDNOTES\FILENAME.EXT \NOTES\NEWNOTES ⏎
```

and between directory trees on different drives:

```
COPY A:\ARCHIVE\FILENAME.EXT C:\NOTES\OLDNOTES ⏎
```

The COPY command can even make a duplicate of a file in the same directory as long as you give the duplicate a file name that is different from the original. You can't give two files in one directory the same name, because DOS would have no way of differentiating between them. Instead, you need to type something like:

```
COPY 1STNAME.EXT 2NDNAME.EXT ⏎
```

Function 2   You can use the COPY command to quickly create new files (small ones, please!) directly from the keyboard. To have it do this, type in COPY CON: and then the name you want assigned to the file. For example:

```
COPY CON: AUTOEXEC.BAT ⏎
```

creates a file called AUTOEXEC.BAT, or overwrites an existing file by that name if there is one. Once this line is entered, type whatever you want to store in the file, pressing ⏎ at the end of each line. When you've finished, press Ctrl-z ⏎ and DOS writes the file to the disk, finishing the job. There's not much flexibility in this approach to making files—you can only edit lines with the backspace key, and you can't edit a line at all once you've pressed ⏎ at its end—but it's a useful feature for making short utility files like the AUTOEXEC.BAT file shown here (see the minitutorial in Chapter 9). Let's say that this file will contain only two lines, CHDIR \MYWORK and CLS, which would change the current directory and clear the screen when the computer boots. To create the file, you would enter:

```
COPY CON: AUTOEXEC.BAT ⏎
CHDIR \MYWORK ⏎
CLS ⏎
Ctrl-z ⏎
```

Function 3   COPY can combine several files into one new one, or add files to the end of an existing one. To create a file named BIG-FILE.TXT composed of the contents of FILEA.TXT and FILEB.TXT, you would type:

```
COPY FILEA.TXT+FILEB.TXT BIGFILE.TXT ⏎
```

To append FILEB.TXT to FILEA.TXT without creating a new file, enter:

```
COPY FILEA.TXT+FILEB.TXT ⏎
```

Any number of files may be combined in this way, and all listed after the first will be appended to the first. This feature of the COPY command is only useful for packing text files into a larger file. There is no point in packing together the complicated data files generated by spreadsheet programs and databases, because application programs couldn't read them later. But combining many old business letters into one giant file might be worthwhile, provided your word processor can read the file. By doing so, directory listings could be simplified and disk space conserved.

Function 4   COPY can print text files. You can achieve this by telling DOS to copy the file to LPT1 (line printer 1), as though LPT1 were the name of a file. For example:

```
COPY FILENAME.EXT LPT1 ⏎
```

sends the file named FILENAME.EXT to the printer. Keep in mind that the file is not processed in any way. Many files contain special codes interspersed among their data. Your software creates these codes for various purposes, sometimes to provide information about how the document should be formatted when it is printed. DOS cannot understand these codes. It sends them straight to the printer as if they were more text. When this happens, the printer can become completely confused, and it may print out utter gobbledygook. For this reason, you should use COPY only to print simple text files, like batch files. You cannot print out database or spreadsheet files this way, nor program files (those named with .EXE or .COM extensions.)

You should also be aware of the existence of the XCOPY and REPLACE commands. XCOPY is an enhanced version of COPY that is specialized for copying many files at once. A single XCOPY command can extend its operations over multiple subdirectories, and even an entire directory tree. Like COPY, it can use global file name characters (section 1.3) to specify many files to be copied by a single command. Unlike COPY, it can copy files on the basis of the dates given to them in directory listings. It also can identify files that have been changed since they were last backed up and copy them over to a diskette. XCOPY is discussed in detail in section 7.8.

REPLACE does just that, it replaces one version of a file with another. Files are transferred from a source directory to a target directory. When a file already exists in the target directory, REPLACE copies the new version over from the source directory. Files not found in the target directory are not copied from the source directory. In this way, many files may be moved without naming them individually. The transfers can be restricted by global file name characters, and the process can even be reversed so that only files not present on the target diskette are copied. Finally, REPLACE can be made to extend its actions across a directory tree, so that a single command can replace a particular file in every subdirectory that holds it. REPLACE is discussed in section 7.11.

7.1 Copying files between disk drives

To copy a file named MYFILE.DOC from drive A to drive B, type:

```
COPY A:MYFILE.DOC B: ⏎
```

There are four parts to this command, which may be interpreted as

1. COPY a file

2. from drive A:

3. named MYFILE.DOC

4. to drive B:.

The expressions A: and B: are called drive specifiers. The first specifier in the command (in this case, A:) indicates the drive where the file is found, and the second (B:) names the drive that will receive the copy. To instead copy the file from drive B to drive A, reverse the drive specifiers by entering:

```
COPY B:MYFILE.DOC A: ⏎
```

When you copy a file from one diskette drive to another, you should check to see which drive is the current drive. If the file to be copied is on drive A and drive A is current, then you can omit the first drive specifier:

```
COPY MYFILE.DOC B: ⏎
```

Conversely, if drive B is current you can dispense with the second drive specifier, but must include the first so DOS will know where to look for the file to copy:

```
COPY A:MYFILE.DOC ⏎
```

DOS won't accept a COPY command like:

```
COPY MYFILE.DOC ⏎
```

Because no drive specifiers are given, DOS looks for MYFILE.DOC on the current drive and, if it finds the file, it attempts to make a copy in the same directory. But a second copy using exactly the same name in the same directory is not allowed.

These examples show the very simplest way of copying files. Matters can become more complicated when a disk has a directory tree—a system in which multiple directories are arranged in a hierarchy starting with the disk's main directory, the root directory. Directory trees are usually associated with hard disks, but sometimes diskettes use them too. You'll know that a directory tree is present when directory listings contain the symbol <DIR>, as in:

```
SUBDIR1     <DIR>      8-22-88  11:18p
```

See the minitutorial in Chapter 5 to learn about directory trees and how DOS commands use them.

The DOS 5.0 Shell   In the DOS Shell, start by selecting the file you want to copy. Then, with the Ctrl key held down, you can drag the file to the symbol of the drive to which the file should be copied. The file will be deposited in whichever directory is currently selected on that drive. You'll then encounter a Confirm Mouse Operation dialog box. Click on Yes or press ⏎ to make the copy.

Alternatively, pull down the File menu and choose Copy. You'll be shown a dialog box (figure 7.1) and prompted to enter the name of the drive to which the copy is transferred. Then click on OK (or press ⏎) to make the copy. A dialog box reports the file name and destination during copying, but for small files on fast computers the dialog box may appear and disappear too quickly to read.

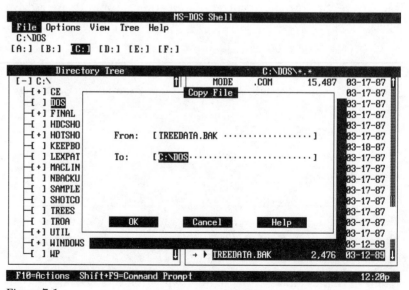

Figure 7.1

When a file of the same name already exists on the target drive, a second dialog box (figure 7.2) may appear to ask you to confirm that the file should be overwritten. You can disable this feature by pulling down the Options menu and choosing File Options. A dialog box will appear displaying a Confirm on replace check box. The confirmation boxes appear only when the check box contains an X. You can toggle the setting on and off by clicking on the check box, or by using the cursor keys to move the cursor to the line and then pressing the space bar.

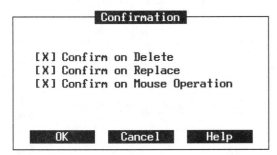

Figure 7.2

Windows 3.1   In Windows, files can be copied by dragging them into a directory tree file folder. This is a little tricky when copying a file between drives. One way is to move to the target drive, select the target directory, and then move back to the first drive, select the file, and then drag it to the target drive's icon at the top of the window. Unlike copying files between subdirectories on the same drive, there's no need to press Ctrl when dragging files between drives. Normally, files are moved rather than copied when Ctrl is not pressed, but files cannot be moved between drives this way.

A second way of copying files between drives is to open a second window to display the tree of the drive to which the copy is directed. This is done by double-clicking on the target disk's icon, which is found at the top of the first window. Then choose Tile from the Window menu so that the two windows will be neatly arranged one above the other. Once this is done, you can scroll the target directory tree on the second drive into view in one window, and then drag the file to it from the other window.

Finally, you can always copy files between drives by choosing Copy from the File menu. You'll be shown a dialog box like the one in figure 7.3, asking you to type in the file's destination using a standard DOS path. When you enter only a drive specifier, like A: or C:, the file is copied to whichever directory is currently selected on that drive.

When a file of the same name already exists on the destination disk, another dialog box (figure 7.4) may prompt you to confirm that the file should be overwritten. This safety feature can be switched on and off by pulling down the Options menu and choosing Confirmation. You'll encounter a number of check boxes, one of which is the File Replace check box. The feature is enabled when an *X* appears in the check box.

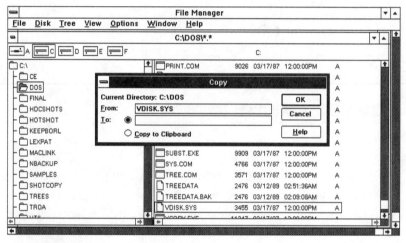

Figure 7.3

Figure 7.4

7.2 Copying files between subdirectories

When you copy a file from a subdirectory in a directory tree, you should first stop to ask which directory is the current directory—the directory to which DOS directs its actions by default. Consider this tree diagram shown in figure 7.5.

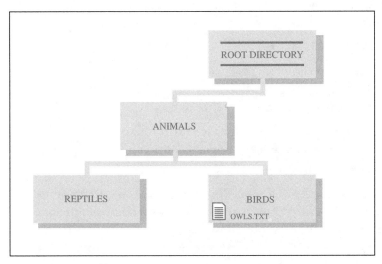

Figure 7.5

Say that there is a file named OWLS.TXT located in the BIRDS subdirectory, and that you want to copy it to ANIMALS. If BIRDS is the current directory, DOS will automatically look for the file there, and you need only specify the directory to which the file will be copied:

```
COPY OWLS.TXT \ANIMALS ⏎
```

However, if any other directory is current, you must specify a directory path to OWLS.TXT also:

```
COPY \ANIMALS\BIRDS\OWLS.TXT \ANIMALS ⏎
```

Of course, you could make BIRDS the current directory (as section 6.3 explains) and then use the simpler command:

```
CHDIR \ANIMALS\BIRDS ⏎
COPY OWLS.TXT \ANIMALS ⏎
```

When the directory in which the copy will be written (the target directory) is the current directory, there's no need to name it at all in the COPY command:

```
COPY \ANIMALS\BIRDS\OWLS.TXT ⏎
```

Since no target directory is named in the command, DOS automatically directs the copy of the file to the current directory.

There is one case where this approach does not work. When the original file is in the current directory, such as when BIRDS is current, then the command:

```
COPY OWLS.TXT ⏎
```

results in the error message:

```
File cannot be copied onto itself
0 File(s) copied
```

because DOS would be copying a file with the same name as the original into the same directory as the original. Since two files in one directory can't have the same name, this action is not allowed.

Drive specifiers   Of course, in any of these examples, you must add drive specifiers when the current drive is different from the one you want to access. For example, if drive A is current, and the tree shown in figure 7.5 is on drive C, then the examples given here would be written as:

```
COPY C:OWLS.TXT C:\ANIMALS ⏎
COPY C:\ANIMALS\BIRDS\OWLS.TXT C:\ANIMALS ⏎
COPY C:\ANIMALS\BIRDS\OWLS.TXT C: ⏎
```

Notice the C: at the end of the last example. It stands for "to the current directory of drive C." When the current directory is other than the one in which you want the file copied, you'll need to either include a path to the proper directory, as in the first two examples, or you'll have to change the current directory of C using the CHDIR command (section 6.3). If you fail to take one of these measures, the copy will not be placed where you expected, and you may end up searching for it.

The DOS 5.0 Shell   In the DOS Shell, begin by selecting the file you want to copy. Then, with the Ctrl key held down, drag the file into the tree diagram of the subdirectory to which you want the copy made. When the target directory is on another drive, move to that drive and select the directory, then move back to select the file and drag it to the symbol for the target drive (just above the tree diagram). Alternatively, choose Dual File Lists from the View menu to bring two directory trees into view. Select the target directory in one and drag the file from the other. Once you've done so, a dialog box will appear to ask you to confirm your choice.

Alternatively, select a file to be copied and then choose Copy from the File menu. You'll be shown a dialog box (figure 7.6) that asks you to enter the DOS path to the drive and directory to which the file should be copied. To make a copy in the current directory of drive D, you could simply enter D:. If you're not sure of the current directory then you should enter the entire directory path, just as if you were using the COPY command from the DOS command line. Remember that the root directory is denoted by a single backslash, such as C:\.

When a file of the same name already exists in the target directory, a dialog box (figure 7.7) will appear to ask you to confirm that the first file should be overwritten. To disable this feature, pull down the Options menu and select Confirmation. A dialog box will appear with a Confirm on replace check box. Select or deselect the option by clicking on the check box or by using the cursor keys to move to it and then pressing the space bar.

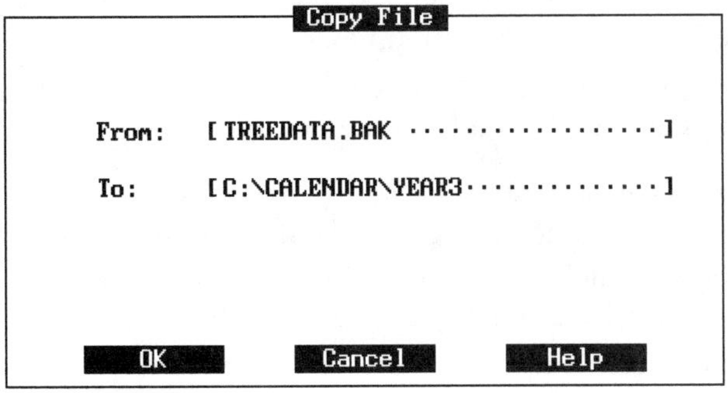

```
┌─────────────── Copy File ───────────────┐
│                                          │
│                                          │
│                                          │
│   From:   [ TREEDATA.BAK ·············· ]│
│                                          │
│   To:     [ C:\CALENDAR\YEAR3 ········· ]│
│                                          │
│                                          │
│                                          │
│   ███ OK ███    ███ Cancel ███   ███ Help ███│
└──────────────────────────────────────────┘
```

Figure 7.6

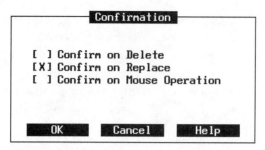

Figure 7.7

Windows 3.1   The easiest way to copy a file is to drag it from a directory listing to a file folder in a tree diagram while holding down the Ctrl key. This action is trivial when the copy is made on the same drive, but is a little harder when the file moves between drives. You have two options in this case. The first method is to move to the target drive, select the target directory, move back to the first drive, select the file, and then drag it to the target drive's icon at the top of the window while holding down the Ctrl key. If you don't press Ctrl, the file will be moved.

In the second method, you open a second window to display the tree of the drive to which the copy is directed. This is done by double-clicking on the target disk's icon, which is found at the top of the first window. Then choose Tile from the Window menu so that the two windows will be neatly arranged, one above the other. Once this is done, you can scroll the target directory tree on the second drive into view in one window, and then drag the file to it from the other window.

The third method of copying files is to pull down the File menu and choose Copy. You'll be shown a dialog box like the one in figure 7.8, asking you to type in the file's destination using a standard DOS path. When you enter only a drive specifier, like A: or C:, the file is copied to whichever directory is currently selected on that drive.

When a file of the same name already exists on the destination disk, another dialog box (figure 7.9) may prompt you to confirm that the file should be overwritten. This safety feature can be switched on and off by pulling down the Options menu and choosing Confirmation. You'll encounter a number of check boxes, one of which is the File Replace check box. The feature is on when an *X* appears in the check box.

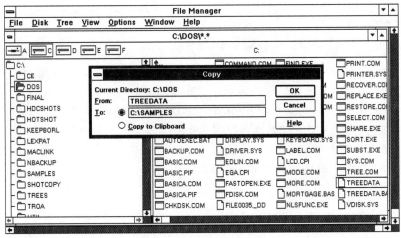

Figure 7.8

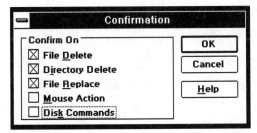

Figure 7.9

7.3 Copying files to and from a root directory

Within a directory tree, files are copied to the root directory exactly as they are to any other directory. The path to the root directory is indicated by a single backslash. So, to copy the file MYFILE.DOC from the subdirectory \MAMMALS\DOGS to the root directory of the same drive, you'd simply type:

```
COPY \MAMMALS\DOGS\MYFILE.DOC \ ⏎
```

or, if DOGS is the current directory, just type:

```
COPY MYFILE.DOC \ ⏎
```

Conversely, if MYFILE.DOC is in the root directory and you want to copy it to the DOGS subdirectory, type:

```
COPY \MYFILE.DOC \MAMMALS\DOGS ⏎
```

or, with DOGS as the current directory, type:

```
COPY \MYFILE.DOC ⏎
```

To copy the file to the root directory of a separate directory tree on drive D, enter:

```
COPY C:\MAMMALS\DOGS\MYFILE.DOC D:\ ⏎
```

Finally, the following example uses global file name characters (section 1.3) to copy all files from the root directory of the current drive to the current directory of drive D:

```
COPY \*.* D: ⏎
```

7.4 ■ Copying files between adjacent subdirectories

DOS provides the dot and double-dot symbols to speed access to adjacent subdirectories in a directory tree. These are nothing more than a single or double-period (.) or (..). They may be familiar to you because they appear as the first two entries of any subdirectory listing. The dot entry refers to the directory itself, the double-dot to the parent directory that holds it. Using these symbols, you may copy files between adjacent subdirectories without typing long directory paths.

Copying to the parent directory   Say that you are working in the directory tree shown in figure 7.10, in which SIAMESE is the current directory, and you want to copy the file CATLIST.DOC from SIAMESE to the parent directory, which is CATS. Instead of typing:

```
COPY CATLIST.DOC \FELINES\CATS ←
```

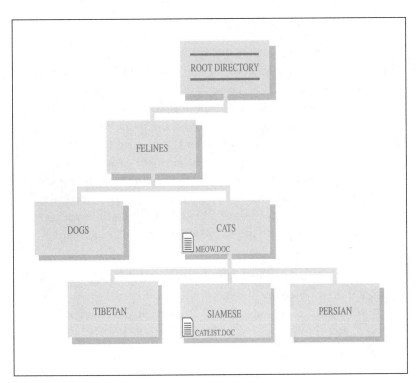

Figure 7.10

you could accomplish the task simply by typing:

    COPY CATLIST.DOC .. [←]

The double-period in this command represents \FELINES\CATS—that is, the whole DOS path up to, but not including, the current directory.

Copying to a directory above   Again using the directory tree shown in figure 7.10, say that CATS is now the current directory, and that you want to copy the file MEOW.DOC to the SIAMESE subdirectory. Instead of:

    COPY MEOW.DOC \FELINES\CATS\SIAMESE [←]

you could use:

    COPY MEOW.DOC .\SIAMESE [←]

Here, the single period represents the entire directory path up to and including the current directory, which is \FELINES\CATS. Alternatively, you could enter:

    COPY MEOW.DOC SIAMESE [←]

In this case, DOS assumes that SIAMESE is a subdirectory named in the current directory. This form of the command can be risky because, if you were to mistype SIAMESE as a word that does not name a subdirectory in the current directory, COPY would instead create a second copy of the file in the current directory and give it the name you actually typed (more on this in section 7.10). Before making a copy like this one, DOS checks the current directory for a subdirectory with the name you entered, and if it finds it, DOS copies the file to that subdirectory. Be careful, because if you make a typing error in the subdirectory name, the error may go unnoticed since DOS won't display an error message and, instead, will copy the file to the wrong directory using the wrong file name.

Copying to a subdirectory at the same level   The double-dot symbol can help you copy files to parallel subdirectories, such as from SIAMESE to PERSIAN, as in figure 7.10. With SIAMESE as the current directory, you could copy CATLIST from it to PERSIAN by typing:

    COPY CATLIST ..\PERSIAN [←]

Again, the double-dot represents the directory path up to but not including the current directory—that is, it represents the parent subdirectory of the current directory. So, this last command is the same as:

```
COPY CATLIST \FELINES\CATS\PERSIAN ⏎
```

7.5 Copying files between directory trees

Sometimes you may need to copy files between two directory trees. Perhaps you are working with two hard disk drives, or a single hard disk that is partitioned to appear as two hard disks, one named C and one named D. Or perhaps a diskette uses a directory tree to organize its files. In either case, you are confronted with two current directories, one for each tree. If the current directory on drive C is \ANIMALS\MAMMALS and the current directory on drive D is \PLANTS\TREES, then the command:

```
COPY C:MYFILE.TXT D: ⏎
```

looks for MYFILE.TXT in \ANIMALS\MAMMALS and copies it to \PLANTS\TREES. This command works whether C or D is the current drive. If drive C were current, you could shorten this command to:

```
COPY MYFILE.TXT D: ⏎
```

Often, you won't be certain which directory is current on the drive to which the file is copied (the target drive). The file will end up in the wrong subdirectory if you make a mistake, so it is important to be sure. One way is to simply name the full DOS path to the subdirectory to which the file is directed. Thus:

```
COPY MYFILE.TXT D:\PLANTS\TREES ⏎
```

or, if MYFILE.TXT is not in the current directory in drive C, then:

```
COPY \ANIMALS\MAMMALS\MYFILE.TXT D:\PLANTS\TREES ⏎
```

If you want to check whether the current directory on the second drive is the correct directory, use the CHDIR command:

```
CHDIR D: ⏎
```

This command won't change the current directory. Rather, it makes DOS display the current directory of the indicated drive, in this case:

```
D:\PLANTS\TREES
```

7.6   Copying groups of files

You can copy groups of files with a single COPY command by using global file name characters, also called wild-card characters. These are two symbols, the asterisk and question mark, that DOS interprets in special ways. Their basic use is simple, but there are complexities worth understanding that are discussed in section 1.3.

The asterisk   When an asterisk is used in a COPY command, it indicates that any match is to be copied. For example,

        COPY *.DOC A: ⏎

indicates that files of any name, but only those with the .DOC extension, are to be copied to drive A. MYFILE.DOC, YOURFILE.DOC, and HER-FILE.DOC would all be included. Conversely:

        COPY TOADS.* B: ⏎

causes DOS to only copy files named TOADS, but with any extension. Thus, TOADS.EXE, TOADS.DOC, and TOADS.BAT would all be copied. Note that the length of the extension does not matter; TOADS.Z would also be included, as would the file TOADS in spite of its having no extension at all.

When an asterisk is used both for the file name and the extension, all files in a subdirectory are copied:

        COPY *.* B: ⏎

Of course, in any of these commands you may include directory paths and drive specifiers when they are required. For example:

        COPY \LIZARDS*.* C:\ANIMALS\REPTILES ⏎

copies all files from the subdirectory \LIZARDS on the current drive to the subdirectory \ANIMALS\REPTILES on drive C.

The question mark   Unlike the asterisk, the question mark refers only to a single character in the file name. In the command:

        COPY CHAPTER?.DOC A: ⏎

the last character of the file name is replaced by ? to indicate that all files are to be copied that share exactly the same name and extension, except for the character replaced by ?. Thus, files named CHAP-TER1.DOC, CHAPTER2.DOC, and CHAPTER3.DOC would all be copied, as would CHAPTER.DOC, despite its lack of an eighth character in the file name. Any number of question marks may be used, and they do not have to be adjacent. The expression:

    COPY CHAPTER?.??? A: ⏎

works exactly like:

    COPY CHAPTER?.* A: ⏎

PITFALLS | The global file name characters do not always work as you might expect. The asterisk may be used to replace only part of a file name or extension, as in:

    COPY CHAP*.TXT A: ⏎

which would copy over files that have names with any number of characters after the initial *CHAP*, such as CHAPTER7.TXT, CHAP6.TXT, or just CHAP.TXT. The asterisk replaces everything from the position it starts at to the end of the file name or extension in which it appears. So, the command:

    COPY *CHAP.TXT A: ⏎

is equivalent to:

    COPY *.TXT A: ⏎

It copies files that have any name with a .TXT extension, not just files like MYCHAP.TXT and YOURCHAP.TXT. The question mark can be made to play the latter role, but it also has certain intricacies. See the discussion in section 1.3 for details.

Renaming while copying   You can rename a file when you copy it. For example:

    COPY OLDFILE.TXT B:NEWFILE.TXT ⏎

renames the copy of OLDFILE.TXT to NEWFILE.TXT as it places it on drive B (the original copy still has the name OLDFILE.TXT). Renaming can also be performed during mass copy operations. The command

    COPY *.DOC B:*.BAK ⏎

copies files ending in .DOC to drive B, changing their extensions to .BAK (for backup). By renaming files, copies can be made in the same directory. Thus, to make backups of all your .DOC files in the same directory as the originals, simply enter:

```
COPY *.DOC *.BAK ⏎
```

The DOS 5.0 Shell   In the DOS Shell, begin by selecting the files that will be copied. Select a consecutive series of files by clicking on the first in the series, and then on the last, while pressing the Shift key. To select files that aren't listed consecutively, click on each while pressing Ctrl. A second click deselects a file. Then, while holding down the Ctrl key, click down on any of the selected files and drag the mouse pointer to the target directory in the directory tree. If the target directory is on another drive, move to that drive and select the directory, and then move back to select the files and drag them to the symbol for the target drive (just above the directory tree). Alternatively, choose Dual File Lists from the View menu to bring into view both the source directory and the target subdirectory; then you can drag the files directly to the subdirectory.

Alternatively, once files have been selected, pull down the File menu and choose Copy. You'll encounter a dialog box (shown in figure 7.11) that asks you to enter the name of the path to the drive and directory to which the file or files should be copied. To place the copies in the current directory of drive D, enter D:. If you're not sure of the current directory then you should enter the entire directory path, exactly as if you were using the COPY command from the DOS command line. Remember that the root directory is denoted by a single backslash, such as D:\. All of the selected files will appear in the dialog box on a single, editable line. Use the cursor keys to scroll the line back and forth.

When a file of the same name already exists in the target directory, a dialog box will appear to ask you to confirm that the first file should be overwritten. To disable this feature, pull down the Options menu and select Confirmation. A dialog box (figure 7.12) will appear with a Confirm on replace check box. Select or deselect the confirmation option by clicking on the check box, or by using the cursor keys to move to it and then pressing the space bar.

```
┌─────────────────[ Copy File ]─────────────────┐
│                                               │
│     From:   [ JOIN.EXE KEYB.COM KEYBOARD.SYS ]│
│                                               │
│     To:     [ C:\DOS······················ ]  │
│                                               │
│                                               │
│                                               │
│        ▐ OK ▌        ▐ Cancel ▌      ▐ Help ▌  │
└───────────────────────────────────────────────┘
```

Figure 7.11

```
┌──────[ Replace File Confirmation ]──────┐
│                                         │
│  Replace File:                          │
│    C:\SAMPLES\JOIN.EXE                   │
│    03-17-87  (8,969 bytes)               │
│                                         │
│  With File:                             │
│    C:\DOS\JOIN.EXE                       │
│    03-17-87  (8,969 bytes)               │
│                                         │
│     ▐ Yes ▌      ▐ No ▌     ▐ Cancel ▌   │
└─────────────────────────────────────────┘
```

Figure 7.12

Windows 3.1   To select multiple files, hold down Ctrl and click on each file's icon. Or, to select a group of consecutive files, click on the file at one end of the range and then click on the other while holding down the Shift key. Then copy the files by any of the methods described elsewhere in this chapter. When dragging files into a directory tree, you'll be able to click down on only one of the files selected. Nonetheless, all of the files will be dragged to the file folder you have chosen.

If you choose the Copy command from the File menu, you can select a group of files by changing the file specification in the From box found inside the Copy dialog box. For example, you could arbitrarily select any file from the directory you want to copy a group of files from. The Copy dialog box would list this file. By replacing the file name with a specification like *.TXT, all .TXT files would be copied in spite of the fact that you hadn't individually selected them in a directory listing.

By default, a confirmation box appears when files are copied over other files of the same name. These confirmations can be annoying when many files are copied. This feature can be disabled by choosing

Confirmation from the Options menu, leading to the dialog box in figure 7.14.

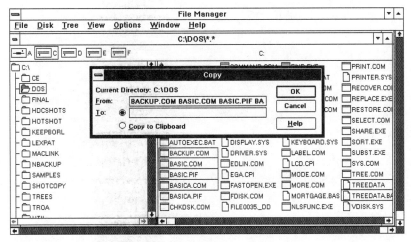

Figure 7.13

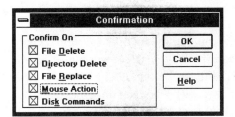

Figure 7.14

7.7 Copying groups of files to multiple diskettes

One shortcoming of the DOS COPY command is that it cannot employ global file name characters (section 1.3) to copy a group of files across several diskettes. When you enter:

```
COPY *.* A: ⏎
```

to copy all files in a directory to a diskette in drive A, you'll encounter a "full disk" error message if the files won't fit. There is no way to change diskettes and continue copying. However, there's a trick by which you can achieve this end, using the DOS XCOPY command.

XCOPY (explained in detail in section 7.8) is a complicated command, one that can extend its range across multiple subdirectories. But it works just like COPY when its advanced features are ignored. Instead of entering:

```
COPY *.* A: ⏎
```

you could type:

```
XCOPY *.* A: ⏎
```

By adding an /M switch to the command, only files whose archive attribute is set (switched on) are copied. The archive attribute, which is discussed in the minitutorial at the beginning of Chapter 22, marks a file as having been changed since it was last backed up (DOS turns the attribute on whenever it writes data into a file). Backup software can locate all files that have their archive attributes turned on and make backups of them. Once a backup is made, the backup utility turns the archive attribute off to exclude the file from the next backup, unless the file is changed again. The command:

```
XCOPY *.* /M A: ⏎
```

copies to drive A all files that happen to have their archive attributes set, and:

```
XCOPY \FISH\SALMON\*.DOC /M A: ⏎
```

copies files from \FISH\SALMON that have .DOC extensions and archive attributes that are turned on.

Like a backup program, XCOPY turns the archive attribute off after it makes the copy, and this is the means by which you can copy files across multiple diskettes. Imagine that all the files you want to copy have their archive attributes set. You enter XCOPY *.* /M A: ⏎ and the copying begins. When XCOPY runs out of diskette space for copying the files, it displays an "Insufficient disk space" error message and quits, just as the COPY command would. But it will have turned off the archive attributes of all files that have been successfully copied. When you change diskettes and reenter exactly the same command, the files already copied will be skipped over. You need only repeat the command as many times as is required to copy over all files.

You can use ATTRIB (discussed in section 4.5) to turn on the archive attributes of a group of files, using the same global file name character specification that appears in the XCOPY command. To switch on the archive attribute of all files in the current directory, type:

```
ATTRIB +A *.* ⏎
```

Another example, the statement:

```
ATTRIB +A \BIRDS\PENGUINS\*.TXT ⏎
```

turns on the archive attributes of all .TXT files in the PENGUINS subdirectory. Notice that you can change +A to -A to turn off archive attributes in selected files. Before starting up XCOPY, you might use this feature to select all files in a directory and then individually exclude a few.

After XCOPY has been used this way, archive attributes may be switched off in files that should be included in a later backup. So always apply ATTRIB once again with +A to turn them all on again. By doing so, you may include some extra files in your backups. But too many files in a backup are far better than too few.

Both XCOPY and ATTRIB are external commands; they are kept in separate files, apart from the main DOS program COMMAND. COM that always resides in memory. If you obtain a "Bad command or file name" error message, you need to specify the locations of the XCOPY.EXE or ATTRIB.EXE files, as in:

```
C:\DOS\ATTRIB +A *.* ⏎
```

Alternatively, name the directory that holds the commands in a PATH command (explained in section 8.1) so that DOS can always find these files, no matter the current directory.

PITFALLS Be aware that both XCOPY and ATTRIB can use the /S switch to extend their operations across multiple directories, so they may be used in tandem for elaborate copy operations from a whole tree at once. But be sure you understand XCOPY thoroughly before trying this. Also, keep in mind that this technique cannot help you copy single files that are larger than what a diskette can hold. To do this, you'll need to use the DOS BACKUP command.

7.8 Copying files between multiple subdirectories

The DOS COPY command can operate upon the files of only one subdirectory at a time. If you wanted to copy all files with .DOC extensions in an entire directory tree, you would need to execute as many COPY commands as there are subdirectories. The XCOPY command works much like COPY, but it can extend its actions across many subdirectories, and even the entire tree.

XCOPY expects to find a parallel tree structure on the disk to which it is making the copies. If it does not find it, it automatially creates subdirectories of the same names as those on the source disk. XCOPY works only in this manner; you can't have it take files from several directories on the source disk and make copies in one directory on the target disk.

In its simplest form, XCOPY works just like COPY. To copy all .DOC files from the current directory (say, of drive C) to drive A, enter:

```
XCOPY *.DOC A: ⏎
```

By adding the /S switch to the command, as in:

```
XCOPY *.DOC A: /S ⏎
```

XCOPY is made to search for files not just in the current directory, but also in all directories beyond—meaning, directories listed in the current directory, directories listed in those directories, and so on. This way, a single branch of the tree can be copied. When the XCOPY command is used while the root directory is the current directory, or when the root directory is entered as the directory to copy from, the /S switch makes XCOPY copy matching files from the entire directory tree.

How the directory tree is copied   XCOPY is not always an easy DOS command to use. Because it can work on just a branch of the source tree, it is essential that you exactly specify the subdirectory that is the starting point of that branch. Just as important, you must tell XCOPY the name of the subdirectory on the target disk at which it should begin transferring copies of files and making new subdirectories to hold them (if necessary). Consider the ominous command:

```
XCOPY C:\CATS\*.* A:\ /S ⏎
```

In this case, all files (*.*) are copied from the directory tree branch on drive C, beginning from and including the subdirectory \CATS. The target drive is specified as A:\. This means that the files contained in the CATS subdirectory are copied into the root directory of the target diskette. XCOPY does not create a subdirectory named CATS on drive A. The subdirectories branching out of CATS on the source disk (drive C) instead branch out of the root directory on the target disk (drive A). When subdirectories of these names (SIAMESE, PERSIAN, TIBETAN) already exist on the target disk in the same positions, they'll be used for the copies instead of for creating new subdirectories. Figure 7.15 illustrates this process.

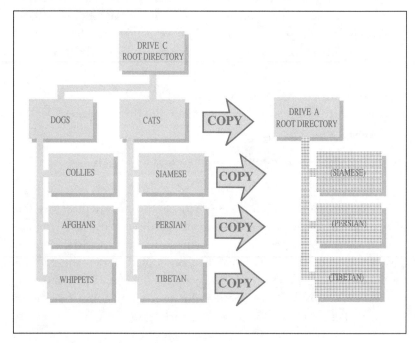

Figure 7.15

You can also specify a directory other than the root directory for files to be saved into on the target disk. For example, the command:

```
XCOPY C:\LEVEL1\LEVEL2\*.* A:\FIRSTDIR /S ⏎
```

places the files from the subdirectory called LEVEL2 into the FIRSTDIR subdirectory on drive A. Subdirectories extending from LEVEL2 on drive C would be created—if they didn't already exist—beginning from FIRSTDIR on drive A. Again, XCOPY will place the file copies in existing directories of the same name, but only if they are in the correct position relative to the starting subdirectory; otherwise, XCOPY will create new subdirectories to accomodate the transferred files.

This example could be simplified by making the source drive the current drive and by making the starting directory on the source drive that drive's current directory:

```
C: ⏎
CHDIR \LEVEL1\LEVEL2 ⏎
XCOPY *.* A:\FIRSTDIR /S ⏎
```

It is essential that you fully specify the beginning target directory. You can rely on defaults—the current directory of the target drive—but if you make a mistake, XCOPY will go right ahead and transfer the files, creating numerous subdirectories in the wrong positions. It can be a lot of work undoing the mistake.

If you want to copy a branch of a tree to a disk that does not contain identical subdirectories, and you'd like the copied branch to originate from the root directory, but don't want any new files actually placed in the root directory, you could use a command like this one:

```
XCOPY *.* A:\EXTRADIR /S ⏎
```

The contents of the current directory on the source diskette are placed in a new subdirectory on the target, EXTRADIR, which XCOPY will create in the root directory.

Advanced features   XCOPY offers a number of features beyond the /S switch that can enhance the command's power. The /D switch copies files on the basis of their dates. See section 7.9 to learn about this feature. Add /P to have XCOPY prompt Y/N? for each file copied—a measure that can help prevent errors but that slows mass file transfers. /V causes DOS to verify that the copy can be read properly. /M and /A cause XCOPY to copy only files whose archive bit is set (see the minitutorial at the beginning of Chapter 4); the /M switch then clears the archive bit, while the /A switch leaves it as it is. These switches make XCOPY useful for some kinds of backups, as section 22.5 explains.

Finally, the /E switch causes XCOPY to copy all subdirectories in the branch of the source directory tree, whether or not they contain files.

Normally, XCOPY copies subdirectories only if they contain files that are being copied. Empty directories leading to a directory containing a file are also created. By using /E, a mirror image of the entire tree branch is created.

7.9 Copying files by date

The XCOPY command, detailed at section 7.8, can copy all files dating from a particular day on. It cannot copy files from a single day. Files are not always well-classified by their dates. The date stamp reflects whatever the system clock was set to when the file was last written to. The date won't match the date of creation if the clock was set incorrectly or if the file was changed since it was first created. You can alter a file's date stamp by temporarily changing the clock setting (see section 17.4), loading the file into the software that created it, and then saving it without making any changes. Various utility software programs, like the FD (File Date) program in the Norton Utilities, can also do the job.

To copy all files dated June 21, 1990 or later to drive A, end the XCOPY command with a /D: switch followed by the date:

        XCOPY *.* A: /D:06/21/90 ⏎

In this command, the characters *.* are global file name characters (explained in section 1.3) that stand for all files in a directory. Notice that the date format shown here is the standard American one; if DOS is configured in your machine to use another country's standard system, use the date format it requires. Global file name characters can also be used to copy, say, all files ending with .TXT and originating on and after the given date:

        XCOPY *.TXT A: /D:06/21/90 ⏎

PITFALL   XCOPY is a complicated command, and it's one that could easily get you into trouble. If you specify a nonexistent path as the destination for a copy, XCOPY will automatically create the necessary subdirectories whether you want it to or not. Be careful.

7.10 Making a copy of a file in the same directory as the original

DOS won't allow two files of the same name and extension in one directory. If you enter the command:

```
COPY ACCOUNTS.TXT ⏎
```

DOS responds with the message:

```
File cannot be copied onto itself
0 File(s) copied
```

Two files of the same name and extension would leave DOS with no way of knowing which to open (or copy, or rename, or erase) if you used the file name in a DOS command. There are times, however, when you may want to make a copy of a file in the same directory. Sometimes you simply need multiple copies of a file to be used for different purposes. And sometimes you may want a short-term backup of a file in case you later have misgivings about modifications you have made.

To make a copy, first decide on a different name for the copy. Then use the COPY command, specifying that name. For instance, if you need a copy of ACCOUNTS.TXT, and want to give the copy the name ACOUNTS2.TXT, then you would enter:

```
COPY ACCOUNTS.TXT ACOUNTS2.TXT ⏎
```

If the file is to serve as a backup file, you may want to give the second copy the extension .BAK:

```
COPY ACCOUNTS.TXT ACCOUNTS.BAK ⏎
```

When the files are in a directory other than the current directory, you'll need to specify the same DOS path for each:

```
COPY \DEPT\ACCOUNTS.TXT \DEPT\ACOUNTS2.TXT ⏎
```

Remember, if the directory of these files is not the current directory, and you don't specify a path for the second copy, it will be saved to the current directory, not to the same directory as the original.

7.11 Replacing one version of a file with another

The REPLACE command provides an unusual but very useful service. It replaces the files on one disk with files of the same name taken from another disk. It can also copy files between subdirectories on the same drive. There is no need to specify the individual files—the command examines directories on both disks and determines which files are to be transferred. Files not present on the target disk are not copied from the source. This saves you the trouble of typing many COPY commands when the files have diverse names and extensions. The REPLACE command is ideal for transferring work to diskettes to take home, and for later restoring the (modified) files to their source. Used this way, you must be very careful to make the transfer in the proper direction, or older versions of files will overwrite newer ones.

To transfer files from the current directory of drive A to the current directory of drive C, enter:

```
REPLACE A:*.* C: ⏎
```

Of course, directory paths may be used also:

```
REPLACE A:\OLDDATA\*.* C:\PROJECT3\OLDDATA ⏎
```

The use of the global file name characters *.* indicates that all files common to the specified directories of each disk should be copied, copying the version on drive A into the version on drive C. You can also limit the file transfer to a subset of those found on each. For instance, to transfer only .DOC files, type:

```
REPLACE A:*.DOC C: ⏎
```

Advanced features REPLACE takes a number of switches that expand its usefulness considerably. First, the /A switch causes RE-PLACE to reverse its usual functioning so that it transfers all files that are not present on the target disk. This stops you from replacing existing files when transferring new ones to a disk:

```
REPLACE A:*.* C: /A ⏎
```

Another useful switch, /S, extends the file transfer to all directories on the target disk. So, if you have multiple copies of a file in a directory tree, you can replace them all at once. In some other DOS commands the /S switch limits the command to the current directory and all directories within and beyond, but in this case it always operates on the whole tree of the target disk. The search remains limited to one directory on the source disk. Note that this switch can't be combined with the /A switch. To replace all instances of the file MONSTER.DAT on drive C with a new version of MONSTER.DAT from drive A, type:

```
REPLACE A:MONSTER.DAT C: /S ⏎
```

Three other switches are refinements that can help keep you out of trouble. Adding the /P switch causes DOS to display the name of each file as it is about to be transferred, and to request your permission before continuing. The /R switch lets REPLACE transfer read-only files, which normally are protected from being overwritten. Be aware that RE-PLACE will not replace hidden or system files. Finally, /W makes REPLACE display this message before beginning:

```
Press any key to begin replacing file(s)
```

This feature is useful when REPLACE is called from a batch file since it gives you a chance to post a screen message to ask the user to insert the proper diskette in drive A.

Note that REPLACE is an external DOS command, meaning that it is held in its own file named REPLACE.COM. If that file is not on hand, you'll need to include a path to it, such as:

```
C:\DOS\REPLACE A:*.* C: ⏎
```

Alternatively, you can provide access to REPLACE.COM through a DOS PATH command (section 8.1).

7.12 Duplicating diskettes

The DOS DISKCOPY command makes an exact copy of a diskette. It's easiest to use when your machine has two disk drives that can hold diskettes of exactly the same capacity (those using 5 ¼-inch diskettes should note that 1.2M drives can write 360K diskettes, but many can't be used reliably with DISKCOPY for anything other than 1.2M copies). When you don't have a matching drive, DISKCOPY can make an exact copy using only one drive. It does this by reading as much from the original as can be stored in the computer's memory chips. Then it prompts you to remove the original from the drive and insert the diskette to which the copy is made. You may need to swap the diskettes back and forth since the contents are transferred in stages.

You should be familiar with the terminology employed by DISKCOPY before starting it up. Its screen messages refer to the source diskette and the target diskette. The source diskette is the original from which the copy is made; the target diskette becomes the copy. The target diskette does not need to be new or empty. For that matter, it does not need to be formatted; DISKCOPY senses that a target diskette has not been formatted and does the formatting itself before it makes the copy.

Once DISKCOPY goes to work, any data that had been on the target diskette is lost forever. It is completely obliterated, and no unerase utility will get it back for you. For this reason, before you start up DISKCOPY you must be dead sure that the target diskette is the one you want to use. There can be no confusion when the diskette is brand new and just out of the box. In all other cases, place the diskette in a drive and request a directory listing to be sure.

DISKCOPY is an external DOS command, meaning that it resides in a file of its own, apart from the main DOS program that stays in memory. This file must be on hand to start up DISKCOPY. The file DISKCOPY.COM should be kept on your hard disk along with all other DOS files. (Note that if your machine lacks a hard disk, you'll need to begin with a DOS diskette containing DISKCOPY.COM in drive A.)

Copying with two diskette drives   When you have two matching diskette drives, begin by typing:

```
DISKCOPY A: B: ←
```

This command means "make a disk copy from the source diskette in drive A to the target diskette in drive B." DISKCOPY starts up and this message is displayed:

```
Insert SOURCE diskette in drive A.
Press any key when ready ...
```

Insert the diskettes in drives A and B and press any key to begin the disk copy. You must be very careful about placing the correct diskette in the correct drive. If you get it backwards, the contents of the target diskette can be copied to the source diskette, destroying its data. When there is doubt, you can press Ctrl-Break to terminate DISKCOPY and start over, but only before pressing a key to begin the disk copy.

```
Once DISKCOPY has finished, it inquires:
Copy another (Y/N)?
```

Press Y when you have a sequence of disk copies to make. You'll again be prompted to place a source diskette in drive A and a target diskette in B, and then to press a key to begin the next copy. To make multiple copies of the same diskette, leave the source in place and change only the target.

When you're finished and you exit from DISKCOPY, you may encounter the message:

```
Insert diskette with \COMMAND.COM in drive A
and strike any key when ready
```

This occurs only in machines lacking a hard disk. The message reports that part of the operating system had to be removed from memory while the copy was made and it now needs to be reloaded. Place your DOS diskette, or any diskette that can be used to boot the machine, in drive A and press any key.

Copying with only one drive   If you have only one diskette drive, you can make disk copies by entering:

```
DISKCOPY A: A: ↵
```

In this case, drive A acts as both the source and target drive. DISKCOPY will tell you when to place the source diskette or target diskette in the drive. If you have a second diskette drive of different capacity, and want to make a disk copy using it, simply change the command's drive specifiers:

```
DISKCOPY B: B: ↵
```

Copying between diskettes of different capacities   You can also copy all files from one diskette to another using the DOS COPY command. When a diskette has only a root directory, and no directory tree, this command copies all files from drive A to drive B:

```
COPY A:*.* B: ⏎
```

COPY is less suitable for duplicating diskettes that have a directory tree: first, you have to recreate the tree on the target diskette with a number of MKDIR commands, and then you have to copy over the files in each subdirectory of the original diskette with a separate COPY command. Instead, use the following XCOPY command (XCOPY is discussed in section 7.8), which automatically creates the tree subdirectories while it copies the files:

```
XCOPY A:\*.* B:\ /S ⏎
```

There is one disadvantage of COPY and XCOPY: if your objective is to make a diskette with exactly the same files as the original, the target diskette must be completely erased before you begin. Another way in which COPY and XCOPY differ from DISKCOPY is that they cannot format new diskettes as they do their work. Also, COPY and XCOPY are usually slower than DISKCOPY. However, in many instances COPY and XCOPY have an advantage. As section 21.3 explains, in a process called fragmentation, disk files may gradually be separated into parts dispersed across the disk surface. Disk drives take longer to read and write fragmented files. But when the files are copied to an empty diskette by COPY or XCOPY, the individual files are reassembled. DISKCOPY, on the other hand, makes an exact copy of the source diskette, so file fragmentation is preserved. This issue is not a concern with the original diskettes (distribution diskettes) you receive with new software. All files on these diskettes will probably be unfragmented and DISKCOPY is almost always the best way to duplicate them.

Copy protection   Some distribution diskettes resist copying. For these, DISKCOPY, COPY, and XCOPY may render error messages, sometimes cryptic ones. When this happens, and you've had no trouble using the disk drives otherwise, you can be sure that you've encountered a copy-protected diskette. The diskette has been modified in subtle ways by the software manufacturer to resist copying and indirectly, thereby, to discourage software piracy. See section 12.2 for a discussion of copy protection.

Verifying the copy   When a copy made by DISKCOPY is complete, you can use the DOS DISKCOMP command to compare the target disk with the source to verify its accuracy. DISKCOMP works just like DISKCOPY. To compare the diskettes in drive A and B, enter:

```
DISKCOMP A: B: ⏎
```

Here, it doesn't matter which disk is in which drive, since neither is changed in any way. DISKCOMP can also verify a copy with a single drive:

```
DISKCOMP A: A: ⏎
```

If all goes well, you'll be shown the message:

```
Diskettes compare OK
```

Otherwise, you'll be told that an error occured on a particular disk side and track. When this happens, make a new disk copy with a fresh target diskette. (It's possible that a second try with the same target diskette may succeed, but the error generally points to a flaw in the disk surface, which in turn suggests that others may crop up later.)

Use DISKCOMP only when you're especially concerned about the data being copied. The DISKCOPY command is quite reliable and the chance of an error slipping by is slim.

Windows 3.1   In Windows, enter the File Manager, pull down the Disk menu, and select Copy Disk. You'll see the dialog box shown in figure 7.16. Just type ⏎ to continue. Additional dialog boxes will then prompt you to insert source and target diskettes.

Figure 7.16

7.13 Verifying that file copies are accurate

Disk drives seldom make mistakes writing data to the disk surface. Ordinarily, a condition that causes an error will be detected on the spot, and one way or another you will have an indication that something has gone wrong. Still, it can happen that a file appears to have been written correctly, but an error has crept in. When crucial data is in the balance, you may want to double-check to see that all has gone well.

DOS can be made to automatically verify that it has written a file correctly. After writing data, it checks to see that what it has just written is readable. If it is, the copy is almost certain to be correct. To have DOS make this extra check, simply enter:

    VERIFY ON ⏎

DOS responds with the message:

    VERIFY is on

Once the command is given, DOS verifies every write operation, whether from a COPY command or when data is written to disk by software. Because DOS has more work to do, disk operations take longer, and in some applications you will notice a significant slowing of performance. For this reason, the verification feature is turned off when you start up the machine. You can turn it on automatically at that time by placing the line VERIFY ON in your AUTOEXEC.BAT file (section 11.1). But it's usually best to only turn verification on for special occasions, and then turn it back off with the command:

    VERIFY OFF ⏎

7.14 Moving files

DOS does not include a command for moving files from one location to another. You're forced to first copy a file, and then erase the original. Combining these functions in one command would make some errors less likely. In many instances the process would also be quicker, because in a file move between subdirectories on the same disk there is no need to actually transfer the file from one disk location to another; simple changes in directory listings do the job.

A batch file can be used to move files, but it must be written and used carefully. At its heart are two statements, one to copy the file and one to erase the original. The danger is that something will go wrong when the file is copied. If the batch file fails to realize that the copy has not been made and goes ahead and erases the original, you'll lose data. Unfortunately, DOS is constructed in such a way that batch files can only detect errors for the XCOPY command and not for COPY. XCOPY, which is described in section 7.8, is more invasive than COPY in that, when you specify a non-existent directory as the file's destination, it will create the directory and all directories leading to it. It would be better to receive an error message in this case, but nothing can be done to change the way the command behaves.

Here is a batch file for moving files:

```
@ECHO off
FOR %%F IN (%2) DO GOTO Begin
ECHO Error! Format for MOVE is:
ECHO MOVE file destination-directory
ECHO For example:
ECHO MOVE c:\level1\myfile.txt a:
GOTO Finished
:Begin
IF NOT EXIST %1 GOTO BadFilename
XCOPY %1 %2
IF ERRORLEVEL 1 GOTO ErrorOccured
ERASE %1
ECHO The file %1 has been moved to %2.
GOTO Finished
:BadFilename
ECHO The file could not be found.
ECHO Please include a path to its directory.
GOTO Finished
:ErrorOccured
ECHO Error!
ECHO The file %1 could not be moved to %2.
```

```
GOTO Finished
:Finished
@ECHO on
```

We'll tell you in a moment how this batch file works, but you don't need to understand it to use it. Just carefully type it into a file named MOVE.BAT. Then, when you want to use the a file to move another file called NOTAGAIN. DOC from its current location to drive A, just type:

```
MOVE NOTAGAIN.DOC A:  ⏎
```

Both the file name and its destination may optionally take directory paths:

```
MOVE C:\LEVEL1\NOTAGAIN.DOC A:\FILEDUMP  ⏎
```

To be useful, you'll want this batch file on line no matter the current directory. Place it in a subdirectory devoted to batch files and specify the name of that subdirectory in a PATH command (section 8.2 explains how PATH commands work).

How the batch file works   This is a complicated batch file; to understand it, you need to know batch file basics, which are explained in Chapter 9. The file begins with a FOR statement that tests whether two parameters (the name of the file to be moved and its destination) have been included on the command line. When a second parameter has not been given, the error message listed on the next four lines is displayed and a jump is made to the end of the file so that it terminates. Otherwise, a jump is made to the :Begin label to copy the file.

Before actually copying the file, a check is made to be sure that the specified file actually exists. This is done with the IF NOT EXIST %1 statement, which looks for the file named by the first command line parameter (represented in batch files by the symbol %1). If the file is not found, a jump is made to the :BadFileName label, the error message on the following two lines is displayed, and a jump is then made to the :Finished label at the end of the file so that it terminates. Otherwise, the batch file goes on to make the copy with the statement XCOPY 1% 2%.

After attempting to copy the file using XCOPY, an IF ERRORLEVEL 1 statement fetches the errorlevel code that is returned by XCOPY to verify that it successfully completed the copy. An errorlevel value of 0 is returned when all has gone well. The expression "ERRORLEVEL 1" refers to any other errorlevel code, as might result from a disk drive error or a full-disk condition. If an error has occured, a jump is made to the :ErrorOccured label, the error message on the following two lines is displayed, and the batch file terminates. However, if the copy has been successfully made, the ERASE %1 statement is executed to delete the original file. Then, the next line of the file displays a message telling you that the file has been moved. In this message, the file name is inserted in place of the symbol %1 and the destination directory is inserted in place of %2. Finally, a jump is made to the :Finished label at the end of the file and the batch file terminates.

| PITFALL | One limitation of this batch file appears when a full-disk error occurs before all files in a mass move are copied. For example, if you specify *.* as the file name (section 1.3) when copying to a diskette, disk space may run short. In this case, some files are copied, but none of the originals are subsequently erased. |

The DOS Shell   In the DOS Shell, begin by selecting the files that will be moved. Select a consecutive series of files by clicking on the first in the series and then on the last while pressing the `Shift` key. To select files that aren't listed consecutively, click on each while pressing `Ctrl`. A second click deselects a file. Then click down on any of the selected files and drag the mouse pointer to the target directory in the directory tree. Files can be moved in this way only if the target directory is on the same drive.

Alternatively, once files have been selected, pull down the File menu and choose Move. You'll encounter a dialog box (shown in figure 7.17) that asks you to enter the path to the drive and directory to which the file or files should be copied. To place the copies in the current directory of drive D, enter D:. If you're not sure of the current directory then you should enter the entire directory path, exactly as if you were using the COPY command from the DOS command line. Remember that the root directory is denoted by a single backslash, as in D:\. All of the selected files will appear in the dialog box on a single, editable line. Use the cursor keys to scroll the line back and forth.

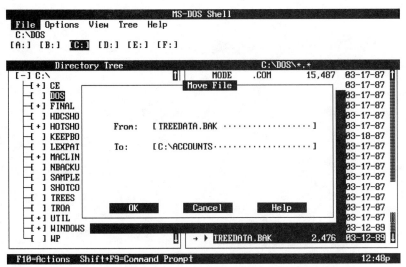

Figure 7-17

Windows 3.1   In Windows, files are moved in nearly the same way that they are copied. After selecting a file, you can either choose the Move command from the File menu, or you can drag the file to the subdirectory to which you want it moved. When dragging files, the Ctrl key is held down to copy the file whereas no key is pressed when the file is moved.

Note that you cannot move files between disk drives by dragging them. If you attempt to do so, the files will simply be copied. For file moves between drives, you should always choose Move from the File menu.

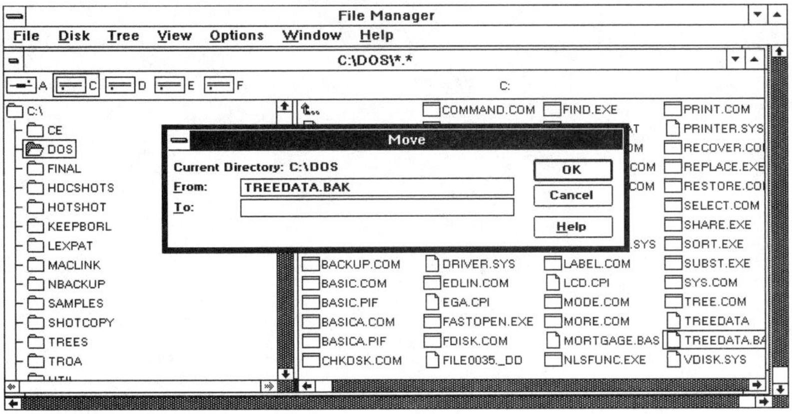

Figure 7.18

Chapter 8

Linking Disk Drives and Subdirectories

- **MINITUTORIAL:** Managing multiple drives and directories
- Making DOS search for program files
- Making DOS search for data files
- Making a disk drive appear like a subdirectory
- Making a subdirectory appear like a disk drive
- Changing a drive's specifier

MINITUTORIAL:

Managing multiple drives and directories

The system of organizing files into directory trees can be frustrating and confusing. Using a tree can require that you remember its structure and repeatedly type in long directory paths. DOS offers a number of features to ease the pain.

Two commands, PATH and APPEND, cause DOS commands and application programs to search for files when they're not found in the current directory. Normally, when you type in only a file name with no directory path to the file, DOS looks for the file in the current directory. If it does not find it there, it returns a "File not found" error message. Using PATH and APPEND, DOS can extend the search to a number of subdirectories you've specified (it won't search the entire tree unless you include every subdirectory in the tree in the PATH or APPEND command, which is not usually possible). Judiciously applied, these two commands can save you a good deal of typing. In some cases they are essential for configuring application software so that it can find the files it needs.

PATH searches only for program files (those with .COM and .EXE extensions) and batch files (.BAT extensions). A PATH command can be placed in your AUTOEXEC.BAT file (section 11.1) so that all the programs you ordinarily use are always available from any directory. Of course, any program can be accessed from any directory by typing in the directory path to it; PATH merely saves you the trouble. External DOS commands—those held in separate files apart from the main DOS program—can also be made constantly available this way.

You can use commands like CHKDSK or TREE at any time without specifying the location of their files on disk. The DOS 4.0 installation program automatically sets up a PATH command for you for this purpose.

The PATH command also makes it easier to manage files. Many users are in the habit of starting up a program by making the directory that contains it the current directory and then entering the program's name. Frequently, directory paths must be typed in when the software opens or creates data files in other directories. If you forget to enter a path when a new file is created, the file may be placed in the wrong directory. Using PATH, the subdirectory that holds the data files you'll use can be made the current directory. When you enter the program name, DOS searches for the program in the subdirectories specified by

PATH and starts it running. You can then load and create files while remaining in the data files' directory.

The APPEND command works in the same way, but it can also cause DOS to look for data files in its searches. Data files required by your programs, such as the spelling checker file used by your word processor, can be placed in remote directories specified in the command. DOS hunts down the files when the program opens them. Similarly, once you've started up a program, when you open a data file that is not in the current directory, you can enter its name without a directory path, and DOS will find it. While this feature sounds attractive, it shouldn't be used as a crutch. There are limits to how much work DOS can do for you, and having solid skill using directory paths is still the best way to make your job easier all-around.

The remaining three DOS commands described in this chapter let you rearrange drives and directory trees in ways that suit your needs. They do not actually rearrange subdirectories or data, but from the user's point of view they appear to. The result is an easier environment for you to work in.

The ASSIGN command lets you change the letter assigned to a particular disk drive. If for some reason you want to refer to drive A as drive B, ASSIGN lets you do it. This command is mostly useful for temporarily configuring old, inflexible software so that it can work on a modern hard-disk machine.

Next comes the SUBST command, which lets you refer to a subdirectory as though it were a disk drive unto itself. For example, the subdirectory \MAMMALS\RODENTS\RATS could be renamed as drive E. Thereafter, you could direct operations upon the subdirectory to E: instead of typing in the long path. This feature is also useful for configuring software, and it comes in handy when you're doing house cleaning and need to access a subdirectory many times in the same work session.

Finally, the JOIN command acts like the opposite of SUBST. It appears to combine two directory trees (and, thus, two drives) into a single tree, with one of the trees essentially transplanted into the root directory of the other. JOIN can be a pleasure to use with two hard disks: A single command can search, analyze, or process all files on both drives, saving you some repetition.

Be warned, however, that the ASSIGN, SUBST, and JOIN commands all tend to make DOS unstable and may create problems using Windows. Things can go wrong when they are in effect, and it is not a good idea to have them operating all the time. PATH, on the other hand, is essential, and APPEND may also become a valuable permanent addition to your hard disk management system.

8.1 Making DOS search for program files

When you enter the name of a program on the DOS command line, DOS ordinarily looks only in the current directory for the file that holds the program. For example, if you try to run a program named OUTLINE by typing:

```
OUTLINE ⏎
```

DOS would look in the current directory for a file named OUTLINE.EXE, OUTLINE.COM, or OUTLINE.BAT. If the file is not found, DOS won't look elsewhere on the disk. Instead, it just tells you:

```
Bad command or file name
```

If you know that the program file is in another directory, you can make that directory the current one and then run the program:

```
CHDIR \SUBDIR1\SUBDIR2 ⏎
OUTLIN ⏎
```

Alternatively, you can run the program without changing the current directory by specifying a directory path to the program file:

```
\SUBDIR1\SUBDIR2\OUTLINE ⏎
```

The second approach is often the better one. If the data files you are planning to work on are not in the same directory as the program file, it's best to have the current directory be the subdirectory holding the data files. That way, the program can find files without making you type in directory paths (file operations within application programs are usually automatically directed to the current directory when no other directory path is specified). This way, you're also assured that new files you create with the software are deposited in a relevant directory.

The PATH command   Ideally, you should be able to move to a subdirectory holding data files and start up the program that uses them without worrying about where the file(s) holding the program itself reside. With only a little effort, it's possible to bring about this state of affairs. The DOS PATH command does the job. It specifies a number of subdirectories for DOS to look through when you ask to run a program. DOS begins the search only after checking the current directory for the sought-after file. To make DOS automatically search the subdirectory \SUBDIR1\SUBDIR2 on drive C, you would type:

```
PATH C:\SUBDIR1\SUBDIR2 ⏎
```

Semicolons separate multiple paths:

```
PATH C:\90TAXES;C:\PLANNING\PROJECT2;D:\ACCOUNTS ⏎
```

Leave no spaces between the semicolons and the next path; otherwise, DOS will issue a "Too many parameters" error message. Be sure to include drive specifiers, such as C: or D: in the paths so that the directories can be found no matter the current drive.

You should avoid naming diskette drives in PATH commands to prevent not ready errors when these drives are empty. DOS begins its search of directories with the first listed in the PATH command. When it still doesn't find the file after searching all listed directories, it issues the usual "Bad command or file name" message.

Each PATH command completely replaces prior PATH commands. You can't add more and more subdirectories to be searched by entering a series of these commands. The limited length of the DOS command line means that only so many subdirectories may be included in this feature. If you run up against the limit, try positioning crucial subdirectories closer to the root directory so that their directory paths will be shorter, and consider using shorter names for subdirectories so that more can fit onto the DOS command line.

The PATH information is stored in a place in memory called the environment. An "Out of environment space" message will appear if the environment is too small to hold all of the information. See section 11.8 if you need to increase the size of the environment. Even when environment space is available, your PATH command can list no more directory paths than can be typed on the DOS command line (127 characters, 63 in early DOS versions). You can fit more directory paths into a PATH command by using short names for important subdirectories.To find out the current PATH setting, simply type:

```
PATH ⏎
```

A list of directories specified by a previous PATH command is displayed. You can cancel the prior PATH command, replacing it with no list of paths at all, by typing:

```
PATH ; ⏎
```

PATH and DOS files   One of the most important uses of the PATH command is to keep all DOS files on line, no matter the current directory. Many parts of DOS are held in files separate from the main DOS program, COMMAND.COM. These external files serve what DOS manuals refer to as external commands, such as CHKDSK, BACKUP, and XCOPY. Generally, it's best to place all DOS files in one subdirectory named DOS located in the root directory. Then include the subdirectory in your PATH command:

```
PATH C:\DOS  ⏎
```

The DOS 4.0 and 5.0 installation programs automatically create a \DOS subdirectory on drive C, places the DOS files in it, and writes this PATH command in the AUTOEXEC.BAT file it creates.

PATH and batch files   PATH is also useful for keeping all batch files within reach of any subdirectory. From the point of view of DOS, files with .BAT extensions are a kind of program to run, and so they can be located and run through a PATH command. Create one subdirectory for all of your general-purpose batch files.

The ability of PATH to find and run batch files has numerous applications. Here is one example. When every subdirectory in a tree has a unique name, you can create a batch file for each subdirectory that will automatically make that subdirectory the current directory. Place in each such batch file a CHDIR statement (section 6.3) followed by the directory path to the subdirectory. So, for the subdirectory \MICE you could create a batch file named MICE.BAT and place in it just two lines to change the current directory to MICE:

```
C:
CHDIR \MAMMALS\RODENTS\MICE
```

All such batch files would be placed in the BATCH subdirectory, and the PATH statement would include this subdirectory, as in:

```
PATH C:\BATCH;C:\DOS;C:\SOFTWARE\WP
```

Thereafter, you would have to only type:

```
MICE  ⏎
```

and the MICE subdirectory would become the current directory (that is, DOS would search for a file named MICE.COM, MICE.EXE, or MICE.BAT, would find the latter in the BATCH subdirectory, and would then execute the DOS commands in that file, making MICE the current directory).

Errors in PATH commands   DOS detects certain errors when you type in a PATH command, such as unwanted spaces, but it won't check to see that the paths you specify actually exist. If you receive an error message like:

```
Bad path or file name
```

you may become confused, knowing that the file name you have just entered is correct, not realizing that the problem could be an improperly specified path typed into a PATH command at some other time.

Limitations of the PATH command   Once you've started a program, a PATH command won't help the program find the data files it needs, including files essential to the program's performance, such as configuration files, overlay files, dictionary files, and so on. Unless configured otherwise, the program is likely to look for these files in the current directory. Since a program located by the PATH command is not usually in the current directory, it may not be able to find the other special files. Starting with version 3.3, DOS offers the APPEND command to help with this problem. It is discussed in section 8.2. Be aware that this command is not a panacea for file-location problems; ultimately, these can only be solved by careful directory tree design.

8.2 Making DOS search for data files

This chapter's minitutorial explains how the DOS PATH command causes DOS to look for program files in directories other than the current directory when no path has been specified for the files at the DOS command line. This feature has been expanded through the APPEND command to allow DOS to search for any kind of file in multiple directories, and even across multiple drives. APPEND can be enormously helpful in organizing the data files that application programs maintain for their own use.

Imagine that you are working in the tree diagram portrayed in figure 8.1. Your main word processor file is in the directory WRITING, but auxiliary files used by the word processor—perhaps a configuration file or a spelling checker data file—are stored in the subdirectory AUXILARY that is just below WRITING. If you make WRITING the current directory and load your word processor, it may have trouble finding the auxiliary files. Most software can be configured to look for related files in other directories, but not always with the desired flexibility. Instead, you could use an APPEND command to cause DOS to automatically seek the auxiliary files in specified directories other than the current one.

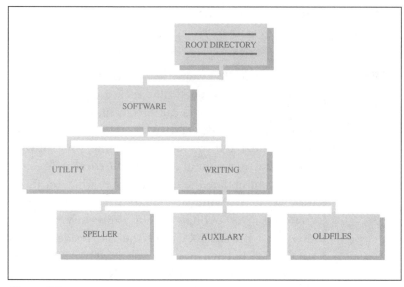

Figure 8.1

If you are familiar with the DOS PATH command, the form of APPEND will be instantly recognizable. You simply write APPEND followed by paths to the directories you want automatically searched, separating the paths with semicolons. Leave no spaces between the semicolons and the next path or DOS will issue a "Too many parameters" error message. For instance:

```
APPEND C:\DOS;C:\ACCOUNTS\1989;D:\  ↵
```

The example specifies three directories: C:\DOS, C:\ACCOUNTS\ 1989, and the root directory of drive D (recall that a lone backslash represents a root directory). It's usually not a good idea to include diskette drives in the command since a "Drive not ready" error message will occur when the drive is empty.

Used in this way, APPEND searches for all kinds of files except for program files, meaning files with .COM, .EXE, and .BAT extensions. You can make APPEND seek these files as well by adding the /X switch to the end of the statement:

```
APPEND C:\ACCOUNTS\1987;C:\DOS;C:\UTILITY /X  ↵
```

The APPEND command was introduced with DOS 3.2 and in that version it is unreliable when the /X switch is used. The command has been improved in subsequent DOS versions. Also, note that APPEND commands are not cummulative. The contents of each command completely replace those of the prior APPEND command. You can find out the current setting by simply typing:

```
APPEND  ↵
```

PITFALL | Be careful of how you use the APPEND command. Because it will automatically track down data files in remote directories, you can specify files by name only, without typing in directory paths. This is fine for looking at a file, but if you then save the file, your software will create a new copy of the file in the current directory rather than update the original file in whatever directory APPEND found it. Matters become even more confused if you wrongly specify a directory path, say, \RODENTS\RATS.TXT, and the file resides not in \RODENTS but in a directory specified by APPEND. In this case, the file is located by APPEND, not by the path you have specified. When you save the file, the altered version would be written into the RODENTS subdirectory and the original would be left unchanged. Starting with DOS version 4.0, you can stop the automatic APPEND search when you specify a directory path with your file name by adding /PATH:OFF to the end of the APPEND command, as in:

```
APPEND=C:\ONEDIR;C:\TWODIR /PATH:OFF ⏎
```

8.3   Making a disk drive appear like a subdirectory

The DOS JOIN command lets you combine the directory tree of one disk with the directory tree of another. Some kinds of software work more efficiently when trees are combined in this way. The entire directory tree from one disk is "transplanted" so that it appears to grow out of the root directory of the disk to which it is joined. Figure 8.2 shows two simple directory trees joined. As you can see, the former root directory of the tree on drive A has become a first-level subdirectory on drive C, its first-level subdirectories have become second-level subdirectories, and so on.

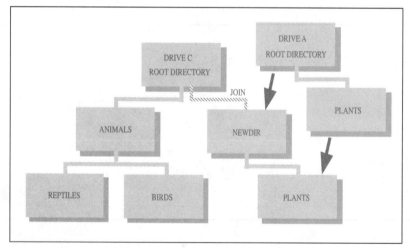

Figure 8.2

It's important to understand that the directory trees of the two disks are not physically grafted. Rather, the change is purely an imaginary one—a trick to make your work easier. Next time you start up the machine, you'll find that both disks and trees are once again separate. However, any changes made in one of the trees while they were joined will be preserved in the tree when it is again independent.

JOIN can be helpful when inflexible software won't let you work easily between two drives. And it can let disk management utilities operate on two disks at once by pretending that they are one. For example, a search for a file of a particular name (as explained in section 20.4) can be performed by one command instead of two. Utilities that navigate and display directory trees can combine all of your data into one presentation, making JOIN an especially useful tool when you add a second hard disk drive to your system (assuming that the utilities use DOS to perform their work).

As figure 8.2 shows, JOIN always inserts the second directory tree into the root directory of the first, and it always transplants the entire tree. Because root directories have no name, you must supply the name by which the temporarily transplanted root directory will be known. Consider the following command:

```
JOIN A: C:\NEWDIR ⏎
```

In this statement, the C: refers to the drive to which the directory tree of the disk in drive A will be temporarily transplanted. Thereafter, drive A will cease to exist for DOS commands to use by that name. If you issue a command directed toward A:, you'll encounter the error message "Invalid drive specification." Finally, the expression NEWDIR specifies that the root directory of drive A will be set up as a subdirectory named NEWDIR appearing in the root directory of drive C.

In this example, drive A has been appended to the tree of drive C. Many people are accustomed to thinking of diskettes as having no directory trees. But the option exists. If no tree were present on drive A, then its root directory would be linked to the root directory of drive C as NEWDIR. (This is to say that you should regard the directory of a diskette as being a root directory, whether or not a directory tree has been created on the disk.)

To undo a JOIN command, type JOIN followed by the name of the drive whose tree was transplanted and the switch /D. The proper expression for the example above would be:

```
JOIN A: /D ⏎
```

To find out whether a JOIN command is in force, simply type:

```
JOIN ⏎
```

In this example, DOS would respond by displaying:

```
A: => C:\NEWDIR
```

Before using JOIN, consider whether the software you are using keeps track of files and expects to find them on particular drives. Batch files can also become completely confused by the JOIN command.

PITFALL | There are a couple of limitations of JOIN that you must keep in mind to avoid perplexing error messages. First, the directory used for the transplanted root directory is permanently created on the tree to which the transplant is made. In the example above, the directory NEWDIR would persist as an empty directory even after the linkage had been broken. (Of course, you could afterwards remove the directory with RMDIR.) If NEWDIR already existed on drive C, it could be used by the JOIN command, but only if it is empty (that is, if it contains no files or subdirectories). A "Directory not empty" error message occurs when you break this rule. You'll do no better if you try to combine the root directories of the two trees with a statement like:

```
JOIN C: A:\ ⏎
```

DOS refuses to meld the two directory contents together. Also, in this case NEWDIR could not be the current directory at the time JOIN is used. It's difficult to remember all of these rules, but at least keep in mind that restrictions exist on the use of JOIN so that you'll know to look them up.

Unfortunately, some DOS commands are not entirely reliable when a JOIN command is in effect. JOIN may cause errors when used after an ASSIGN command (section 8.5) or a SUBST command (section 8.4). And a JOIN command should never be active when using FORMAT, DISKCOPY, DISKCOMP, BACKUP, or RESTORE. Also, JOIN cannot be used to connect disk drives across a local area network.

8.4 Making a subdirectory appear like a disk drive

One way of avoiding repetitive typing of directory paths is to use the DOS SUBST command to temporarily rename an often-accessed subdirectory as though it were a disk unto itself. For example, the subdirectory BALEEN in the path \MAMMALS\AQUATIC\WHALES\ BALEEN could be made to appear simply as drive E:. In that case, the command:

```
COPY FLIPPER.TXT \MAMMALS\AQUATIC\WHALES\BALEEN ⏎
```

would be reduced to:

```
COPY FLIPPER.TXT E: ⏎
```

The first version of DOS did not use directory trees. Once trees were added, software written for earlier versions could only get at files in the root directory of a tree. The SUBST command was introduced to get around this limitation. Today, virtually all software can access tree subdirectories, and so this application has become obsolete. However, this feature remains useful for housekeeping on a hard disk.

Use the DOS SUBST command to make a drive assignment by typing:

```
SUBST E: C:\MAMMALS\AQUATIC\WHALES\BALEEN ⏎
```

substituting the path of the subdirectory you want to use in place of the path shown here. BALEEN could thereafter be accessed either as drive E or still as a subdirectory on drive C. If instead you were to write:

```
SUBST A: C:\MAMMALS\AQUATIC\WHALES\BALEEN ⏎
```

diskette drive A would be inaccessible until you undid the substitution by typing:

```
SUBST A: /D ⏎
```

The /D switch stands for delete. It deletes the association of the subdirectory with drive A.

Error messages   When you apply SUBST, DOS may respond with the error message:

```
Invalid parameter
```

Normally, DOS can create only drive specifiers between A: and E:. The message may result when you use a higher drive specifier without first reconfiguring DOS to handle it. This reconfiguring is done with the LASTDRIVE command, which is discussed in section 11.6. To reconfigure DOS to handle drive letters up to, say, *J*, place the line:

```
LASTDRIVE = J
```

in the CONFIG.SYS file that DOS automatically reads when it is loaded (section 11.1). Then reboot the computer to bring the command into action.

PITFALL | There are situations in which the SUBST command can confuse DOS, leaving it not entirely reliable. The DOS manuals repeatedly warn against using SUBST with certain commands, notably ASSIGN, BACKUP, DISKCOMP, DISKCOPY, FDISK, FORMAT, JOIN, LABEL, and RESTORE. It's not a good idea to place SUBST commands in your AUTOEXEC.BAT file, applying them on a permanent basis. Instead, use the command when there is special housekeeping to do, such as a reorganization of files that requires lots of typing. Then turn the command off when you've finished the job.

8.5 Changing a drive's specifier

You may occasionally encounter software that requires certain files to be located on certain disk drives. Generally, such software was written before the days of inexpensive hard disks, when the typical IBM PC had only two diskette drives, A and B. These days, most computers have a diskette drive as A and a hard disk drive as C, with no drive B at all, and old software may not run.

To correct this situation, DOS lets you rename a drive, so that, for example, drive C will be called B and will show a B> prompt on the screen instead of C>. This change is made by the ASSIGN command. To rename drive C as drive B:

```
ASSIGN B=C ←
```

In this case, an existing physical drive B would be cut off from access by DOS until the assignment is undone. Thereafter, drive C could be accessed either as C: or B:. More than one drive can be renamed in a single command:

```
ASSIGN A=C B=D ←
```

To undo all assignments that have been made, just type:

```
ASSIGN ←
```

PITFALL | The ASSIGN command is intended only for emergency situations. Generally, software that is so inflexible as to require the use of ASSIGN is probably too primitive to bother with (and possibly too dangerous to entrust your data to).

It's not a good idea to execute other DOS commands once ASSIGN has been used. Commands like ERASE and COPY can become confused and cause DOS to behave erratically. For this reason, keep the ASSIGN feature active only while it is required. Execute an ASSIGN statement, load the program that needs it, and then cancel the assignments by entering ASSIGN ← the moment you quit the program.

Chapter 9

Batch Files

- MINITUTORIAL: All about batch files

- Creating a batch file

- Controlling batch file screen echo

- Displaying screen messages from batch files

- Passing file names to batch files

- Making batch files interactive

- Repeating batch file commands

- Using IF/THEN commands in batch files

- Making batch files respond to program errors

- Making one batch file run another

- Creating menus with batch files

MINITUTORIAL:
All about batch files

Batch files provide a way of using a series of DOS commands over and over again without retyping them. Let's say that there is a series of files that you want to regularly back up from your hard disk drive to a diskette. Each time you make the backup you would need to type:

```
COPY FILE1.TXT A: ⏎
COPY FILE2.DOC A: ⏎
COPY FILE3.* A: ⏎
COPY FILE4.TXT A: ⏎
```

and so on. To avoid constantly retyping these commands, you could write them all into an ordinary text file, like the one created by a simple word processor. The file could be given any name—say, MYBACKUP—so you will be able to easily remember its contents. In addition, the extension .BAT must be appended to the file name: MYBACKUP.BAT.

Once the file has been created, you need only type:

```
MYBACKUP ⏎
```

on the DOS command line and DOS will carry out the commands the file MYBACKUP contains in the order they appear. It is the .BAT extension that causes DOS to treat the file this way, and so this extension must never be used with any other kind of file. Note, however, that you do not need to type in the .BAT extension when you run the file. Either:

```
MYBACKUP ⏎
```

or:

```
MYBACKUP.BAT ⏎
```

would do the job.

DOS offers a number of features by which you can make batch files much more powerful than a mere sequence of DOS commands:

■ A batch file may be passed one or more words from the DOS command line. In this case, when starting up MYBACKUP.BAT, you could type:

```
MYBACKUP *.DOC ⏎
```

The expression *.DOC could be sent to the batch file where it would be used to choose files to backup. At another time, a different expression, like *.TXT, could be passed to the file to make it operate on a different set of files. You can create general-purpose batch files in this way, as section 9.4 explains.

■ The FOR command (section 9.6) lets a batch file repeat a command many times. You can use it to reduce several commands to a single one.

■ Batch files can test whether a particular condition is true, such as whether or not a file exists, and then act one way if so, and another way if not. This technique (explained in section 9.7) is called conditional branching, and it lets you create very flexible batch files that can deal with a variety of situations. Using errorlevel codes (section 9.8), batch files can learn that a program has not run properly and can then respond differently than if all had gone well.

■ Batch files can display messages on the screen to prompt for a certain action. You also can annotate batch files so that you can later understand how they are designed.

■ To some degree, batch files may be made interactive. After prompting you for input, the batch file can interpret incoming keystrokes and behave one way or another.

■ Batch files can run other batch files. So, you can share the special functions of one batch file with several others.

One batch file—AUTOEXEC.BAT—is enormously useful. The commands in this file are automatically carried out whenever the machine is turned on or rebooted. It can load memory-resident programs you always use, configure the machine in various ways, and move you to any drive and directory you wish to start work in. You can learn more about AUTOEXEC.BAT in section 11.1.

Windows 3.1   Batch files can be run in Microsoft Windows. They appear in directory listings using the same icon as program files. Batch files are regarded as non-Windows applications, which means that for every batch file you must create a program information file (PIF) to inform Windows about the batch file's characteristics. See section 18.5 to learn how to set up a PIF. Once done, you can start the batch file by clicking on either its icon or that of its PIF.

Windows can use a batch file called WINSTART.BAT much as DOS uses AUTOEXEC.BAT. The file is automatically executed when Windows starts up in 386 enhanced mode. WINSTART.BAT has limited utility.

Its job is to automatically load memory-resident programs. WIN-START.BAT is not automatically created by Windows or the Windows installation program, and it does not replace AUTOEXEC.BAT.

9.1 Creating a batch file

A batch file is an ordinary text file that contains DOS commands. There are two basic ways to create one, either with a text editor or word processor, or through a special use of the DOS COPY command.

Creating a batch file with the COPY command   Let's say that the batch file will be named QUICKBAK.BAT, and that it will contain three COPY commands to make backups on drive A of files with extensions .DOC, .OL, and .TXT. To create the file, move to the directory where it will reside and type:

```
COPY CON: QUICKBAK.BAT ⏎
```

or, to place the file in a directory other than the current directory, say C:\BATCH:

```
COPY CON: C:\BATCH\QUICKBAK.BAT ⏎
```

The words COPY CON: mean, "copy what I type on the console (that is, the combination of keyboard and screen) to a file of the following name." Nothing happens when you press ⏎ after this command except that the cursor moves to the line below to await further input. You then type in the DOS commands one by one, pressing ⏎ at the end of each line. Once you press ⏎, you cannot go back to edit the previous line, so you must be careful to avoid typing errors. After you enter the last command, press Ctrl-z-⏎. This tells DOS that you have finished. You'll hear the file being written to disk and then the DOS prompt returns to the screen. In this example, then, what you'd type is:

```
COPY CON: QUICKBAK.BAT ⏎
COPY *.DOC A: ⏎
COPY *.OL A: ⏎
COPY *.TXT A: ⏎
Ctrl-z ⏎
```

Creating a batch file using a text editor or word processor   The obvious advantage of using word processing software to create batch files is that you can easily edit the file. Indeed, for any but the shortest of batch files, it is usually best to use a text editor, particularly when you want to make a change in an existing batch file. The COPY CON: command explained above can't change only part of a file—it completely replaces the former version of the file. Using this method you must retype the entire batch file each time you make a change.

Text can be entered and altered in batch files using a text editor or a word processor. There is a difference between the two. Ordinarily, text editors don't automatically wrap words from line to line. They operate on one line of text at a time, and allow a line to extend to any length, even if the text must be scrolled horizontally. Text editors place only text in their files and not formatting codes. They are used mostly by computer programmers, but you'll find them in some utility packages. Many DOS shells, such as the Norton Commander, also offer an editor, although the DOS Shell that accompanies DOS 4.0 does not. All DOS versions include a primitive text editor called EDLIN. It requires that you learn a dozen commands to do the work that can be performed in most other editors with only a few. Nearly everyone has a better editing tool on hand.

You can also use an ordinary word processor to create a batch file. Unlike text editors, word processors can use wordwrap and fancy formatting. It is important to understand that many full-featured word processors introduce special codes into files. These are used to format the text for printing, to keep track of special fonts, and so on. Such codes are unique to the word processor that creates them. If DOS encounters them in a batch file, it will issue an error message and possibly refuse to go on. So you must be sure that your word processor saves the file to disk as a plain ASCII text file. (ASCII—the American Standard Code for Information Interchange—refers to an industry-wide system for representing text.) Virtually all word processors that use special codes have an alternate save option that lets you store the file on disk in ASCII form. If you can find no such option, your word processor probably relies entirely upon the ASCII system and you should have nothing to worry about. To be safe, however, read the documentation that came with your software before you entrust your files to a batch created with a word processor.

PITFALL | You must never apply special word processor features to batch files. Don't use special fonts and don't introduce any formatting codes. It's OK to use the search and replace options, but not features that would maintain the text as an outline, hook notes on to it, and so on. You can print out a copy of the batch file using the word processor in any way that you like, but you must save it on disk in the plain, ASCII form.

Viewing and printing a batch file   No matter how a batch file is created, it is easy to view its contents and print it. To view the file QUICKBAK.BAT, type:

    TYPE QUICKBAK.BAT [←]

Or, if the file is found in a different drive and subdirectory, say, C:\BATCH, type:

    TYPE C:\BATCH\QUICKBAK.BAT [←]

To print out a batch file, direct the copy to LPT1 (line printer 1) by typing:

    COPY QUICKBAK.BAT >LPT1 [←]

or, again:

    COPY C:\BATCH\QUICKBAK.BAT >LPT1 [←]

You may need to use the symbol COM1 or COM2 instead of LPT1 if you have a serial printer (most laser printers work as serial printers). Alternatively, load the batch file into a word processor or text editor and print it, or use a printing utility like the LP (Line Print) program in the Norton Utilities.

9.2 Controlling batch file screen echo

As the commands in a batch file are executed one after another, they are normally displayed on the screen, each at its own DOS prompt, just as if they had been entered by hand. Other messages may appear following each command, depending on the command's nature. For example, a batch file that contains these two lines:

```
DIR A:
DIR B:
```

first displays the line DIR A:, then a directory listing from drive A, and then the line DIR B:, followed by its directory listing. If you'd just like to see the listings, and not the commands, you could make the commands invisible by starting each line with the @ symbol:

```
@DIR A:
@DIR B:
```

Instead of beginning lines with @, you can make all commands invisible by inserting the line:

```
@ECHO OFF
```

and later, to cause commands to again be displayed:

```
ECHO ON
```

The @ECHO OFF command begins with @ to stop it from being displayed before going into effect. ECHO ON doesn't need a leading @ because it follows ECHO OFF and so it isn't displayed. Using these two commands, you can turn the echo feature on and off as you wish. Generally speaking, not all commands should be made invisible, because in many cases you would have no way of interpreting an error message should the command go awry. Some people prefer to always use @, and never ECHO OFF. This approach makes clear which lines are shown and which are not.

9.3 Displaying screen messages from batch files

There are several ways to cause batch files to display a screen message. The best way is to include the command @ECHO followed by the words you want written on the screen. To display the message "Roses are red, but as for violets...," you would type:

```
@ECHO Roses are red, but as for violets...
```

When you want to display a full-screen message, consider saving your long message as a short text document in your word processor. Then use the DOS TYPE command to display it, perhaps first clearing the screen with CLS. Here is an example in which just such a document has been stored in the file INTROSCR.DOC:

```
@CLS                          clear the screen
@TYPE C:\BATCH\INTROSCR.DOC   display the message
@PAUSE                        wait for a keystroke before moving
                              on—more on this at section 9.5
@CLS                          clear the screen again and proceed
```

CLS clears the screen and places the cursor on the first line of the display, so TYPE begins displaying your document from the top of the screen. To center the message, add some blank lines at the top of the document so that the text will appear balanced between the top and bottom of the screen. Make a plain text document that uses no formatting codes.

Sometimes, you'll want to write notes to yourself in a batch file so that you can later understand how it works. This is done by starting each line of notes with @REM (REM stands for REMark). For example:

```
@REM This batch file was created on December 27,
@REM 1989 for making occasional backups of the
@REM financial analysis data.
```

TIP

You can make your batch file messages look much nicer by using a utility like the BE (Batch Enhancer) programs in the Norton Utilities. BE lets you create windows for messages to appear in. You can draw boxes and lines in any color to make your screens clearer and more pleasant to the eye. Most important, BE can position the cursor anywhere on the screen so that messages can be centered and nicely formatted. The Batch Enhancer also includes a BEEP program that can beep the computer's speaker in a variety of ways if a batch file needs to draw attention to a message it displays.

9.4 Passing file names to batch files

Let's say that your word processor always creates two documents of the same name, one ending with the extension .DOC and the other with .OL. If you had created a file named CHIMPS that repeatedly needed to be copied over to drive A, you could save keystrokes by making a batch file to do the job. The batch file might be named CHIMPS.BAT and would contain the lines:

```
COPY CHIMPS.DOC A:
COPY CHIMPS.OL A:
```

If you created another document named GIBBONS, you would need to make another batch file to handle the job, and one each for GORIL-LAS, ORANGS, and so on.

However, a single batch file can do the job. It would look like this:

```
COPY %1.DOC A:
COPY %1.OL A:
```

We'll explain how these lines work in a moment. Since the batch file is used for files with many different names, you'd want to give it a more general name, such as QUIKCOPY.BAT. Then, when starting the batch file, instead of typing just:

```
QUIKCOPY  ⏎
```

you would include the name of the relevant files:

```
QUIKCOPY CHIMPS  ⏎
```

or:

```
QUIKCOPY GIBBONS  ⏎
```

The word following the batch file name in the two examples above is called a parameter, and it is passed to the batch file to substitute for the symbol %1. So, when you type QUIKCOPY CHIMPS ⏎, the word CHIMPS is substituted for %1 wherever it occurs in the batch file. The two statements:

```
COPY %1.DOC A:
COPY %1.OL A:
```

become:

```
COPY CHIMPS.DOC A:
COPY CHIMPS.OL A:
```

And when you run the batch file with the parameter GIBBONS, as in QUIKCOPY GIBBONS ⏎, the lines of the batch file are temporarily converted to:

```
COPY GIBBONS.DOC A:
COPY GIBBONS.OL A:
```

Passing multiple parameters   You can even use more than one parameter if you like. A batch file started by the command:

```
QUIKCOPY GORILLAS PRIMATES ⏎
```

might contain these lines:

```
COPY %1.DOC A:
COPY %2.DOC A:
```

The resulting commands would be:

```
COPY GORILLAS.DOC A:
COPY PRIMATES.DOC A:
```

So, the first parameter corresponds to the symbol %1, and the second to %2. You can also use the symbols %3, %4, and so on up to %9. They may be used any number of times in the same batch file, any number of times on the same line, and in any order. A file containing the commands:

```
COPY %2.DOC A:%1.TXT
DIR A:%1.TXT
```

would, when run with the command QUIKCOPY CHIMPS PRIMATES ⏎, result in:

```
COPY PRIMATES.DOC A:CHIMPS.TXT
DIR A:CHIMPS.TXT
```

In this case, the batch file would copy the file PRIMATES.DOC from the current directory to a file named CHIMPS.TXT on drive A, and would then give a directory listing for the latter file.

PITFALLS Once you've set up a batch file with multiple parameters, it's up to you to remember how many parameters it takes and the order in which they are entered. Obviously, if the parameters are entered in the wrong order, the wrong operations will be performed upon the wrong files. Serious errors can result.

Problems also may occur when two few parameters are included on the command line. DOS executes batch file commands one after another. If a third parameter is required, but not until the fourth command in the file, DOS will let you know that there is a problem only after the first three commands have already been executed. If it was the second of the three parameters that was omitted, all sorts of errors may have occurred before your error becomes evident. Be careful!

Testing the number of parameters It's possible to test that a sufficient number of parameters have been written on the command line when a batch file is run. Consider the following:

```
@FOR %%F IN (%2) DO GOTO Begin
@ECHO Error!
@ECHO This batch file requires two parameters.
@GOTO Finished
:Begin {batch file content begins here}
   .
   .
   .
:Finished {last line of the file}
```

The first line uses a FOR construction, which repeats an action until some condition is met—in this case, that a second command parameter is found (if you're not familiar with FOR, see the discussion in section 9.6). The %2 symbol calls upon a second command line parameter. If one exists, the command GOTO Begin is executed and DOS starts executing commands starting from the :Begin label. Otherwise, the FOR command stops executing—having failed to meet the condition that a second command line parameter must exist—and DOS moves on to the second line in the file. From there, an error message is displayed, and a jump is made to the end of the file without executing any other commands. The @ symbols keep the commands from being displayed (section 9.2).

Command formatting   It's important to notice that parameters exactly replace the symbols %1, %2, and so on. The examples above contain commands like:

```
COPY %1.DOC A:
```

in which no space is left between the %1 and the following .DOC. A space left between the two would result in the command:

```
COPY CHIMPS .DOC A:
```

resulting in an error message because of the space inserted into the file name.

Using the % character   When DOS sees the % character in a batch file, it assumes that it is encountering a parameter reference and it becomes confused when the % is not followed by a number. This character, however, is a legitimate file name character. If you must refer to a file that contains % when writing a batch file, double the character. For example, instead of writing the line:

```
COPY MONKEY%.TXT A:
```

write:

```
COPY MONKEY%%.TXT A:
```

Do this even when the file name already has eight characters:

```
COPY MONKEYS%%.TXT A:
```

9.5 Making batch files interactive

Often it's desirable to construct a batch file that works in different ways in different cases. Sometimes one group of commands would be executed, sometimes another, depending on what the user types in. Unfortunately, DOS does not allow much flexibility in this matter, although utility software can extend its capabilities.

The basic means of interacting with batch files is the PAUSE command, which causes a batch file to stop executing, display a message, and then wait for your response. The message is written immediately after the word PAUSE. The command is particularly useful for notifying someone that a diskette must be changed. When the command:

```
PAUSE Please change the diskette in drive A
```

appears in a batch file, DOS displays the message and then adds the line "Strike a key when ready...." In this case, the result is:

```
Please change the diskette in drive A
Strike a key when ready...
```

At that point, you change the diskette at your leisure and then strike any key to send the batch file on to the line following the PAUSE command.

You may also use this feature to terminate a batch file before all its commands have been carried out. For instance, in the file:

```
DIR *.DOC
PAUSE Press Ctrl-Brk do not have these files copied, otherwise
COPY *.DOC A:
```

DOS first displays a directory listing of files with a .DOC extension. This is followed by the message:

```
Press Ctrl-Brk do not have these files copied, otherwise
Strike a key when ready...
```

If you press Ctrl-Break, the batch file terminates without automatically copying the files to drive A. (When a batch file is terminated by Ctrl-Break, the message appears "Terminate batch job (Y/N)?," and you must type Y in response.)

Utility software   It's hard to imagine a more primitive form of interactivity than that offered by the PAUSE feature. What's really needed is a way of branching within batch files, so that various responses would lead the batch file to move on to various groups of commands. Utility software can add this capability to batch files in a variety of ways. Some programs completely replace the DOS batch file processing facilities with an elaborate programming language. Other efforts are more modest, but quite effective.

For example, The Norton Utilities includes a small program called ASK. It lets you control which parts of a batch file are executed and which are skipped over. ASK operates by means of the errorlevel feature, which is discussed in section 9.8. This feature lets batch files respond to errors that occur within programs that are run by the batch file. The program sends DOS an errorlevel code when it terminates, and the batch file is able to fetch this code and decide what to do next, depending on whether or not the program successfully performed its task. When the ASK program is run from within a batch file, it displays a numbered list of menu choices and waits for a corresponding keystroke: ①, ②, ③, and so on. Once a choice is made, the program quits and sends DOS the number of the menu choice as an errorlevel code. The batch file then examines this code and branches to the commands associated with the menu choice. (The example in section 9.8 shows how to organize a batch file this way.)

9.6 Repeating batch file commands

Sometimes the same command is used again and again in a batch file. Perhaps you'd like to use the COPY command to print out a group of files. This is usually done by directing the copy to LPT1, which stands for line printer 1 (you may need to use COM1—communications port 1—if your printer is connected to a serial port). You can print out the files using a separate COPY command for each file:

```
COPY THISFILE LPT1
COPY THATFILE LPT1
COPY WHATFILE LPT1
```

You'd save yourself some typing by reducing these statements to a single line using a FOR command. Here is how it looks for the three files:

```
FOR %%F IN (THISFILE THATFILE WHATFILE) DO COPY %%F LPT1
```

The symbol %%F is a variable; it takes the value of first THISFILE, then THATFILE, and then WHATFILE. Replacing %%F with these values, the statement is converted to something like this:

```
FOR THISFILE DO COPY THISFILE LPT1
FOR THATFILE DO COPY THATFILE LPT1
FOR WHATFILE DO COPY WHATFILE LPT1
```

As you can see, the end of each line matches the three individual commands written above. The one-line statement has been converted by FOR into three separate commands.

Here are the steps for making a FOR command in a batch file. First, write FOR %%F IN. Follow it with the list of files to be operated upon, placing them within parentheses with spaces (not commas) separating them. Then write DO and, finally, the desired DOS command, writing %%F a second time in place of the file the command operates upon (that is, COPY %%F LPT1 instead of COPY FILE1 LPT1).

Applications   At first sight, FOR appears complicated and hardly seems worth the trouble. But it has valuable applications when used with global file name characters (discussed in section 1.3). These let you specify a group of files that share common names or extensions. For instance, *.DOC refers to all files in a directory that end with the .DOC extension. Some DOS commands cannot use global file name characters. The following TYPE command, for example, won't work:

```
TYPE *.DOC
```

TYPE displays files, and it expects the name of only one. The FOR command can get around this limitation:

```
FOR %%F IN (*.DOC) DO TYPE %%F
```

This single statement could potentially replace dozens of individual commands. Even better, you could create a batch file in which the expression within the parentheses is transmitted to the file at the time it is started up from the DOS command line. Section 9.4 gives details of how this is done. In this case, *.DOC could be replaced by %1:

```
FOR %%F IN (%1) DO TYPE %%F
```

For a batch file named TYPEIT, you'd start up the file by naming it on the DOS command line, following the name with the file group you want displayed:

```
TYPEIT *.DOC  ⏎
```

The expression *.DOC would be transmitted to the file, where it replaces the %1 inside the parentheses, and so all files with .DOC extensions would be displayed. The batch file is ready to display any group of files. You could as easily type:

```
TYPEIT *.TXT  ⏎
```

Used in this way, the FOR command is immensely powerful. You need concern yourself with its intricacies only while writing the general-purpose batch files. Thereafter, you can forget how it works but still be served by it.

TIP

You can use FOR in commands entered directly on the DOS command line. But in this case, use the symbol %F instead of %%F:

```
FOR %F in (*.DOC) DO TYPE %F  ⏎
```

9.7 Using IF/THEN conditions in batch files

Often it is desirable to have a batch file vary what it does depending on what it encounters. Consider a batch file that copies files from one disk to another. Rather than blindly try to copy over a particular file, the batch file could first check that the file is present. If so, it makes the copy. If not, the batch file could look for the file in other directories and then copy it. If it still couldn't find it, it could display an error message telling the name of the missing file. Batch files designed in this way are more useful than simple ones, which would generate an ambiguous "File not found" error message.

To construct a batch file in this way, you must first create a test, and then tell the batch file what to do if the test succeeds or not. For copying files, the test would be whether or not the file exists. Here is how the batch file works:

- First Test: Does the file exist?
  No: Jump ahead to the second test
  Yes: Copy it and jump to end of batch file to quit

- Second Test: Is the file in a second directory?
  No: Jump ahead to display a message
  Yes: Copy it and jump to end of batch file to quit

- Message: Display an error message with the file name

And here is the actual batch file code (@ signs begin each line to stop the command from being displayed):

```
@IF NOT EXIST %1 GOTO TEST2
@COPY %1 A:
@GOTO FINISHED

:TEST2
@IF NOT EXIST C:\LEVEL1\LEVEL2\%1 GOTO MESSAGE
@COPY C:\LEVEL1\LEVEL2\%1 A:
@GOTO FINISHED

:MESSAGE
@ECHO Could not find the file named %1

:FINISHED
```

This example is not as hard to understand as it may first appear. First, the symbol %1 refers to the name of the file that has been passed to the batch file from the DOS command line. If the batch file were named COPYIT.BAT, when you start the batch file, you would specify on the command line that the file MYFILE.TXT should be copied:

```
COPYIT MYFILE.TXT ⏎
```

In this case, the name MYFILE.TXT would replace the symbol %1 everywhere in the batch file. The statement IF NOT EXIST %1 GOTO TEST2 becomes IF NOT EXIST MYFILE.TXT GOTO TEST2 and the statement ECHO Could not find the file named %1 becomes ECHO Could not find the file named MYFILE.TXT. See section 9.4 for a detailed discussion of using parameters like %1.

The first line of the file is the first test. If says, "if MYFILE.TXT does not exist, jump ahead to the label named TEST2." A label marks a point in a batch file for GOTO statements to jump to. A file may have any number of different labels. As you can see, the label itself is written with a leading colon (as in :TEST2). The colon is omitted, however, in references to the label (as in GOTO TEST2). Only the first eight characters after the colon are significant, so :ErrorResponse1 and :ErrorResponse2 would be treated as identical and could cause problems if used together. Note that the labels are case-sensitive. This means MyLabel, mylabel, and MYLABEL are regarded as different labels.

When the first test succeeds; MYFILE.TXT does NOT EXIST in the current directory, the batch file jumps ahead to the label :TEST2 and proceeds from there, starting with the following line. Otherwise, the test has failed and it is not the case that MYFILE does NOT EXIST, so the second line of the file is executed, copying the file over to drive A. With the desired task performed, the third line jumps ahead to the :FINISHED label at the end of the file, the batch file ends, and the DOS prompt appears.

If MYFILE.TXT is not immediately found and control jumps to the label :TEST2, a second test it made. It is just like the first, but it looks for the file in the directory \LEVEL1\LEVEL2. Notice how the %1 symbol combines with the directory path to actually create \LEVEL1\ LEVEL2\MYFILE. TXT. Again, if the result of the test is that the file does not exist, control jumps ahead to a label, in this case to :MESSAGE.

Otherwise, the file is copied from the LEVEL2 subdirectory and then a jump is made to the :FINISHED label at the end of the file.

Should neither test find MYFILE.TXT, control ends at the :MESSAGE label. It is followed by an ECHO command (explained in section 9.4) which displays the message "Could not find the file MYFILE.TXT." From there, flow continues directly to the end of the file. Note that labels, such as the concluding :FINISHED label, have no role except to mark positions in the file. Nothing happens when :FINISHED is encountered after the ECHO command.

Other kinds of tests   The example above uses the expression IF NOT EXIST as a test. You can also use IF EXIST if that fits the situation. Besides the EXIST symbol, you can perform tests based on equality using ==. For example, the statement:

```
IF %1 == MYFILE.TXT GOTO FINISHED
```

tests whether the file name passed from the command line (represented here by %1) is the same name as MYFILE.TXT. If so, the batch file jumps to the label :FINISHED. This line might cause a batch file to refuse to copy this particular file. Similarly:

```
IF NOT %1 == MYFILE.TXT GOTO FINISHED
```

rejects all files except MYFILE.TXT.

Problems can arise if you forget to include the required parameters on the command line. In this case, an expression like IF %1==MYFILE.TXT GOTO FINISHED is read as "if (nothing) equals MYFILE.TXT" and the batch file stops with an error. When appropriate, you can stop the batch file from terminating by placing an extra character on both sides of the double equals sign, as in:

```
IF x%1 == xMYFILE.TXT GOTO FINISHED
```

When MYFILE.TXT is named on the command line, this expression changes to:

```
IF xMYFILE.TXT == xMYFILE.TXT GOTO FINISHED
```

Although the file name is altered, a match is made and the file jumps to the :FINISHED label properly. However, if no parameter is entered, the equation becomes:

```
IF x == xMYFILE.TXT GOTO FINISHED
```

Correctly, no match is made in this situation, and the GOTO statement is ignored. But, because at least the letter *x* remains at the left of the equation, no error condition occurs, and the batch file is able to continue.

TIP

It's a good idea to test that a sufficient number of parameters have actually been written on the batch file command line before carrying out the batch file commands. When there should be two parameters, start the file with the lines:

```
FOR %%F IN (%2) DO GOTO Begin
ECHO Error!
ECHO This batch file requires two parameters.
GOTO Finished
:Begin
   .
   .
   .
:Finished
```

The first line tests to see if a second parameter was typed (denoted by %2) and, if so, jumps ahead to the :Begin label to start the file commands. When no parameter is found, an error message is displayed and a jump is then made to the :Finished label at the end of the file, terminating it.

Testing errorlevel codes   You can also make tests on the basis of errorlevel codes. These are codes that application programs hand to DOS when they terminate. They tell whether the program was forcibly terminated by an error. A batch file can use a line like:

```
IF ERRORLEVEL 1 GOTO ERRORMESSAGE
```

to find out whether a program it has run has completed its work correctly; if not, it can display an error message and behave accordingly. See section 9.10 to learn more about errorlevel codes.

Finally, notice that the IF statements in the batch file shown here all end with GOTO followed by a label. In these cases, the action taken in response to the test result is to jump, or not to jump, to another position in the batch file. Instead of GOTO, you can also use a DOS command as the result of a test. For example, instead of:

```
IF EXIST MYFILE.TXT GOTO FINISHED
```

you could write:

```
IF EXIST MYFILE.TXT COPY MYFILE.TXT A:
```

In the second case, once the file has been copied to drive A, the batch file proceeds on to the next line.

It takes a little work to figure out the logic of batch files using IF. But once you've got it right, you'll be able to create files that are much more flexible than straight-through files that execute their lines from first to last.

9.8 Making batch files respond to program errors

When you run a program from within a batch file, that program will eventually terminate and return control to the batch file, whereupon the next statement in the batch file will be executed. Sometimes the usefulness of the remaining statements in the file depend on the program's having successfully finished the work it was to do. If the program ran into some sort of trouble and had to be terminated prematurely, possibly because you typed Ctrl-Break, the batch file needs to know about it. Otherwise, the batch file may continue on to process faulty data. In the worse case, when the program is a utility that does not show itself on the screen or interact in any way, the fact of the program's error may go completely unnoticed.

For these reasons, it is sometimes useful for a batch file to check whether programs run by it have successfully performed their job. This is done using the errorlevel feature. When a program terminates, it may send DOS an errorlevel code, which is nothing more than a number from zero up that indicates how the program ended. Usually, a zero indicates that everything went well. The meanings of other code numbers are set by the program's designers; sometimes no codes are sent at all. You'll need to consult each program's documentation to find information about its errorlevel codes, if any. Only a few DOS commands return an errorlevel code, most notably XCOPY and BACKUP.

In batch files, you can use the error level information with IF and GOTO statements to alter the path DOS takes through the file. Consider these two batch file lines:

```
THEPROG
IF ERRORLEVEL 0...
```

First, the program named THEPROG is run. An ERRORLEVEL statement immediately follows to check the error level code returned by THEPROG. This (incomplete) ERRORLEVEL statement means "if the errorlevel code was zero, then..." Follow the expression with GOTO and a label:

```
IF ERRORLEVEL 0 GOTO ProgramSuccessful
```

This means, "if the error level code was zero, then, instead of just executing the next line in the batch file, jump ahead to the label :ProgramSuccessful and continue executing commands from there. The label appears later in the file, on a line of its own:

```
IF ERRORLEVEL 0 GOTO ProgramSuccessful
...
...
...
:ProgramSuccessful
...
...
...
```

When the program terminates without error, the lines following the :ProgramSuccessful label are executed, but the lines in the ERRORLEVEL statement are jumped over. Conversely, when ERRORLEVEL is not zero, the lines immediately following the ERRORLEVEL statement are executed. Two more lines must be added to the batch file to make it operate correctly:

```
IF ERRORLEVEL 0 GOTO ProgramSuccessful
...     program error instructions go here
...
...
GOTO AllDone
:ProgramSuccessful
...     program success instructions go here
...
...
:AllDone
```

The line GOTO AllDone causes DOS to jump to the label :AllDone, which has been added as the last line to mark the end of the batch file. This will prevent the batch file from executing the commands listed under the :ProgramSuccessful label. You don't want these run because, under the conditions we established, the program wasn't successful. You can expand this to include multiple ERRORLEVEL statements, each directing DOS to a different block of code. For example:

```
IF ERRORLEVEL 0 GOTO AllOK
IF ERRORLEVEL 1 GOTO Error1
...     Errorlevel=2 case
...
GOTO Finished
```

```
:Error1
...     Errorlevel =1 case
...
GOTO Finished

:AllOK
...     Errorlevel = 0 case
...

:Finished
```

9.9 Making one batch file run another

Sometimes the same series of DOS commands is used in more than one batch file. Rather than write those commands in each batch file, you can place them in their own file and then call that file from other batch files. For example, say that you've created a batch file named COPY-FILE.BAT that copies a number of files from one directory to another. Perhaps it contains the lines:

```
COPY C:\BIGFILE D:\BACKUPS
COPY C:\SMALFILE D:\BACKUPS
COPY C:\NOFILE D:\BACKUPS
```

Then you could add the line:

```
CALL COPYFILE
```

in another batch file so that the commands in COPYFILE.BAT would be executed at the point in the file that CALL COPYFILE appears. So, the batch file:

```
DIR *.TXT
CALL COPYFILE
C:
```

would be carried out as:

```
DIR *.TXT
COPY C:\BIGFILE D:\BACKUPS
COPY C:\SMALFILE D:\BACKUPS
COPY C:\NOFILE D:\BACKUPS
C:
```

Be sure to add a drive specifier and/or directory path to the CALL statement if there is any chance that the COPYFILE batch file is not in the current directory:

```
CALL C:\BATCH\COPYFILE
```

TIP

You don't have to bother with the CALL command when you want
to use it as the last line of a batch file. In this case, just name the
batch file you want called as if it were software that you wanted to
run. Instead of:

```
DIR *.TXT
CALL COPYFILE
```

you could write:

```
DIR *.TXT
COPYFILE
```

The reason this approach works only when a batch file is called as
the last command in another batch file is that DOS does not
return to the original calling file when the word CALL is omitted.
In the file:

```
DIR *.TXT
COPYFILE
C:
```

DOS would stop processing the batch file and return to the DOS
prompt after executing the last line of COPYFILE.BAT; the
command C: would never be carried out.

9.10 Creating menus with batch files

A primitive menu system can be established using nothing more than DOS batch files. Of course, there are much better ways of building a menu system. The DOS 4.0 Shell, Microsoft Windows, and the Norton Commander all let you construct menus in some way. If you have no utility software at your disposal, there's a roundabout way of making menus using batch files.

Any program can be launched by a batch file simply by including the program name in the file. To start up WordPerfect this way, you would create a batch file named, say, WORDPROC.BAT and place in it nothing more than the line:

```
WP
```

or, to include the directory path to the file:

```
C:\SOFTWARE\EDITOR\WP
```

Now, let's say that you wanted to create a menu offering three choices: 1-2-3, WordPerfect, and Excel. Begin by starting up your wordprocessor to create a new batch file named MENU.TXT (in fact, just about any name will do). Using tabs and blank lines, create a single file that looks something like this:

```
                MAIN MENU

    Select one of the following programs:

            (1) Lotus 1-2-3
            (2) WordPerfect
            (3) Excel

    Type in the option number and strike <Enter>
```

Save the file as MENU.TXT, then create a batch file named MENUS.BAT. It contains only two lines:

```
CLS
TYPE MENU.TXT
```

Finally, create three batch files like the WORDPROC.BAT file shown above, each loading one of the programs listed in the menu. Give each file this line after the program name, however:

```
MENUS
```

Name the files 1.BAT for the Lotus 1-2-3 file, 2.BAT for the WordPerfect file, and 3.BAT for the Excel file. Because the file 2.BAT loads Word-Perfect, it would contains lines like:

```
C:\SOFTWARE\EDITOR\WP
MENUS
```

Place all five files in the same directory—one that DOS always searches through its PATH command (section 8.2).

That's all there is to it. You start up the menu screen by typing:

MENUS ⏎

The CLS command clears the screen and TYPE displays the menu selection held in MENU.TXT. The MENUS.BAT file then terminates, and a DOS prompt appears at the bottom of the display. When you type a number from one to three followed by ⏎, DOS interprets the number as the name of a program or batch file. Accordingly, it runs one of the three batch files you've made—1.BAT, 2.BAT, and 3.BAT—and the batch file in turn loads the appropriate program. After the program quits, the second line in these files is executed. This line is MENUS, and so the main menu screen starts up again.

This system is obviously limited in what it can do, and it cannot gracefully respond to errors. Note, however, that it can be extended to include submenu screens, and even sub-submenus. Just have one or more of the batch files loaded by the main menu display another screenful of options. You'll need to use different numbers or letters in each screen, since there can only be one 1.BAT, and so on. It might be useful to use numerals for the main menu and the 26 letters of the alphabet in the submenus. (Actually, you could use the same numbers or letters more than once by including CHDIR commands in the system to shift over to batch files in different directories—directories not included in your PATH statement. But when matters become this complicated, you're far better off purchasing a menu program and doing the job right.)

Part II

Making Everything Work Together

Chapter 10

Hardware Configuration

- MINITUTORIAL: Principles of hardware configuration
- Determining installed equipment
- Setting PC and PC/XT dip switches
- Configuring serial and parallel ports
- Configuring video hardware
- Using the keyboard
- Using a foreign language keyboard
- Using keyboard macros
- Using a mouse

MINITUTORIAL:
Principles of hardware configuration

One of the virtues of IBM personal computers is that they can be extensively customized. A PC can use any of a dozen video systems, from simple black-and-white text to high-resolution color graphics. Similarly, there are several kinds of diskette drives available, and scores of hard disks, not to mention other types of media, such as removable hard disk drives and tape storage units. In addition, an extraordinary assortment of devices can be connected to the machine—mice, trackballs, scanners, printers, bar code readers, joysticks, and much more. Many of these devices connect to the machine through ports—electronic pathways to the outside world. Finally, there are three kinds of memory that a machine can use and the allowed quantity of each varies.

Confronted with such diversity, when the machine is turned on it must have some way of finding out what is connected to it. It does this by consulting information that is stored in the computer during a process called hardware configuration. Hardware configuration is performed by setting internal switches on early PCs, or by running special configuration software that accompanies later models. It's something that any PC user can learn to do. Don't confuse hardware configuration (telling the computer what equipment it contains) with software configuration (telling your software what equipment it has at its disposal). Chapter 12 is concerned with software configuration. There's also more on hardware configuration in Chapter 13 (modems), Chapter 14 (printers), and Chapter 15 (memory).

Hardware configuration is something you must think about whenever you add expansion boards to your machine's slots, or remove them. At that time you may need to reconfigure the machine so that whenever it is turned on it will be aware of the hardware changes. For many users, particularly those who do not modify their machines, hardware configuration is a task they never encounter because the computer vendor does it for them. But you still may need to know what equipment is installed in your computer so that you can understand software manuals and can discuss problems with software support people. We'll discuss some configuration concerns.

Memory   The machine minimally needs to know how much conventional memory it holds (see Chapter 15 for more information about the three kinds of memory). This may range from as little as 256K (kilobytes—that is, thousands of bytes) in some very early PCs up to the

640K limit imposed by DOS, always in increments of 64K. Machines using the 286, 386, or 486 microprocessors (that is, any machine other than an original PC or PC/XT-style machine) also need to know how much extended memory is installed, if any. The third kind of memory, expanded memory, is not assessed during hardware configuration. Rather, it is located and initialized by a device driver (see section 11.11) each time the computer is started up. So long as you follow the installation instructions properly, the machine will have no trouble using it.

Memory must be reconfigured whenever you add or remove a memory-expansion card to or from one of the computer's slots. Memory must also be reconfigured after adding additional memory chips in empty sockets on the computer's motherboard—the main circuit board upon which the expansion slots are mounted. Besides reconfiguring the computer, you may also need to configure the memory board itself—section 15.2 tells how.

Note that memory is not reconfigured when you change some other kind of card, such as a video adapter, that has many memory chips. Reconfiguration would not be required even after adding additional memory chips to a video board, although switches on the board itself might need to be altered.

Video   Nearly all video adapters can operate in more than one video mode. For example, an Enhanced Graphics Adapter (EGA) offers an ordinary 25× 80-character text mode, a high-resolution 16-color graphics mode, and so on. The computer needs to know which video mode to start up in. Also, most adapters support a variety of screen resolutions, including some that may exceed the capability of the video monitor attached. For this reason, the adapter itself may need to be configured (by setting tiny switches on it) to inform it of such limitations.

Ports   Computers connect to printers and other devices through ports. Serial ports and parallel ports are the most common. Other types exist for video game peripherals, networks, scientific instruments, and other special equipment. Virtually all computers have at least one parallel port, and most have at least one serial port as well. It is not uncommon for a computer to have two parallel ports and two or three serial ports.

Every port in a machine has a unique name so that software can identify and use the port. Parallel ports are named LPT1 (line printer 1), LPT2 (line printer 2), and so on. As you can tell by the name, this kind of port most often connects to a printer. For this reason, LPT1 is also sometimes referred to as PRN. Serial ports are named COM1 (communications port 1), COM2 (communications port 2), and so on, with COM1 sometimes called AUX (auxiliary port). Again, the name of the port hints at a common use: Serial ports connect to modems for communication across phone lines. You'll often encounter these port names when configuring hardware and also when using certain DOS commands.

The computer doesn't need to be told how many ports there are of each kind when it is configured. It finds them on its own when it starts up. But the adapter cards that hold the serial and parallel ports may themselves need to be configured when they are installed so that, for example, two serial ports will not both be named COM1.

Diskette drives   Over the years, IBM has released a variety of diskette drives that use diskettes with various formats and different data storage densities. The first drives held either 360 kilobytes or 1.2 megabytes of data on 5 ¼-inch diskettes. These have gradually been supplanted by 720-kilobyte and 1.44-megabyte 3 ½-inch drives introduced with the PS/2 machines. Again, the machine must find out from hardware configuration the number of drives present and the characteristics of each. Because you can't always tell a drive's capacity just by looking at it, you may need to turn to the computer's documentation to find out.

Hard disk drives   Hard disk drives are not as standardized as diskette drives. They pose special problems in installation that are discussed in the minitutorial at the beginning of Chapter 16. In some cases, the number of hard disk drives mounted in the machine may not even be obvious, because they may be hidden inside the machine without showing a front panel, or they may be completely contained on an expansion card. You can count the drives by taking the lid off the computer.

Unfortunately, a greater difficulty awaits. There is a system of numbers indicating the drive type, and in some cases you must be prepared during hardware configuration to tell the machine the drive type of all hard disks installed. You can learn this number by consulting the documentation for each drive, or by contacting the disk's manufacturer or vendor. Alternatively, you can use special hard disk installation software to protect yourself from these intricacies.

So how is hardware configuration actually performed? Owners of PS/2 Micro Channel machines have good news on this front: the machines are entirely self-configuring. This is one of the advantages of the Micro Channel bus (a bus is the system of circuitry that ties together different parts of the computer, including its expansion cards). This advantage also applies to the alternate EISA bus used by some IBM clone manufacturers. You just run the configuration program that is shipped with the machine and it figures out what equipment is installed and makes a record of it. If you alter the hardware, even by so little as moving a card from one slot to another, the machine will detect the change at start-up and request that you rerun the configuration program.

Three approaches to configuration   Owners of IBM AT-style machines, including numerous 286 and 386 clones, perform hardware configuration using a special program called SETUP that comes on the machine's Diagnostics diskette. At the same time, the program performs a number of checks on the machine to be sure that everything is running well. SETUP senses the installed equipment, but less thoroughly and with less certainty than the PS/2 or EISA configuration programs. It asks you to confirm that its analysis is correct. You may blindly accept its judgement and hope that all will go well, or better, you can inspect the inside of the computer to be completely sure. If you have a hard disk drive, SETUP will query you about the drive type as mentioned above, so be prepared with the number; you can get it from the drive's documentation or by a call to the vendor or manufacturer. Also, have a blank diskette on hand for the diskette-drive test. Be aware that AT-style machines contain an internal switch that tells whether to start up in a monochrome or color video mode. The switch is normally located on the computer's main circuit board next to the center of the back panel. Push the switch toward the rear of the machine for monochrome, toward the front for color.

The earliest IBM machines, PCs, PC/XTs, and other models that use the 8088 microprocessor, are configured using dip switches found inside the computer. There are one or two banks of these tiny switches, some having to do with the video adapter, others with the amount of memory installed, and so on. We discuss these switches in detail in section 10.2.

PC-style machines are the least convenient to configure. Even the AT's SETUP program can be an annoyance since the entire configuration procedure must be redone to change a single setting. Because hardware configuration is hardly ever performed, these disadvantages are not grave. But those who constantly change equipment (as from one video system to another) will be glad to have a self-configuring machine.

10.1 Determining Installed Equipment

Sometimes you'll need to know what equipment is installed in a machine in order to ascertain whether certain software can be run, or peripherals connected. As with the task of hardware configuration, there are three cases, depending on whether the machine is a simple PC or PC/XT-style machine, an AT or AT-style 386 or 486 clone, or a self-configuring PS/2 or EISA machine. It's very easy to find out installed equipment in PS/2 and EISA machines, a little harder in ATs, and sometimes quite a job in the earliest PCs.

The simplest method in any kind of machine is to run a utility like the SYSINFO program in the Norton Utilities. It reports the numbers and kinds of video adapters and disk drives, counts serial and parallel ports, and figures out if a math coprocessor chip is installed. It informs you of how much of each type of memory is installed and how much is available at the moment. And it reports the DOS version, the current video mode, and—when it's possible—what kind of machine you're using. (SYSINFO can also run performance tests to tell you how fast your machine runs relative to a stock IBM PC-XT.)

PCs and PC/XTs   Except for finding out the amount of installed memory (section 15.1), there is no standard way of determining equipment in a PC or PC/XT using software. You must open the case and look around inside the machine. Sometimes it is necessary to remove adapters from their slots in order to find out what they are, perhaps then to consult their documentation. Or you might try reading the dip switch settings (as explained in section 10.2) to find out certain information.

AT-style machines   On an IBM AT or compatible, as well as on many AT-style 386 or 486 compatibles, you can determine what equipment is installed by running the SETUP program just far enough to see its listing of equipment, but not far enough to actually make any changes in the configuration settings. Do this by rebooting the machine with the Diagnostics diskette in drive A (the diskette is shipped with the machine). Select Setup from the main menu, and then quickly move through the section that sets the time and date of the internal clock. Next you'll see a screen resembling this:

```
The following options have been set:

Diskette Drive A   -   High Capacity
Diskette Drive B   -   Not Installed
Fixed Disk Drive C   -   Type 3
Fixed Disk Drive D   -   Not Installed
Base memory size   -   640KB
Expansion memory size   -   0KB
Primary display is attached to:
   - Monochrome Display Adapter

Are these options correct  (Y/N)?
```

At this point, you may type N to change any of the settings, or Y to move on to reset the machine. Instead of proceeding in either way, remove the Diagnostics diskette from drive A and reboot the machine in the normal way using Ctrl-Alt-Del. Notice that this listing does not tell you very much about the video adapter; there could well be a second adapter installed but not used at start-up.

PS/2 and EISA machines   Simply run the configuration program that accompanies the machine (it's on the Reference Diskette in PS/2 machines). A menu choice in the program leads to a detailed summary of installed equipment. Unlike in IBM ATs, you can view the configuration information without reconfiguring the machine. Here's a sample from the PS/2 configuration program:

```
Total System Memory
   Installed Memory ................... 3072 KB (3.0 MB)

Built In Features
   Installed Memory ................... 1024 KB (1.0 MB)
   Diskette Drive A Type ............... 1.44MB 3.5"
   Diskette Drive B Type ............... Not Installed
   Math Coprocessor ................... Not Installed
   Serial Port ........................ SERIAL_1
   Parallel Port ...................... PARALLEL_1

Slot1 - Empty

Slot2 - IBM 2 MB 16-bit Memory Adapter
   Installed Memory ................... 2048 KB (2.0 MB)
```

10.2 Setting PC or PC/XT dip switches

Pre-IBM AT machines are referred to as IBM PCs and IBM XTs. While XTs are most obviously distinguished from the original PCs by a hard disk, they also have more slots and a slightly different circuitry design. Both kinds of machines are configured by setting dip switches—small boxes that hold a bank of eight tiny switches. The switches are numbered from 1 to 8, and can be pushed between on and off positions with the point of a pen.

True IBM PCs have two dip switch banks, using the second bank of eight switches to specify how much memory is installed. They are found on the machine's main circuit board with either the number 1 or 2 printed beside the bank to identify it. XTs have only one switch bank; they automatically sense how much memory is present. A so-called PC/XT compatible may be based on either design. Here are how the various settings are made:

System memory   These settings report the number of 64K blocks of memory, from 64K to a full 640K. They were originally devised to support the original IBM PCs that used the now-obsolete 16K memory chips and thus they entail using switches that have the same setting no matter how much memory is installed. Five switches are always turned off. On dip switch bank 1, switches 3 and 4 are off; on dip switch bank 2, switches 6, 7, and 8 are off. In addition, switches 1 through 5 on dip switch bank 2 must be set as follows:

	1	2	3	4	5
64K	on	on	on	on	on
128K	on	off	on	on	on
192K	on	on	off	on	on
256K	on	off	off	on	on
320K	on	on	on	off	on
384K	on	off	on	off	on
448K	on	on	off	off	on
512K	on	off	off	off	on
576K	on	on	on	on	off
640K	on	off	on	on	off

On single-bank PC/XT systems, set switches 3 and 4 to ON-ON for 64K, OFF-ON for 128K, ON-OFF for 192K, and OFF-OFF for 256K and above.

Disk drives   Only the number of diskette drives is configured. Hard disks are detected by the operating system at start-up. The setting for diskette drives is made in dip switch bank 1. When one diskette drive is present, turn both switches 7 and 8 on. When two are present, switch 7 is on and switch 8 is off. Additionally, switch 1 must be turned off in either case.

The video adapter   This setting is made on dip switch bank 1. For a monochrome adapter (or a monochrome Hercules Card), turn both switches 5 and 6 off. For a color graphics adapter, turn switch 5 on and switch 6 off. For either an EGA or VGA adapter card, turn both switches 5 and 6 on. When more than one video adapter is in the machine, this setting determines which is used at start-up.

A math coprocessor chip   If you have installed a math coprocessor chip (see section 12.4) you must inform the computer of its presence by setting switch 2 of dip switch bank 1 (or switch 2 of the only dip switch bank in an XT-style machine). Set the switch to off when a coprocessor is installed; otherwise, leave it on.

10.3 Configuring serial and parallel ports

Ports are gateways between the computer and the outside world. Printers, plotters, digitizers, modems, and mice are all connected to the printer through either a serial port or a parallel port. Parallel ports transmit data one character at a time using eight lines, while serial ports operate in a more complicated fashion over a single line.

The number of serial and parallel ports varies from machine to machine. All PS/2 machines and some AT-style clones have at least one serial and one parallel port built in. More ports of either kind may be added through expansion boards placed in the computer's slots.

Serial ports are named COM1 (for communications), COM2, and so on, while parallel ports are dubbed LPT1 (for line printer), LPT2, etc. As these names imply, serial ports are often used for modems, and parallel ports for printers. When two serial devices (such as modems) are attached to the machine, one goes to COM1 and one to COM2. Similarly, two printers might be hooked up to LPT1 and LPT2.

When you install expansion boards that contain ports, the boards must be configured so that each port has a unique name. For example, if each of two boards contains a parallel port, one of the ports must be made to act as LPT1 and one as LPT2. It neither matters which is which, nor which slot the card resides in. Boards are usually shipped with their ports set as COM1 and/or LPT1, but most can be reset as another port.

Counting ports   It's not always easy to count the number of ports in the machine. Some ports are on expansion boards, such as an IBM AT-style serial/parallel adapter, which provides one port of each of those types. Memory expansion boards also frequently come equipped with extra ports, and video cards sometimes have a parallel port. PS/2 machines have one serial and one parallel port built right into the main circuit board of the machine, as do some AT-style clones. (PS/2 machines also have a mouse port.) For every port there is normally a socket at the back of the machine, usually protruding from the adapter card that holds it. But sometimes special cables are connected to a spot on the surface of an expansion board, with a standard socket affixed at the end of the cable (this occurs when the board offers so many features that there is not enough space for all its sockets on the back edge). If you are not certain how many ports your computer currently has installed, check the documentation for each board and the machine itself.

The number of ports in a machine can be further complicated by the special nature of certain devices, particularly mice and modems. Both are sold in two forms, one with a port built in, one that uses a port already installed in the machine. Thus, you might acquire an external modem, which connects to an existing serial port or, instead, you could buy an internal modem that fits in a slot and adds another serial port to the machine. During hardware configuration, you need to remember to count an internal modem as another serial port. Similarly, a parallel mouse comes with its own adapter board that fits into a slot to add a parallel port to the machine (it is also sometimes called a bus mouse since the slots are connected to circuitry called the bus.) A serial mouse does not take up a slot, but instead connects to a preexisting serial port. When slots are scarce, the kinds of ports used may become an important consideration when you're considering the purchase of new equipment.

Configuring ports   Port settings are made either by tiny dip switches or jumpers found on circuit boards. The switches are numbered and are easily set with a pointed object. Jumpers are more primitive. They consist of minuscule spikes protruding from the board surface over which fit tiny links that may be inserted either to connect or disconnect the spikes. Designs vary from board to board, and the only way to know how to set the dip switches or jumpers is by consulting the accompanying documentation. It will tell you the locations of the dip switches or jumpers, and the settings that should be made to give a port a particular name (such as COM1 or COM2). This documentation is often little more than a flimsy manual of only a few pages. Be careful to keep all of your documentation or you won't be able to reconfigure an expansion board at some later date if you change the equipment in the machine or if you get an entirely new computer.

Software may also need to be configured so that it will direct its communications to the proper port. For example, if a modem is connected to COM2, it is essential that your communications software accesses COM2, and not COM1 by default. Similarly, printer output is generally directed to LPT1 unless you specify otherwise. If you want to use a second parallel printer that is connected to LPT2, you'll need to direct your software to use that port, or will need to acquire utility software that can switch the port assignments so that DOS treats LPT2 as LPT1 and the former LPT1 as LPT2.

10.4 Configuring video hardware

Video hardware consists of a video controller (the video circuitry) and the video monitor (or video display) attached to it. The video controller used in PS/2 machines is built into the computer. Most other machines keep the video controller in one of the machine's expansion slots (as a video adapter). No configuration is usually necessary, but in certain cases video hardware must be specially set up before it can be used.

All video controllers have a certain amount of memory installed. This video memory (or video RAM) holds the video image displayed on the screen. Video modes that use many colors or work in high-resolution require that the video controller have lots of memory. Sometimes a video card may be shipped with less than its full memory complement installed. In this case, it can't display its most advanced video modes and you must buy additional memory to gain access to these features. Increasingly, the full complement of memory is installed on new cards, but the memory on older models may be expandable. If you find that your software is unable to use an advanced video mode, inspect the video adapter for empty chip sockets. Sometimes memory is added on a piggyback card that fits into a long socket on the side of the video card.

While a video controller can detect how much memory it holds, it may not be able to find out the capabilities of the video monitor to which it is connected—whether the monitor is capable of color, the highest resolution the monitor can display, and the monitor's screen dimensions.

Configuring video adapters   Some video adapters have dip switches, tiny banks of numbered switches by which you can configure the card. By setting the switches, you can specify information about the video adapter's and video monitor's characteristics. Not only does the adapter use this information to organize its own activities, but it also can pass the information along to software, which can then configure itself to make the most of your available hardware.

Configuring a video display   The video display may also require configuration, particularly if it is a multisync monitor. These monitors are designed for flexibility. The various kinds of video adapters—MDA, CGA, EGA, MCGA, VGA, 8514/A and XGA (all of which are described in section 12.3)—require monitors tailored to certain technical characteristics. A multisync monitor can detect the speed at which an adapter transmits video data and adjust itself accordingly, thus allowing itself to be used with a variety of adapters. These monitors are usually equipped with switches that let you specify what kind of non-multisync monitor they should work like, such as a 16-color CGA monitor or a 64-color EGA monitor.

Many multisync monitors can also be switched between digital and analog modes. The digital mode restricts the number of colors that can be displayed; analog mode allows a broad spectrum of colors. VGA, MCGA, and 8514 video controllers use a monitor in analog mode, and all other standard PC adapters use digital modes. The switches on a monitor, if any, vary by manufacturer and model. You'll need to consult the monitor's documentation to make the proper settings.

PITFALL | Be aware that some monitors can be damaged when they are connected to an unsuitable adapter or are improperly configured. So read the documentation carefully. This is one instance in which you shouldn't experiment with hardware by trying out different combinations of switch settings.

Screen savers   Most desktop video displays produce an image by aiming an electron beam at a phosphorescent film at the front of the picture tube. With time, individual points on the screen can burn out to leave tiny black holes in any image displayed. It normally takes years for this process to begin, but it is accelerated when parts of the screen are constantly kept brightly illuminated. If you keep the same program on the screen around the clock, screen borders and the menu bar may be perpetually illuminated, and ultimately points at this part of the screen will burn out.

You can postpone this kind of damage by using a utility program called a screen saver. Screen savers keep an eye on the keyboard and mouse. When no input occurs for a specified period of time (typically a few minutes), the program assumes that no one is using the computer and it blanks out the screen. When the mouse or keyboard is subsequently moved, the screen is instantly restored to exactly as it was. Instead of leaving the screen completely blank, many screen savers display a decorative moving pattern, such as bursting fireworks, to let you know that the computer is working.

A number of screen savers are available in Windows 3.1. To select one, choose the Desktop icon in the Control Panel. Then open the Name list in the Screen Saver area. Then select a screen saver from the displayed list. Enter in the Delay box the time you want to pass before the screen saver comes into action.

Screen savers may also incorporate security features. A blanked-out screen prevents passersby from snooping into your work when you're away from your desk. To prevent someone from restoring the image by moving the mouse, some screen savers let you set up a password. Once blanked out, the screen image won't be restored until the password is typed in (doing this has no effect on the software running in the machine).

10.5 Using the keyboard

A computer keyboard is much more complicated than a typewriter keyboard. Several kinds of keys are dedicated to different purposes, and sometimes their functions overlap. What's more, there are keys that shift or toggle parts of the keyboard from one role to another. It's important to understand the keyboard well since accidental keystrokes can misdirect software and create great confusion.

The keyboard is divided into either three or four parts. Most familiar are the ordinary typewriter keys with the alphabet, numerals, and punctuation marks. To the left or above is a bank of keys marked F1 , F2 , and so on. These are the function keys, which perform special services that vary with the software you're using. To the right of the typewriter keys lies the numeric keypad, which lays out the numerals in the familiar adding-machine positions for fast entry of numeric data. These keys duplicate the number keys in the top row of ordinary typewriter keys and usually may be used interchangeably. Four of the keypad keys double as cursor keys that can move the cursor on the screen. For simplicity, all newer keyboards have a separate set of cursor keys apart from the keypad. What follows is a description of all the keys and their interrelations.

Typewriter keys   Most of the typewriter-style keys are familiar. Two distinctions are worth noting. First, there are three pairs of brackets: ( ), { }, and [ ]. In computer literature these are respectively referred to as parentheses, braces, and brackets (or square brackets). Keep in mind that computers tend to be sensitive to the differences between these characters. When computer documentation tells you to use a brace, don't substitute a parenthesis or bracket. Second, notice the difference between the standard slash (/) and the backslash (\)—the backslash leans from upper left to lower right. Both of these characters are used in DOS commands, and you'll encounter error messages if you confuse them. The apostrophe also comes in its usual form (') and a reverse form (`). One other symbol worth noting is the vertical bar (|) which is used in some DOS commands.

The return key   The return key parallels the carriage return key on an electric typewriter. Just as a carriage return means "end of line," pressing ⏎ means "end of command" on the DOS command line.

When you type in instructions for software or DOS, the command is not interpreted and responded to until ⏎ is pressed.

The function keys   There are either ten or twelve function keys (F1, F2, F3, and so on) on all IBM keyboards. These keys do not type in a character or perform a particular task. Rather, these keys are specially programmed by the software currently in use. For example, in one word processor, striking the F3 key might cause the document to be reformatted. In another word processor the key could have an entirely different meaning, such as to save your work to disk. Because the meanings of the keys change from program to program, you'll need to learn them from each program's documentation. Many programs that use the function keys include a set of stickers or templates you can put above or to the side of the keys to help you remember what each function key does.

Additional function key keystrokes are made through combinations with the ⇧, Ctrl, and Alt keys. Striking Ctrl-F3 has a different meaning than striking F3 alone. Few programs use all function key combinations, and some don't use the function keys at all (in which case nothing happens when you press one of the keys). It is a widespread practice to use the F1 key as a way to ask the software to display Help information. Sometimes pressing F1 takes you to a menu of the uses of the other function keys.

The cursor keys   The role of the cursor keys also varies between programs. Generally, the four arrow keys (←, →, ↑, and ↓) move the cursor by one character or one line on the screen. The combinations Ctrl-← and Ctrl-→ often move the cursor by one word to the left or right. The Home and End keys usually display the beginning or end of a document, while PgUp (page up) and PgDn (page down) scroll the display by one screenful. Not all software operates upon text, however, and software authors have used the cursor keys every way imaginable.

The shift keys   There are three kinds of shift keys on IBM keyboards. You'll find a pair of keys marked ⇧ or Shift that operate just like typewriter shift keys. And there are the Ctrl (control) and Alt (alternate) keys, which work in combination with most alphabetical keys and function keys, but not all. Keystroke combinations that use the Ctrl or Alt keys are generally used to send commands to software. For example, Ctrl-S could mean "save my work," and Alt-F7 might mean "reformat the document." Their meanings vary from program to program.

In most cases, these key combinations don't result in characters shown on the screen. However, the combinations of Ctrl and the letters *A* through *Z* sometimes display the symbols, ^A, ^B, ^C, and so on. These are read as control A, control B, etc. Occasionally, computer documentation will instruct you to enter a code like ^S, which means that you should type Ctrl-S.

The toggle keys   Four keys toggle the keyboard between two states, just as the shift lock on an ordinary typewriter shifts all characters to uppercase when you strike it once and returns them to lowercase when you press the key again. Here are the four toggles:

- **The Caps Lock key**   This key is roughly equivalent of an ordinary typewriter shift lock. However, it affects only alphabet keys and not numeral or punctuation keys. On keyboards that have indicator lights, the Caps Lock indicator lights up when the keyboard is set to uppercase, and it goes out when you toggle back to lowercase. Note that lowercase letters result when the Caps Lock feature is set to uppercase and you hold down a ⇧ key.

- **The Num Lock key**   The numeric keypad at the right of the keyboard serves two purposes: to input numbers and to move the cursor. The Num Lock key toggles the numeric keypad between these two states. When Num Lock is toggled on, the keypad is locked to inputting numbers, and your keystrokes on the numeric keypad are interpreted as numerals rather than as cursor moves. Conversely, when Num Lock is toggled off, the keypad keys move the cursor and perform the operations associated with Home, End, PgUp, and PgDn. Most keyboards have an indicator light that switches on when the keypad is set for inputting numbers. Note that holding down a ⇧ key temporarily reverses the Num Lock status.

- **The Scroll Lock key**   This key also toggles between on and off states. It is intended to modify the function of the cursor keys. When Scroll Lock is on, the cursor keys move the cursor up and down the screen. When Scroll Lock is off, the cursor keys instead scroll the display (scrolling has been unlocked). Few programs actually use ⌷Scroll Lock⌷ this way; many don't use this key at all.

■ **The Ins key**   The ⌷Ins⌷ key usually toggles word processors between two input modes: insertion mode and overwrite mode. In insertion mode, keystrokes are inserted into text at the cursor. In overwrite mode, each keystroke is written left to right on top of characters already displayed. However, this key is sometimes used for very different purposes. Keyboards do not ordinarily provide an indicator light for it.

Finally, there are a host of keys and keystroke combinations to handle special functions.

The backspace and delete keys   In addition to the standard typewriter backspace key (⌷←⌷), the keyboard also offers a deletion key (⌷Del⌷). Both remove a character from the display. The difference between the two is that ⌷Del⌷ deletes the character upon which the cursor rests, while ⌷←⌷ deletes the character immediately to the left of the cursor.

The Esc key   The ⌷Esc⌷ (escape) key varies in its role from program to program. Generally, it is used to undo or reverse a situation. For instance, when you select a submenu, pressing ⌷Esc⌷ will usually return you to the menu above. Sometimes the escape key will get you out of trouble if you become lost in unfamiliar software. ⌷Esc⌷ can also be used to cancel DOS commands before you have pressed ⌷←⌷.

The Sys Req key   This key, which stands for system request, is not found on all keyboards and is generally meant to be used when the machine is linked with other computers through a network. It calls up the central managing software to make a request of one sort or another. Alternatively, this key may be active when the computer uses an operating system other than DOS. Usually, the key does nothing at all on machines that are not networked, but some computers may assign it a special role.

The PrtSc key   ⌷Prt Sc⌷ (or ⌷⇧⌷-⌷Prt Sc⌷ on older keyboards) causes the current contents of the screen to be copied over to the printer. See section 14.8 to learn the details of this feature. When you type ⌷Ctrl⌷-⌷Prt Sc⌷, something entirely different happens. The computer is toggled into a state in which all interactions with DOS are printed (echoed) on the printer. For example, if you press [Ctrl]-[PrtSc] and then enter the command:

```
COPY MYFILE C: [←]
```

the printer writes the line:

```
COPY MYFILE C:
```

Striking [Ctrl]-[PrtSc] a second time turns this printing feature off.

PITFALL The [Ctrl]-[PrtSc] feature can lead to confusion. If you accidentally type [Ctrl]-[PrtSc] without noticing it, the computer will try to write to the printer the next time you enter a command. If the printer is turned off or if no printer is connected, you'll receive an error message and the computer will freeze up. To get out of this situation, turn on the printer, let the line print, then type [Ctrl]-[PrtSc] to toggle the printer echo off.

Ctrl-Alt-Del This unusual key combination uses three keys to make it virtually impossible to type by accident since [Ctrl]-[Alt]-[Del] reboots the computer. This feature is useful if your software goes haywire and you lose control of the machine. The feature also comes in handy when you've changed the files that automatically configure DOS when it starts up (CONFIG.SYS and AUTOEXEC.BAT—explained in section 11.1) since the changes won't come about until you reboot.

PITFALL Many beginners use [Ctrl]-[Alt]-[Del] as a sort of panic button that they press whenever they feel they have lost control. Do not get into the habit of doing this since you can lose data. In particular, never use [Ctrl]-[Alt]-[Del] while a disk drive is reading or writing data (you can hear the drive mechanism moving or see the drive's indicator light flicker). Data will quite likely be lost if you do.

Ctrl-Break [Ctrl]-Break is an especially important keystroke combination. It causes a program to stop in its tracks, returning you to the DOS prompt (in some cases, however, it does absolutely nothing). [Ctrl]-Break can be very handy when you lose control over software and want

to exit the program without rebooting the machine. You can also use
Ctrl-Break when you've entered a DOS command and want to stop the
command prematurely.

PITFALL | Don't use Ctrl-Break as a panic button. Data can be lost
when an application program is not terminated through
its normal channels. However, if you must terminate a
program as it runs, always try Ctrl-Break before Ctrl-
Alt-Del since the former is less likely to harm your data
(and you're spared waiting for the machine to restart).
Note that Ctrl-Break is not always able to terminate a
program; sometimes Ctrl-Alt-Del is the only choice
(and sometimes even that won't work, in which case you
must turn the machine off).

Pause (or Shift-Num Lock)   DOS, and some programs, write
information onto the screen continuously. The data may scroll out of
view before you can absorb it. In this case, you can temporarily halt the
output by striking Pause (or ⇧-Num Lock on older keyboards). The
screen freezes and stays that way until you strike any key to get it going
again. This feature is less useful on high-powered PCs where the
scrolling occurs so quickly that the Pause key may not be fast enough
to stop the scrolling in time.

Finally, note that any keyboard key except a shift and toggle key will
repeatedly enter the same character if you hold it down continuously.
Hold down A and you'll get a long line of As. The rate at which
characters are repeated is called the typematic rate in IBM parlance.
The typematic rate has two aspects: the delay time between a key being
pressed and repetition beginning and the actual repetition rate. Some
people find the usual values too fast; others find them too slow. DOS
won't let you change the typematic rate, but utility software like the
NCC (Norton Control Center) program in the Norton Utilities can. Or
it can be done from Windows by choosing the Keyboard icon in the
Control Panel window.

10.6 Using a foreign language keyboard

There are dozens of keyboard layouts in the world. Languages vary in the characters they use, punctuation marks, and, in many cases, accents. Different customs prevail even for keyboards supporting the same language. Any PC keyboard can be customized to use a different language layout using the KEYB command. The version of the command described here requires DOS version 3.3 or later; earlier versions lacked this command, or used a different form that you'll find described in your DOS manual.

KEYB employs one of the two-character codes found in the following list:

Australia	US
Belgium	BE
Canada (English)	US
Canada (French)	CF
Denmark	DK
Finland	SU
France	FR
Germany	GR
Italy	IT
Latin America	LA
Netherlands	NL
Norway	NO
Portugal	PO
Spain	SP
Sweden	SV
Switzerland (French)	SF
Switzerland (German)	SG
United Kingdom	UK
United States	US

The KEYB command also requires that the DOS file KEYBOARD.SYS be on hand, either in the current directory, or accessible via a PATH statement (section 8.1). To adapt the keyboard to the format used in France, type:

```
KEYB FR,,KEYBOARD.SYS ⏎
```

Once you've entered this command, try typing number keys at the top of the keyboard to see various French accented characters. Appendices in the back of your DOS manual tell about the various character sets and keyboard layouts.

The above example shows a simplified use of the KEYB command. It becomes much more complicated if you make use of a relatively new DOS feature called code paging. Code paging is beyond the scope of this book. Its workings are hard to understand, and best left to computer experts. However, in many cases code paging must be used to make the proper characters appear on the screen, and to print them out. Be aware that not all printers can handle the various character sets (certain IBM printers are specially designed to support them). If you require foreign-language support, begin by finding a printer that supports your needs. Then acquire a copy of DOS 4.0 or 5.0. Its installation program will configure the computer for the language of your choice.

10.7 Using keyboard macros

Frequently repeated sequences of keystrokes can be reduced to a single keystroke by using keyboard macros (a macro is computer parlance for the condensation of many actions into one). For example, if you frequently type, "Sincerely yours," you can easily program any key on the keyboard to output this expression. If you were to associate the expression with F10 then everytime you strike F10, the sequence "Sincerely yours," will be entered just as if you had typed it by hand. If you are working in a word processor, the two words would instantly appear in your document.

Keyboard macros can just as easily express sequences of command codes (the codes used to tell software what to do next, such as to load or save a file) and this is how they are most useful. Let's assume that a program loads a file by having you type Ctrl-L, then the file name (say, MY-FILE.DOC), and then ↵. This entire sequence of keystrokes could also be linked to F10 or any other key. Once accomplished, you could press F10, and **MYFILE** would be loaded.

Some application programs include a keyboard macro facility, but keyboard macros are generally made using special software that is not included with DOS. These programs are widely available. A keyboard macro program is a memory-resident program (section 15.4), meaning that it is loaded into memory when you start up the machine and it stays there while you work with other software. You can make a macro at any time by awakening the macro program through a special keystroke combination called a hot key. The program comes into action and displays messages on the screen, covering up data written by the application program you have been using. When you are finished, the macro program's screen messages disappear and you can continue work with the application.

Using a keyboard macro program   A macro is made by recording a desired sequence of keystrokes such as the "Sincerely yours," we mentioned above. Once you have pressed the hot key to activate the keyboard macro program, you enter a command telling that you want to make a new macro, and specify which key it should be linked to. The macro program then returns you to the application you were working in, but it stays awake to record every keystroke you make, including combinations with shift keys. Once the sequence is done, you enter a special code to signal that the macro is done. Thereafter, the macro is automatically entered whenever you strike the designated key combination.

To make these concepts clearer, here is an example using the SuperKey program from Borland International. The program resides on disk as KEY.COM. It is loaded when you start up the computer, either by entering KEY ⏎, or by naming the program in the AUTOEXEC.BAT start-up file (see section 11.1) so that it loads automatically. The program prints a short message on the screen when loaded and you're immediately returned to the DOS prompt to enter another command.

Let's say that next you load your wordprocessor and are ready to open the file MYFILE.DOC. Because you open (and close) this file dozens of times a day, you want to make a keyboard macro of the command sequence Ctrl-L MYFILE.DOC ⏎, tying the macro to the F8 key.

First, you must activate SuperKey by pressing its hot key combination, which is Alt-\. This action brings the SuperKey menu to the screen. Then, from a menu of options, you have SuperKey make a new macro by typing ⏎ twice. The program responds by asking which key to tie the macro to. The key is specified simply by pressing it. Then, the SuperKey menus disappear and you are returned to the word processor. But SuperKey is still active, watching your every keystroke. You type in Ctrl-L MYFILE.DOC ⏎. and your wordprocessor opens MYFILE.DOC accordingly. But before going on to work on the file, you type Alt-- to cause SuperKey to stop recording. Now the keystroke sequence has been made into a macro, and the next time you need to open MYFILE.DOC, you need only strike F8 when you would otherwise have had to type Ctrl-L MYFILE.DOC ⏎.

Keyboard macro software lets you save a group of macros to a disk file. Not only can you save your macros for another day, but you can create groups of macros tailored to a particular program.

Advanced features   Some macro programs let you create macros that load other macro files. Using this feature, you can set up a system where one keystroke closes down the program you are working in, opens another, and loads the macros designed for the new program. The new macro file contains a macro that can reverse the procedure. In this way, you can toggle between two programs in DOS using only a single keystroke.

While keyboard macro programs will allow you to assign macros to virtually any key, or any combination using a ⇧, Ctrl, or Alt key, many keys are unsuitable for macros. Obviously, the usual character keys—like A or 1—should be left alone. You also must take care not to assign macros to function keys that are already given special uses by the software in which the macros will be used. While most software uses the function keys, few use all combinations of ⇧, Ctrl, and Alt with the function keys. Check to see which are available for macros. Similarly, many programs receive commands as combinations of Ctrl, but not Alt, and a letter of the alphabet. In such cases, you can confine the macros to Alt key combinations to avoid confusion. Alt key combinations are generally better than function keys for macros because you can assign mnemonics to the keystrokes—Alt-C for copy, Alt-S for save, etc.

Sometimes it takes a combination of keyboard macros to perform a task. Perhaps you'll need to enter a key sequence that is always the same except for a file name at its center. In such cases, write one macro for the keystrokes preceding the file name, and one for the keystrokes that follow. Then strike the key for the first macro, type in the file name, and strike the key for the remainder. Some macro programs offer a pause feature to accommodate this process in a single macro.

PITFALLS | Keyboard macros can be dangerous! Ordinary keystrokes can cause plenty of mischief when an error invokes an unintended operation. Should the faulty keystroke be linked to a long keyboard macro, several wrong turns can be taken in the blink of an eye. You can protect yourself by attaching macros to keystroke combinations that are difficult to press accidentally.

Macros in DOS 5.0   DOS 5.0 introduces the Doskey program to provide macros. Unlike the single-key macros described above, Doskey lets you define any word you like to represent an entire DOS command. You just type in the word and press ← to have DOS execute the command. Say that you often use the command:

```
DIR *.TXT /W
```

to display directory listings tailored to a particular need. Doskey lets you tie this command to any expression you please, such as QD for quick directory. Then all you need to enter is QD and the above command is executed (unfortunately, the Doskey macros won't work from within batch files). This particular macro would be set up the command:

```
DOSKEY QD=DIR *.TXT /W
```

You can assign multiple commands to the macro by listing them all with the symbol $t inserted between. Also useful are the symbols $1 through $9, which represent any additional information you want the macro to use. For example, you could rewrite the above Doskey command to read:

```
DOSKEY QD=DIR *.$1 /W
```

Now, when you use the QD macro you would need to specify what $1 stands for. If you want a directory listing of .TXT files, you'd enter:

```
QD txt
```

and Doskey would convert the file specification to *.TXT. When you want .BAT files displayed, you'd enter instead:

```
QD bat
```

You may set up as many macros as you like, but Doskey normally limits them to as many as will fill its 512-byte buffer. To expand the buffer to, say, 2 kilobytes, add a /BUFSIZE switch the first time you use Doskey:

```
DOSKEY /BUFSIZE=2048
```

If you wish to use your macros again and again, write them into a batch file as a succession of Doskey commands. To see a listing of the macros, enter:

```
DOSKEY /DMACS
```

To make a batch file of the macros, add the > symbol and the desired batch file name to the command, as in:

```
DOSKEY /DMACS > MYMACROS.BAT
```

Then use a text editor to open the MYMACROS.BAT file. You'll see all of the commands, but without the word "Doskey" at the beginning of each macro. Type Doskey at the start of each macro so that each line will become a full-fledged Doskey command. Then save the file. Thereafter, you have only to enter:

```
MYMACROS
```

to have each Doskey command in the file executed so that every macro will be at your finger tips.

Windows 3.1   Keyboard macros are less useful in a graphical environment like Windows. You need software that can track mouse movements too. Windows includes the Recorder program for this purpose.

To record a macro, choose the Recorder icon from the Accessories group. You'll encounter a Recorder dialog box in which you pull down the Macro menu and choose Record. This action opens a Record Macro dialog box like the one shown in figure 10.1. You can enter a name for the macro at the top of the dialog box and a description of its function below, and may optionally specify a shortcut key by which the macro can later be started up. Type in the key that will be used and select Ctrl, Alt, or Shift as the shift key it will be combined with. This is all that's required in most instances; other settings offered by the dialog box are for special situations.

Once you're ready to go, click on the Start button. Then perform the mouse actions and type the keystrokes that form the action you want to make into a macro. When you're done and want to stop recording, click on the Recorder icon or type Ctrl-Break. A dialog box appears asking you whether you want to save or discard the macro.

When a shortcut key has been declared, macros are played back by opening the Recorder window and selecting the desired macro. Then switch to the application in which the macro will be used and press the shortcut key once the cursor has been set. Alternatively, begin by setting the cursor in the application, then move to the Recorder window, select the macro, and click on Run.

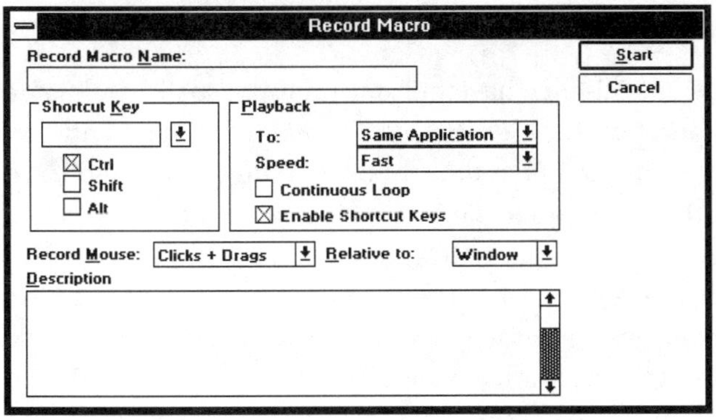

Figure 10.1

10.8 Using a mouse

A mouse is a device that makes it much easier to move the cursor across the screen. A mouse looks like a box, a few inches square, that rests on the desk next to the computer keyboard. It's connected to the back of the computer by a cable. A second cursor appears on the screen—the mouse cursor—when a mouse is operating. Typically, the cursor appears as an arrow when the display operates in a graphics mode, and as a solid block the size of a character when operating in a text mode. You push the mouse across the desk surface using one hand. Pushing the mouse to the right moves the cursor to the right on the screen, and so on.

A mouse lets you work more quickly, especially when editing text or tables of numbers, where you must move the cursor to screen positions far apart. It's virtually essential for freehand composition in many graphics programs, including desktop publishing programs. A mouse can also make software easier to use by allowing simple point and shoot selection of menu items. Combined with a DOS Shell like the Norton Commander, a mouse can make DOS much easier to work with.

Mice also have disadvantages. To use a mouse, you must move your hand away from the keyboard and then move it back to typing position. Repeated hundreds of times in a day, this simple action can be tiresome and annoying. Generally speaking, it takes less effort to move the cursor far across the screen by using a mouse instead of keyboard commands. But the keyboard is much less tiring for short cursor jumps to adjacent characters or words (once you've mastered the software's keyboard codes). Similarly, menu selections can be faster through the keyboard once you know your software well.

Mouse buttons   All mice have buttons on top, usually two. Some have three buttons, but the middle button is seldom used by software. The buttons are simple switches that are pressed down to turn on and let go to turn off. In computer slang, pressing these buttons is called clicking the mouse. Pressing a button twice quickly is called double-clicking. The buttons are used in various ways, often to make a selection from a menu of options a program provides. This is done by first moving the mouse to point the cursor to a menu item on the screen, and then clicking a mouse button to make the program respond to the selection.

A mouse can also be used to move objects across the screen. Do this by shifting the mouse cursor to the object, pressing a mouse button, and then moving the mouse with the button held down. This is called dragging.

Mouse drivers   A mouse is managed by a mouse driver, which is a kind of device driver (section 11.11). The mouse driver is built into the machine in computers that have a dedicated mouse port (including all PS/2 machines). Otherwise, the mouse runs through a serial or parallel port and the mouse driver must be installed in memory every time the computer starts up. In this case, a mouse won't work if for some reason its driver is no longer loaded by CONFIG.SYS (section 11.1) during booting. The driver is usually held in a file called MOUSE.COM.

Software support   Software works with a mouse only when it has been specially designed to do so.The software is said to "support a mouse." Most software written for IBM PCs still does not support a mouse, but many major application programs do. Among programs that do support a mouse, some offer only rudimentary features, such as cursor placement, while others let you use the mouse to edit text, make menu selections, and so on. Some programs may have trouble working with older versions of mouse drivers. If you own a mouse, or are planning to purchase one, mouse support becomes another consideration when shopping for software.

To find out whether the software you presently own supports a mouse, look at the documentation for each application. The introductory section that explains how to install the software may contain a section concerning installation for use with a mouse. Or check mouse in the documentation's index. As a last resort, call the software maker's support line and ask.

There is no problem in running software that does not support a mouse even when a mouse is connected to the machine. Once installed, the mouse is left connected at all times. Nothing happens when you move the mouse while using software that does not support it. Conversely, on IBM PCs, nearly all software that supports a mouse can be run without one, using only keyboard commands. Even when a mouse is connected, you can usually use these keyboard commands instead of the mouse, depending upon which you find more convenient.

Configuring the mouse in Windows 3.1   To customize the mouse in Windows 3.1, select the Mouse icon in the Control Panel window. You'll then see the dialog box shown in figure 10-2. Change the settings for the Mouse Tracking Speed and Double-Click Speed by dragging the square in its respective bars to a different position. The tracking speed determines how quickly the mouse cursor travels relative to mouse movements. Slower speed makes for greater control but more work in moving the cursor long distances. The double-click speed sets the maximum duration between clicks for which the clicks are interpreted as a double-click. If you find that your double-clicks are sometimes interpreted as two single clicks, move this setting toward slow. You can test that the setting is right for you by attempting a double-click in the box marked TEST; the box darkens when a double-click is detected.

The dialog box also displays two check boxes for customizing mouse usage. Select Swap Left/Right Buttons to make the right mouse button the primary one—a welcome feature for the left-handed. Or select Mouse Trails if you are having trouble seeing the mouse cursor on a laptop computer's liquid crystal display (LCD). Once selected, a momentary trail of cursors is left behind every cursor motion to make it easy to follow.

TIP

Don't make the double-click setting too slow or you'll slow down software response to single clicks. Whenever a click occurs, software waits until the specified double-click duration has passed to see if another click is coming. Software has no way of knowing that you intend only a single click. So a tiny delay is added to every mouse operation. Don't make the delay unnecessarily long.

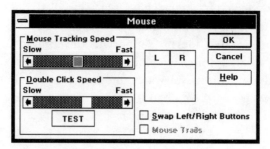

Figure 10-2

Chapter 11

Configuring DOS

- MINITUTORIAL: Steps to configuring DOS

- Setting up AUTOEXEC.BAT and CONFIG.SYS

- Customizing the DOS prompt

- Setting the number of DOS buffers

- Setting the maximum number of opened files

- Setting the number of file control blocks

- Setting the maximum number of drive specifiers

- Setting stack resources

- Setting environment variables

- Enabling the Ctrl-Break feature

- Setting country-specific information

- Installing a device driver

- Reconfiguring the computer quickly

MINITUTORIAL:
Steps to configuring DOS

To configure DOS means to get DOS ready to handle the software you will be running on the computer. When software runs, it constantly has DOS perform certain tasks, including reading and writing data to and from disk drives. When an unusual request is made, such as opening a large number of files at once, DOS must be ready to accommodate it. If DOS is not ready, it issues an error message, and in some cases it may even freeze, forcing you to reboot the machine.

Configuration is performed primarily by the CONFIG.SYS file that DOS automatically reads when the machine is started up. CONFIG.SYS is an ordinary text file containing a number of configuration commands, most of which are discussed in this chapter. Having this file is optional, although it would be unusual not to have one. When there is not at CONFIG.SYS file, DOS uses default values for its configuration—that is, rule-of-thumb values that are suitable for most users. When a CONFIG.SYS file is created, it only needs to contain configuration commands for those aspects of DOS that you wish to change from the default values.

Some of the commands discussed in this chapter can be placed in either CONFIG.SYS or in AUTOEXEC.BAT, which is the second file that DOS automatically reads when it is loaded. Certain configuration commands work only in CONFIG.SYS; others only in AUTOEXEC.BAT. Commands that must be placed in CONFIG.SYS can only be used when the computer starts up. Those that can be placed in AUTOEXEC.BAT are usually (but not always) commands that can be reused later in a work session to reconfigure DOS for a particular task at hand.

Four commands are specifically concerned with disk drives and files. DOS has two systems for accessing files, the details of which are of interest only to software programmers. The first system, which uses file control blocks, was the only system in early DOS versions. Later, with the advent of directory trees, a second way of accessing files appeared using file handles. Both systems require DOS to put aside a small amount of memory for each file that may be opened. These memory spaces can only be set aside when DOS starts up, and for this reason the maximum number of files that can be opened under either system is set during booting. If the maximum number is too low, software may be unable to open as many files as it needs to, or as you would like it to. Sections 11.4 and 11.5 explain how to change the maximums for the two file-access systems.

Similarly, when it boots, DOS sets aside a number of spaces in memory to act as file buffers. These are temporary holding areas through which information passes on its way between memory and disk drives. In some DOS versions, the default number of file buffers is too small for machines with hard disks and it must be reconfigured (see section 11.3). As a default, DOS also limits the number of disk drives it can recognize to five drives (named A> through E>). As section 11.6 explains, there are times when five is not enough, even if there are not that many actual disk drives installed in the machine. You can change the allowed number with a statement in CONFIG.SYS (section 11.1).

Another configuration command that is extremely useful is the PROMPT command (section 11.2), which lets you change the form of the DOS prompt. It is simple to make the DOS prompt show the name of the current directory in a directory tree. This feature is of enormous value in keeping you oriented as you move about the tree.

There are other commands, such as JOIN and PATH, that can temporarily alter the structure of the directory tree, or have DOS search several subdirectories for programs and data. Strictly speaking, these commands are not configuration commands, because they are not placed in CONFIG.SYS, but they are important. They are discussed in Chapter 8. Be sure to read the minitutorial at the beginning of that chapter.

Finally, you may need to deal with miscellaneous concerns. Machines connected to unusual peripherals may encounter a problem called stack overflow, as section 11.7 explains. The Ctrl-Break feature may be modified so that it can more easily terminate a running program. And you can change the format used by DOS when it displays times and dates in directory listings (These are discussed in sections 11.9 and 11.10 respectively.)

Many computer users happily work without ever being concerned with these features and the DOS commands that control them. However, hard disk owners using a DOS version earlier than 3.3 definitely should create a CONFIG.SYS file containing settings for the number of DOS buffers and the number of files that may be open at once. Section 11.1 explains how the file is made, and sections 11.3 and 11.4 explain the specifics. As mentioned, the PROMPT command is also indispensible. Otherwise, you may be able to get away with ignoring the contents of this chapter, at least until an error message comes your way and you are forced to make the necessary adjustments.

11.1 Setting up AUTOEXEC.BAT and CONFIG.SYS

When DOS starts up, it looks in the root directory of the boot disk for two files, one named CONFIG.SYS and one named AUTO-EXEC.BAT. You won't find these files on the DOS diskettes that accompany the DOS manual. Rather, in all DOS versions prior to 4.0, they must be created by you, the user, to get the most out of DOS. (The files are created automatically by the DOS 4.0 installation command, but there may still be occasions when you'll need to make one on your own.) The two files serve separate, but related, purposes.

CONFIG.SYS   CONFIG.SYS contains instructions for how DOS should be configured, that is, how DOS should prepare itself to handle the software that will be run on the machine. This includes matters like setting the maximum number of files that software may open. The minitutorial at the start of this chapter gives an overview. CONFIG.SYS makes settings that can't be changed after the computer has started up.

AUTOEXEC.BAT   AUTOEXEC.BAT (automatically executing batch file) is a batch file. As Chapter 9 explains, a batch file is nothing more than a file containing a list of DOS commands that are carried out one after another when the file is run (this is when the file's name is entered on the DOS command line). There are a few commands that may appear in AUTOEXEC.BAT to configure DOS, but mostly the file contains various start-up operations that you would like to have performed automatically each time the machine boots. For example, a CHDIR command in AUTOEXEC.BAT can set the current directory to whichever directory you mostly work from, saving you the trouble of typing in the command each time you start up the machine.

Both CONFIG.SYS and AUTOEXEC.BAT are optional; the computer will run without them. You may be able to dispense with CONFIG.SYS if you use DOS version 3.3 or later. This is because, starting with this version, DOS began to make large enough allocations for DOS buffers (section 11.3) and for the maximum number of files that may be opened at any one time (section 11.4). For earlier DOS versions, a CONFIG.SYS file should be created containing at least these two lines:

```
FILES = 20
BUFFERS = 20
```

Or, if memory is scarce:

```
FILES = 12
BUFFERS = 12
```

Several other commands may be needed in CONFIG.SYS, depending on how your software works, and on how you use DOS. All of these commands are explained individually in this chapter. One requirement that may force you to create a CONFIG.SYS file even if you use a current DOS version is to load one or more device drivers. These are small programs that are permanently loaded into memory to control devices like printers, mice, or unusual video hardware. A DEVICE command (section 11.11) in CONFIG.SYS does the job.

Although a CONFIG.SYS file is not always strictly necessary, you'll need one in order to use many valuable DOS features, especially some that make a hard disk work faster. The more you know about DOS, the larger your CONFIG.SYS file will become.

While CONFIG.SYS often is not really optional, AUTOEXEC.BAT always is. But for efficiency's sake, the file is indispensable. If you use memory-resident programs (section 15.4) for calendars, calculators, keyboard macros, and so on, they should be listed in AUTOEXEC.BAT to avoid having to type in their names each time the computer is started. The contents of AUTOEXEC.BAT exactly matches what you would type in at the DOS prompt. For example, say that you want to automatically load the two memory-resident utilities SideKickPlus and SuperKey (named SKPLUS and KEY, respectively), here assumed to be in the \UTILITY subdirectory. Also, say that you want to change the DOS prompt with a PROMPT statement so that the current directory is always displayed (as explained in section 11.2), and that you then want to move to the directory \PROJECT1\MEMOS, making it current. Here's what the batch file would contain:

```
\UTILITY\KEY
\UTILITY\SKPLUS
PROMPT $p$g
CHDIR \PROJECT1\MEMOS
```

TIP

Programs run by an AUTOEXEC.BAT file (SKPLUS and KEY in the above example) need not be in the root directory along with AUTOEXEC.BAT. Just specify a path to the directory holding the program, as the \UTILITY directory is specified in the example above. Be aware, however, that some programs need to start up with their home directory set as the current directory so that they can find auxiliary files. Use CHDIR commands in the file when this is the case.

There are two basic ways of creating either CONFIG.SYS or AUTO-EXEC.BAT: by a text editor or word processor or through the DOS COPY command.

Using a text editor   To create one of the files with word processing software, just make a new file in the root directory of the disk from which DOS (COMMAND.COM) is booted, naming it CONFIG.SYS or AUTOEXEC.BAT. Then write in the commands, one to a line, pressing the ⏎ key at the end of each line, including the last line. Save the file as a simple text-only file, and you're done.

Many utility packages contain simple word processors called text editors. (DOS includes a primitive text editor called EDLIN, but it's not worth learning if you already have a good word processor on hand). Text editors are ideal for creating these files, since they don't place extra formatting characters in the files. Full-featured word processors may load the files with special codes used for formatting and other features. DOS won't be able to read a file laden with these codes. If there is a problem, it won't be immediately obvious because the word processor won't show the codes on the screen. Instead, use the DOS TYPE command to display the file after you have quit the word processor. Just enter:

```
TYPE \CONFIG.SYS ⏎
```

or:

```
TYPE \AUTOEXEC.BAT ⏎
```

DOS will display the file, including characters you did not type in. To get rid of the codes, check your word processor's documentation for a way of saving the file in plain-text, ASCII form.

Using the DOS COPY command   The DOS COPY command can create or replace a new file on disk, but in a way that is both clumsy and unforgiving of mistakes. Here is how it is done.

First, move to the drive from which the computer will boot (here, drive C), and make the root directory the current directory by entering:

```
C: [←]
CHDIR \ [←]
```

Next, type in COPY CON: followed by the file's name. These words mean, Copy what I type on the console (that is, the keyboard and screen combined) to the following file. For instance, to create AUTO-EXEC.BAT, type:

```
COPY CON: AUTOEXEC.BAT [←]
```

Once you press [←], the cursor will move to the next line of the screen and wait for you to type in the first command for the file.

Type in the commands one by one, pressing [←] at the end of each line. If you make a mistake, you can change it only by backspacing to the point at which it occured, and then retyping what you have just erased. Even then, once you press [←] there is no going back to a line above to make corrections; you must start over.

Finally, after the last line has been typed in and [←] pressed, type [Ctrl]-[z]. This action adds an end-of-file marker to the file. Once done, the disk drive's indicator light will go on as the file is written and DOS will then display the message "1 File(s) copied." You're finished, and the DOS prompt returns to the screen for your next command.

Here is what you would type to enter the sample AUTOEXEC.BAT file discussed above:

```
COPY CON: AUTOEXEC.BAT [←]
\UTILITY\KEY [←]
\UTILITY\SKPLUS [←]
PROMPT $p$g [←]
CHDIR \PROJECT1\MEMOS [←]
[Ctrl]-[z] [←]
```

Altering CONFIG.SYS and AUTOEXEC.BAT   To alter a CON-
FIG.SYS or AUTOEXEC.BAT file, just open it with your word processor, make the change, and save it again as a text-only ASCII file. (Note
that the COPY command can't edit existing files; you have to type in
everything from the start). Once a change has been made in CON-
FIG.SYS, you must reboot the machine to bring it into action. A change
in AUTOEXEC.BAT can also be activated by rebooting, or, from the
root directory, you can just type:

> AUTOEXEC ⏎

on the DOS command line. The latter approach doesn't always work,
because commands in the file will be executed a second time since
booting. Attempts might be made to load second copies of memory-
resident programs or to execute DOS commands that should only be
used once. Rebooting avoids these problems by starting everything
from scratch.

▮11.2▮ Customizing the DOS prompt

Ordinarily, the DOS prompt merely shows the name of the current drive: A>, B>, C>, and so on. The DOS prompt may be customized to include other information such as the date or time. Most valuable, you can make the DOS prompt display the name of the current directory. For example, instead of just showing:

C>

the DOS prompt could be:

C:\SOFTWARE\DATABASE>

This feature is of inestimable value in guiding you through a complicated directory tree.

The DOS prompt is changed by using the PROMPT command. This command employs a number of special metacharacters that cause the command to display special information. For instance, the letter *t* makes the command display the current time at the DOS prompt (providing the system clock is accurately set—see section 17.4). The current directory is indicated by the letter *p*. Metacharacters are always preceded by a dollar sign ($). Thus:

PROMPT $p ⏎

would give a DOS prompt like:

C:\SOFTWARE\DATABASE

Notice that the drive specifier (C:) is automatically included with the DOS path created by $p. The drive letter alone can be obtained with the metacharacter $n. To add a > character at the end of the line, add $g:

PROMPT pg ⏎

Now the prompt becomes:

C:\SOFTWARE\DATABASE>

when the subdirectory \SOFTWARE\DATABASE is current. Note that a single backslash represents the root directory:

C:\>

TIP

A directory path printed within the DOS prompt tends to blend with DOS commands typed thereafter. To keep matters clear, type a space or two after the $g. Alternatively, try adding some dashes before the final >:

```
PROMPT $p--$g ⏎
```

The result:

```
C:\SOFTWARE\DATABASE-->
```

Use $t and $d for the time and date, respectively. Rather than pack everything onto one line, you can insert a carriage return on the line using the underscore character preceded by $. Thus,

```
PROMPT $t$_$p--$g ⏎
```

creates a two-line DOS prompt that would look like this:

```
11:24:33.45
C:\SOFTWARE\DATABASE-->
```

The metacharacter *h* represents the backspace. Use it, if you wish, to get rid of the hundredths of a second part of the time (three h's) and possibly the seconds reading as well (three more) as in:

```
PROMPT $t$h$h$h$h$h$h$_$p--$g ⏎
```

The result would be:

```
11:24
C:\SOFTWARE\DATABASE-->
```

Finally, you can type any normal characters into a PROMPT statement. For example:

```
PROMPT The time is $t$_The date is $d$_$p--$g ⏎
```

gives this DOS prompt:

```
The time is 11:24:33.45
The date is 12/18/89
C:\SOFTWARE\DATABASE-->
```

Of course, it would be inconvenient to type such a complicated command every time you start up the machine. So place it in the AUTO-

EXEC.BAT file that DOS reads at start-up (see section 11.1). The PROMPT command is so useful that the DOS 4.0 installation program writes PROMPT pg in the AUTOEXEC.BAT file it creates automatically. So, in DOS 4.0 and later, you may never see a plain DOS prompt like C>.

You can return to a normal DOS prompt (such as C>) at any time by simply entering:

PROMPT [←]

11.3 Setting the number of DOS buffers

Data is stored on disks in 512-byte blocks called sectors. When DOS transfers information to and from disk drives, it moves the data one sector at a time through a temporary holding area in memory called a DOS buffer. Like disk sectors, a DOS buffer holds 512 bytes. As a program writes a sector of data to disk, the information is actually written into a DOS buffer. Only when the buffer is full is its data actually written into a disk sector. Similarly, when a program reads data from a file, a whole sector is read into a buffer, even when less than 512 bytes of data are required.

DOS operates on only one file at a time at any given moment (when more than one file is open at once, DOS moves from one to another). For this reason, one DOS buffer ought to be enough to handle all file transactions as sector after sector passes between drive and memory. But normally several DOS buffers are used. This is done because some kinds of software tend to repeatedly access the same disk sectors. By keeping the most recently accessed disk sectors in DOS buffers, there is a high probability that repetitious read/write operations will be avoided in the disk drive. The software finds the information it needs already stored in memory (in the buffers), and so it can run more quickly.

The ideal number of DOS buffers depends on the kind of software you are using, and the speed of your computer and its disk drives. DOS documentation recommends the following number of buffers:

Disk Size	Recommended buffers
under 40M	20
40M to 80M	30
80M to 120M	40
over 120M	50

These numbers are approximate, and can be reduced if memory is scarce (50 buffers take up 25K of memory!). Note that you'll only need one buffer if you use disk caching, which is discussed in section 21.9. Machines lacking a hard disk can make due with three buffers.

Set the number by including a BUFFERS statement in the CONFIG.SYS file that DOS automatically consults when it is booted (explained in section 11.1). DOS buffers can only be created when the machine starts up. To set the number of buffers to 20, add to CONFIG.SYS the line:

```
BUFFERS = 20
```

The buffers are normally placed in conventional memory (that is, in the 640K normally available to DOS). Starting with DOS 4.0, you can add an /X switch to a BUFFERS command to place the buffers in expanded memory (see the minitutorial in Chapter 15).

When no BUFFERS statement is found in CONFIG.SYS (or no CONFIG.SYS file exists), DOS creates a default number of buffers. This value varies both by the DOS version, and by the capacity of the disk drives and the amount of memory in the machine. In DOS 3.3, for example, the number of buffers created varies from 2 for a machine with little memory and low-capacity drives, to 15 for a well-outfitted computer with additional memory and a hard disk.

It is tempting to create a very large number of buffers to hasten disk operations. In many cases, the ideal way of handling disk files would be to read the entire file into numerous DOS buffers, operate on it there, and then write it back to disk in one operation. In fact, there is a kind of software called disk caching software that does something like this (it is explained in section 21.9). But two factors limit the number of DOS buffers that are practical:

- The buffers take up scarce memory. Enough buffers to hold a 100K file would, by definition, take up at least 100K of memory. Not all of us have so much memory to spare. As mentioned above, DOS couldn't place buffers outside of conventional memory until version 4.0.

- Whenever a disk read or write operation is performed, DOS must scan all buffers to see what they contain. Particularly in slower computers, the time required to scan many buffers can exceed the time needed to just read or write the sector on the disk drive. (Caching software, on the other hand, uses a much more elaborate means of detecting which sectors are in buffers, and in prioritizing which sectors should remain in buffers. In a word, caching software is smarter than DOS.)

Efficiency concerns   A large number of DOS buffers is of no benefit when your application software works by reading a whole file into memory, operating on it, and then writing the whole file back to disk. Word processors and spreadsheet programs are good examples of this kind of software. By comparison, databases usually use random access files that are read and written in bits and pieces, rather than as a whole. Such software gains much from operating with numerous DOS buffers. More and more, all kinds of software use a multitude of auxiliary files, and these files often benefit from having many buffers on hand.

TIP

Should a special occasion arise where you can't quite fit data in memory, reducing the number of DOS buffers is a convenient ploy for temporarily obtaining an extra 8 or 9K of memory. Just set BUFFERS = 3, and then put up with slower disk access until the job is done.

11.4 Setting the maximum number of opened files

When DOS boots, it sets aside a number of small blocks of memory by which to control files. For every file that is opened, a block of memory must be allocated. If software attempts to open more files than have been provided for, DOS is unable to meet the request. It sends an error message to the software (not to you, the user), and if the software is well constructed, it will inform you that it could not open any more files. When this happens, you should quit the program and insert a FILES command in the CONFIG.SYS file that DOS automatically reads at start-up to configure itself (section 11.1). The FILES command can increase the number of files that may be opened up to 255, or even 65,535 in recent DOS versions. To set the number of files to 20—a good number to start with—include in CONFIG.SYS the line:

```
FILES = 20
```

You'll need to reboot the machine to bring the new command into effect.

Without a FILES command, DOS sets the number of files that may be opened to 8. This is the number of files that may be opened at any one time. There is no limit to how many files may be opened and then closed in sequence. Eight files is often enough for a single application program, but not for a system that uses much auxiliary software, such as memory-resident programs. The files you open from within your application programs, such as multiple documents within a word processor, are only part of all files that may actually be opened. Here are some other sources of invisibly opened files:

■ Certain standard DOS functions are adminstered as if they were files, including output to the printer and screen. For this reason, five of the eight files allowed by default are already taken before you have loaded a program. Devices such as print spoolers and network links also may function as files.

■ Application programs may be partially stored in files that are separate from the main program file. This is done partly to conserve memory. Seldom used sections of a program called overlays may be read in from their individual files while the program runs. And drivers, such as a printer driver that operates a particular brand of printer, may need to be opened and loaded.

■ Software may open files it keeps to configure itself. It also may need to open auxiliary files, such as spelling checkers, font libraries, and so on.

■ Memory-resident programs, including editors, calendars, and calculators, all have their own files. The total number of files that can be opened at one time must be increased because these utilities run while application programs run, and while application programs continue to keep their own files open.

■ Software sometimes generates temporary files. These are files that hold data created during processing. For example, when a long list is sorted, it may be necessary to create a file to hold partially sorted data. Once the sort is completed, the file is erased.

Determining the optimum number of files   For hard disk owners, the value for FILES should normally be set to 20. Systems limited to diskette drives may need as many, but usually they do not since they simply can't keep as many files available on disk (which is to say that some features in advanced software simply can't be used unless you have a hard disk). Experimentation is often the only way to find out the required number. Don't just set FILES to the maximum allowed value of 255 (or 65,535 starting with DOS 3.3). For each file that may be opened, 48 bytes of memory are set aside. To specify 255 files when you actually need 20 would be to waste 11,280 bytes of memory.

Note that the size of your hard disk has no bearing on the appropriate value for the maximum number of files. It is the kind of software you use, and the number of programs you run at once that matters.

An alternate method of accessing files   DOS has two ways of reading and writing files. The first method, using file control blocks, was employed by early DOS versions. DOS later added a second method that uses file handles. Today, nearly all software uses the latter method, although the file control block method is still supported. The FILES command sets the maximum number of files that may be opened using file handles. To enable an old program that uses file control blocks to open more files, you must use the FCBS command, which is explained in section 11.5.

11.5 Setting the number of file control blocks

When software needs to read a file or write to a file, it makes a request to DOS and DOS does the actual reading and writing. Early DOS versions communicated with software through a table of information called a file control block. This expression is abbreviated as FCB. A file control block had to be created in memory for every file opened. Later DOS versions introduced a different method of accessing files, and FCBs are seldom used today. Still, there is a chance you may encounter older software that requires them.

When the computer starts up and DOS boots, four file control blocks are automatically created in memory just in case you run a program that uses them. Ordinarily, you would run a program and never know that it uses FCBs. But if the software should attempt to open more than four files, DOS would be unable to accommodate it, because it can only create FCBs at start-up. An error message would appear.

When you encounter this error, you should save the work you have done and exit the software. Then you must add a line to the CONFIG.SYS file that DOS automatically reads when it is booted. This file, discussed in section 11.1, instructs DOS how to configure itself. To make it configure eight FCBs instead of the default number of four, you would insert into the file the line:

```
FCBS = 8,0
```

The easiest way to modify CONFIG.SYS is to load it into your word processor or text editor. Place the FCBS statement on a line of its own. Then save the file and reboot the computer. Thereafter you may return to your application and run it successfully.

As you can see, there is a second number given with the command, the 0 separated from the number 8 by a comma. This value tells DOS how to handle FCBs in multiuser systems where files on one disk are shared between multiple users. There's no need to concern yourself with how it works. Just be sure to include it, because this parameter is not optional.

Every file control block takes up 44 bytes of memory. Since most users have no software that requires file control blocks, you can save a little memory by placing a FCBS statement in CONFIG.SYS to have DOS create less than the default number. For technical reasons, the minimum is 1 FCB, not 0. (The maximum number, incidentally, is 255—a tremendous waste of memory.)

11.6 Setting the maximum number of drive specifiers

Normally, DOS can identify five disk drives, giving them the names A: through E:. Most machines have one or two diskette drives, drives A and B, and one or two hard disk drives, C and D. There are occasions, however, when DOS may need to be able to identify more drives, perhaps a drive F, a drive G, and so on. Here are some applications:

- High-capacity disk drives may be divided into two or more logical disk drives. This means that the disk's capacity is split into two or more sections, each acting as an individual disk drive with its own root directory. One physical drive becomes two or more logical drives (more on this in section 16.4).

- You may be working on a local area network (discussed in Chapter 19) and have access to several remote disk drives.

- You may wish to create one or more RAM disks. These set aside a portion of memory (possibly extended or expanded memory, as explained in the minitutorial at the beginning of Chapter 15) to hold files. Great efficiency can be achieved in this way, for RAM disks operate much faster than real disk drives. From the point of view of the user, and of software, a RAM disk is just one more disk drive. Each RAM disk is given its own drive specifier, such as E: or F:. See section 15.3 for a detailed discussion of RAM disks.

- You may apply the DOS SUBST command. This command lets you assign a drive specifier to a subdirectory in a directory tree. By doing so, you avoid constantly retyping the directory path to the subdirectory. For example, \ANIMALS\MAMMALS\PRIMATES\ APES\CHIMPS could be replaced by G:. The expression COPY MYFILE G: would copy MYFILE to the CHIMPS subdirectory. The SUBST command is discussed in section 8.4.

In all of these cases, DOS may be required to generate drive specifiers higher than E:. When DOS is booted, however, it sets aside a little bit of memory to manage each drive. If no memory has been set aside for additional drives, subsequent attempts to create RAM disks or apply the SUBST command for such drives will be greeted with a DOS error message.

Increasing the number of allowed drive specifiers

To make DOS set aside memory for additional drives, use the LASTDRIVE command, which specifies the name (letter of the alphabet) of the last drive specifier that DOS can use, counting upward from *A*. The command is placed in the CONFIG.SYS file that DOS automatically reads at start-up to configure itself (section 11.1). You must reboot to activate the new command. To specify F as the last drive, simply add to your CONFIG.SYS file the line:

```
LASTDRIVE = F
```

The highest drive number allowed is Z. Specify only as many drives as you are likely to use. Don't arbitrarily specify the highest value, because valuable memory will be wasted. LASTDRIVE can't reduce the setting to a drive specifier lower than E.

11.7 Setting stack resources

When the computer's microprocessor is at work, it may be interrupted at any time by a variety of hardware devices, such as modems or printers. The microprocessor stops what it is doing and takes care of the request coming from the device. To do this, it must save the byproducts of the work it is doing; later, it fetches these byproducts and returns to the task at hand. The place in memory that it saves the byproducts is called a stack. Several stacks may be kept in memory at once. Sometimes many demands may be made upon the microprocessor at the same time, and there is more to put in the stacks than there is room. DOS does not handle this situation gracefully. It simply displays the message:

```
FATAL: Internal Stack Failure, System Halted
```

This means that the computer has hung itself; it has frozen in its tracks. Any work that you had been doing and hadn't saved is lost. To restart, you must reboot the computer.

This error is rare, and usually only occurs in complicated systems. When it does happen, you can avoid a recurrence by placing a STACKS command in the CONFIG.SYS file (section 11.1). The command takes two numbers, the first specifying how many stacks to create, and the second giving their size. The appropriate numbers vary widely, and only a computer expert can decide on optimal values. However, you can experiment to find a value that works, but that is not so large as to waste lots of memory. Try beginning with the minimum value of 8 stacks of 32 bytes each. In your CONFIG.SYS file, include:

```
STACKS 8,32
```

The first number, the number of stacks, may be no larger than 64, and the second number, the bytes in each stack, is limited to 512.

PITFALL | Don't opt for the maximum allowed number of stacks just to play it safe. By doing so, 32 kilobytes of conventional memory would be set aside and lost to your programs.

11.8 Setting environment variables

DOS sets aside a small area of memory for maintaining an environment. This is a list of specifications that are made available for all programs to read. As such, it constitutes an environment for all software running in the machine. Certain of the specifications are standard to DOS. For example, when you enter an alternate form for the DOS prompt using the PROMPT command, the entire command, including the word PROMPT, is stored in the environment. Similarly, subdirectories specified by a PATH statement are placed in the environment. In these cases, both PROMPT and PATH are said to be environment variables. The words are written in the environment followed by the information provided, allowing DOS or application programs to find out whether any such specification exists, and if so, what it is.

Sometimes information is introduced into the environment so that it will be available to programs that have been specially designed to look for it. For instance, the directory to which programs should look for particular files could be specified in the environment. In this case, the environment variable will be a word not specified by DOS, such as TRGETDIR. Software would use the variable only if it was specifically designed to. This feature is not often used. But when it is, you need to know how to insert variables into the environment.

The SET command does the job. It can be entered on the DOS command line or included in your AUTOEXEC.BAT file (or some other batch file). To set the variable TRGETDIR to \UTILS\SUB1 you would enter:

```
SET TRGETDIR=\UTILS\SUB1 ↵
```

There must be no spaces on either side of the equals sign. It does not matter whether the characters are entered in uppercase or lowercase, or any combination of the two. A second command that sets TRGETDIR would replace the first:

```
SET TRGETDIR=\UTILS\SUB2 ↵
```

On the other hand, if you just name the variable without giving a value for it, as in:

```
SET TRGETDIR ↵
```

the variable is removed from the environment. Typing:

SET ⏎

alone makes DOS list all variables currently held in the environment.

Increasing the environment size   DOS sets aside only 127 bytes of memory for the environment. In some instances the environment can fill, resulting in the message:

Out of environment space

To increase the environment size, say, to 320 bytes, include this command in your CONFIG.SYS file:

SHELL = C:\COMMAND.COM /E:320 /P ⏎

You'll need to reboot before the new command will come into effect.

11.9 Enabling the Ctrl-Break feature

The Ctrl-Break key combination lets you escape from a program and return to DOS. It's not a good idea to use it to exit from application programs. They often need to do some housekeeping before quitting, and Ctrl-Break robs them of this chance. But often Ctrl-Break is a perfectly legitimate way to return to the DOS prompt, such as when running a batch file you want to stop prematurely. And when software malfunctions, Ctrl-Break may be the only way to recover without rebooting the machine.

As software runs, it constantly calls on DOS to perform certain functions, such as reading and writing data on disk. It's during these moments that DOS checks to see if Ctrl-Break has been pressed. The rest of the time, the computer remembers that Ctrl-Break has been struck, but it is unable to communicate the news to DOS. Even when software activates DOS, it must make a particular kind of request to get DOS to react to the Ctrl-Break status. Thus, it sometimes happens that you may desperately wish to exit a program, but Ctrl-Break has no effect.

The BREAK command causes DOS to respond to Ctrl-Break more often. When it is used, you stand a better chance of getting out of your programs, although you may still encounter situations where Ctrl-Break is ineffective. To turn the BREAK feature on, type:

```
BREAK = ON ←
```

To find out the current status of the BREAK feature, just enter:

```
BREAK ←
```

TIP

The BREAK status is initially switched off; this is because it takes DOS a little longer to fulfill every request when it must perform the Ctrl-Break check. The degree to which it makes your computer run slower depends on how your software works. Only rarely is the difference perceptible. Still, you should be aware that turning BREAK on slows the machine very slightly.

11.10 Setting country-specific information

The time and date are specified in different ways in different countries. Americans are accustomed to the date being expressed as month/day/year, but other nations may use day/month/year or year/month/day. You can make DOS observe these details and others by placing a COUNTRY command in the CONFIG.SYS file (section 11.1) that DOS automatically reads at start-up. The command requires a code number specifying the country or language whose standards you wish to use. (See section 10.6 to set the keyboard layout in use.) Here is a list of the codes:

Arabic speaking	785
Australia	061
Belgium	032
Canada (English)	001
Canada (French)	002
Denmark	045
Finland	358
France	033
Germany	049
Hebrew speaking	972
Italy	039
Latin America	003
Netherlands	031
Norway	047
Portugal	351
Spain	034
Sweden	046
Switzerland	041
United Kingdom	044
United States	001

To set the country format to France, place this line in CONFIG.SYS:

```
COUNTRY = 033
```

The COUNTRY command employs a file named COUNTRY.SYS that is found on one of the DOS diskettes. You can place it in the root directory of the boot disk to ensure that it can be found. Alternatively, you may include a path to the file as part of the COUNTRY command. For example, if COUNTRY.SYS is on drive C in a subdirectory named DOS, then enter:

```
COUNTRY = 033,,C:\DOS\COUNTRY.SYS
```

Notice that there are two commas in this command; both must be present.

11.11 Installing a device driver

A device driver (sometimes just called a driver) is a program that is kept in memory at all times to control a device, that is, a piece of hardware. Everything connected to the computer is a device: the keyboard, the display, printers, disk drives, modems, scanners, mice. There are multiple designs for each of these devices. For example, hard disk drives vary in their capacity and the arrangement of sectors on disk surfaces. Similarly, various printers use different systems to draw graphics. No computer could possibly be designed to handle every device, in part because most devices are invented after the computer is designed.

For this reason, IBM-compatible computers have a generic way of interacting with devices. The manufacturer that develops the device creates software, a device driver, that is kept in system memory. When the computer needs to interact with the device, it sends a command to the device driver, telling it in a general way what it wants done. Then the device driver takes over and actually manipulates the device using the special knowledge it has of the device's design.

For example, software running in the computer could tell a printer device driver to start printing in italics. A driver for a dot-matrix printer might then translate the incoming text to a different font, whereas a daisy wheel printer that has no such font would be instructed to underline the text. In this way, software may be designed to handle various dissimilar devices, including some that have not yet been invented. The exact details of controlling the device are left to those who write the device driver, and these are usually the same people who designed the device.

Certain devices, most notably diskette drives, have standard designs. The computer has built-in drivers for such devices, and so there is no need for you to load a device driver into memory. In other cases, such as when you connect a scanner or plotter, you must install a driver. Drivers are usually short programs, typically about 5K, often named with a .SYS extension. You'll know when you need to install a driver because the device will be shipped with a diskette containing the driver, and the installation instructions for the device will tell you about the driver.

Hard disks sometimes require the installation of a device driver, although most do not. There are scores of hard disk designs, including some very unusual ones for high-capacity drives. Most PCs have drivers built-in for standard hard disk designs in the 10-80 megabyte capacity range. But not all designs can be accommodated. If you acquire an unusual drive, you may find that it has been shipped with a driver that you must install.

Loading a device driver Device drivers can be loaded only when DOS boots. This is done with a **DEVICE** statement, which must be placed in your CONFIG.SYS file (section 11.1). If the device driver is held in the file XYZ.SYS, then the statement

```
DEVICE = XYZ.SYS
```

does the job. You may need to use a drive specifier and directory path to tell DOS where to find the driver:

```
DEVICE = D:\DRIVERS\XYZ.SYS
```

Once the driver is loaded, any software that uses it will be able to find it. Usually, the driver takes up roughly as much space in memory as its file takes up disk space. This much memory is wasted when software is used that does not use the driver. There is little that you can do about the waste of memory since device drivers cannot be removed or reinstalled without rebooting.

TIP

When memory is scarce and a large driver goes unused, you may want to temporariliy modify CONFIG.SYS and then reboot (or use the technique explained in section 11.12). When a device is physically disconnected from a computer, be sure to remove its DEVICE statement in CONFIG.SYS to avoid wasting memory.

DOS device drivers DOS is shipped with a number of standard device drivers that may optionally be installed if you have software that uses them. One that is widely used is ANSI.SYS, which gives programs a standard way of gaining more control over the keyboard and screen. There are also drivers named DISPLAY.SYS, DRIVER.SYS, PRINT-

ER.SYS, VDISK.SYS SMARTDRV.SYS, and so on. These are discussed elsewhere in this book under relevant headings.

Windows 3.1 The Windows Setup program installs the standard Windows device drivers at the time Windows is first installed on your hard disk. However, not all Windows device drivers are used since many support features (like sound cards and videodisc players) that most computer setups do not have hardware for. You may also need to introduce a device driver that does not come with Windows. This is particularly true of printer device drivers, which translate Window's graphics language into commands matching your printer's capabilities.

To install a new device driver, choose the Drivers icon from the Control Panel menu. The dialog box shown in figure 11.1 appears with a list of all currently installed drivers. Click on the Add button to see the Add dialog box, which lists all drivers available on the Windows distribution diskettes. If you want to activate one of these drivers, select it and click on OK. On the other hand, if you're installing a non-Windows driver not found in the list, choose Add Unlisted or Updated Driver.

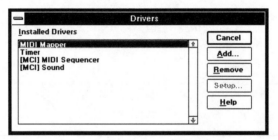

Figure 11.1

To install the device driver, insert the diskette holding the driver into drive A or enter the DOS path to the subdirectory on your hard disk that holds the driver (choose Browse if your need to search your hard disk for the file). After clicking OK, you'll encounter a final dialog box that may ask you for information to configure the driver. Configuraion information can sometimes be quite technical. For example, you may be asked which input-output port or microprocessor interrupt to use. This information is required so that two pieces of hardware do not connect to the computer in a way that they'll interfere with each other. For help, turn to the documentation that accompanied your hardware.

When you have finished, you will need to choose Restart Now if you want the driver to go into operation immediately.

If you later need to reconfigure a driver, choose the Setup button once you've selected a driver listed in the Installed Drivers list. You'll encounter the same configuration dialog box as when you first installed the driver. Again, you must choose Restart Now to have the changes come into effect at once.

Drivers can be removed by selecting them in the Installed Drivers list and choosing the Remove button. The driver is merely deactivated; its file remains on disk and the driver can be reinstalled easily.

11.12 Reconfiguring the computer quickly

When you are pushing the limits of the 640K of memory allowed to DOS, you may find that a particular DOS configuration works well for one application program, but not for another. One program may use particular device drivers, a RAM disk, or a special memory-resident program, while another has different requirements. You can handle such varying needs by creating multiple CONFIG.SYS and AUTOEXEC.BAT files tailored to the task at hand. The computer is then reconfigured by rebooting using the desired configuration files.

The appropriate versions of the files are activated by copying their contents into the CONFIG.SYS and AUTOEXEC.BAT files kept in the root directory. The alternate files are stored in some other directory. There is no need to name them CONFIG.SYS and AUTOEXEC.BAT. For example, one file holding CONFIG.SYS contents could be named DATABASE.CCC. A similar file holding AUTOEXEC.BAT commands could be in DATABASE.AAA. When it's time to reconfigure the machine for your database program, enter the commands:

```
COPY DATABASE.CCC C:\CONFIG.SYS ⏎
COPY DATABASE.AAA C:\AUTOEXEC.BAT ⏎
```

These two commands could be placed in a batch file named DATABASE.BAT. By including the directory that holds the batch file in a PATH statement (section 8.1), the file will be available no matter the current directory. Then, at any time, you can type:

```
DATABASE ⏎
```

and then reboot to completely reconfigure the machine.

If you set up such a system, be sure to create a plain vanilla version of CONFIG.SYS and AUTOEXEC.BAT that simply boots the machine in ordinary fashion. Before shutting down the computer for the day, you'll probably want to call the batch file that establishes this version so that the computer will boot in a simple way when you start up again.

Chapter 12

Configuring Software to Work with Hardware

- MINITUTORIAL: Steps to installing and configuring software

- Installing software on a hard disk

- Dealing with copy protection

- Matching software to your video hardware

- Working with a math coprocessor

- Configuring software to your printer

MINITUTORIAL:

Steps to installing and configuring software

When you acquire new software, you will need to both install and configure it to the particular machine it will work on. Installation generally refers to the process of copying required files to a hard disk and creating a subdirectory structure that will allow the files to find and access each other. Configuration, on the other hand, refers to the process of tailoring the software to your hardware. The software needs to know what kind of video system the machine uses, the type of printer connected, whether a mouse is available, and so on. The software should be able to figure out much of this information itself once it is running (although many programs cannot). However, you will always need to at least specify the printer type if a printer is used.

Today, most software is shipped with an Install program that both sets up the files and prompts you for the required configuration information at the same time. Complicated programs may maintain a separate configuration program so that you can go back any time to change the configuration settings (for example, when you change the printer in use). While Install programs are generally easy to use, be sure to read the software documentation carefully. Pitfalls abound, so also see section 12.1 to learn about problems you may encounter.

There are a few important steps to take before running the install program. Perhaps it is because these steps are so obvious that they are so often overlooked:

- Make copies of the distribution diskettes. You may skip the tutorial diskette if you like, but all others should be copied. Never write files to the originals; use only the copies. Be aware that diskettes can go bad, particularly after a few years have passed, even if only left in storage.

- Fill out the registration form and send it in. Once registered, you'll hear about upgrades and bug fixes (repairs) to the software. Also, some companies require registration before they will give you assistance over the phone.

- Write the serial number from the diskettes on the inside front cover of the program's manual, along with the support telephone number.

- Keep the packaging in good-as-new condition until you are certain everything is in working order. Should problems arise, it will be a lot easier to return the software if the packaging is in good shape.

■ Store the manual(s) with your other computer documentation. Many products are shipped with several manuals and inserts, some of which seem obscure when you begin using the software, but which later may turn out to be crucial. You will be very unhappy if you can't find them when you need them. Consider keeping odd-sized documents, along with keyboard templates and other such things, in large, clearly labeled manila envelopes.

■ Finally, before installing the program, be sure to sit down and read the part of the documentation concerning installation. Don't just type INSTALL $\boxed{\leftarrow}$ to see what happens. All kinds of problems can arise from doing so.

12.1 ◼ Installing software on a hard disk

When you acquire a new piece of software, you must almost always install it before you can begin to use it. Installation means to set up the files that hold the program (or that are used by the program) so that they can find each other. You may also need to configure the software so that it works with your particular printer, video system, extended or expanded memory, and other equipment.

As software has become more complicated, it has come to be shipped with dozens, sometimes hundreds of files, filling many diskettes in some cases.

Most software includes an installation program. You simply run this program (the software's documentation will tell you how) and it prompts you to insert the distribution diskettes one by one. Usually the program will ask you questions about your system or the kind of work you will be doing and on that basis it selects certain files to copy out of the many contained on the diskettes. While an installation program would seem to protect you from every problem, many things can go wrong, in part because installation programs are sometimes badly designed. Keep the following suggestions in mind.

Suggestion 1   Place the software in appropriately named sub-directories. Frequently, the software's installation program will create these directories for you, but you may be instructed to create sub-directories of particular names at particular positions in the directory tree. Don't rename directories made by the installation program unless the documentation specifically allows it since the program may be designed to look for files in a subdirectory of that name only.

You might be inclined to try copying all files into the root directory of the hard disk, as though the disk were a giant diskette. This way of organizing a hard disk will soon come back to haunt you because the root directory can hold only so many files and will quickly fill. See section 5.1 to review the essentials of directory tree organization.

Suggestion 2   Once the software's subdirectories have been created (either by you or by the installation program), add a subdirectory for data files. Don't get into the habit of placing data files in the same subdirectory as the program files. Data files should go into their own subdirectories so that they can be conveniently viewed in their own directory listings. By keeping them apart from program files, you will also avoid future confusion about the identity of various files. And when you later need to install an updated version of the software, you can do so without confusion and without endangering your data.

Suggestion 3   Make copies of your AUTOEXEC.BAT and CONFIG.SYS files before running the installation program. Many installation programs open these files and insert lines into them. For example, they may place a DEVICE statement in CONFIG.SYS to cause a device driver to be loaded when the computer is booted. Unfortunately, not all installations are well behaved in this regard. They may write statements in the files that nullify those that you have written yourself. In the worst case, the file may simply be replaced with one generated by the installation software. By making copies of the two files before running the program, you'll be able to quickly recover if undesirable changes are made.

Be particularly wary of changes made by installation programs to a PATH command (section 8.2) in your AUTOEXEC.BAT file. Some programs require this command for proper operation. Installation programs may simply replace the existing command with one of their own. When this happens, other software in your system may mysteriously stop functioning.

Suggestion 4   Avoid placing unnecessary files on the disk. It is astonishingly easy to fill up a 20- or 40-megabyte hard disk. So be sure that the files you place on it are actually used. Printer drivers are particularly wasteful of disk space. These are the small files that let software work with the printer you own. There may be more than 100 shipped with the software, but you will be using only one or two. Most installation programs ask for the name of your printer and install only the appropriate file. Still, you should verify that the disk has not been packed with useless printer drivers. A file holding a printer driver usually has a name resembling that of the printer it serves.

Other candidates for elimination are software tutorials and software demonstration files. Run the tutorial and then delete it from the disk. The same applies to demonstation files, which are ready-made data files that can be loaded into the software to show it in action. These often are included for software salespeople rather than software customers. Again, take a look and then get rid of them.

TIP

When you are unsure whether a file can be eliminated or not, rename it and then see if the program runs properly. A good way of doing this is to change just the first character of the file name to the next highest letter of the alphabet. For example, the file WHATSIT is renamed to XHATSIT. If you find that you need the file after all, you'll have no trouble remembering what the original name was. Be sure to make a thorough run through of the software before eliminating files, including using it for printing.

Suggestion 5   Keep a sharp eye out for files that use the same names as those employed by other programs on your hard disk. Certain names tend to be used again and again. If two programs use a file named STARTUP, you certainly don't want them to read the wrong file since they would probably become fatally confused and cause the machine to freeze up. Even when the two files are safely tucked away in their own subdirectories, a poorly thought-out PATH command (section 8.1) or APPEND command (section 8.2) could lead to confusion.

12.2 Dealing with copy protection

Although it is increasingly rare, some software manufacturers still copy protect their software, making it impossible or very difficult to use on more than one computer. There's some justification in this measure since some companies estimate that ten or more illegal copies of their software exist for every original paid for. For them, copy protection is not a matter of greed, but of survival. It's sometimes hard to remember this since consumers often spend several hundred dollars for some documentation and a few diskettes. What is hidden from view, though, is the vast sums of money required to develop, upgrade, and support software.

Unfortunately, copy-protection schemes can sometimes interfere with the normal use of your computer. In the worst case, they can even cause data loss. Most schemes are variants upon two basic approaches: one that modifies the diskette upon which the software is originally shipped and one that modifies the hard disk upon which the software is installed.

Diskette modification   In this approach, one of the diskettes packaged with the software documentation must be placed in a diskette drive, normally drive A, when the software is started up. It's usually called the key disk. The program may still be installed on a hard disk, but before it begins full operation, it checks that the key disk is in place and refuses to operate if it's not. The key disk cannot be copied by the DOS DISKCOPY command or any other conventional means. The key disk may force you to swap diskettes unnecessarily and in some cases can prevent the diskette drive from being used for other purposes. It also slows software loading.

Hard disk modification   Software used from a hard disk may effectively be copy protected by limiting the number of times the program can be installed upon a hard disk drive. Like a key disk, one of the software distribution diskettes is made so that it cannot normally be copied. When crucial files are installed from this diskette to a hard disk, the diskette itself is modified so that another copy cannot be made. Often, two installations are allowed from the diskette so that a backup will be on hand. Sometimes you can deinstall the software; the installation software removes the files from the hard disk and then gives itself permission to make another installation at some later time.

In this approach, the hard disk is also modified during installation, often by establishing certain disk sectors as key sectors similar in function to the key disk we mentioned earlier. When the program starts up, it checks for the presence of the key and refuses to work if the key isn't there. Because the key is created by code on the diskette—code that cannot be copied or used more than once or twice—the software cannot be pirated by copying the program files from the hard disk to another diskette.

PITFALLS | The problem with any kind of hard disk modification is that it can interfere with the use of other software, particularly utility software. Defragmenters and other kinds of disk optimization software (discussed in Chapter 21), which reorganize the distribution of files on a disk to improve efficiency, can wipe out the copy-protection key, as can utilities designed to find and repair bad disk sectors. To avoid problems, you're forced to deinstall the software every time you use such a utility and then reinstall the protected software afterward. Other difficulties arise when using backup programs, which may fail to replace the key when restoring the disk after a serious data loss.

Circumventing copy protection   A few software companies have specialized in creating software that circumvents copy-protection measures. The stated purpose of these utilities is to help users avoid problems arising from copy protection. The utilities let you create a second, standby copy of the original distribution diskette (if a key diskette fails, you must stop work until the manufacturer sends you another—something they may be willing to do only after you've returned the original). Such utilities allow unlimited installations to a hard disk and, in some cases, they can trick a computer into thinking that a key diskette is present when it is not. These utilities are widely available in retail stores and through advertisements in computer magazines.

New copy-protection techniques are constantly developed, and the manufacturers of software that overcome these techniques must repeatedly upgrade their product to handle the new ploys. Some even sell an add-in disk controller board for cracking the toughest protection schemes. You may require a new edition of the copy-protection program every time you upgrade your copy-protected software. These utilities are usually targeted at best-selling application software titles. Each manufacturer keeps a list of programs they are sure their utility can crack. You can phone them to find out about your particular need. Copy-protected software not on the approved list may or may not be successfully breached by the utility.

It must be emphasized that breaking copy-protection schemes for purposes of software piracy is not only immoral and illegal (successful lawsuits are on the books), but also unwise. The value of the time you devote to using a program will ultimately far outweigh its cost in dollars and cents. Only by owning and registering the program can you receive proper documentation, telephone support, updates with new features, and bug fixes. Equally important, your computer is protected from accidentally acquiring computer viruses (see section 23.6) as pirated software is passed from machine to machine. And, by supporting the company that makes the software, you see to it that the company stays in business and improves the tools upon which you rely.

12.3 Matching software to your video hardware

A video system is the combination of a video display and a video adapter that operates the display from one of the computer's expansion slots (or, in PS/2 models and some AT-style clones, from the computer's main circuit board). There are seven video systems widely used in IBM microcomputers. They vary in many ways, chiefly by screen resolution, by whether they support graphics, by whether color may be used, and, if so, by the number of colors available. The seven main systems are:

- Monochrome Display Adapter (MDA): This is a text-only, black-and-white system still common on many PC- or XT-style clones.

- Hercules Graphics Card (HGC): Also an early video standard, this is the only non-IBM standard to have been widely adopted. It is essentially a monochrome display adapter that can also perform monochrome graphics. Many clones follow this standard under the name monographics card.

- Color Graphics Adapter (CGA): This is a text and graphics system that must be used with a color monitor. It can display up to 16 colors at once in low resolution or two colors in medium resolution.

- Enhanced Graphics Adapter (EGA): This more advanced system includes all of the features of the monochrome adapter and the color graphics adapter, plus higher-resolution graphics modes, some allowing up to 64 colors. It can also run simple text and graphics modes on a black-and-white monitor.

- Video Graphics Array (VGA): This is the video system built into all IBM PS/2 MicroChannel models and is available for earlier PCs as add-in cards. It includes nearly every feature of the EGA, plus graphics modes of higher resolution, and it allows up to 256 colors on the screen at once. Independent hardware manufacturers have devised the Super VGA standard, which, unlike an ordinary VGA, supports 256 colors in high-resolution modes. Unfortunately, this standard varies between manufacturers; software designed to support the SuperVGA may prove to be incompatible in some cases.

■ MultiColor Graphics Array (MCGA): This is a slightly reduced version of the VGA that lacks the VGA's most advanced graphics modes. This standard is built into PS/2 models 25 and 30 and is found nowhere else.

■ 8514/A adapter: Named after a high-resolution color monitor, this is an expansion board that extends graphics modes to 256 simultaneous colors at 1024×768-dot resolution. Targeted at engineering design work and desktop publishing, it is relatively slow and has not found a wide audience.

■ Extended Graphics Array (XGA): This is the coming PC video standard. Like the 8514/A adapter, it can handle 1024×768-dot graphics in 256 colors, but it is much faster. XGA circuitry includes a graphics processing chip optimized for Windows. The XGA operates only in 32-bit machines (386 computers and later). It is backward compatible with the VGA standard, but unlike the VGA, you can have up to eight XGAs running a machine at the same time. This is possible because the XGA's video buffer is placed high in extended memory where there are no practical limitations on buffer size.

All of the seven above-mentioned video systems are nothing more than circuit boards that are built into the machine or placed into an expansion slot. Each has its own range of video modes (or screen modes) that it supports, including text-only modes in black-and-white or in color and graphics modes in black-and-white or in color. However, just because the card has a particular capability, does not mean that you will always be able to use it.

One limitation is that the video monitor you use with the card must be capable of as high a resolution as the card's most advanced video mode; if not, the monitor will work only with the card's less-advanced modes. Similarly, some monitors generate no more than 16 colors, some no more than 64, and some are unlimited.

A hindrance to using advanced video hardware is that software may not support it. It is quite difficult to design software that works with many video modes, and virtually no program supports all modes offered by the EGA or VGA. More and more, software is able to figure out for itself what video hardware is present. It then runs in the most advanced video mode that both it and the hardware are capable of. When installed, less-sophisticated software may require that you specify the video equipment you have. If you're not sure, turn off the machine, open it, and carefully remove the card connected to the video monitor (section 24.3 explains how to insert and remove expansion cards). The name of the video system should be written somewhere on the card.

PITFALLS

There are two common problems that you may encounter in early video systems, one with the CGA and one with the EGA. The CGA was designed for economy and, as a result, it is impossible for it to respond to software quickly without causing snow on the screen. Snow is a kind of interference during which the screen briefly appears to be filled with hundreds of dots (snow). It is extremely annoying and may make software virtually unusable. There are ways that some software can avoid snow, but only by making screen operations painfully slow.

As mentioned above, all CGA screen modes are supported by both the EGA and VGA (or MCGA). These more advanced systems don't cause snow. Increasingly, software authors have simply given up on the CGA. They'll write software for CGA modes with no protection against snow. The result is high-performance on an EGA or VGA, but misery on a real CGA. When you encounter this problem, there is really nothing helpful to do except to replace the CGA with a more advanced card. Occasionally you may encounter software that allows you to specify whether or not to protect against snow. If you are not sure if your video card has a snow problem, try running the software without snow protection. You will be rewarded with higher performance if it works.

A second problem has to do with a design flaw in the EGA. It is not possible for software to find out what graphics mode an EGA is operating in. When a memory-resident program is brought into action, it opens a window on the screen to communicate with you. If it can't determine the screen mode, it can't figure out how to properly save the information on the screen that it overwrites. Consequently, when you exit from the memory-resident program, it may improperly restore the former screen image of the application program from within which it was opened. Again, there is no general solution to the problem. It is one more reason to invest in a VGA adapter.

12.4 Working with a math coprocessor

A math coprocessor is a special chip that lets a computer process some kinds of mathematical calculations much more quickly, often by a factor of 50 or more. Nearly all PCs have an empty socket in which the optional coprocessor chip is inserted. The chips are not standard because not everyone needs one, and they can be expensive. Machines that use an 8088 microprocessor (such as an IBM XT) require an 8087 math co-processor. Similarly, machines using 80286 and 80386 microprocessors take 80287 and 80387 math chips (actually, a 386 machine can use either a 287 or 387 chip). The math coprocessing circuitry is built into the 80486 microprocessor, so there is no need for a separate chip.

The coprocessor chip must be rated fast enough to work with the main microprocessor. For example, an 80386 computer that runs at 25 megahertz needs a math coprocessor designed to run at this speed. The faster the coprocessor, the more expensive it is.

Performance gains   Math coprocessors boost performance when software spends much time processing numbers by multiplication and division or by using trigonometric and transcendental functions. These kinds of operations are common in scientific and financial calculations and in the production of complex graphics where the position of each point on the screen or printed page must be calculated.

A math coprocessor can perform operations in only a few steps that the computer's microprocessor requires dozens of steps to achieve; the coprocessor can also work with greater accuracy in decimal calculations. Calculations comprising mostly additions and subtractions usually benefit little from a math coprocessor. Performance gains of 50 times or more do not occur continuously. A typical spreadsheet recalculation would not be accelerated by nearly so much. The only way to find out the actual performance gain is by trying it for yourself.

Installation   A coprocessor chip is easy to install. You merely insert it into its socket. Instructions accompanying the chip tell which way to place the chip in the socket, so there should be no danger of installing it backwards. But, if you have never handled chips before, you could bend one of its pins or, worse, expose it to static electricity, so be careful. On PC- or XT-style machines, you must inform the computer of the chip's presence by turning off switch 2 of dip switch bank 1 (the only dip switch bank in an XT). AT-style and PS/2 machines automatically sense the presence of the chip, so there is no need to reconfigure the computer. Once installed, plan on leaving the chip where it is. It is very easy to damage a chip when pulling it out. A math coprocessor cannot be shared between machines.

Software support   Not all software supports a math coprocessor. While the machine's microprocessor does the same things a coprocessor would, the coprocessor needs special instructions. Increasingly, the tools programmers use to build software automatically generate the instructions used by the coprocessor chips. When coprocessor support is included in a product, the maker usually advertises it. Sometimes you will see an expression like 80x87 support, meaning support of any co-processor chip, whether 8087, 80287, 80387, or the math circuitry on the 80486 chip. Software that supports one coprocessor chip supports them all. Programs that require a math coprocessor are rare.

Software that uses a math coprocessor can almost always sense that a coprocessor is present. On rare occasions you may need to manually reconfigure the software. Check the software's documentation to find out how this is done (look in the manual's index under configuration, coprocessor, and math).

12.5 Configuring software to your printer

When software sends text to a printer, it has much more to do than just output one character after another. It ensures that margins are correct and that the paper is forwarded periodically. It switches between special fonts and print styles like italics; it may need to draw graphics on the page as well. The software exerts this control by sending special codes to the printer. Unfortunately, except for the simplest documents, there is no universal code system that every printer uses. Printers have become even less standardized with the introduction of laser printers since laser printers require special languages (such as PostScript) as well as simple codes to draw fancy graphics and variably sized type.

The people who write software are engaged in an uphill battle to make their products work with as many printers as possible. Ideally, they would make full use of every feature offered by every printer. But, as a practical matter, they are forced to confine their efforts to features that are universal to all printers of a particular kind. For example, your printer may be able to create outline letters, while most printers cannot. Because few printers can print them, software authors are unlikely to let you use outline letters in their applications. In this way, an attractive capability of the printer ends up being worthless.

Printer drivers   Even when printers have the same capabilities, the way that the capabilities are controlled may differ substantially. Software may need to send different codes to the printer to perform the same actions, and may need to sequence the codes in different ways. To handle these differences, software writers usually create a number of printer drivers that accompany their programs. A printer driver converts general printer commands from the software into exact commands that the particular printer can understand.

Ordinarily, there is a unique printer driver for every printer the software supports. Each resides in its own file on one of the diskettes on which the software is distributed. An individual printer driver is usually only two or three kilobytes in size. Since some programs are shipped with more than 200 drivers, they cannot all be incorporated into the main program, because they would fill precious memory with superfluous code. Instead, the particular driver required for your printer is installed at the same time you install the program itself on the machine.

Printer driver installation   As section 12.1 explains, most software installation is handled by an Install program found on one of the distribution diskettes. It transfers the software to a hard disk, or rearranges it on diskettes for systems lacking a hard disk. During the installation process, the program is likely to ask you the type of printer attached to the machine, usually by presenting a list of all supported printers. Once the choice is made, the driver is automatically installed into the software. Alternatively, there may be a special configuration program for installing the driver separately from an Install program. The documentation will explain how it works. You'll need to know about this program if you change to a new printer and need to reconfigure the software to work with it.

Installing printers in Windows 3.1   To install a printer in Windows, choose the Print Manager from the Main window. After the Print Manager window opens, pull down its Options menu and choose Printer Setup. The dialog box shown in figure 12.1 will appear. Select a printer from the scrollable list at the bottom of the box and click on Install. You'll then encounter an Install Driver dialog box that will tell you which Windows distribution disk to place in drive A. Having done so, click on OK and wait for the printer driver to be installed. The selected printer will be listed in the Installed Printers box above, along with any others that have been selected. Software will let you specify which printer you want to use at the time you print. You can make any of the installed printers the default printer by selecting it and clicking on Set As Default Printer. Click on Close once you've finished.

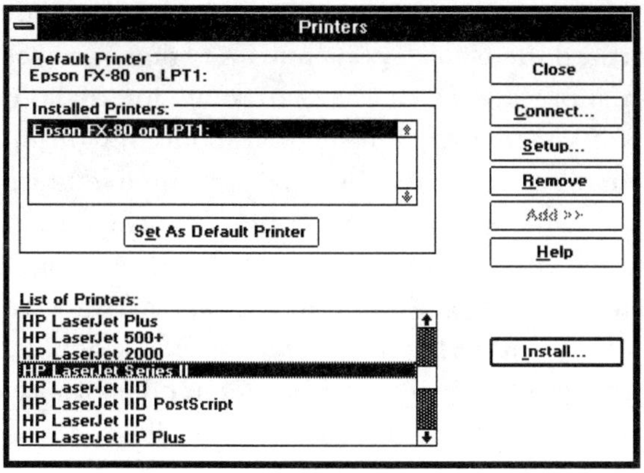

Figure 12.1

Other approaches to printer control   Some software confines itself to simple printer operations and may not come with a library of printer drivers. Instead, during installation the software reconfigures itself in small ways to handle the printer you specify. If your printer isn't supported, you may be prompted to type in specifications for the printer you have. For example, the software may need to know the codes that initiate and cancel italics printing. These codes are usually called escape sequences, since they consist of more than one character, with the first always being the escape character.

The printer's documentation ought to list the escape sequences the printer uses. Italics printing might be turned on by Esc-B and turned off by Esc-C. The software you configure will allow some way of entering these codes, usually by typing `Esc`-`B` and `Esc`-`C`. Sometimes the software requires code numbers, rather than characters, and you must type in the numeric equivalent of each character in the escape sequence. Esc is always 27, and B happens to be 66, so you would enter 27,66 in whatever way the software proscribes. Again, the documentation should provide you with the numbers you need to enter.

These days, configuration at this level is a rarity. But there is a little technical gobbledygook that you may need to deal with even if your printer is explicitly supported by the software you want to use. While running the software Install program, you may be asked for the following information:

- ◼ Line-feeds: The software installation or configuration program may ask, "Should the program add line-feed characters during printing?" If you answer yes, the software will issue a command for the printer to forward the paper by one line every time it makes a carriage return. Most printers can be set through internal dip switches (see Chapter 14 for more information about configuring printers) to automatically make the line-feed every time software orders a carriage return. Normally, this feature is turned off in printers, so the usual answer to the above question is yes. But, if the printer's auto-line-feed feature is turned on, the software should be instructed to withhold the line-feed; otherwise double-spacing occurs. Conversely, if neither the printer nor the software make the line-feed, the printer will print line after line without ever advancing the paper.

■ I/O ports: If the software asks whether you want to use operating system I/O (input/output), it is offering to let you send the printer output through some channel other than parallel port 1, which is also known as LPT1. By answering no, you'll be offered a selection of serial and parallel ports to choose for the printer output, depending on the hardware the software finds installed in your machine. The minitutorial at the beginning of Chapter 10 discusses ports and how serial and parallel ports differ.

■ Cut sheets: You may be asked whether the printer uses cut sheets—single pages of paper—or continuous paper. This tells the printer whether to stop after each page and wait for you to insert another page before continuing.

■ Default settings: You may be asked to input a number of default settings that determine how the printer operates when no specifications are given for the document you're printing. You might be asked for the default font, default line spacing, and so on.

If you have printer trouble after your software appears to have been properly configured, stop to consider whether the printer itself has been improperly configured. All printers have a number of dials, buttons, or switches that must be set properly before the printer can work with any software, including DOS. The surest way to test that the printer is working is to type ⃞PrtSc⃞ (or ⃞⇧⃞-⃞PrtSc⃞ on older keyboards) to print out an image of all that is written on the screen (laser printer owners may then need to press the form-feed button to have the page ejected). If nothing happens, set aside your concern with software configuration until the printer is properly communicating with the machine. See section 14.1 for more information.

Chapter 13
Configuring and Using a Modem

MINITUTORIAL:
Communications basics

Two computers can communicate across an ordinary phone line using a modem. Basically, all modems work in the same way, although some are placed in one of the computer's slots or are built into the machine (internal modems), while others reside in their own box that connects to a serial port at the back of the machine (external modems).

A modem cannot do anything until it is put under the control of communications software. You start the software like any other program, whereupon it takes control of the modem and follows your commands for sending and receiving information. This software can be purchased separately from the modem or may accompany the modem.

Both communicating computers must have a modem and software, but neither the modems nor the software need be identical. That's because nearly all modems and software adhere to certain standards that ensure that they can work together. Once a modem is installed (section 13.1) you probably won't need to deal with it again. But communication software is used again and again. At first sight this software can be intimidating because of all the jargon it uses—things like baud rates and parity bits. It's worth taking the trouble to understand these new terms, however, because once you do, you'll find that modem communication is not at all difficult. Moreover, a solid conceptual understanding will allow you to deal more effectively with modem problems and errors.

How data is transmitted   A modem sends data across a phone line by converting it into a series of sounds. At any moment, the modem either sends a high tone (corresponding to on) or a low tone (off). A byte of data consists of eight bits, each of which is either turned on or off. For example, the letter *B* consists of the bit pattern:

    ON-OFF-OFF-OFF-OFF-OFF-ON-OFF

A modem would communicate *B* by sending a corresponding pattern of highs and lows across the telephone line:

    HIGH-LOW-LOW-LOW-LOW-LOW-HIGH-LOW

While this principle is simple enough, in practice matters become much more complicated. The receiving modem encounters a continuous stream of HIGHs and LOWs. It needs to know how long the HIGH or LOW pulses will last. If the pulse period is 1/100th of a second and the receiving modem thinks information is coming its way at twice that rate using 1/200th of a second pulse, it will read a 1/100th-second pulse twice, and thus interpret one HIGH as being two HIGHS or one LOW as being two LOWs. Conversely, if the receiving modem expects 1/50th of a second pulse when the transmission rate is actually 1/100th, it will sample the line too slowly and miss every other pulse.

For this reason, the two communicating modems must operate at the same speed. The speed is measured in bits per second, or bps. Common speeds are 1200, 2400, and 9600 bps. At 1200 bits per second, the modem can transmit 1200 HIGHs or LOWs per second across the telephone line. This value is also sometimes (often incorrectly) referred to as the baud rate (pronounced "bawd"), thanks to a certain Monsieur Baudot who first formulated the concept.

Even when the modem speeds match, the receiving modem cannot easily decipher the stream of incoming data. Confronted with a steady stream of HIGHs and LOWs, it requires a frame of reference by which to know where each byte of data begins and ends. In addition, the modem needs some way of starting and stopping communications, and of dealing with momentary interruptions in data transmission.

Asynchronous communications   To deal with these concerns, most PC modems are designed for asynchronous operation. A synchronous modem would simply start up a flow of HIGHs and LOWs and treat every eighth pulse as the start of a new character. Asynchronous communications, on the other hand, are prepared for constant starts and stops. Rather than communicating a long sequence of bytes end to end, an asynchronous modem transmits and receives data one byte at a time, stops for a breather, and then prepares to start all over again on the next byte.

Figure 13.1 shows how the system works. Between sending bytes of data, the transmitting modem keeps the tone signal on the line HIGH. The receiving modem monitors the HIGH signal and waits. Then the sender suddenly drops to LOW to signal that the transmission of eight bits will begin with the next pulse. This initial LOW pulse is referred to as the start bit. The following eight pulses go HIGH and LOW to describe the bit pattern of the character being sent, and the receiving modem captures them and assembles them into a character of data. The communications program operating the modem takes the character and transfers it to memory, possibly writing it on the screen or to a disk file. Then the transmitting modem sets the line HIGH again until the next character is transmitted.

Once the line goes high, a minimum time must pass before the next character is transmitted. This time is typically one or two pulses, and these pulses are referred to as stop bits.

Parity checking   In addition, after the data bits and before the stop bits, an extra pulse is sometimes inserted for error checking. This bit is called the parity bit. When the transmitting modem sends a byte, it counts how many of the eight bits are ON. Using a scheme called even parity, the parity bit is itself turned ON when the sum of ON bits is even, otherwise OFF. In odd parity, the parity bit is turned ON when the sum of ON bits is odd.

In either case, when the receiving modem acquires a byte, it independently calculates the parity bit. It compares this calculation to the parity bit transmitted with the byte. If the two are not in accord, it means a transmission error has occurred. In many cases, this will cause the modem to issue a request to have the byte retransmitted. Parity checking can catch single-bit errors quite well, but double-bit errors—two bits wrong—will fly right by. For this and other reasons, parity checking leaves much to be desired as an error-checking scheme, which is why it has often been superseded by far more effective methods. But any modem supports this feature. The communications software you use will ask whether or not it is required. Figure 13.1 summarizes the various communications parameters.

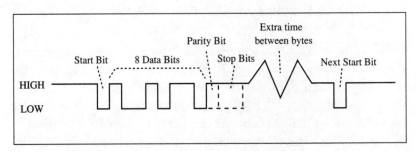

Figure 13.1

Communication protocols   In reality, communications software can apply the basic principles presented here in far more complicated schemes that can deal with frequent errors and constant changes in the direction of communication. Various codes are used by the modems to communicate which station is to transmit and which is to receive. When files are transferred, data is often transmitted in packets of bytes that end with error-checking codes much more elaborate than simple parity bits. Of course, both communicating computers must work in the same way at this level as well, and so standard systems of codes and procedures called protocols have been devised. Section 13.5 discusses the most popular of the PC protocols.

13.1 Configuring a modem

When you install a modem, it will either fit in a slot in the machine, or it will connect to a port in the back (ports are discussed in Chapter 10). Modems that connect to a port in the back always use a serial port. Because the port is already installed, no configuration is required. But when the modem is internal, it adds another serial port to the machine, and you must be certain that it is set to act as a different port than any other.

Serial ports are numbered as COM1, COM2, COM3, and COM4. Many internal modems built for PC XTs and PC ATs come configured as COM1. If an installed serial port already acts as COM1, either that port or the modem must be reconfigured. It's best to reconfigure the modem. Because PS/2 machines have a built-in serial port called COM1, PS/2 modems tend to be preconfigured as COM2. The configuration procedure varies from modem to modem. You'll need to consult the documentation to learn what to do. A modem may be configured by setting minute dip switches found on the modem. Alternatively, you may need to change jumpers, which are tiny boxes that fit over protruding pins to connect them. In either case, the documentation will tell you the location and proper settings. Modems designed for PS/2 Micro Channel machines will be assigned a port setting by the machine's configuration program.

Once the modem is installed, be sure that your communications software is directed to the proper port. If the modem has been configured as COM2, or connected to a serial port that acts as COM2, then the software must also be set to use COM2. The method for changing the setting varies from program to program and must be learned from the documentation. Be sure to save the setting in the program's self-configuration file so that it will be remembered in subsequent sessions.

13.2 Configuring communications software

When you start communications software, you'll need to specify certain settings (parameters) that will match the performance of the modem to that of the modem on the other end of the line. These settings are technical and can be intimidating at first sight. Read the minitutorial at the beginning of this chapter to acquire a general understanding of them. The communications program will probably offer default parameters—commonly used settings that will be employed if you specify no others. We'll discuss the basic parameters.

Setting the bits per second   As the minitutorial explains, the bits per second setting determines the speed of communication. The measure bits-per-second is abbreviated as bps. Today, 1200 bps and 2400 bps are the most common modem speeds, but the industry is moving toward 9600 bps as a standard. (The earliest PC modems worked at 300 bps.)

The number of bits required to send a character of data depends on various parameter settings, such as the number of stop bits, whether a parity bit is used or not, and so on. As a rule of thumb, count on 10 bits per character. Thus, a 1200 bps rate communicates roughly 120 characters per second. At 80 characters to a line, a full screen of text requires about 16 seconds at this pace. Half this time is required at 2400 bps.

Your communications software must be set to operate at the bits-per-second rate used by the computer you are calling. This information is usually published along with the telephone number of on-line services. When you are communicating with another microcomputer, you'll need to agree in advance on what speed to use. You also will need to hang up and start over if you dial up at the wrong speed unless you have a modem that can adjust automatically. A mismatched bits-per-second rate produces gobbledygook on the screen.

Setting the number of data bits   Generally speaking, one character of data requires one byte to hold it. Since a byte consists of eight bits, eight bits are sent across the telephone line to communicate one character. In this case, the modem is said to be using eight data bits.

However, normal English text uses only the first seven of the eight bits in a byte. Communication can be hastened by sending only seven bits across the line. So, communications software is often configured to use seven data bits. Again, the setting must match that used by the remote station.

Setting the number of stop bits   Stop bits mark the end of a character. The usual setting is 1; you may also encounter the values 0 and 2, and even 1 1/2 (the latter is possible because, in this application, a bit refers to a measure of time).

Setting parity   As the minitutorial explains, a parity bit may be added to the end of each byte of data communicated to test for transmission errors. The receiving modem tests the parity bit to see that the data was received correctly. This system is primitive and unreliable. Today, most communications software relies on much more elaborate coding systems to ensure faultless data transmission. For this reason, when communications software asks you to set the parity feature, the correct response is almost always no parity or none.

Setting the duplex mode   Normally, of the two communicating modems, one is set to full duplex mode and one to half duplex mode. This determines which computer is responsible for echoing the characters you type—that is, responsible for displaying the characters on your screen as you type them. The computer set to full duplex doesn't directly display the typing done on it. Rather, this computer waits for the remote computer to send back the typing as it receives it, and only then does the computer set to full duplex display the typing. Conversely, the computer set to half duplex displays characters as they are typed, and echos back characters received from the remote computer. Since most on-line services are set to half duplex, you should normally configure your software to full duplex.

The proper parameters vary between on-line services. If you have received documentation in the mail, consult it for the settings. Citations in newspapers or magazines of the telephone numbers of services invariably include these specifications. When you are transferring data between two PCs, call the person at the remote station and agree on the standards you will use. Once parameters have been entered, your communications program will most likely provide some way to save them to a disk file so that they'll be on hand next time you start the program. You should be able to link a set of parameters to the name of a service so that in the future you can select the service from a menu and have the parameters set automatically.

There is one more standard communication setting. You must configure the communications software to address the proper port (COM1, COM2, etc.) through which the modem relays data. See section 13.1 to learn how.

Windows 3.1   Windows includes a relatively simple communications program called Terminal. To configure the program, just click on the Terminal icon in Accessories. You'll see the dialog box shown in figure 13.2. Terminal assumes that COM1 will be a modem; if it isn't, all options will be disabled until the proper port has been selected. Then you can set the communications parameters as required. You'll find more information about Terminal later in this chapter.

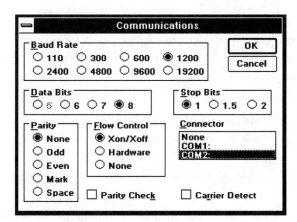

Figure 13.2

13.3 Operating a modem

A number of modem designs exist, each with its own special features, some of which are nearly indispensable, and others that are useful only in certain types of applications. Some features can be used only if a certain brand or type of modem operates at both ends of the line. Here is a sampling of some features:

■ Auto dial and auto answer: Nearly any modem possesses these abilities, which let it dial a number on its own, and answer the phone when the phone rings. Of course, the phone line must be connected to the modem. Most modems can dial using either tones (touch tones) or pulses (the older rotary system); a few modems can sense whether tone dialing is supported and adjust themselves automatically. Another useful feature is the ability to pause during dialing to await transfer to a long distance service or across a PBX.

■ Auto redial: When you can't get through on a phone line, an auto redial feature keeps trying at periods you specify. A few systems offer dial backup, in which the modem automatically redials if a connection is accidentally broken and then continues its transmissions.

■ Automatic speed adjustment and fall back: Some modems can sense the speed at which the remote system is operating. A few can even detect when line noise is too severe for efficient transmission and automatically fall back to a slower, more suitable transmission speed.

■ Voice/data switching: Some modems can be switched between voice and data transmission, allowing you to alternate between voice-telephone and computer. This feature must be present in the modems at both ends to be of use.

■ Data compression: Some modems automatically compress data as they transmit it, and uncompress data as they receive it. Since fewer bytes of data need to be transmitted, time is saved. This feature is only useful when supported by both modems. Data compression can be switched on and off.

■ Automatic hangup: Modems equipped with this feature automatically hang up when they lose contact with the modem with which they are communicating (in modem parlance, the modem loses the carrier signal). This can avert situations in which your modem sits idle, running up long-distance charges, with you unaware of the problem. Most modems have this feature.

Controlling a modem   Modems are mostly controlled by software. Some external modems offer a few switches to handle certain features, such as a change between voice and data transmission. But software must take command before these switches are of use. You can control your modem and communications software in much the same way you use other software: either by selecting commands from menus, or by typing one command after another on a command line. The menu approach is the easiest and is adequate for most jobs. Once communications parameters have been set (as explained in section 13.2), a single menu selection causes the software to carry out one command after another until the modem successfully connects with another.

Alternatively, working from a command line, you can type individual commands, telling the modem to wait for a dial tone or to hang up. A standard system of these commands is used by many modems and communications programs. Most of the commands begin with the letters AT followed by a single character and then ⏎. For example, ATA ⏎ sets the modem to answer mode so that it awaits a call from another modem. Additional characters act as modifiers to specify subcommands. Thus, while ATD1234567 ⏎ causes the modem to dial the phone number 123-4567, the addition of P in ATDP1234567 ⏎ makes the modem use pulse dialing, and the addition of T in ATDT1234567 ⏎ selects tone dialing. If your modem uses the Hayes AT standard—and most do—your modem documentation will contain a listing of all such codes, and your communications software will pass the codes you type on the command line to the modem.

Sometimes it's useful to monitor how the modem is performing. Most external modems have a number of indicator lights for this purpose. In addition, communications software displays status information in some way. Certain information is often labeled with established abbreviations, including the following:

- MR (modem ready): The modem is ready to send or receive data.

- CD (carrier detect): A signal has been detected from the remote modem.

- OH (off hook): The modem's telephone line is in use.

- RD (receiving data): The modem is receiving data.

- SD (sending data): The modem is transmitting data.

This sort of information is helpful in analyzing problems when the modem can't establish a connection, or when the connection breaks off prematurely. Still, for most users it is the quality of your communications software that determines whether or not you'll avoid problems.

Windows 3.1   Once the Windows Terminal program has been configured (as explained in section 13.2), you can specify modem commands by choosing Modem Commands from the Settings menu. You will see the dialog box shown in figure 13.3 with a Hayes-compatible modem as the default. Select one of the other standards or None if you need to enter the commands individually. Then click on OK.

To specify a phone number, choose Phone Number from the Settings menu. The dialog box in figure 13.4 is displayed. Normally, you need only type in a number and click on OK. Then choose Dial from the Phone menu to go on-line. See section 13.5 to learn about file transfers through the Terminal program.

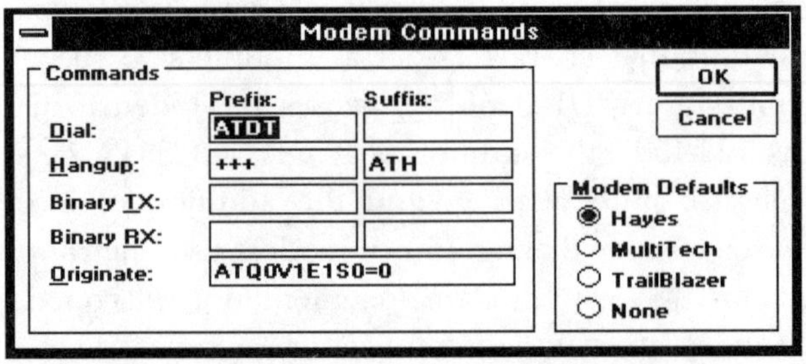

Figure 13.3

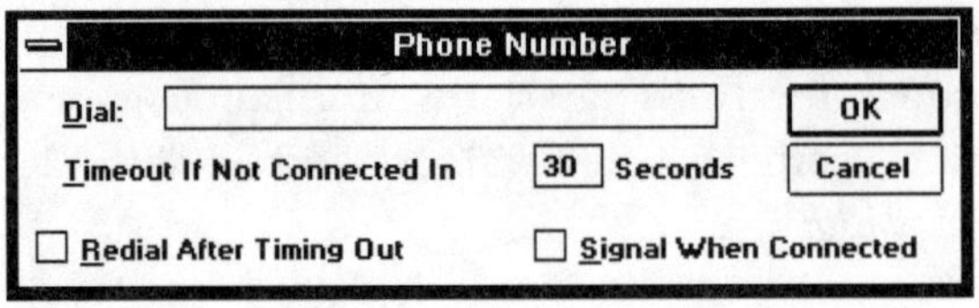

Figure 13.4

13.4 Going on-line

If you've read the entire chapter up to this point, you know enough to go on-line. Here is a summary of the steps to follow once you've physically connected the telephone line to the modem and started your communications program.

From documentation sent to you by on-line services or by prior agreement with individuals who you'll be communicating with, set the necessary communications parameters, including:

- The bits per second rate, usually 1200 or 2400.

- The number of data bits, usually seven or eight.

- The number of stop bits, usually one or two.

- Parity status, either no parity (the most common setting), even parity, or odd parity.

- The duplex setting, almost always full duplex.

- The port used by the modem, usually COM1 or COM2.

Have the modem dial the number by selecting the appropriate menu item or by directly controlling the modem from a command line by entering:

    ATDT1234567 ⏎

for the number 123-4567 using a touch-tone phone, or:

    ATDP1234567 ⏎

to dial the number if you're using a pulse-dial line.

Once a connection has been established to an on-line service, you'll be prompted to enter your registered name and the password you have been given. You'll then see the service's main menu and can proceed from there. Use the on-line help system for guidance. Alternatively, if you're connecting to another microcomputer, you can use the communications software features to transmit files. Each program works differently, so you'll want to begin by reading the communications software's documentation.

When you disconnect from an on-line service, be sure to do it via the proper quit command offered by the on-line service. Otherwise, on-line services may continue their connection with you even though you've hung up, and you'll be charged for that time. Many services will automatically disconnect if your modem accidentally hangs up.

13.5 Transferring files

Once you've gone on-line, you may wish to transfer files to or from the computer you are communicating with. Sending a file to another computer is called uploading; receiving a file is called downloading. The copy of the original file is read from a disk drive on one computer, sent across the phone line, and deposited on a disk drive in the receiving computer. All communications software can transfer files, but, as with any software, the exact commands used vary from program to program.

The simplest method of file transfer is sometimes called ASCII or text-file transfer. ASCII refers to an industry standard for coding ordinary text documents. An ASCII file transfer is one in which any document is treated like a text document, whether it is one or not (thus, program files or database files also could be transmitted). The text is transmitted character by character with little or no error-checking.

The communications programs that send and receive the file control the process by inserting special codes into the transmission to report that an error has occured, that transmission has finished, and so on. Unfortunately, some of these codes may happen to already reside in the file that is transmitted; when the receiving computer detects them, it treats them as if they were signals from the transmitting computer's communications software. The resulting errors won't hurt the original file, but they can make the transmission of some files by the ASCII text method impossible.

Communication protocols   Among their other functions, communications protocols are used to provide sophisticated error-checking for file transfers. A protocol is simply a method of transferring file data in blocks, with intercomputer messages inserted between the blocks at well-defined points so that they cannot be confused with data. The data is sent in packets (say, of 128 bytes) that end with a series of bytes that contain special error-checking codes. When noise on the phone line scrambles the data, this error-checking code is much more likely to catch the problem than a simple parity-checking scheme would (explained in the minitutorial at the beginning of this chapter) that might be used in ASCII file transfers. Good error-checking is essential for some kinds of data, because the existence of the errors may not otherwise be obvious. It's obvious when a text file—such as a letter—is faulty, since you can see it's filled with gobbledygook. But altered numeric data might still appear as numbers—they'll just be the wrong numbers. And, if you're transferring program files, good error-checking is absolutely essential because the smallest error can render a program unusable.

One other advantage of communications protocols is that they can speed up data transmission. By working in packet units, they can strip out the start and stop bits (discussed in the minitutorial) used in byte-by-byte transmissions. Some also may compress the data before it is sent, using special techniques that can pack, say, 1000 bytes of data into 800 bytes. Of course, the data must be uncompressed at the receiving end by a modem and communications software that has the exact same features as the sending modem.

TIP

Many compression utilities are available to make files smaller on disk to preserve disk space. Some kinds of files, particularly spreadsheet files, can be reduced to a fraction of their original size in this way. If you send a lot of files across the lines, you'll save on phone charges by transmitting them in compressed form. Of course, the receiving end must also have a copy of the compression utility so that the files can then be decompressed before use. (See section 20.3, Compressing files, for more information on this topic.)

Protocol differences   Protocols vary in how they handle data flow and error recovery. An important issue is how the protocol buffers data—that is how it manages the flow of data between modem messages. It is inefficient for a communications program to read some data from disk, then transmit it, then go back and wait for the disk again, and so on. Clever programming can allow the computer to simultaneously access the disk and send data across the telephone line.

A second issue is packet size. Generally speaking, the larger the data packet, the faster the transmission, since less time is wasted on the processing that goes on between the sending of packets. When errors occur, an entire packet must be retransmitted. Hence, large packets make for proportionately longer error recoveries; smaller packet sizes are better on noisy lines.

Two of the more common protocols are Xmodem and Kermit. Ymodem and Zmodem also are popular. There also are many proprietary protocols. They are devised by the manufacturers of particular modems or communications programs, and work only with their hardware or software. They are called proprietary because their internal specifications have not been made public, and thus can't be copied by others for inclusion into any communications program. Other protocols, like the Hayes protocol and Crosstalk protocol, were developed by particular manufacturers, but have been released for others to use. Other standards have their virtues in particular situations or applications.

Using protocols   Any major communications program will contain a number of protocols. Kermit and Xmodem are offered widely. When you dial up an on-line service and request a file transfer, you may be asked to specify the protocol you wish to use. Then you begin the file transfer using that protocol. There's no need to specify a protocol until the file transfer begins, since protocols are not ordinarily used while you exchange messages with the remote station. The exact steps to transferring a file depend on both the design of your communications software and the system used by the service or the computer to which you connect. Be sure to carefully read the documentation sent to you if you're using an on-line service. When problems arise, look for the remote system's help menu, which should provide detailed instruction. Failing that, call the service's technical support number. Endless experimentation will not necessarily bring you the desired results, and much time can be wasted trying to solve communications problems if you lack an adequate grasp of what's going on.

Windows 3.1   The Terminal program in Windows can transfer plain text files or binary files using either the Kermit or XModem/CRC protocols. For text files, you can begin by choosing Text Transfers from the Settings menu. You'll see the dialog box shown in figure 13.5, which lets you determine the method by which text is to be transferred. The default Standard Flow Control is usually the best method; the others are more appropriate when the telephone line is noisy. Text files may then be sent or received by choosing Send Text File or Receive Text File from the Transfers menu. This menu also offers View Text File for viewing files before or after their transmission.

For all three menu choices, you will see a dialog box like the one in figure 13.5. Files are listed on the left, with a directory tree on the right. You can change drives by clicking at the bottom right, and can narrow the directory listing by entering a specification at the bottom left. Once a file has been selected to send, or a subdirectory has been set to receive, click on OK to start the transfer.

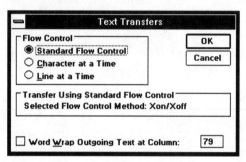

Figure 13.5

When transferring binary files, choose Binary Transfers from the Settings menu. You'll see the dialog box in figure 13.6. Select the desired protocol and click on OK and then choose Send Binary File or Receive Binary File from the Transfers menu. You'll then encounter dialog boxes like those for text file transfers, and can transmit or receive files in the same way.

Figure 13.6

13.6 Dealing with communications errors

Communications can go wrong in countless ways. Many kinds of errors are sensed and corrected by your communications software. But sometimes the software behaves as if everything is going correctly, even though data is not being transferred properly. These situations usually arise from faulty parameter settings. Here are the most common cases:

- Nothing but garbage appears on the screen. When the screen is filled with total nonsense, including graphic characters that would not normally be part of a text message, the likely culprit is a mismatch of the bits-per-second rate (discussed in the minitutorial at the beginning of the chapter). For instance, you may have set your communications software to operate the modem at 1200 bps (bits per second) when the station you have called is operating at 2400 bps. The software captures data, but groups it incorrectly, so that nonsense is generated. This error also occurs when the computers do not use the same number of data bits (for example, if one computer uses 7-bit data and one uses 8-bit data). Watch for odd spacing when this occurs.

- Partially garbled text appears on the screen. The two stations are probably using different parity settings.

- Your typing appears doubled on the screen. When outgoing text appears with every letter doubled, aass iinn tthhiiss eexxaammppllee, the problem is that both your modem and the remote modem are set to half duplex mode (explained in the minitutorial). Reconfigure your communications software for full duplex. If this doesn't solve the problem, look for a setting called local echo or just echo and make sure it is set to off.

- Your typing doesn't appear on the screen. In this case, both your modem and the remote modem are set to full duplex mode. Change your software to half duplex mode. If this doesn't work, look for the echo setting and make sure it is set to on.

- The communications software fails to find a dial tone. If the phone is properly connected to the modem, you probably have forgotten to specify the proper port as the modem port. See section 13.1 for details.

Chapter 14

Configuring and Using Printers

MINITUTORIAL:
All about printers

There are two basic kinds of printers: line printers and page printers. A line printer is one that prints out data line-by-line starting from the top of the page. Page printers, on the other hand, receive all data for an entire page before printing it. Dot-matrix printers and ink jet printers are line printers; laser printers are page printers. Despite the differences in their functioning and quality of output, in many respects these printers work in the same way. By default, they expect to receive a stream of text. Alternatively, software can program the printer to work in a graphics mode to draw graphics in various resolutions.

Software controls printers by sending special codes. For example, there are codes to set page margins or to specify that text should be written in bold face. There is no single system of codes that all printers follow. In fact, no single system is possible because printers vary greatly in their capabilities. However, printer designs have gradually coalesced around four systems of codes, or standards. They are:

- The Diablo standard: Named for the American company that developed it, this is the earliest and most primitive of the standards. It is oriented toward daisy-wheel printers. Its only graphics capability is in striking the page repeatedly with the period symbol. So much business software supports this standard that many printers provide an operating mode in which they emulate it.

- The Epson standard: This is the dot-matrix standard found in the printers offered by IBM for the first PCs. It was developed by a Japanese company, Epson, and its basic commands are found in most Japanese printers. Lots of bells and whistles have since been added to this standard. More printers support this standard than any other.

- The ISO standard: Formulated by the International Standards Organization, the ISO standard is essentially a superset of the Epson standard. Its advanced features include the ability to rotate and invert fonts, and to report certain kinds of information, such as font widths, to the program using the printer.

- The PCL standard: The PCL (Printer Command Language) standard was developed for the Hewlett-Packard LaserJet printers. This language is really nothing more than a system of simple codes like those used in line printers. The LaserJet printers normally operate as text-oriented page printers that can handle graphics on part of the page (or all of the page in some recent models).

Hewlett-Packard's LaserJet printers so dominate the IBM PC laser printer market that many programs support no other laser printer standard. Many manufacturers have cloned these printers, and even radically different laser printers, such as the Apple LaserWriter printers, provide LaserJet emulation modes. The LaserJet printers use a control language developed by Hewlett-Packard and called the Printer Control Language, or PCL. As the printers have evolved, so has PCL, and today there are three main levels (versions) of the language:

- PCL 3 is found in the earliest LaserJets, it does little more than print high-quality text and handle simple graphics.

- PCL 4 is used in the LaserJet Plus and the immensely successful LaserJet II printers. It adds support for downloaded fonts. More advanced models of the LaserJet II add a few extensions to this standard, such as the ability to choose paper trays. PCL4 is the de facto laser printer standard for PCs. It serves the vast majority of LaserJet printers in use.

- PCL 5 was introduced with the LaserJet III printers. PCL is radically revised in this version, with the addition of a powerful graphics language called HP-GL/2 that supports scalable fonts (fonts that can be drawn in nearly any point size).

Laser printers use two methods of writing text. In both cases, the printer keeps a dictionary of every character of every font it will use. When it needs to write an *A*, it looks up the form of that character and then prints it. In the simplest method, the actual pattern of the character (its bitmap) is stored in the dictionary. Fonts of this kind are called bitmap fonts. In the alternate, more advanced method, the shape of each character is stored as a mathematical formula that is used to generate the character. This system produces scalable fonts (also called outline fonts, since a character's outline is drawn according to a formula and then the outline is filled in). In the first case, characters can be printed only in those sizes for which there are bitmaps available. In the second, characters can be printed in virtually any size.

Software can print a font only when the printer is equipped with that font, either as a bitmap font or as a scalable font. All printers have a certain number of fonts built in—perhaps only one in a dot-matrix printer, but normally at least a dozen in a laser printer. These built in fonts are called printer fonts. Particularly in laser printers, additional fonts may be added by plugging in cartridges. These are called cartridge fonts. Finally, the data for even more fonts can be downloaded from the computer to the printer's internal memory. These are soft fonts which disappear when the printer is switched off. You acquire a soft font on disk, transfer it to your hard disk, and then use a downloading program to send it to the printer.

A printer can hold only as many soft fonts as it has room in memory. A printer's memory is also required for constructing graphic images, and so space is limited. In a small type size, a bitmapped soft font might require 16K. But larger type sizes require lots of memory. When asked to print a document requiring several soft fonts, a printer can be overwhelmed.

Scalable fonts take up much less space in a printer's memory. However, a printer that uses scalable fonts requires its own processor chip to construct each character. In essence, these printers are specialized computers themselves. But scalable fonts can also be used with laser printers that do not support them. This is managed by having the computer (rather than the printer) create a bitmap from a character's outline formula, and then having that bitmap sent to the printer as a soft font.

Fonts also come with files holding screen bitmaps that let software display the font on screen. Like printer bitmaps, you are limited to type sizes for which a screen bitmap is on hand. However, software may interpolate bitmaps to produce an approximate image of intermediate type sizes. This approach has been carried further with the TrueType scalable fonts issued with Windows 3.1. They generate high-quality bitmap images for screen and printer in any type size. Because both screen and printer bitmaps arise from the same source, you see on the screen exactly what will be printed (hence the name TrueType). Remember that having a font on screen does not mean that your printer is necessarily ready to print it. It is up to you to see to it that the font has been properly downloaded or installed in the printer if it is not a built-in printer font.

14.1 Configuring a printer to your computer

No kind of computer hardware varies so much as printers. There are many kinds in use—dot-matrix printers, daisy-wheel printers, ink jet printers, laser printers, plotters—offering a bewildering variety of features. Still, there is some degree of uniformity in printer design, as indeed there would have to be for a computer to be able to use them all. Certain brands of printers that have sold hundreds of thousands of units have become de facto standards; so, you may hear of the Epson standard, the Diablo standard, and the HP LaserJet standard.

Printer configuration can be a major source of headaches for computer users. It is important to have a clear grasp of what configuration means in this case. You need to both configure the printer to your computer so that the computer can communicate with it electronically and configure the printer to work together with individual programs. Nearly always, the printer is configured to the computer by setting switches on the printer itself. It is configured to software on a program-by-program basis during software installation. It is the former case that we are concerned with here (see section 12.5 about configuring software to printers).

Dip switches   Almost all printers have a variety of dials or buttons by which the printer is operated. Many also contain a hidden bank of minuscule switches (dip switches). The dip switches may be concealed behind a snap-open panel, or it may take a screwdriver to get at them. The switches are numbered, usually from zero upward, with each switch set to either on or off. They can be moved with the point of a pen.

The purpose of each switch is explained in the printer documentation. It varies with the printer and the features the printer offers. Some laser printers let you make similar settings by programming the printer through front-panel buttons. Here are some typical uses:

- Most printers offer a number of character sets which can be specified to suit the country in which the printer is being used. Dip switches control this setting.

- Various default modes for the printer may be set, such as the width of characters used. Software may override this default specification, but simple printer operations, such as when DOS is made to print information, will adhere to the default setting.

■ Some printers can adjust to more than one protocol. This means that, depending on the protocol the printer is set to, it will interpret incoming formatting codes and other information in accordance with that standard. In this way, a new laser printer can act like an older daisy-wheel printer, and thus use older software that does not support the laser printer's advanced features. Dip switches may control which standard is in effect.

■ Certain mechanical features may be set, such as how the printer deals with an out-of-paper condition, whether continuous feed paper is used, and so on.

■ The way the computer employs its internal memory is sometimes set through dip switches. You probably won't ever need to worry about making this setting.

■ A dip switch can determine whether the printer will automatically make a line-feed (advance the paper by one line) every time it makes a carriage-return, or whether it should be up to software to issue the line-feed command.

Normally, the printer dip switches are set at the factory for the typical computer system. Most people never need to touch them. But occasionally a program's documentation will tell you that the printer must be configured in a particular way. When this happens, you should be prepared to look at the printer documentation, find out about the location and assignments of the dip switches, and perform the necessary reconfiguration.

When a printer appears to malfunction, the problem is often caused by an incorrect dip switch setting. A common complaint is that a printer will make two line feeds for every line, creating double-spaced text. This error occurs because a dip switch is set to cause the printer to insert its own line-feed even though the software using the printer is doing the job itself. This is a good example of a situation where the configuration is actually set by both the software and the hardware. Either the printer or the software could be reconfigured to solve the problem. Since you have only one printer but will probably use many programs with it, you may need to check the programs' documentation to see whether a majority of the programs require the printer to provide its own line-feeds, or whether most supply a line-feed from the software. Then, change either the software or the printer settings, depending on which is less work for you. For example, if you use seven programs and only one has a line-feed requirement that the other programs do not have, it would be much less work to change the way that one program operates—if you can, that is—than to change the six other programs or the printer switches.

Front panel controls   Similar problems may arise when the printer has dials by which you can set the print width, spacing, and so on. These are useful when DOS prints out information without any control over formatting. But on some printers, the dial settings can interfere with the formatting commands sent to the printer by software. Again, it is advisable to maintain the printer with one series of settings and solve the problem with software.

The worst situation to find yourself in is where the problem you confront can only be solved by reconfiguring both the printer and the software using it. With several possible settings for each, there are many combinations to test. It's not uncommon to waste an entire day trying to get a printer to work properly.

When faced with this situation, the best approach is to try to reset the printer to the standard dip switch settings it was shipped with and then solve the problem through software reconfiguration. Many printer manuals list the factory settings for the dip switches. If you can't locate this information, call the manufacturer. You should always take this step when you acquire a used computer and configuration problems crop up.

Software configuration   When a printer operates correctly long enough to successfully print some words and lines and then goes completely wild, churning out gobbledygook, the problem is almost certainly not in the printer settings, but rather lies in the configuration of the software using the printer. Such errors can occur when the software does not correctly understand the system of formatting codes used by the printer. To learn more about this problem, see section 12.5.

Finally, you should be aware that certain nonstandard hardware is sometimes shipped with special software required for its use. This software is called a device driver. It provides a bridge between the way application software thinks a printer works and the way it actually does. Device drivers must be installed when the machine is booted. See the discussion in section 11.11 for details. It is unlikely that you'll need to install a device driver for a printer; if you do, the printer's installation documentation will tell you about it.

14.2 Configuring a serial printer

A printer is connected to the computer through either a serial port or a parallel port. A port is an electronic gateway between the machine and the outside world. From the user's point of view, it is nothing more than a socket at the back of the machine that a cable can be plugged into. The port sockets may reside on the back edges of expansion cards that have been inserted into the machine's slots, or they may be built into the machine itself. Thus, the number of serial and parallel ports available depends on the equipment you have installed.

Some video adapters provide a single parallel port, because this is the kind of port printers are usually connected to, and the kind of port toward which software normally directs its printer output. Older memory expansion cards also may include serial or parallel ports. Some add-in boards do nothing but provide extra ports. The machine counts the ports of each kind when it starts up and numbers them. Serial ports are labeled COM (for communication ports) and are named COM1, COM2, and so on. Similarly, parallel ports are labeled LPT (for line printer), and they are named LPT1, LPT2, etc. You can learn more about ports in the minitutorial at the beginning of Chapter 10.

Most printers are parallel printers, meaning that they use a parallel port. But some printers, notably laser printers, use serial ports, and accordingly are called serial printers. By default, most software directs printer output to LPT1. When you configure software to work with a serial printer (section 12.5), the software will see to it that output is directed to COM1, rather than LPT1. But sometimes the software fails to make this provision. The solution is simple. Just enter:

```
MODE COM1: 12,,,,p ⏎
MODE LPT1 = COM1 ⏎
```

Should the serial printer be connected to COM2, enter:

```
MODE COM2: 12,,,,p ⏎
MODE LPT1 = COM2 ⏎
```

The printer documentation may give instructions similar to these. For optimum performance, follow those instructions instead. It's usually a good idea to include these commands in your AUTOEXEC.BAT file so that the printer port will be automatically configured everytime you switch on the machine, but if your printer documentation gives you other directions, follow its instructions instead.

14.3 Switching between printers

If you have two printers connected to the machine, one hooked up to a parallel port and one to a serial port, you can direct output from your software to one or the other without changing the printer cables. Printer output is normally directed to parallel port 1, which is called LPT1 (or PRN) by DOS. Similarly, output to a serial printer is normally directed to serial port 1, which is COM1 (or AUX). You may use the DOS MODE command to redirect output from one port to the other. Serial ports must be initialized (prepared) before use. To initialize COM1 to the proper settings for most printers, enter:

```
MODE COM1: 12,,,,p ⏎
```

This command sets up the serial port for 1200 bits-per-second data transmission. Then type in another command to redirect printer output from LPT1 to COM1:

```
MODE LPT1 = COM1 ⏎
```

Later, to switch back to the parallel printer, enter:

```
MODE LPT1 ⏎
```

Be aware that these commands will not work if the software you use doesn't employ DOS as a channel of communications to the printer. Some programs directly control the parallel and serial ports, and they'll pay no attention to the MODE command. However, you'll find that many programs let you specify which printer port to send output to. When this feature is not available, you can recable the printers each time you need to switch between them, or can purchase a special printer switch that lets you do the job with the turn of a dial. Alternatively, certain printer-control utility software can do the job of switching between multiple parallel printers or multiple serial printers.

Microsoft Windows   In Windows, the Print Manager will let you direct output to any installed printer. Enter the Print Manager by choosing its icon in the Main group, then choose Printer Setup from the Options menu. You'll encounter a list of installed printers. Select the desired printer and click on the Set As Default Printer button below. This action is seldom necessary, however, because normally you can choose a printer from within Windows programs.

14.4 Operating a printer

The first step to using a dot-matrix printer or some other kind of line printer is to align the paper so that it is at the top-of-page position. This should be done before the printer is turned on. Of course, no such adjustment is required for printers that automatically feed single pages, such as laser printers. But printers that use continuous-feed paper are unable to tell what position on a page they are writing upon. It is only by aligning the paper properly that text and graphics will be correctly positioned.

The part of the printer that moves back and forth to do the writing is called the print head. Some printers have markings on or near the print head to mark the top of page position. You just turn the printer platen (roller) to bring the leading edge of the paper to this position. Other printers have no markings, and you must find the top-of-page position through experimentation. Even then, you may find that the best paper alignment varies from program to program, because each application formats a page differently, and because applications are designed to work with many printers and may not be perfectly optimized for yours.

Once the paper is positioned properly, turn on the power switch. Printers vary greatly in how they act when this is done. Some hardly make a sound; others shuttle back and forth to test the equipment; some laser printers print out a sample page to show that everything is working well. Once this process is complete, the printer is said to be initialized. It is ready to receive data from the computer; there are generally no buttons or dials on the printer that you need to adjust before printing begins.

With the exception of laser printers, virtually all printers have three control buttons: the Select button, the Line Feed (LF) button, and the Form Feed (FF) button. The Select button determines whether the printer is on-line, that is, whether it is ready to receive data from the computer and print it. When the printer is ready, it is said to be selected or on-line, and when it is not, it is deselected or off-line. Pushing the select button toggles the printer between the two states. Turning on the printer leaves it selected, pressing the select button deselects it, pressing it again selects it once more, and so on.

The reason the printer can be deselected—made not ready—is so that you can handle the printer paper without having the computer try to use the printer at the same time. Only when the printer is deselected can you use the other two buttons, the line-feed and form-feed buttons. These do exactly what they say: advance paper through the printer, either one line at a time or all the way to the top of the next page. To move the paper by part of a page, you can either press the line feed button repeatedly, or you can simply turn the platen. (Note that some printers won't let you turn the platen when power is on, or they will require you to push a button as you make the turn. Never force it.)

Remember that turning the platen will throw the paper out of alignment, so that a form-feed will no longer take the paper to the top of a new page. You can reset the paper at any time by realigning a page to the top of page position, turning the printer off for a few seconds, and then turning it back on. (Some printers can be reset without actually turning it on and off, either through a special reset button, or by pushing some combination of the three basic buttons—check the documentation for your printer.)

It's worth understanding what happens when you reset a printer. All printers have some internal memory called a buffer that holds data between the time it is received and the moment it is printed. Some printers have buffers that store only a few dozen characters; others can hold many pages of text. When you press the select button to deselect the printer, the information stored in the buffer is preserved. When you strike select again to reselect the printer, the printer continues printing the buffer contents, if any. For this reason, when the printer goes haywire, it's not enough to just deselect the printer and then reselect it. You must reset it (turn it on and off) to clear the buffer.

Most printers beep when they run out of paper. Well-designed software can detect that the printer has run out of paper, and it may display a message on the screen to inform you. After you have introduced more paper, laser printers can normally continue with the job at hand. But many continuous-feed printers lose track of where they are and require you to start the print job over. Again, it may be the quality of the software you employ that makes the difference.

Some printers present a variety of dials for making certain settings, like character width or line spacing. These controls can be useful when you are printing data that is not formatted in any special way. Any printing performed by DOS commands is of this kind. Usually, software takes complete control of the printer. If the printer is well designed, the control settings should have no effect on the software's formatting. If the controls do have an effect, you will need to experiment to find settings that give good results.

Finally, you should be aware that most printers contain hidden switches (dip switches) that are used to configure the printer. These play a variety of roles. They may cause the printer to adhere to a particular printer protocol, causing it to interpret formatting information according to one of several industry-wide standards. Or the switches may be changed to control a variety of printer features. Most computer users never have to touch these switches, because the factory settings are adequate in most cases. Laser printer owners may find that, in place of dip switches, printer features may be programmed using push-button switches on the front panel. Read section 14.1 to learn about configuring the printer to the computer and section 12.5 about configuring software to the printer.

Using an HP LaserJet printer   HP LaserJet printers have a control panel that includes a number of buttons and a liquid crystal display readout. Among the buttons are the On Line and Form Feed buttons found on-line printers. There is also a Continue/Reset button. Pressing it causes the printer to resume printing after it has been taken off-line for some reason, such as to change the paper tray. This button will reinitialize the printer if it is held down for several seconds (the display will indicate when the reset occurs).

Another button on a LaserJet control panel is marked Print Fonts/Test. Pressing this button when the printer is off-line makes the printer generate a sample page of all internal fonts. Holding the button for several seconds causes the printer to perform a self test in which it issues a page containing text in various sizes and some graphics.

Finally, settings for the default font, point size and pitch, paper size and orientation, and other features can be set through the menu system. Normally, these things are specified within applications programs which send the settings to the printer as the are required. Generally you'll only need to use the menuing system when you dump plain, unformated text to the printer. Even in this case, the default settings

(12 point Courier) ought to do the job. Selections are made by pressing the Menu to cycle through the various options, each of which is displayed in turn. Then press the ⊞ or ⊟ keys to increment or decrement the value assigned to the option, such as the point size or font number. Once the proper setting is in view, press the Enter button to put it into effect.

Downloading fonts to an HP LaserJet printer   There are various font installer programs available. They differ in how they work, but they are easy to use. Microsoft Windows can also install fonts. Enter the Print Manager by selecting its icon in the Main group. Then choose Printer Setup from the Options menu. The Printers' dialog box will appear, offering a list of installed printers. Select the printer you want to install fonts to, and then click on the Setup button. In the next dialog box that appears, click on the Fonts button; the Font Installer window then appears. It reports fonts currently installed in the printer and lets you add new ones. This feature is available only for PCL (HP LaserJet-compatible) printers.

All installed fonts are listed in the Fonts dialog box that appears when you choose the Fonts icon in the Control Panel. Screen fonts for the fonts built into your printer are installed when you install the printer driver for the printer. The screen fonts for cartridge fonts or soft fonts are installed by software that accompanies these fonts. When no installation software is available, you can use the Font dialog box to install additional fonts, including TrueType outline fonts. Just click on the Add button. An Add Fonts dialog box will appear. It offers a Drives list in which you can select the drive and directory containing the fonts you wish to add. A list of new fonts appears in the List Of Fonts box. Select the individual fonts you want, or click on the Select All button. Then click on Ok. Fonts are removed by selecting them in the Fonts dialog box and clicking on the Remove button.

Be aware that TrueType fonts take up additional memory. You may want to disable them when they are not in use. This is done by clicking on the TrueType button in the Fonts dialog box. Another dialog box appears and offers a check box for making this setting. It also lets you specify that only TrueType fonts be used in applications. If you select this option, no other fonts will appear in font lists in your applications. You are saved the trouble of remembering which type sizes are available in non-TrueType fonts. You can work freely in your applications knowing that everything you do will be rendered in high-quality type.

14.5 Printing files

Normally, files are printed by the program that creates them. If you have created a file with your word processor, you print it by starting up the word processor, loading the file, and using the program's Print command. However, there may be occasions when you want to print a file without using an application program. For example, you might find an unidentified text file on a diskette and want a printout. You could probably load the file into your word processor and print it, but it may be easier to have DOS do the job. To print a text-only file named WHATSIT.TXT, you'd type:

```
COPY WHATSIT.TXT LPT1 ⏎
```

or:

```
PRINT WHATSIT.TXT ⏎
```

The COPY command works by sending a copy of WHATSIT.TXT to a printer instead of to a new disk file. The expression LPT1 at the end of the command specifies that the data will be sent to the first parallel port—the one most printers are connected to. You could instead write PRN for exactly the same effect, or LPT2 if the target printer is hooked up to a second parallel port. Similarly, you may write COM1 in place of LPT1 if the printer is hooked up to serial port 1. However, the serial port must first be prepared for use in this case. See section 14.2 to learn how.

The PRINT command works differently, since it sets up a print spooler in memory to print one or more files in the background while you perform other work on the machine. This command is discussed in more detail in section 14.5. As the example shows, the command does not usually require a specification of which printer port to use. Rather, the port is specified only the first time the command is used by adding a /D switch. One way to set the port is to execute an initial PRINT command that does not print a file:

```
PRINT /D:LPT1 ⏎
```

Alternatively, add the /D switch the first time you use the command to print a file:

```
PRINT /D:LPT1 WHATSIT.TXT ⏎
```

You will be prompted to name a port if you leave out the /D switch the first time PRINT is used. Note that PRINT (unlike COPY) is an external DOS command, meaning that it is kept in a separate file apart from the main DOS program COMMAND.COM. When the file PRINT.COM is not in the current directory, you must begin PRINT commands with a path to the subdirectory that holds this file, as in:

```
C:\DOS\PRINT /D:LPT1 WHATSIT.TXT ⏎
```

Alternatively, list the subdirectory holding the file (in this case, C:\DOS) in a PATH statement (section 8.1) so that DOS can find it automatically.

COPY and PRINT can be used this way only to print simple text files. Spreadsheet files, database files, and the like are out of bounds. The commands also cannot print text files that contain formatting codes. These are special characters that word processors introduce into files to control features such as typefaces, margins, and so on. You can tell whether a file contains formatting codes by having DOS display it with the TYPE command (section 2.6). When the displayed text contains extra characters, or appears in odd ways, formatting codes are present. Another sign of formatting codes is that the computer may beep as it displays the file (press Ctrl-Break to stop the display).

On the other hand, some programs include formatting using ordinary characters. For example, a program might italicize the word *heaven's* in for heaven's sake by having you write:

```
for @italics(heaven's) sake
```

Since all of the characters are ordinary text, DOS will have no trouble printing out files formatted in this way. But the printout would contain no italics; instead, the text would appear exactly as it does on the screen.

Word processors that employ special formatting characters each have their own system. When a program prints a file, it converts the codes into the instructions required by the particular printer in use. DOS, on the other hand, simply sends the codes to the printer as if they were part of the text. The printer becomes confused and prints out random characters; it may interpret certain codes in the wrong manner and begin formatting the text in bizarre ways; or the printer may run wild, beeping and spewing out paper.

No harm is done to your equipment or files when such mistakes occur. However, you may have difficulty regaining control of the machine and the printer. The proper way to deal with an out-of-control printer is first to strike Ctrl-Break to stop DOS from transmitting data. Once the DOS prompt returns to the screen, turn off the printer, wait a few seconds, and then turn it back on. Don't deselect the printer using one of the buttons on the printer case. Although it has stopped moving, the printer will continue to hold characters DOS has sent to it, and it will again run amuck when you strike the select button a second time. The printer must be reinitialized to regain control of it; turning it off and on is the easiest way of accomplishing this. (Many printers can be reinitialized by using the printer control buttons; consult your printer documentation to learn whether this is an option.)

Another disadvantage of using DOS to print files is that it does not insert page breaks into the text. If your printer uses continuous-feed paper, a lengthy text document is printed in a long scroll. Text may fall on top of the crease where the paper is torn apart. Sometimes you can get around this problem by setting dials on the printer to force automatic page breaks. But not all printers have this capability. Note that PRINT advances the printer paper to its top of form position when it finishes printing a file; COPY just stops mid-page.

Generally, DOS is best used for printing single-page files for quick reference. The COPY and PRINT commands offer a convenient way of printing system files, including CONFIG.SYS, AUTOEXEC.BAT, and other batch files. Any other kind of file is best printed out by the software that created it so that it may be properly formatted. (See section 14.5 to learn a trick by which COPY or PRINT can be used for formatted text.) There also are utility programs that can print simple text files and format them to a limited extent. For example, the LP (Line Print) program in The Norton Utilities lets you set page margins and line spacing, and lets you add page headers, page numbers, and so on. But this kind of utility cannot interpret formatting codes that are kept within the text to mark italicized words, alternate fonts, and so on.

Microsoft Windows   When programs run under Windows, printing is performed normally through the program's Print command. Non-Windows programs use none of the printing facilities offered by Windows' Print Manager. However, Windows applications send print jobs to a print queue—a list of work that is currently being printed or is waiting to be printed. There are two kinds of queues, a local queue reporting on a printer connected directly to your machine, and a network queue that reports on printers connected via a local area network (LAN). The latter topic is discussed in section 19.2.

To view a printer queue, choose the Print Manager icon from the Main group. A dialog box that names the printer opens, tells what port (or network path) it operates through, and whether the printer is currently active. Below, you will find a description of each job in the queue, including its title, time it was submitted, and the percentage completed if printing is in progress. The print jobs are referred to as files since the data sent to the printer is stored in temporary files.

You can change the order or any file in the queue so long as the file is not currently printing. Simply drag the file's entry in the queue to the desired position. To delete files from the queue, select the file and then click on the Delete button at the top of the window. The queue can be cleared by choosing Exit from the View menu and then clicking on the OK button in the dialog box that appears asking for confirmation. The Print Manager window also offers Pause and Resume buttons for temporarily suspending printing.

14.6 Printing files while you work

Printers, particularly slow printers, can tie up the computer while software is printing documents. Printing takes time because it is a mechanical activity; the computer would be able to print much more quickly if only printers could move faster. When a computer prints data, it spends most of its time waiting for the printer to become ready for the next fragment of data. Only a small fraction of the computer's power is required by a typical dot-matrix printer.

This waste of time can be avoided by a process called spooling. Software called a print spooler is loaded into memory. The DOS prompt then reappears and you may begin work. When you have an application program print out a document, the spooler captures the entire document and sets it aside, either in memory or in a temporary disk file. From the program's perspective, it is as if the printer was operating at terrific speed, so that the software never needed to wait for it. In reality, the printer output has been placed in storage. The application program quickly announces that printing is complete, allowing you to go on working, or to quit the program and move on to another. Meanwhile, the spooler patiently prints out the document from the place where it has been stored, even as you are doing other work with the machine. So long as memory or disk space allows, you may queue several documents for the spooler to print.

This process is sometimes called printing in the background. The spooler operates by repeatedly taking over the computer for minuscule fractions of a second, during which it outputs more data to the printer. The entire process is invisible, and occurs so quickly that you don't realize that your software is being incessantly halted and restarted.

Many manufacturers offer spooling programs. A spooler is often included on the diskette that accompanies memory-expansion boards, since these boards provide the considerable memory that many spoolers require to handle large files. You can also buy special hardware print spoolers, which combine spooler functions with expansion memory in a box that is connected between the printer and the computer. Finally, some application programs include a built-in spooler.

The DOS PRINT command   A primitive print spooler is provided by the DOS PRINT command. Unlike sophisticated spoolers, it cannot directly intercept printer output from your application programs. Instead, it prints documents directly from files. Some limitations in its use are discussed below.

A simple text-only file named BIGIDEA.TXT could be printed in the background by entering:

> PRINT BIGIDEA.TXT ⏎

Use a directory path if BIGIDEA.TXT is not in the current directory:

> PRINT C:\PLANNING\BIGIDEA.TXT ⏎

You may queue several files by listing them all with a space between their names:

> PRINT BIGIDEA.TXT HUGEIDEA.TXT TINYIDEA.TXT ⏎

Or, you may use global file name characters (section 1.4) to name several related files:

> PRINT *.TXT ⏎

The first time you use PRINT after booting, you must specify to which printer port the output is to be directed. This may be done by inserting /D:LPT1 into the command, as in:

> PRINT /D:LPT1 BIGIDEA.TXT ⏎

In this case the first parallel port is specified. Use /D:LPT2 for a second parallel port, and /D:COM1 or /D:COM2 for the first or second serial ports. PRINT will prompt you if you forget to specify a port.

Be aware the PRINT is an external DOS command, meaning that it is kept it its own file that DOS must be able to find to get it running. When PRINT.COM is not in the current directory, either include a path to it in the command:

> C:\DOS\PRINT TINYIDEA.TXT ⏎

or set up a PATH command to find it, as explained in section 8.1.

Once the PRINT command has been executed, printing begins and continues until all specified files have been output. A form feed is inserted at the end of each file. Thereafter you may type in additional PRINT commands to add or remove files from the print queue. These commands don't need to include the /D: switch used in the first PRINT command. To add a file to the queue, follow it with a /P switch:

```
PRINT ZEROIDEA.TXT /P ⏎
```

To remove a file from the queue before it has started printing, or to stop it from printing once it has started, use /C (for cancel) instead:

```
PRINT HUGEIDEA.TXT /C ⏎
```

Finally, to clear the queue of all files and terminate printing, type:

```
PRINT /T ⏎
```

Restrictions of using PRINT   When files contain special formatting codes, PRINT cannot interpret the codes to format the document. Instead, it sends the codes to the printer as if they were additional text; often, the printer runs amuck and prints out nonsense. But you may be able to use PRINT to print your word processor documents in the background in spite of this limitation. Many word processors let you redirect printer output to a disk file. This means that the word processor interprets the formatting commands and converts them into the instructions the printer uses. But instead of sending the data to the printer, it dumps it into a disk file. Then PRINT can sometimes send the file to the printer where it will be perfectly formatted, exactly as if it were printed by the word processor itself.

Say that you have a text file named WHATELSE.TXT that you want printed in the background. You would ask your word processor to print it using the file-output option (assuming it has one). You might name the output file WHATELSE.PRN. Then the software would create the file in much less time than it takes to print it. Thereafter, at any time you could start the file printing by entering:

```
PRINT WHATELSE.PRN ⏎
```

Be aware that printer output files can sometimes become much larger than the text files they originate from. Also, remember that the output to the file is formatted for the particular printer that your word processor is currently configured for (see section 12.5 concerning printer configuration). If you create a printer output file and send it to a friend, you must be certain that he or she is using the same printer as you, or one of very similar design.

The PRINT command offers a number of complicated technical features for optimizing interactions between the machine and the printer. Your DOS manual lists these features, but they are not easily understood. If you will be doing a lot of printing in the background, it is much wiser to acquire a good spooling program rather than waste time toying with the limited capabilties of PRINT.

14.7 Echoing DOS messages to a printer

Early computers resembled teletype machines in certain respects. Everything typed in by the user, and every response from the machine was printed on a continuous sheet of paper. Although it is not very useful, this feature still lies hidden in IBM microcomputers. When it is enabled, the echo mode prints out anything written on the screen by DOS, including commands typed in. It does not output the information displayed by application programs. The echo mode is turned on by pressing Ctrl-PrtSc. Pressing the key combination again toggles the feature off.

The echo feature can be useful during a general housecleaning of your hard disk or floppies. It provides a paper trail of file movements and erasures, lest you forget what you have done. It also can be used to make hardcopy of directory listings and other DOS output. However, this sort of output is better achieved using redirection, in which you write >LPT1 at the end of a DOS command.

Pitfall

The best reason for knowing about the echo mode is that it can be accidentally activated through faulty typing. It is quite perplexing to suddenly have the printer start writing without your having issued a command for it to do so, and if the printer is switched off, you will encounter the error message, "Printer not ready," or perhaps a "Printer out of paper" message. Once this happens, the computer won't let you move on until the printer is turned on and the waiting output is printed. You can halt the output midway by typing Ctrl-Break. Then strike Ctrl-PrtSc to toggle the echo off.

People who don't know about this lurking demon often end up needlessly rebooting the computer. Make a mental note of this problem so that you can recognize it when it occurs.

14.8 Printing the screen image

It is easy to print out an exact copy of the screen contents. Simply type `Prt Sc` or, on older keyboards on which the `Prt Sc` key is also marked with an asterisk, type `⇧`-`Prt Sc`. Be sure the printer is turned on and selected first (see the minitutorial at the beginning of this chapter). If it is not, the print screen feature will not wait; you must turn on the printer and then press `Prt Sc` or `⇧`-`Prt Sc` again.

Printing a graphics screen   Print screen normally works only for screens displayed in a text mode, as opposed to a graphics mode. It's easy to become confused in this regard, since the screen may contain only text even when it is using a graphics mode. Because most software operates in a text mode, the simple `Prt Sc` or `⇧`-`Prt Sc` command usually does the job. When it doesn't, you must prepare DOS for printing out graphics screens by typing at the DOS prompt:

    GRAPHICS `←`

Since this is a DOS command, it must be used before starting up the application program from which you want to make screen shots. This feature is not made available automatically because it takes up a small amount of memory and there is no point in wasting memory on a seldom-used command.

Printers vary in their graphics capabilities; some can even print out color displays using `Prt Sc`. The GRAPHICS command optionally takes a parameter telling what kind of printer is connected to the machine, as in:

    GRAPHICS COLOR4 `←`

for a printer using a four-color ribbon. These parameters include COLOR1, COLOR4, COLOR8, COMPACT, GRAPHICS, and THERMAL. The parameters all refer to the operating characteristics of certain IBM-made printers. Because most people use non-IBM printers, some experimentation may be necessary to find out which setting is best (it's possible that none will work at all). When none is named, the GRAPHICS setting is in effect, and it corresponds to the popular IBM Personal Graphics Printers and Proprinters. Be aware that not all high-resolution graphics modes are supported; a nonstandard video system can make your printer run amuck, although no harm is done and the printer is easily reset by turning it off and back on.

The GRAPHICS command can also be customized to print in special ways. By appending /R to the end of the command, as in:

```
GRAPHICS /R ←
```

the printer will reverse the screen image, printing black where the display shows white, and vice versa. Since most displays show white letters on a black background, the usual printout is not true to life: it prints black letters on the white paper. The /R switch gives WYSIWYG (what you see is what you get) printing. Similarly, appending /B to the GRAPHICS command when it will be used with a color printer causes the printer to print the background color, rather than leave the background as unprinted white paper.

Be aware that the GRAPHICS command is an external command, meaning that is it held in a file named GRAPHICS.COM apart from the main DOS program that is always in memory. To use the command, this file needs to be in the current directory. Alternatively, add a directory path to the command to tell DOS where the file is located. For example:

```
C:\DOS\GRAPHICS ←
```

Or, list the directory that holds the file in a PATH command (section 8.1) so that DOS can find the file automatically.

Applications   The PrtSc feature is remarkably useful. When comparing data that cannot be brought to the screen at once, Print Screen lets you grab one part of the data so that it may be on hand after switching over to displaying other data to which it must be compared. Print Screen can also be used in a pinch for data recovery. If you have a file that has been corrupted in some way and cannot be copied or printed out in any way, your last resort may be to display segments of the data one after another and dump them on to the printer using ⌈PrtSc⌉ or ⌈⇧⌉-⌈PrtSc⌉. Then you can type the data into a new file. There usually is a better way to recover data, but when worst comes to worst, you will be glad to have Print Screen on hand.

Chapter 15

Managing Memory

- MINITUTORIAL: The three kinds of memory
- Finding out installed and available memory
- Configuring memory-expansion boards
- Using a RAM disk
- Using memory-resident programs
- Resolving conflicts between memory-resident programs
- Using memory management software

MINITUTORIAL:
The three kinds of memory

Don't confuse memory with the information held on diskettes and hard disks. Memory is an invisible realm to which information from disks and the keyboard is transferred. Data is held by memory chips, of which there are several kinds:

■ Random access memory (RAM): Most memory in your machine is RAM. This memory is empty when your machine starts up and is then filled with data. Data is read from disk storage, placed in RAM, modified by software, and later written back to the disk. Programs, which are also kept on disks, are loaded into RAM as well. To run a program means to load it into memory and turn control of the machine over to it. RAM may hold many things at once, including parts of DOS and Windows, permanently loaded utility programs, one or more application programs you are running, and data on which the programs operate. RAM is erased when the computer is turned off or rebooted.

■ Read-only memory: This kind of memory uses a different kind of memory chip, one that is preprogrammed with computer code that it continues to hold even when the machine is turned off. All computers have ROM chips that hold crucial parts of the operating system (the Basic Input-Output System, or BIOS, as it's called on IBM PCs). When the machine is booted, this software comes into action and, among other things, gives the machine the ability to read disk drives so that it can load the main DOS file, COMMAND.COM.

Read-only chips are relatively slow compared to RAM chips. This can be a considerable disadvantage because certain routines held in ROM may be executed many times, and that may mean that the chip is repeatedly accessed. For example, a ROM routine that writes single pixels on the screen may be called again and again to display an image. To make ROM code run faster, sometimes it is virtualized. This means that the code is copied into RAM which is then made to represent the same address range as the ROM. This device is called shadow RAM.

■ Flash memory: This is a special kind of RAM that does not lose its data when the machine is turned off. Banks of flash memory chips can be used as a kind of virtual disk drive. Files are stored in the chips in the same way that they are organized on disk, and DOS then stores and retrieves the files as if an actual disk were present. Because the device is entirely electronic, it works much more quickly than disk drives.

You will hear of three kinds of memory in IBM personal computers running DOS: conventional memory, extended memory, and expanded memory. The distinction between the three has nothing to do with the kind of memory chips used, but rather with the system by which the microprocessor at the heart of the computer communicates with memory chips. Here are the main differences:

■ Conventional memory: This is the main memory used by DOS. The quantity of any kind of memory is measured in kilobytes (K)—nominally 1,000 bytes, but actually 1,024. Originally, conventional memory was limited to 640K, but today matters have become more complicated.

A simple IBM XT-class machine uses a microprocessor, the 8088, that cannot create memory addresses higher than one megabyte. This range of addresses is referred to as the chip's address space. When DOS was designed, it was decided that only the lowest 640K of memory would be available for programs. The rest of the addresses are used for various purposes, such as mapping images onto the video display. This part of the address space stretching from 640K up to the 1 megabyte mark is referred to as the upper memory area. The lower 640K is the lower memory area. In addition, in later microprocessor designs it is possible to play a trick with memory addressing and gain an additional 64K of memory space above 1 megabyte. This is called the high memory area.

■ Extended memory: PCs using 286, 386, 486, and 586 processors can use a different memory addressing scheme to access much more memory—16 megabytes for 286 machines and a virtually unlimited amount for the others. When a machine uses this addressing scheme, it is said to be working in protected mode. By comparison, the original 1-megabyte scheme is referred to as real mode.

In protected mode, only memory above the 1-megabyte mark is accessed. However, DOS is a real-mode operating system and it must reside in conventional memory. Software can use both conventional and extended memory at once, but this must be done by constantly switching the microprocessor between real mode and protected mode. For example, a program can be run from extended memory, but whenever it needs to call on DOS, the machine must switch to real mode, have DOS do its work, and then switch back to protected mode to return control to the program.

To make matters even more complicated, a versatile memory management feature called paging is found on 32-bit processors (386, 486, and 586 chips). In this scheme, any 4K stretch of memory (a page) can be assigned any range of addresses. Memory that physically starts at the 2-megabyte mark can be made to appear as if it starts at the 1-megabyte mark or the 256K mark. What's more, the same addresses may be assigned to different blocks of memory. This feature provides the basis for virtual 86 mode in which the processor divides extended memory into a number of blocks, each of which appears as a separate instance of conventional memory. Real-mode applications may be multitasked, with one allocated to each memory block. From the application's point of view, it is merely running by itself in conventional memory, with all of conventional memory allocated to it.

Paging can also be used to fill in the upper memory and high memory areas above the 640K usually devoted to conventional memory. The low end of this range is normally occupied by video memory, and the high end of upper memory is filled by ROM chips. Areas between may hold ROMs for disk drives, networks, and other devices. Between, large blocks may go unused. A 386, 486, or 586 machine can reassign some extended memory pages, so that they fill these blocks with usable memory addresses. Then, with proper memory-management software, the blocks can be occupied by device drives, memory resident programs, or whatever, that would otherwise take up space below the 640K mark. Although the blocks are outside 640K, they are still within conventional memory, and so can be reached by a processor running in real mode.

■ Expanded memory: This kind of memory is a system for giving more memory to programs that run under DOS and are ordinarily confined to 640K. Software must be specially designed to use it (such software is said to support expanded memory). Expanded memory allows you to work with very large files, such as giant spreadsheets. In addition, operating environments like Windows and DESQview can use expanded memory to keep several large programs in memory at once and let you shuttle back and forth between them. Up to 32 megabytes of memory may be added to a PC XT or 286 machine in this way, and a virtually unlimited amount can be used in 386 and 486 machines. Note that expanded memory slows down software somewhat; the degree to which it slows depends on how the software is designed. Expanded memory also goes by the name Expanded Memory Specification, or EMS. The standard was invented by three companies—Lotus, Intel, and Microsoft—and so you will also hear of the LIM standard.

Expanded memory makes use of the fact that certain ranges of addresses in the upper memory area go unused. Expanded memory reserves a 64K block of addresses through which it presents 64K of memory that the processor can read and write. Through various means, the microprocessor can instruct the memory hardware to show a different 64K block at the same position. In this way, pages of memory are swapped in and out of the same address range. It's up to the software to keep track of which page is in view and which data is on which page. The page swapping can be slow on older hardware. For this reason, performance may lag when the processor must process widely dispersed data.

Today there are actually two expanded memory standards. In the more recent and more technically advanced LIM 4.0 standard, expanded memory does not require a continuous 64K block in memory, as it does in LIM versions 3.2 and earlier. Instead, it can use a varying number of 16K blocks located in different memory positions. This system makes installation more complicated but more flexible. Not all software written for the earlier standard works with LIM 4.0. And because not many machines possess the more modern LIM 4.0 hardware, software may not use its advanced features in order to remain compatible with earlier expanded memory boards. LIM 4.0 includes elements of a second earlier standard, the Enhanced Expanded Memory Specification (EEMS), which has not achieved widespread popularity. Some people (incorrectly) use the term EEMS when referring to LIM 4.0.

Because 386, 486, and 586 machines can page extended memory (as described above), these computers can easily emulate expanded memory using extended memory. So, while expanded memory requires special hardware in 8088 and 286 machines, it is done entirely through software in more advanced computers. Actually, it is much more efficient for these computers to store data as extended rather than expanded memory. They may use expanded memory only because software has not yet been updated to use extended memory.

Memory expansion boards   Many add-in memory boards can be set up to act as conventional memory, as extended memory, as expanded memory, or as a combination of two or three. Once your system is equipped with 640K of conventional memory, no more can be added of this kind. Whether the remainder should be allocated to extended memory, expanded memory, or both, depends on the software you are using. Extended memory is generally more useful. In PC/XT-class machines the microprocessor cannot access extended memory, and so expanded memory is the only choice. Conversely, 386 and 486 machines emulate expanded memory in extended memory and do not require expanded memory hardware. Only on 286 machines must you decide how to divide a memory expansion board between extended memory and expanded memory.

If you have extended or expanded memory, put it to good use. DOS is increasingly able to use these kinds of memory for its commands. This is particularly true of DOS 5.0, in which the main DOS program can be moved to the high memory area, and in which various DOS memory requirements, such as for DOS buffers, can be directed toward expanded or extended memory.

The complexity of the PC memory system can lead to all sorts of exasperating software conflicts. A genre of utility software called memory managers have been devised to overcome these problems. The last section of this chapter is devoted to this topic.

15.1 Finding out installed and available memory

It's worth knowing how to find out how much memory is available in a computer so that you can diagnose problems and make judgements in configuring the machine. Available memory can mean two things. First, there is the absolute quantity of memory, set by the number and size of memory chips in the computer. Most PCs are equipped with 640K (kilobytes, or thousands of bytes) of conventional memory, which is the maximum that DOS can use directly. Second, there is the amount of conventional memory left over after DOS has been booted and various memory-resident programs have loaded.

The CHKDSK (Check Disk) command tells how much conventional memory is available. Just enter:

    CHKDSK ⏎

to obtain a listing of information about the current drive, or:

    CHKDSK B: ⏎

to obtain information about some other drive (in this case, drive B). After analyzing the drive, CHKDSK displays several lines of information. The last two lines of this information refer not to the drive, but to conventional memory. Here is a typical reading:

    655360 bytes total memory
    456608 bytes free

The first line tells how much conventional memory is installed; the second reports how much is free for your programs. The difference between the two figures reflects the memory taken up by DOS and other memory-resident software.

DOS version 4.0 introduced the MEM command for quickly determining available memory. It provides the same information about conventional memory that CHKDSK does, but includes a third line telling the file size of the largest application program that can be run. MEM also reports the quantity of extended memory it finds, and the quantity of expanded memory as well—provided that an expanded memory device driver was loaded when the machine was booted. To use MEM, simply enter:

    MEM ⏎

By adding the switch /PROGRAM or /DEBUG, MEM can be made to generate a detailed listing of memory usage that is useful, but difficult to decode without a technical background. The /DEBUG version is cryptic to the nonprogrammer.

TIP

You may sometimes find that the amount of memory available for application programs is not as great as you expected. Perhaps you tallied the size of the main DOS file, COMMAND.COM, and of the memory-resident programs you loaded, subtracting the total from the amount of memory installed. Be aware that any program can allocate memory to itself when it is run and keep that memory to itself. DOS, for example, sets aside DOS buffers (see section 11.3), which can easily take up 10K of memory. DOS also sets aside small blocks of memory for controlling each disk drive, managing files it has opened, and so on. Memory-resident programs may allocate quite large work areas to themselves because they may not be able to obtain necessary memory when they are awakened while an application program is running. Many memory-resident programs will let you set the size of the work area during loading. The size you set will determine how large a file you can load into your memory-resident text editor, and so on.

15.2 Configuring memory expansion boards

A memory expansion board is a circuit board inserted into one of the computer's slots in order to expand the amount of memory available to your programs. Many memory expansion boards can be configured to provide varying amounts of two or three of the three kinds of memory used in IBM PCs. See the minitutorial at the start of this chapter if you don't know about the three kinds of memory.

When you configure a memory expansion board, you must not only specify which kind or kinds of memory the board is to provide, but also must set the starting address of each kind of memory. To understand what a starting address is, you need to know that memory is arranged as a sequence of addresses counted from 0 upwards, with one byte (one character) at each address. Say that you have an IBM AT with 512K of RAM installed. Roughly speaking, memory addresses 0 through 512,000 are already filled in this machine. If you want to add an additional 128K to bring conventional memory up to a full 640K, you would need to specify that the starting address of the 128K of additional memory is the first byte followng the 512,000 memory addresses already used. Similarly, when expanded memory is first installed, you would need to specify the starting address in high memory where the 64K window used by expanded memory will be located. Because extended memory resides above the first megabyte of memory addresses, its starting addresses are always numbers greater than one million.

Switches and jumpers   Memory expansion boards are customized either by using dip switches or jumpers, which are mounted on the board surface. Dip switches are banks of very tiny switches that are set to either an on or off position. They are too small to get at with your fingers; use the tip of a pen. Jumpers are more primitive. They consist of a tiny removable box that fits over two spikes protruding roughly a quarter of an inch from the board. The jumper connects the pins, thus acting as an on switch. The jumper box can be removed and reinserted over just one spike to break the connection (you should never remove the little boxes from the board, because they are easily lost). Occasionally three spikes are found in parallel, and the box can be fit over either of the two adjacent pairs, or to the side, making for three possible settings.

The documentation that accompanies the memory expansion board will tell you where to look on the board for dip switches or jumpers. Often, an identifying code is printed on the board just beside the switches or jumpers. There is no need to understand what the individual switches or jumpers do—just follow the instructions.

Hexadecimal numbers   Addresses are expressed in hexadecimal numbers. These are base-16 numbers, which means that, instead of counting from 0 to 9 and then carrying 1 to the ten's place to make a second column of digits (7...8...9...10), you count all the way to 15 before carrying. Since ordinary numerals stop with the 9, the series is extended with the letters A through F, with A representing 10, B as 11, and F as 15 (9...A...B...C...D...E...F...10). There is no need for you to learn to count in this system, but you should be accustomed to numbers that contain alphabetic characters, such as 9EA6, if you are going to be configuring memory boards. To distinguish hexadecimal numbers, they are usually written with a trailing x or h, as in 9EA6x. Because memory is often regarded in 64K blocks, the following list is useful for finding the hexadecimal starting address for each 64K segment:

64K Block Number	Total Memory	Starting Address (Hex)
Block 1	64K	0000
Block 2	128K	1000
Block 3	192K	2000
Block 4	256K	3000
Block 5	320K	4000
Block 6	384K	5000
Block 7	448K	6000
Block 8	512K	7000
BLock 9	576K	8000
Block 10	640K	9000
Block 11	704K	A000
Block 12	768K	B000
Block 13	832K	C000
Block 14	896K	D000
Block 15	960K	E000
Block 16	1024K (1 MB)	F000

If you were to add 128K to 512K (512K equals eight 64K blocks) of conventional memory already installed, the starting address would be 8000 since that is the starting address of the ninth 64K block of memory.

Positioning expanded memory   When installing expanded memory, you need to find an unused 64K segment of memory addresses in high memory—that is, above the 640K allowed to conventional memory. The highest 64K block, at F000, is at least partially occupied by read-only memory chips (the ROM BIOS), and so it should be avoided (read-only memory chips take up address space just like ordinary erasable memory chips). Usually, the address E000 is ideal for expanded memory. But problems may arise in computers that are networked, or that possess advanced video systems, because these may populate various stretches of high memory with chips used to hold video images, or with additional read-only memory chips.

Sometimes the 64K segment can't be positioned on a 64K boundary (as shown in the list) because of heavy memory use by other hardware. In this case, you may need to enter hexadecimal numbers that indicate a starting point within one of the 64K blocks. Again, the numbers can be confusing. To indicate a starting address half way between D000 and E000, enter D800. One-quarter of the way would be D400, and three-quarters of the way is DC00. Similarly, you could write CC00 or E400.

PITFALLS | If you encounter persistent difficulty in finding a 64K open span of memory space for installing expanded memory, you will need to consult the documentation of your video cards and other slot hardware. Video memory normally begins in the B000 address range, but it may start from A000 (that is, just after the 640K of conventional memory) and extend to high addresses. Advanced video boards are sure to add some read-only memory to the system, and this may be positioned apart from the video memory used to hold the screen image. The sizes and addresses of the memory used by any card ought to be present in the user documentation. Unfortunately, some documentation can only be deciphered by those with technical background. There should be no harm in experimenting even if you're not sure of exactly what's going on, but you can waste a lot of time this way. In the end, you may need outside help if your system is a complicated one.

Extended memory addressing　　Extended memory is installed at memory addresses above the sixteen 64K blocks shown in the list on the previous page. The hexadecimal numbers used to describe extended memory addresses require a fifth digit, with the bottommost address at 10000. The second megabyte of extended memory begins at 20000, the third at 30000, and so on. Intermediate addresses are usually counted in 256K blocks, rather than 64K blocks, because memory chips smaller than 256K are not used. Counting this way, the boundaries are at 10000, 14000, 18000, 1C000, 20000, 24000, etc. In every other respect, configuring extended memory is exactly like configuring system memory.

Device drivers　　Expanded memory is managed by a device driver (see section 11.11) that must be loaded by CONFIG.SYS when the computer starts up. DOS includes its own driver starting with version 4.0. It is held in the file XMA2EMS. It is designed for IBM-made expanded memory hardware. Expansion boards from other manufacturers will have their own driver that works in its own way. XMA2EMS is loaded by placing in CONFIG.SYS a statement like:

```
DEVICE=C:\DOS\XMA2EMS.SYS FRAME=D000
```

This statement sets up the expanded memory window at memory address D000. The XMA2EMS program presents many pitfalls; if you have trouble installing it, consult the lengthy discussion in the DOS 4.0 manual.

DOS 4.0 also offers a driver that emulates expanded memory in 386 machines. It is called XMAEM.SYS. To have all of extended memory used as expanded memory, you would write into CONFIG.SYS the line:

```
DEVICE=C:\DOS\XMAEM.SYS
```

Alternatively, you may specify that only part of extended memory be used this way by giving the number of 16K pages of memory that should be allocated. An entire megabyte of extended memory is equal to 64 pages, and it would be allocated by the statement:

```
DEVICE=C:\DOS\XMAEM.SYS 64
```

15.3 Using a RAM disk

A RAM disk, sometimes called a virtual disk, is a sort of phantom disk drive constructed in computer memory. On disk drives, data is stored in disk sectors, with 512 characters (bytes) of data to a sector. These 512-byte chunks can just as well be stored in series of 512 positions in memory. When software needs to access the 512 bytes, it can read or write them more quickly than on an actual disk drive, since no time is spent in moving read/write heads to the proper position over the disk surface, or in waiting for the desired sector to revolve around. For this reason, RAM disks are primarily used to increase a computer's performance.

A RAM disk is created by special utility software. When you run a RAM disk program, it puts aside a specified amount of memory to be used as disk sectors, and sets up a main directory (root directory) and other structures that DOS uses for keeping track of files. There is no need to format a RAM disk. The RAM disk is then assigned a drive specifier, such as B: or D:. Thereafter, you may use it exactly as if it were an actual disk drive. You can copy files to it, ask for a directory listing, or have programs create data files within it. Of course, the disk is empty when it is created, exactly as if it were a newly formatted disk.

Ideally, all data would be kept in RAM disks instead of on actual disk drives. But RAM disks have one terrible disadvantage: if the electricity goes out for even a fraction of a second, everything stored in memory, and thus everything stored on the RAM disk, is lost. You would lose all of your data every time you turned off the machine! Some manufacturers make special memory boards (nonvolatile RAM disks) that are powered separately from the machine, and which have a backup battery for when the lights go out. Unfortunately, these boards are expensive, and they use so much power that the backup battery does not last long enough to weather a long power outage. In the future, very high-capacity memory chips that use little power may make disk drives obsolete.

Creating a RAM disk   RAM disk software generally comes as a device driver, a special type of utility program (discussed in section 11.11) that is automatically loaded when the computer is booted. This is done by including a DEVICE statement in your CONFIG.SYS file (see section 11.1). The program creates a RAM disk, which stays in memory until the machine is turned off or rebooted. Some RAM disk programs can be run at any time, not just when the machine starts up. These utilities may let you remove the RAM disk from memory without rebooting or even changing its size. This approach is preferable because you can more readily reconfigure the machine for a particular application program you wish to run.

You may create several RAM disks, but there generally is no need since a RAM disk can be as large as you like provided you have enough memory installed. These days, most RAM disk software can create RAM disks in expanded memory or extended memory (explained in the minitutorial at the beginning of this chapter). If your machine has a memory expansion card that can be employed for expanded or extended memory, it may have been shipped with a diskette containing a RAM disk program that can make use of it in this way. So, you can have the best of both worlds: a full 640K of conventional memory for your programs to use, plus a large, super-fast RAM disk in expanded or extended memory.

Once a RAM disk has been created, the first order of business is to copy files onto it from an actual disk drive. Commands in AUTOEXEC.BAT (see section 11.1) can copy the files automatically every time the machine is started up. Because data kept on RAM disks is always in danger, they are not a good place to keep data files. Rather, use them for non-data files that are frequently read, such as a spelling-checker file. Section 21.8 gives suggestions for the optimum use of a RAM disk. If you do choose to place data files on a RAM disk, create a batch file (explained in Chapter 9) that will automatically copy the files to an actual disk for safe keeping. Then get in the habit of frequently backing up the RAM disk as you work. Remember that any kind of malfunction that crashes the machine, including a software hang up, will cost you all the data on your RAM disk.

The DOS RAM disk program   DOS includes a RAM disk program named VDISK in PC DOS and RAMDRIVE in MS DOS. It is held in the file VDISK.SYS or RAMDRIVE.SYS. The program can only be used when the computer is booted. This is done by adding a line to your CONFIG.SYS file. To create a 128K RAM disk in conventional memory, write:

```
DEVICE=VDISK.SYS 128
```

or:

```
DEVICE=RAMDRIVE.SYS 128
```

If the program file is not in the root directory, you will need to include a directory path for it, as in:

```
DEVICE=C:\DOS\VDISK.SYS 128
```

The drive specifier assigned to the RAM disk will be the next available above the highest drive specifier currently used. For example, if you have a floppy drive A and a hard disk drive C, and no drive B, the RAM disk will appear as drive D even though B is free.

Creating a 128K RAM disk this way means that 128K of conventional memory will no longer be available for your programs. If you have extended memory installed in your machine then you can have the RAM disk placed there instead. Just add /E at the end of the statement:

```
DEVICE=VDISK.SYS 128 /E
```

Be aware that placing a RAM disk in extended memory may cause problems with communications hardware, such as modems and network adapters. You can be sure of compatibility only by experimenting.

A RAM disk can also be placed in expanded memory by appending an /X switch in PC DOS (version 4.0 or later) or an /A switch in MS-DOS:

```
DEVICE=VDISK.SYS 256 /X
```

or:

```
DEVICE=RAMDRIVE.SYS 256 /A
```

The /X and /A switches may not be used in the same statement as an /E switch.

You may make the RAM disk as large as you please within the confines of available memory. However, VDISK and RAMDRIVE won't let you shrink remaining conventional memory to less than 64K. Note that the actual size of the RAM disk will be slightly smaller than the amount you specify, because some space must be devoted to the directory and other DOS structures.

Unless specified otherwise, DOS limits the number of drive specifiers it can use to the letters A through E. In a complicated system, or in networked computers, you may need to extend this range to accomodate one or more RAM disks. You can do this with the LASTDRIVE command, which is explained in section 11.6.

15.4 Using memory-resident programs

DOS is designed to run only one program at a time. You load a program into memory, use it, and then quit the program, effectively clearing it out of memory. Only then can you run another application. On the other hand, the successor to DOS, OS/2, can load many programs at once and let you switch back and forth between them at the press of a key. What's more, this kind of multitasking operating system can keep programs running even when out of view, so that, for example, a database can be sorted while you continue work in your word processor.

While DOS cannot multitask, it does support memory-resident programs. These are utility programs that are loaded into memory and stay there while application software runs. Such utilities are often called TSRs, for terminate and stay resident, meaning that the program immediately terminates when it is loaded, but remains in memory.

Pop-up programs   TSRs were originally accommodated by DOS to solve certain technical needs. There is a way that software can call upon them to perform special tasks. However, software designers quickly discovered that TSRs could be designed as pop-up programs. These are utility programs that pop up on the screen when you press a special keystroke combination. For example, a TSR might act as a memory-resident calculator. The calculator is normally hidden from view, but by pressing a hot key—the special keystroke combination that brings it to the foreground—the image of a calculator instantly pops up on part of the screen. After you have finished using the calculator, you exit from the TSR as you would from any other program, and the calculator disappears from view, leaving the screen exactly as it was when you pressed the hot key. But the calculator remains in memory and it can be brought into action any number of times.

In most cases, the hot key is actually a combination of keys, typically a shift key (such as Alt) and an out-of-the-way symbol key, such as . It's easiest to design a TSR that uses two shift keys as the hot key, and sometimes two programs will want to use the same keystroke combination. To avoid such conflicts, well-crafted TSRs allow you to select the hot key.

Loading TSRs   Memory-resident programs are run like any other program: you type in its name at the DOS prompt and press ⏎. TSRs usually load and automatically terminate themselves, doing no more than showing a message announcing that they have been successfully loaded into memory. Thereafter, you can activate the program at any time using the hot key, whether you are working in DOS (at the DOS prompt) or from within a program. Some TSRs can be removed from memory without restarting the machine. The point of doing this is to free up memory for use by application programs or other TSRs. Ordinarily, when several TSRs are in use, the TSR you remove from memory must be the last loaded for this feature to be useful.

There are many kinds of memory-resident programs in existence: calendars, notepads, and telephone directories, as well as a slew of technical utilities that speed disk access or compress data. The most popular have been combined into single TSRs that provide a dozen or more functions at a touch of the hot key. But such convenience comes at a price. Here are some problems you should be aware of.

Memory allocation   TSRs take up memory, and memory is often scarce. As application programs become more complicated, they require more memory to operate efficiently, or to operate at all. Many TSRs take up 50K each, and it is not at all hard to fill up a third of the 640K allowed to DOS with one's favorite utilities. Indeed, many of the most important tools for improving a computer's performance or your work efficiency rely on TSRs. You may be forced to chose the most valuable.

Software manufacturers have come up with two partial solutions to the memory-shortage problem. First, they have developed software that manages TSRs. Such software sets aside a certain amount of memory for TSRs without actually loading any into it. When you strike a hot key, you are presented with a menu of TSRs on hand. You make a selection, and only then is the TSR loaded from disk. When you have finished with the TSR, it is removed from memory to make room for another.

This approach to TSR management comes in two basic forms. Some manufacturers offer their own extensive collection of TSRs managed in this way. The TSR management software comes with a TSR library, and (generally) no other TSRs can be used with it. Other companies sell a management program without including specific memory-resident utilities. The advantage of the latter is that you can then use TSRs from a number of manufacturers.

The second solution to the memory shortage problem (affectionately known as RAM-cram) has been to redesign TSRs so that they can make use of expanded memory or extended memory if the computer is equipped with either. These special kinds of memory are discussed in the minitutorial at the beginning of this chapter. In brief, they allow DOS programs to work with memory beyond the 640K limit, albeit with certain limitations in its use and speed of access. TSRs can store data in expanded or extended memory, reducing their requirements for conventional memory. Even better, some TSRs can store themselves in expanded memory, running from there, or temporarily copying themselves into conventional memory when they are called up. Such TSRs still take up a small amount of RAM, typically only a few kilobytes, to intercept the hot key and bring the TSR into action.

When you consider the purchase of a TSR, find out how much memory it requires. There usually will be a range, depending on how much power you wish to give the utility. You should be able to learn the memory requirements from the TSR's documentation. Don't accept the file size of the TSR program as a measure of how much memory it takes up. It may grab several times as much memory when it is loaded, reserving that memory for its own use.

PITFALLS A TSR may sully the computer display, especially when an Enhanced Graphics Adapter (EGA) runs your video monitor. When you call up a TSR with a hot key, it writes on the screen on top of whatever your application program may have written. When it quits, it should restore the screen to exactly as it was so that you can resume work in the application. To do this, the TSR makes a copy of the part of the screen image that it overwrites. Quite a bit of memory can be required for this when the machine is running in a color graphics mode; sometimes the image is temporarily stored on disk. Unfortunately, the EGA video system was designed in such a way that it is sometimes impossible for the TSR to find out the current video mode. Without this information, the TSR cannot save and restore a screen image properly. There is really not a lot that you can do about this problem except upgrade to the more advanced VGA video system (introduced with the IBM PS/2 computers, and available as an add-in adapter for older machines).

Multitasking TSRs   While TSRs cannot truly multitask in DOS, there is a primitive mechanism by which they can invisibly come alive roughly 18 times a second to carry out a task. They do this so quickly that you will never notice that the operation of the application program you are using is constantly being suspended. One kind of TSR that works this way is a print spooler, which sends data to a printer while you continue to use the machine for other purposes. You'll find more on this topic in section 14.5.

15.5 Resolving conflicts between memory-resident programs

As a TSR is loaded, it latches itself into the operating system in some way. When another TSR is loaded, it may attempt to attach itself in the same manner, thus disconnecting the first. This may happen even when the two programs use different hot keys. To counter the problem, manufacturers frequently state in their documentation that their utility should be loaded last if others are used. Since only one TSR can be last, you are faced with a quandary. One prominent manufacturer has taken the problem into its own hands by designing a TSR that essentially cuts in line in front of TSRs loaded after it, potentially disconnecting them.

As a result of this and other problems, some memory-resident programs are incompatible with others. One TSR may never be able to operate with another, or the two may be used together only when loaded in a particular order. It's not hard to recognize when a conflict has occured, because the computer frequently hangs—it freezes up and you'll need to reboot to get it running again.

However, it may not be obvious that a TSR is causing the machine to hang, for faulty equipment can also cause this problem. Generally, if a TSR is going to make trouble, the trouble will occur while the TSR is in use, or immediately after you close the pop-up window and return to the program you are running from DOS. This does not necessarily mean that the particular TSR you have been using is the one that is at fault. Another may be the source of the mischief.

To find the culprit, remove all TSRs except the one that appears to have failed and see if it works properly while running alone. It's possible that a conflict exists between the TSR and the application program in which it is opened, rather than with another TSR. So test the suspect TSR within the same program it crashed, using the same program features.

If the problem TSR passes this initial test, try loading each of the remaining TSRs along with it, one at a time. Because most TSRs are loaded through AUTOEXEC.BAT when the computer is booted, the temptation may be to modify AUTOEXEC.BAT again and again. Rather than go through this trouble, temporarily remove the names of all TSRs from your AUTOEXEC.BAT file and then manually load the

TSRs immediately after the machine has booted. You'll need to reboot for each test.

TIP

Be aware that certain TSRs are invisibly active even when they have no presence on the screen. TSRs that use your modem can be an example, as are those that spool output to a printer while you do other work. These processes depend on very precise timing. They may operate perfectly for long periods, and then suddenly crash. In this case, the problem is sometimes an incompatibility with the application software running at the same time as the TSR; alternatively, the TSR may be fundamentally incompatible with the particular brand of hardware in your machine.

You can proceed in three ways once you've narrowed your TSR conflict down to two suspects. Try the solutions in the following order.

Solution 1   Try loading the programs in a different order. Reread the program manuals to find out which emphasize loading order and which do not. The ones that appear least sensitive to loading order should be the first loaded. Because there are many combinations, a lot of time can be wasted in experimentation with more than three TSRs. So begin testing the order of only the problem TSRs, and then add the rest, loading each additional one first if possible, or, if that fails, loading it last.

Solution 2   Call the technical support lines of the companies that made the TSRs, starting with the TSR that crashed. Describe the problem you have had and tell them of other programs with which you suspect their TSR is having compatibility problems. Then ask whether they have had similar reports and whether they know of any solutions. Frequently, you'll find that technical support personel are very familiar with the idiosyncrasies of not just their own product, but those of their competitors. Sometimes, companies work together to assure intercompatibility. Perhaps your problem can be solved by obtaining an upgrade (more recent version) of a TSR. If not, ask how you should proceed to solve the problems you are having.

Solution 3   When all else fails, you can get almost any TSR to work with any other by acquiring a special utility tailored to just this purpose. These utilities are themselves TSRs, and they can help you unload one TSR and load another in the same memory space without rebooting. A number of such products are available as stand-alone utilities. You'll find similar abilities in some operating environments (discussed in the minitutorial at the beginning of Chapter 18) like Windows and DESQview. These environments allow you to run multiple programs and TSRs at once, and they treat TSRs like any other application. But be aware that they may slow down your application software if you load too many TSRs, or configure them improperly.

15.6 Using memory management software

The minitutorial at the beginning of this chapter describes a very complicated memory system that has evolved from the original system of having everything kept in the lowest 640K of conventional memory. Today, conventional memory is expanded to include the upper memory area (from 640K to 1 megabyte) and the high memory area (the first 64K block above 1 megabyte), which actually is extended memory that is treated as conventional memory. Starting with 286 computers, extended memory may be present, but the paging facility is available only on 32-bit (386, 486, and 586) machines. Expanded memory is implemented in 8088 and 286 machines using special hardware, but in 32-bit computers it is created by software from extended memory.

All of these kinds of memory must work together, and must do so as memory-resident programs and multiple applications simultaneously try to grab memory for themselves. To cope with this complexity and prevent conflicts, a genre of utility software has evolved called memory managers.

Both DOS and Windows are accompanied by a program called HIMEM.SYS whose job is to allocate extended memory to competing applications, including for the purpose of using the first 64K of extended memory as a high memory area. HIMEM.SYS is a device driver (a topic discussed in section 11.11), and it must be declared in your CONFIG.SYS file. In most cases, all you need to write is:

```
DEVICE=C:\DOS\HIMEM.SYS
```

or:

```
DEVICE=C:\WINDOWS\HIMEM.SYS
```

depending on where the HIMEM file is located. This command should be one of the first in your CONFIG.SYS file. It must preceed the loading of any other device drivers or software that use extended memory, including SMARTDRV or RAMDRIVE. This command takes a number of optional switches for fine-tuning HIMEM, but it's not likely you'll need them.

If you use software that requires expanded memory, you probably have already installed an EMS device driver if you are using an 8088 or 286 machine that has expanded memory hardware installed. But if you're using a 386, 486, or 586 machine, you'll need to load software that emulates expanded memory hardware by allocating extended memory. This is done by another device driver, EMM386.EXE. Like HIMEM.SYS, EMM386 is loaded by CONFIG.SYS using a DEVICE statement such as:

```
DEVICE=C:\DOS\EMM386.EXE
```

The statement must follow the HIMEM statement. EMM386 also takes a number of optional configuration parameters that, among other things, specify the location in conventional memory where the expanded memory page frame should reside. As with HIMEM, your best bet is to initially dispense with the switches and let the program configure itself. However, you probably will want to specify how much extended memory will be given over to expanded memory. The default value is 256K, which is not very much for most applications. Simply type the number of kilobytes after the command. To allocate 750K, write:

```
DEVICE=C:\DOS\EMM386.EXE 750
```

The functions of both HIMEM.SYS and EMS386.EXE are combined in a popular program called QEMM386.SYS (from Quarterdeck Office Systems). It has a number of advantages:

- While the Windows version of EMM386 can provide expanded memory only for DOS applications running inside Windows, QEMM386 will do this even when Windows is not running.

- QEMM386 can stop Windows from appropriating all extended memory to itself so that non-Windows programs that use extended memory will have some available.

- By playing some clever tricks, QEMM386 can open up even more conventional memory for use by applications programs.

- QEMM386 can locate memory-resident programs in extended memory when these programs would otherwise take up conventional memory.

The QEMM386 program can do all of this, and yet consumes less memory than HIMEM.SYS and EMM386 combined. Its installation program automatically modifies your CONFIG.SYS file by adding a DEVICE command that loads the program.

Chapter 16

Disk Formatting

MINITUTORIAL:
Disks and disk formatting

Disks, whether diskettes or hard disks, are divided into concentric rings called tracks, with each track divided into a number of equal-sized segments called sectors. IBM PCs store data in one-sector units of 512 bytes. When a PC needs to read a particular piece of information, it figures out on which track the information resides and then sends the disk's read/write heads to that position over the disk surface. The data is read when the required sector swings beneath the read/write head.

No tracks or sectors are defined on a disk's surface when it is new. They are created by laying down magnetic markings in a process called formatting. The format markings assign a unique number to each disk sector so that DOS can identify it. It's possible to buy preformatted diskettes, but usually you must format them yourself. Hard disks are often delivered already formatted by computer stores, but not when the disk is bought from a mail order house. Even if the disk arrives formatted, there may be future occasions when you'll need to reformat it. See section 23.5 to learn about unformatting accidentally reformatted drives.

Besides marking sectors and tracks, formatting also sets up certain disk sectors to hold information DOS uses to keep track of the files that will later be written on the disk. Three structures are created:

■ Sectors are set aside for the disk's root directory. The number of sectors depends on the capacity of the disk; the fewer the sectors, the smaller the number of files that may be listed in the root directory. (The root directory is exactly the same thing as what many people call the directory of a diskette. All disks have this base directory located in particular disk sectors. You may then optionally construct a directory tree on top of it, as the minitutorial in Chapter 5 explains.)

■ Two copies of a file allocation table (FAT) are created. This table keeps track of which sectors are in use, and which sectors belong to which file. A second copy is made for safety's sake, because total data loss usually results if the file allocation table is destroyed.

■ Optionally, formatting may introduce information on the disk so that the disk can be used for booting the computer. The minitutorial in Chapter 17 explains how booting works. With this option, formatting writes a boot record in one sector, two hidden

DOS files in some others, and then adds the main DOS file, COMMAND.COM.

Thus, there are two kinds of formatting. Defining tracks and sectors is called low-level formatting. Adding directories, file allocation tables, and other structures is called high-level formatting. When you use the DOS FORMAT command to format a diskette, it does both, first performing a low-level format, and then a high-level format. However, when applied to a hard disk, FORMAT only carries out the high-level format. Beforehand, you may need to use a special low-level formatting program that is shipped with the disk (DOS includes no such utility).

There are two reasons why low-level formatting is performed separately on hard disks. First, the design of hard disks is not standardized, and the DOS FORMAT program would not be able to handle all hard disk models; second, an extra step, called partitioning, is added in formatting hard disks. Partitioning does just what it says: it divides the disk into parts. One reason for doing this is to keep a second operating system on the disk. For example, the computer might run using DOS some of the time, and UNIX the rest of the time. Part of the disk would be used by DOS, part by UNIX. A structure called the partition table is initialized by the partition software. It informs the computer where each partition begins on the disk, and tells which partition should be used for booting when the machine is switched on.

Another reason for partitioning a disk is to deal with a limitation imposed by early DOS versions. Before version 3.3, DOS could not handle a hard disk larger than 32 megabytes. This limitation arose because DOS uses a two-byte number to keep track of disk sectors. The largest number that two bytes can hold is 65,535, with each number assigned to a disk sector. When a disk contains a greater number of sectors, no number is available to identify those beyond 65,535. With 512 bytes per sector, and 65,535 sectors, the largest possible disk holds 32 million bytes, or 32 megabytes.

Using special utility software or DOS 3.3, you may partition a large disk drive into a number of units that are 32 megabytes or smaller, assigning a drive specifier to each, such as C, then D, then E, and so on. Thus, it seems that there are multiple hard disks when, in fact, there is just one large one. DOS 4.0 acquired the ability to create a single partition of any

size so that an entire high-capacity drive may be accessed under a single drive specifier.

Even when using only DOS on a hard disk, you still must partition the disk between performing the low-level and high-level formats. In this case, the entire disk may be given over to a single partition, and so the disk is not actually partitioned in the sense of being divided into parts. The disk still requires partitioning in this case so that DOS can identify it and boot from it.

16.1   Formatting a diskette

A brand new diskette cannot be used until it has been formatted. Formatting places magnetic markers on the disk surface to define the sectors in which data is stored. When DOS encounters a disk that doesn't have these markers, it issues an error message like:

```
General Failure error reading drive A
Abort, Retry, Fail?
```

(Press A to return to the DOS prompt when this happens.) Formatting also creates a main directory (the root directory) and file allocation tables by which DOS keeps track of the placement of files.

A newly formatted disk is ready to hold files of any kind, including program files and data files. However, the disk may not necessarily be used to start up (boot) the computer. For the disk to have this capability, it must have certain DOS system files transferred to it during formatting, as explained below. Whenever you format a new diskette, you should begin by deciding whether or not you want to make it a bootable diskette; doing so reduces the available space on the diskette, typically by about 30K (the amount varies with the DOS version).

Those who own hard disks will usually want to boot from drive C, and generally have no need of any bootable diskettes. On the other hand, machines having only diskette drives always boot from drive A. Theoretically, a single boot diskette is all that is needed in this case—use the diskette to boot and then remove it from the machine. But much disk swapping can be avoided by making other diskettes bootable.

Basic formatting   To format a diskette in drive A, simply enter:

```
FORMAT A: ←
```

In some cases a more complicated command is required, as explained at the end of this section. The FORMAT command is carried out by a part of DOS that is kept in its own file called FORMAT.COM. If your DOS files are on a hard disk, you must see to it that this file is available, either via the PATH command (see section 8.1), or by typing a directory path to it, as in:

```
FORMAT C:\DOS\FORMAT A: ←
```

If you are working from diskette drives, the FORMAT program can be found on the main DOS diskette. Place the diskette (actually, a copy of the diskette, since you should not normally use the original) in drive A. Then enter the command FORMAT A: ⏎. To follow these instructions can be alarming, because it appears as if DOS will proceed to reformat the DOS diskette in drive A, destroying its contents. But after loading the FORMAT program, whether from a diskette drive or a hard disk, DOS will pause and display the message:

```
Insert new diskette for drive A:
and strike ENTER when ready
```

You can then place the diskette that is to be formatted in drive A and press ⏎ to begin formatting, or Ctrl-Break if you have changed your mind.

The chief reason for sometimes striking Ctrl-Break instead of ⏎ is a nagging uncertainty that the disk placed in the drive for formatting is really the one needing it. When the diskette is not taken straight from a box of new ones, be sure to inspect it before starting up the FORMAT command. Just place it in drive A and use the DIR command to see what's on it. Once you are sure that you want to proceed, label the diskette so that it won't be mistakenly exchanged for some other while it is not in the machine.

PITFALLS The FORMAT command can operate on any disk drive in the machine, including a hard disk. Because FORMAT effectively destroys all data on a disk that has been previously formatted and used, you must be alert and careful not to accidentally direct the command to the wrong drive. In the worst case, vast amounts of data can be obliterated on a hard disk drive. DOS has been steadily improved to make it harder and harder to commit such an error, but it still occurs all too frequently when someone presses forward without really understanding the FORMAT program. This is one command that you should not wildly experiment with just to see what happens.

You can make formatting diskettes less risky by replacing the DOS FORMAT program with a utility like the Safe Format program in The Norton Utilities. This program formats diskettes in the same way that FOR-

MAT formats hard disks, but without destroying data. If a diskette has been accidentally reformatted using Safe Format, you can use another Norton Utility, UnFormat, to recover some—perhaps all—of your data, provided that no new data has been transferred to the diskette in the meantime. We discuss unformat programs in section 23.5.

Making the diskette bootable   To cause FORMAT to transfer the DOS files used to boot the computer, simply append /S to the end of the format command:

```
FORMAT A: /S ⏎
```

Diskettes are often set up for booting when formatted. The SYS command, which is discussed in section 17.1, can make a disk bootable at a later date. However, only in DOS 4.0 can SYS make any diskette bootable. In earlier DOS versions the diskette must be specially prepared for this during formatting by adding a /B switch to the command. This feature is useful to software manufacturers, but not to the general user.

Volume labels   All disks formatted by DOS may optionally be given a volume label, which is nothing more than a name of up to 11 characters that identifies the diskette. A volume label can be invaluable for keeping track of diskettes. The volume label is shown at the top of any directory listing. It also can be found at any time by the VOL command, as in:

```
VOL A: ⏎
```

to which DOS might respond:

```
Volume in drive A is BACKUP13
```

or:

```
Volume in drive A has no label
```

The volume label is hidden in the disk's main directory (the root directory). The DOS LABEL command (section 16.6) can change the volume label at any time or add one if none was created during formatting. Sometimes software creates or alters volume labels, particularly backup software that uses volume labels to number each backup diskette in a series.

Prior to DOS 4.0, to cause FORMAT to create a volume label you must append /V to the command:

```
FORMAT A:  /V  ⏎
```

DOS will then prompt you to enter the label before formatting begins. Starting with DOS 4.0, FORMAT always prompts you for a label. In this case, you may specify the label right in the command:

```
FORMAT A:  /V:MYLABEL  ⏎
```

Format types   Besides /S and /V, FORMAT can use a number of other switches to cause a high-capacity drive to format a diskette at a lower capacity for use in other drives. For example, a 1.2-megabyte floppy disk drive can be made to create 360K floppies, or even single-sided floppies with half that capacity. Use /1 to make a diskette single-sided (this works only with 5 ¼-inch disk drives). Use /8 to give a disk eight sectors per track, the original IBM standard for low-capacity floppies. Most useful, /4 causes a 1.2M IBM AT-style disk drive to format a 360K diskette:

```
FORMAT A:  /4  ⏎
```

Or, to format a 720K 3 ½-inch diskette in a 1.44M drive, enter:

```
FORMAT A:  /N:9  /T:80  ⏎
```

Alternatively, in DOS 4.0 and later you may use the /F switch to specify diskette capacity. To create a 720K diskette in a 1.44M drive, you would enter:

```
FORMAT A:  /F:720  ⏎
```

Of course, you may combine switches in a single command so long as they are not contradictory:

```
FORMAT A:  /S  /V  /4  ⏎
```

Be aware that some early 1.2M drives cannot reliably format 360K diskettes. It may be impossible to read back data written on such a diskette, whether by a 360K drive or a 1.2M drive.

DOS 5.0 features   DOS 5.0 completely revamps the FORMAT command. Whereas in prior DOS versions FORMAT always destroys all data on diskettes; in DOS 5.0, FORMAT normally treats a diskette the same way it treats a hard disk, reformatting the root directory and file allocation tables, but nothing else. By doing so, DOS 5.0 opens the option of unformatting the diskette to recover data it previously held. DOS 5.0 introduces the UNFORMAT command for this purpose; we'll explain how it works in Chapter 9. Although FORMAT does not erase disk sectors when it is used this way, it does check each sector to see that it holds data properly.

If you want a full low-level format, add a /U switch (for unconditional format) to the command. The /U switch is useful when you want to obliterate all data on a disk for security reasons. Otherwise, anyone wielding data-recovery software can piece together your erased data. You also should use this option if you've been receiving read and write errors while using the disk and want to make the disk safe for further use.

DOS 5.0 also introduces the /Q switch (for quick format). A quick format is like an ordinary one in that FORMAT merely erases the disk's root directory and file allocation tables. But a quick format doesn't bother to test all disk sectors. Interestingly, you can combine the /Q and /U switches for an even faster format. In this case, data is not obliterated. Use the /U switch alone to expedite formatting of previously unformatted disks.

The DOS 5.0 Shell   Diskettes are formatted in the DOS shell by choosing Disk Utilities from the main program list (not from the File Manager). Then choose Format . You'll encounter a dialog box containing a Parameters box into which you can type a drive specifier other than A: or switches used by the FORMAT command. Once you choose OK, the same messages are displayed as occur when you use FORMAT. You'll be prompted for a volume label when formatting is complete.

Windows 3.1 To format a diskette in Microsoft Windows, insert the diskette in a drive and choose Format Disk from the Disk menu in the File Manager. You'll be shown the dialog box in figure 16.1. You can specify the diskette capacity and a volume label, and can direct the command to a drive other than A if desired. You also can select Make System Disk to make the disk bootable, or Quick Format to reformat a disk that has been formatted previously. In the latter case, the disk's root directory and file allocation tables are cleared, and the tracks are left untouched so that nothing is written over existing data. Thus, a quick format is equivalent to a mass erasure of files. Choosing this option means there is a possibility of recovering old files if a mistake was made. But it also means that confidential data may be left on the disk for anyone to view who has a file recovery software.

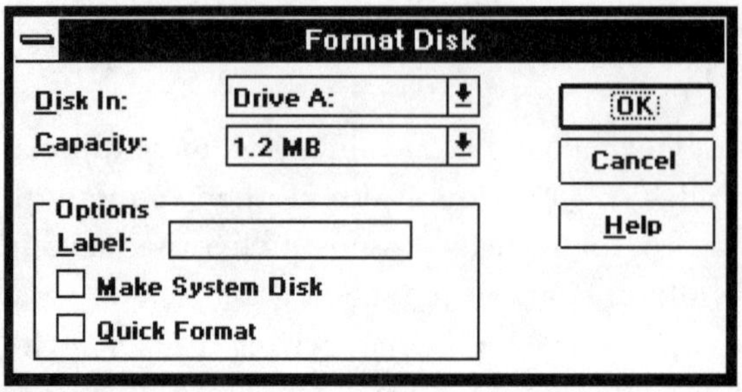

Figure 16.1

16.2 Formatting a hard disk: low-level formatting

As the minitutorial at the start of this chapter explains, hard disks undergo formatting in two distinct steps. In low-level formatting, the magnetic lines that define disk sectors are laid down on the disk surface. Later, in high-level formatting, the various DOS structures, such as the root directory, are established, and DOS files required for booting may be added.

Hard disk formatting is divided into stages for two reasons. First, while the DOS FORMAT program can easily carry out high-level formatting on any diskette or hard disk, it cannot perform all low-level formats. To do this, it would have to deal with all possible drive geometries, that is, all possible combinations of numbers and sizes of disks, and all possible patterns of tracks and sectors that disks can hold. Instead of having FORMAT do the job, the drive manufacturer supplies its own formatting program tailored to the idiosyncracies of the disk.

Second, a two-stage formatting scheme lets you partition the disk into more than one section. Each partition appears as a disk drive unto itself with its own drive specifier (C, D, E, and so on); from your point of view, there are several disk drives present when in fact only one physical disk drive exists. A disk's partitions may be divided between more than one operating system, say with one given a high-level format by DOS, and another by UNIX. Or, all partitions may reside under DOS. One reason for the latter choice is that, until DOS 4.0, DOS could not handle partitions larger than 32 megabytes. One way of using high-capacity disks has been to partition them into two or more segments of less than 32M and have DOS treat each as a unique disk. (The intricacies of disk partitioning are discussed in the next section. Note that partitioning is obligatory even for hard disks used only with DOS.)

Formatting programs   Ordinarily, hard disks come preformatted when purchased at a retail store. Mail order disks, on the other hand, tend to be delivered unformatted. In either case, you should be sure that the drive is accompanied by a diskette holding a low-level formatting program for the disk. One would think that a disk would not require a low-level format more than once in its life. But there are occasions, particularly following some kinds of disk failures, where the only way to get the drive up and running again is to reformat it at low level. If you have no low-level formatting program on hand, you may be forced to purchase utility software to do the job because DOS contains no equivalent.

Occasionally, a hard disk's low-level format program is held on the disk drive itself in a read-only memory chip (ROM). The program is started up by the DEBUG program that comes with DOS. Instructions that accompany the drive tell you how. While having the program on board stops you from losing it, you'll still be in trouble if you don't keep track of the instruction sheet over the years during which it is not needed.

Owners of PS/2 computers are fortunate in this regard, because a low-level formatting program is shipped with every machine. Just boot the machine from the Reference Diskette and then press Ctrl-A at the main menu. You'll be led to the Advanced Diagnostics, which offers low-level formatting as a menu choice. The Advanced Diagnostics exist for other PCs, but they must be purchased separately.

Using the format program   Once the low-level format program is launched, it prompts you for various information. It usually begins by asking for the drive name or number. Drive names may be C, D, and so on. Note that the first hard disk drive in a system is always C; B goes unused even when there is no second diskette drive. Because a single disk drive can be used as two or more virtual drives with, for example, one partition acting as C and another as D, this way of specifying the drive can lead to confusion. Thus, some format programs ask for the drive number, which always refers to an actual physical disk drive, no matter how it's disk capacity is divided. The numbers, from 1 upward, count only hard disk drives, not diskette drives. The first hard disk installed in the system is number 1, the second number 2, and so on.

Specifying the drive is no problem when you are installing a computer's first hard disk. Many formatting programs will sense that there is no hard disk and help you along. But you must be very careful when adding a second disk, lest you accidentally set the format program loose upon the wrong disk drive. Read the instructions accompanying the format program meticulously before you begin.

Bad tracks   The next concern is the bad track table. This is a list of tracks (rings of disk space) that were found to be imperfect during factory testing of the disk. The format program will see to it that these tracks go unused. The disk surfaces in a hard drive are not always perfect. It's not unusual for 5 or 10 tracks to be bad. At 15 sectors per track, and 512 bytes per sector, each bad track would cost you about 8K of disk space. So, usually, only a tiny fraction of the disk's total capacity is lost in this way.

The bad track table is usually written on a label affixed to the drive case. The formatting program will prompt you for the information from the table. The tracks are specified by their side and their track number. The side refers to the platter side inside the drive. Virtually all hard disks have multiple platters whirling around in tandem. Since each platter has two sides, the total number of sides is double the number of platters. The sides are numbered from zero upwards; so, a three-platter disk drive will have sides 0 through 5. The track numbers refer to the concentric rings of disk space. They are also counted from zero upward.

TIP

It's easy to forget about the bad track table when you install a hard disk. If it's not in view when you start up the format program, you'll need to reopen the computer, and possibly even remove the drive. Think about this in advance and make a copy of the table if necessary.

Setting the interleave   A low-level formatting program requires one more piece of information: the disk's interleave. The speed at which a disk drive operates is set as much by the computer's electronics as it is by the rate at which the platters turn. Only very fast PCs can keep up with the data flow when one sector after another along a track is read or written. A slower computer reads a sector, pauses momentarily while it transfers the data it finds there, and then reads the next. During the pause, the disk platters continue to turn so that by the time of the second access, several sectors may have gone by the read/write heads that hover over the disk surface. For optimal performance, the next sector of data that needs to be read should be positioned at whatever sector is coming to the read/write heads when the computer is next able to transfer data. Thus, instead of placing a body of data in

consecutive sectors along tracks, it is laid out at (for example) every third sector. This distribution of data is known as the disk's interleave.

When data is set apart by three sectors, the disk is said to have a 3:1 interleave, or simply an interleave of 3. In the case of 1:1 interleave, the data is laid out in adjacent sectors. A low-level formatting program needs to be told a disk's interleave in part because the proper interleave depends on the speed of the computer as much as the speed of the disk drive. There are rules of thumb about what interleave to use for a machine of a particular type—6:1 for older PC/XTs; 3:1 for an original AT running at 6 MHz; 2:1 for a fast 286 or slow 386 machine; and 1:1 on fast 386 and 486 machines. But many variables determine the proper interleave, and it is nearly impossible to reason it through. Consult the documentation for your disk controller card for suggestions.

Optimum interleave   It's worth understanding the effects of an incorrect interleave. When the interleave factor is too large, time is wasted waiting for the next sector to swing around to the drive's read/ write heads. A too small interleave is even worse. The next sector of data passes by the read/write heads before the electronics are ready, and so the computer must wait through a whole turn of the disk to get back to that sector.

Unfortunately, it's difficult to judge gradations of hard disk performance just by watching a drive's indicator light. It is very impractical in any case to try formatting a new hard disk with several interleaves and running tests with a stop watch. The documentation that accompanies the disk drive should contain at least some advice about what interleave to use. You may find a table of interleave values for different speed machines, because a 10MHz (megahertz) machine would use a tighter interleave than a 6MHz machine.

When documentation and phone support is inadequate, you can buy an interleave optimization utility that will try out various interleaves on a single track and determine the best to use. Several companies sell interleave-optimizing, low-level format programs, and others market programs that can go back and change a disk's interleave at a later date—without harming the data the sectors hold. Recent versions of the Norton Utilities include the Calibrate program for this purpose. See section 21.6 for more information about interleave optimization.

Time requirements   Once it has been given all the information it requires, the low-level formatting program goes to work. It takes much longer to format a hard disk than a floppy. The time varies with the formatting program, since some perform thorough tests on each disk sector after formatting it, while others do very little. The formatting time also varies by the speed of the computer. As a very rough measure, expect to wait one minute for every megabyte of disk space. When the job is finished, move on to partitioning (section 16.3) and high-level formatting (section 16.5).

16.3 Formatting a hard disk: partitioning

Once low-level formatting is complete, a hard disk must be partitioned. This is done by the FDISK program, which is found on one of the DOS diskettes as FDISK.EXE. The program is usually run from drive A. To start FDISK, simply enter:

    FDISK ⏎

Alternatively, FDISK can be run automatically by the SELECT program that installs DOS on drive C.

The capabilities of FDISK have varied considerably between DOS versions as partitioning has become more flexible. For reasons explained in the minitutorial at the beginning of the chapter, DOS was not originally designed to handle hard disks larger than 32 megabytes. Of course, the capacity of many disk drives far exceeds 32 megabytes. Special techniques have been devised to let DOS use entire high-capacity drives. DOS itself introduced certain methods beginning with version 3.3, and other approaches are available through utility programs made by independent software houses. Finally, starting with version 4.0, DOS introduced partitions not limited to 32 megabytes.

Primary and extended partitions   Starting with version 3.3, two partitions may belong to DOS, a primary partition and an extended partition. The primary partition is exactly like DOS partitions in earlier DOS versions, and it is used for booting. Extended partitions hold data but can't be booted from. Second hard disk drives may only have an extended partition. An extended DOS partition can be as large as the drive itself, but it may be subdivided, with each subdivision, or volume, acting as a logical drive. This means that each volume is given a drive specifier from D: to Z: and, from the user's point of view, each volume acts as an independent drive with it's own directory tree. In DOS 3.3, a volume may be as small as a single cylinder, and as large as 32 megabytes, but no larger. Hence, the 32-megabyte limit on partition size (and thus on file size) remains in force. Only starting with version 4.0 can you exceed the 32-megabyte limit in DOS.

Figure 16.2 diagrams this system. In the diagram, logical drives C: through E: are contained on a single hard disk. Note the introduction of logical drive tables. These are analogous to the partition table in the master boot record. They reside in the extended boot record that begins each volume of the extended DOS partition (note that calling these boot records is a misnomer, since they're not for booting). The logical drive table for the first volume tells the location of the next, etc.

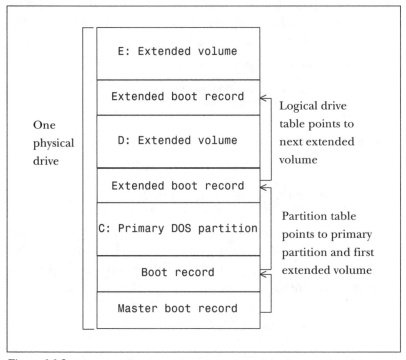

Figure 16.2

The FDISK menu In our examples here, we'll look at FDISK in DOS versions 3.3 and 4.0. The same system continues in DOS 5.0. The exact wording of the menus varies between versions, but the functions are the same. DOS versions prior to 3.3 will lack the menu choices for extended partitions. Here is the basic start-up menu.

```
FDISK Options
Current Fixed Disk Drive: 1
Choose one of the following:
    1. Create DOS partition
    2. Change Active Partition
    3. Delete DOS partition
    4. Display Partition Information
    5. Select Next Fixed Disk Drive
Enter choice: [1]
```

The current fixed disk drive tells which drive FDISK is about to partition. The number 1 refers to the first drive in the machine (nominally drive C). If you need to partition a second drive you've just installed, select menu choice 5 to direct FDISK to that drive (this menu choice doesn't appear when only one hard disk drive is installed).

The usual menu choice, 1, is preselected, so you only need to press ⏎ to get started. Then you're shown a second menu:

```
Create DOS Partition
Current Fixed Disk Drive: 1
   1. Create Primary DOS partition
   2. Create Extended DOS partition
Enter choice: [1]
```

Creating a first partition   For a first partition on a first hard disk, you'll choose 1, otherwise 2. The message appears:

```
Do you wish to use the maximum size
for a DOS partition and make the DOS
partition active (y/n)........? [Y]
```

If your disk holds 32 megabytes or less, again, just press ⏎ to select yes. But if you have more capacity, you have two options. If you're working in DOS 4.0 or later, you can type Ⓨ, and DOS will make an oversize partition automatically. You'll see a message like:

```
System will now restart
Insert DOS diskette in drive A:
Press any key when ready. . .
```

When you strike any key, DOS reboots from drive A, presenting the usual date and time queries. The process takes only a few seconds since only a few sectors on the disk are affected. When DOS 4.0 or over creates an oversize partition, it displays the message:

```
WARNING! SHARE should be loaded for large media
```

This reminds you that your oversized partitions require that you load the DOS SHARE command when the computer starts up. Do this through your CONFIG.SYS file by adding the line:

```
INSTALL=SHARE
```

The file takes up about 7K of memory.

Creating multiple extended partitions   Oversize partitions can confuse utility software, and even some application software. If your software has not been modified to deal with oversize partitions, you may want to confine yourself to creating multiple extended partitions of 32 megabytes or less. You do this by typing N when asked if you want to use the entire disk for the primary partition. FDISK then tells you how large the disk is:

```
Total disk space is 819 cylinders.
Maximum space available for partition
is 642 cylinders.
Enter partition size.........: [642]
No partitions defined
```

It's up to you to decide how many cylinders to use. This example is for a 40-megabyte drive that will be split into two 20-megabyte partitions. FDISK displays the maximum number of cylinders that will fit in 32 megabytes—642. In this case, you'd type 410 over this value (half the 819 cylindrs) and then press ↵. The partition is created and the following message displayed:

```
Create Primary DOS Partition
Current Fixed Disk Drive: 1
Partition Status Type    Start  End    Size
C: 1      PRI    DOS   0      409    410
Primary DOS partition created
Press ESC to return to FDISK Options
```

This status information shows that logical drive C has been created, that it is the primary DOS partition (the one used for booting) and that the partition extends from cylinders 0 to 409. You press Esc to return to the main menu and then go on to make an extended partition from the remaining cylinders. Again, you select the first menu choice to Create DOS partition and then select Create Extended DOS partition. The message appears:

```
Create Extended DOS Partition
Partition Status Type    Start  End    Size
C: 1      PRI    DOS   0      409    410
Total disk space is 819 cylinders.
Maximum space available for partition
is 409 cylinders.
Enter partition size.........:[ 409]
```

As before, you are shown status information, and this time told how many cylinders are left. You can divide the remaining space into as many segments as you like, each with its own drive specifier, starting from D. FDISK specifies 409 cylinders as the obvious choice, and you select it by pressing ↵. Now the partitioning information reflects the new partition:

```
Partition Status Type   Start  End   Size
C: 1      PRI    DOS    0      409   410
   2      EXT    DOS    410    818   409
Extended DOS partition created
```

Setting the drive specifier   Notice that the second partition is not yet marked by the symbol D: to indicate its drive specifier. This is accomplished in the next step. FDISK displays the message:

```
Create Logical DOS Drive(s)
No logical drives defined
Total partition size is 409 cylinders.
Maximum space available for logical
drive is 409 cylinders.
Enter logical drive size........:[ 409]
```

At this point, just press ⏎ and you'll see:

```
Create Logical DOS Drive(s)
Drv Start End  Size
D:  410   818  409
All available space in the Extended DOS
partition is assigned to logical drives.
Logical DOS drive created,
drive letters changed or added
Press ESC to return to FDISK Options
```

You will encounter the following warning:

```
WARNING! No partitions marked active
```

Specifying which partition to boot from   The message means that you must tell DOS which partition to boot from. This task is performed automatically if you don't create an extended partition. But in our case, we must return to turn to the main FDISK menu (by pressing Esc) and selecting the second menu choice (Change active partition). The usual status information appears:

```
Partition Status Type   Start  End   Size
C: 1      PRI    DOS    0      409   410
   2      EXT    DOS    410    818   409
```

You're asked for the number of the partition to make active. You type 1 and press ⏎, and that's that. If you choose this selection again, you get the message:

```
The only bootable partition on Drive 1 is already marked active.
```

Deleting a partition   You're finished. The drive has been partitioned and now requires a high-level format. But before moving on to that topic, let's look at the other two options in the FDISK main menu.

First, you may want to delete a partition from a disk. In this example, we'll delete an extended partition. Choose option 3 (Delete DOS Partition) from the main menu and you'll be shown a screen like this one:

```
Delete DOS Partition
Current Fixed Disk Drive: 1
Choose one of the following:
   1. Delete Primary DOS partition
   2. Delete Extended DOS partition
   3. Delete logical DOS drive(s) in
      the Extended DOS Partition
Enter choice:[ ]
```

To delete an extended partition (menu choice 2), you must first delete the logical drive assignment by selecting 3. Status information is displayed:

```
Delete Logical DOS Drive
Drv Start End  Size
D:  410  818  409
Total partition size is 409 cylinders.
Warning! Data in the logical DOS drive
will be lost. What drive do you wish
to delete.....................? [ ]
```

You type in the drive specifier (in this case, D) and press ⏎. DOS responds with the message:

```
Are you sure.....................? [n]
```

Type Y and ⏎, and FDISK displays:

```
All logical drives are deleted in the Extended DOS partition
```

Then press Esc to return to the main menu. Select option 3 again (Delete DOS Partition). The same menu appears, but this time with only two choices:

```
   1. Delete Primary DOS partition
   2. Delete Extended DOS partition
```

After selecting 2, FDISK displays:

```
Delete Extended DOS Partition
Current Fixed Disk Drive: 1
Partition Status Type  Start  End   Size
C: 1      PRI    DOS    0      409   410
   2      EXT    DOS    410    818   409
Warning! Data in the Extended DOS
partition will be lost. DO you wish
to continue................? [N]
```

Just type Ⓨ and ⏎ and the partition is deleted.

Getting partition information   You can find out the current partitioning of a drive at any time by selecting option 4 from the FDISK main menu (Display Partition Information). You're shown the same information displayed by the other FDISK options. For example:

```
Display Partition Information
Current Fixed Disk Drive: 1
Partition Status Type   Start  End    Size
C: 1      PRI    DOS    0      409    410
D: 2      EXT    DOS    410    818    409
Total disk space is 819 cylinders.
The Extended DOS partition contains
logical DOS drives. Do you want to display
logical drive information? [Y]
```

Press ⏎ to see:

```
Display Logical DOS Drive Information
Drv Start End  Size
D:  410   818  409
```

Partitioning utilities   Prior to the appearance of DOS 3.3, large drives had to be partitioned with utility software that could create multiple DOS partitions on a disk, or partitions larger than 32 megabytes. These required that you load a device driver from your CONFIG.SYS file when the machine boots. Some of these utilities can pull off an even more amazing trick: they can span a partition across two hard drives. That is, two physical drives become one logical drive, accessed through one drive specifier, and one directory tree. This setup does not hinder disk performance, and in some cases actually helps it since the single logical drive has two sets of read/write heads.

To work this magic, these programs must take the disk through every step of formatting, both low- and high-level. Because they are often applied to super-high-capacity drives, they are specially designed to deal with the problems of unusual drive geometries. They can, however, be used with drives of any size. Your involvement in disk formatting is limited to entering bad track numbers and installing the DOS files through the SYS command. The rest is a breeze.

These utilities are gradually falling from favor as DOS acquires more capability. If you use one, you should be aware that some can interfere with the operation of certain kinds of software, particularly when they use a nonstandard sector size. You may find that utility software like file defragmenters and disk repair programs won't work with drives formatted and partitioned this way. In some cases, the makers of partition extension programs have issued their own equivalents to some of these utilities.

16.4 Formatting a hard disk: high-level formatting

At high-level, hard disk formatting is identical to that of diskettes, as explained in section 16.1. Place a copy of the DOS diskette in drive A so that the FORMAT.COM program will be on hand and enter:

FORMAT C: /S ⏎

The /S switch causes FORMAT to set up the disk for booting the computer; this switch is not required when formatting a second hard disk in a machine, because that disk would not be used for booting. You may also append the /V switch to the command so that DOS will prompt you for a volume label for the disk. DOS 4.0 will ask you for a volume label whether you use this switch or not. Unlike diskettes, for which an indexing scheme using volume labels can be valuable, there usually isn't much point in labeling a hard disk. However, backup software (discussed in Chapter 22) may sometimes use a hard disk's volume label to associate backup files with the disk.

Unlike with diskettes, when FORMAT is directed at a hard disk, it displays a warning message explaining that it is not a diskette that has been designated. The message can help you recover from a mistyped FORMAT command. Formatting begins immediately when you press E; there is not so much as a fraction of a second in which to change your mind, so proceed carefully.

PITFALLS | Many hard disk utility packages include a so-called unformat program designed to reverse the effects of accidentally using FORMAT on a disk already full of data. These utilities are discussed in section 23.5. Do not become nonchalant about your use of the FORMAT command with the idea that, should an error occur, you can apply one of these utilities to get out of trouble. There are two reasons why you should not feel so assured. First, such utilities must be purchased and properly installed in your system before the accidental reformatting occurs. Otherwise, they can make only a limited and messy recovery of your data. Second, even when such a utility has been installed, a perfect recovery is unlikely. Files changed in the hours immediately preceeding the accidental reformatting may be corrupted. In the case of complex data files, such as spreadsheet files, the corruption may be enough to result in the loss of all data in the file.

16.5 Changing a disk's volume label

A volume label is a name of up to 11 characters that identifies a disk. A disk's volume label is displayed at the top of every directory listing taken from the disk; it also can be viewed by entering:

VOL ⏎

Add a drive specifier to view the label of a drive other than the current drive:

VOL A: ⏎

DOS returns a message like:

Volume in drive C is HARDDISK 1

Starting from version 3.0, DOS provides the LABEL command for changing a disk's current volume label, or for giving a label to a disk that wasn't given one during formatting (section 16.1 explains how volume labels are added during formatting). To add the label HARDDISK to drive C or to replace the current label with this one, enter:

LABEL C:HARDDISK ⏎

The label is always written in uppercase letters. If you exceed the 11-character limit, or if you just enter:

LABEL ⏎

DOS responds with a message reporting the current volume label (which reads FIXED DISK in this case):

Volume in drive C is FIXED DISK
Volume label (11 characters, ENTER for none)?

You can then type in a new label (in this case, if you enter more than 11 characters, DOS will use the first 11 for the new label). Alternatively, just press ⏎ to delete the current label, whereupon DOS will inquire:

Delete current volume label (Y/N)?

Respond by pressing Y to delete the label.

Windows 3.1   To change a disk's volume label in Windows, select the disk drive's icon. Then choose Label Disk from the Disk menu, type in the new label, and choose OK.

Chapter 17

Getting Ready To Boot

- MINITUTORIAL: Starting up the computer
- Making a floppy disk bootable
- Booting the computer
- Rebooting the computer
- Setting the system time and date
- Finding out the current DOS version
- Rules for turning the machine on and off

MINITUTORIAL:
Starting up the computer

When you switch on the computer, some seconds pass before a DOS prompt appears. During this time, indicator lights blink, disk drives turn, and cryptic messages may appear on the screen. This process is called booting the computer, meaning metaphorically that the computer lifts itself by its bootstraps. Of course, it is impossible to lift yourself into the air by pulling at your bootstraps, but the expression is used with computers to indicate that something very clever is happening. The main task of booting is to load the main DOS program, COMMAND.COM, into memory from a disk drive. Yet it is COMMAND.COM that controls disk drives. How can the disk drives load COMMAND.COM without already having COMMAND.COM in memory?

The computer is able to load DOS because it keeps a small piece of DOS at a particular position on the disk from which the computer boots (the boot disk). There is software built into the machine that is just smart enough to cause the disk drive to find this part of DOS and turn control over to it. This part of DOS is called the boot record.

The boot record makes the machine a little more intelligent. After reading the boot record, it is able to find another file on the disk, IBMBIO.COM (IO.SYS in MS-DOS), load it, put it in charge, and then find yet another file, IBMDOS.COM (MSDOS.SYS in MS-DOS). With this last file brought into memory, the machine is smart enough to load COMMAND.COM. Once loaded, COMMAND.COM is permanently put in charge of the machine. It configures itself using the CONFIG.SYS file, performs the commands it finds in the AUTOEXEC.BAT file, and then displays a DOS prompt, waiting for you to enter a DOS command, or to type in the name of a program to run.

The boot record, IBMBIO.COM, IBMDOS.COM, and COMMAND.COM may be placed on the disk when it is formatted. Only COMMAND.COM appears in directory listings of the disk, but all must be on the disk to be able to use it for booting. Normally, you decide when you format a disk whether it can be used for booting or not. In machines with one hard disk, which always appears as drive C, the disk is always made bootable.

Machines with no hard disk always boot from diskette drive A. You can keep one boot diskette and remove it immediately after start-up, or you can make numerous diskettes bootable, add application software, and go to work without changing diskettes. The latter approach is convenient, although a significant portion of a diskette's space might be taken up by the DOS files.

For many application programs it is important to keep a copy of COMMAND.COM in the drive from which the computer has booted. When COMMAND.COM is loaded in memory, it locates itself in two areas. One part contains critical software that must always be in memory while programs run; the other part can be dispensed with while software is running, but must be on hand when programs terminate and return control to DOS. This latter part is referred to as the transient part of DOS.

When application programs require lots of memory, DOS lets them overwrite its transient part; later, when the program finishes, DOS reloads the transient part from the COMMAND.COM file. It looks for the file in the same disk as it booted from. Since the hard disk is always in place, DOS always finds the file when it boots from a hard disk. But the boot disk may have been removed when the machine has been booted from a diskette in drive A. In this case, DOS displays a message asking that you insert a DOS diskette in drive A. It then reloads the transient portion of COMMAND.COM and returns to the DOS prompt. Thereafter, you may switch back to the diskette that was in the drive. To avoid unnecessary diskette swapping, you can place a copy of COMMAND.COM on a diskette that was not made bootable during formatting or you can follow a special technique that lets a computer reload COMMAND.COM from a different drive or directory than the one from which DOS was booted.

17.1 Making a floppy disk bootable

It's tiresome to insert and remove a DOS diskette every time you start up a diskette-only machine. You can get around this annoyance by making a diskette bootable. This means that the diskette contains three files required for booting. COMMAND.COM is one of these files, and it is easily moved to a diskette with the COPY command. But the second two files have a special status: they are hidden files that cannot be seen in directory listings and cannot be moved by COPY. For this reason, the three files that make a diskette bootable are usually installed when the diskette is formatted. This is done by adding /S to the format command, as in FORMAT A: /S ⏎. The format command can destroy data when wrongly used, so be sure you are familiar with the discussion found in section 16.1.

The SYS command   Some software manufacturers would like to make the diskettes they distribute bootable. But the three special DOS files are under copyright, and so they cannot be packaged with the software. As a DOS owner, however, you are free to copy the files over from your DOS diskette. Some manufacturers create their program diskettes in a way that the special disk locations used by the two hidden files are kept unoccupied. After copying the original program diskette, you can transfer the hidden files to it using a command called SYS. You'll need to place the DOS diskette in one drive, say drive A, and the diskette you want to make bootable in the second drive, drive B. Then enter:

```
SYS B: ⏎
```

The two hidden files are copied from the DOS diskette to the special locations. However, the third file, COMMAND.COM, is not transferred automatically. You must move it separately by entering:

```
COPY COMMAND.COM B: ⏎
```

Starting with DOS 4.0, a diskette does not require special preparation to apply the SYS command; any diskette can be made bootable anytime.

Reloading   Some software requires so much memory that it intrudes on parts of DOS, and when the program has finished, those parts of DOS must be read back into memory from disk. The missing parts are taken from COMMAND.COM. DOS expects to find the file on the same disk it booted from. If it finds the information it needs, the DOS prompt reappears and you can proceed to your next task. But if the machine was booted from drive A and the boot diskette has been removed, the machine responds with a message asking you to insert a DOS diskette (bootable diskette). You can avoid swapping diskettes by transferring COMMAND.COM to any program diskette that is used from drive A. The other boot files aren't required in this situation.

TIP

Except for installing software on a hard disk, you should not use the original diskettes on which you received your software. Originals should always be copied and then placed in safe storage so that you'll have a reliable backup should harm befall the diskettes you use day to day.

Microsoft Windows Windows makes the Sys command available through the File Manager. Choose Make System Disk from the Disk menu and you'll encounter the dialog box shown in figure 17.1. The command is always directed to drive A.

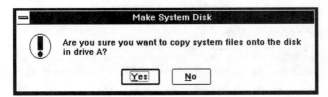

Figure 17.1

17.2 Booting the computer

Provided that everything is set up properly, when you turn on your computer it will boot. (The minitutorial that begins this chapter explains what happens during booting.) Once the machine has booted, the DOS prompt appears on the screen, and you can start entering DOS commands and running programs. Normally, there is nothing for you to do while booting proceeds. However, before switching on the machine you must be sure that it is ready to boot. There are two ways to boot an IBM PC, depending on whether the machine has a hard disk or not.

Computers with a hard disk   The first hard disk installed in a computer is always named drive C, even if there is no second diskette drive named B. The machine will boot from the hard disk only after the disk has been formatted in a way that it is set up for booting. (See section 16.5 to learn how to prepare a hard disk this way.)

Even with a hard disk installed, the machine still begins by trying to boot from drive A. For this reason, that drive must have no diskette in it when the machine is switched on; or—if a diskette is present—the drivedoor (lever) must be open. Once the computer fails to find a diskette in drive A, it moves on to drive C and boots. If the door to drive A is closed and it contains a diskette that can't be booted from, the machine issues the message:

```
Non-System disk or disk error
Replace and press any key when ready
```

In this case, the machine does not then go on to boot from drive C. You must open the door of drive A and then restart the computer by pressing any key.

Occasionally, there may be a bootable diskette in drive A when you boot a computer that has a hard disk. Even in this case, you should open the door to drive A so that booting takes place on drive C. This is because the disks in the two drives may not use matching DOS versions. The machine may boot properly, but later you could have trouble when you find yourself using DOS files from drive C that don't match the DOS version booted from drive A. Also, DOS may later need to access one of the boot files again, and won't be able to find it if the diskette is removed.

Computers without a hard disk   Computers lacking a hard disk always boot from a diskette in drive A. The door (lever) at the front of the drive must be closed, and the disk inside the drive must be a boot diskette. This is nothing more than a diskette that has been prepared for booting during formatting (as explained in the minitutorial at the beginning of the chapter) or by the SYS command (section 17.1). Be aware that just copying the main DOS file, COMMAND.COM, to a diskette does not make it a boot diskette. When you switch on the machine and the diskette inside drive A is not a boot diskette, the computer displays the message:

```
Non-System disk or disk error
Replace and press any key when ready
```

Place a boot diskette in the drive, close the drive door, and press any key to begin booting.

PITFALLS | The various kinds of IBM machines behave differently when booting fails. On IBM-made PCs, XTs, and ATs, you'll encounter a screen like the one shown in section 24.1. This is the BASIC Interpreter, a programming language built right into the machine. Clones will display an error message instead. PS/2 machines show a diagram of a computer indicating that you should insert the boot diskette and press F1 .

No matter what appears on the screen, don't panic. Just place a proper boot diskette in drive A and press F1 to reboot (or press Ctrl - Alt - Del if you encounter the Basic Interpreter). Note that this situation can arise even on computers that have hard disks and that normally boot from the hard disk. It might occur, for example, if something has happened to one of the files used in booting, as when COMMAND.COM has been accidentally erased.

17.3 **Rebooting the computer**

There are several reasons why you may need to reboot the computer, thereby clearing memory of software and data, and loading a fresh copy of DOS from disk. They are:

■ Software may have malfunctioned such that keyboard commands no longer get through, or no longer give you control over the software. In this state, the machine is said to have hung, or to be frozen.

■ You may be lost in software that you are not familiar with and are unable to exit.

■ You may need to reboot after making a change in the CONFIG.SYS or AUTOEXEC.BAT files that DOS automatically consults when it starts up. Rebooting activates changes in these files.

■ You may wish to reconfigure the machine for work you are about to do. By rebooting with different CONFIG.SYS and AUTO-EXEC.BAT files, you may change the general DOS configuration, load or remove device drivers from memory, add or delete RAM disks and memory-resident programs, and so on. Section 11.12 discusses this strategy.

Rebooting is done in two ways, either by pressing the Ctrl, Alt, and Del keys at once, or by switching the machine off and then back on. The first method is called a warm boot and the latter a cold boot. A warm boot skips over most of the diagnostic tests that normally occur at start-up. Striking Ctrl-Alt-Del does the job on all occasions except when the machine hangs through a severe software problem.

PITFALLS Ctrl-Alt-Del is vastly overused by PC users. Do not get into the habit of using it as a panic button ("I'm lost. I'll just start over again"). Software needs to keep its house in order, and many programs record important information on disk when you quit through the proper exit command.

No matter how the software works, you must be careful to not press Ctrl-Alt-Del when a disk drive is running (as shown by the indicator light on the drive or on the front panel of the machine). If a file has been only partially written to disk when Ctrl-Alt-Del is pressed, it may be destroyed. Rebooting is no substitute for knowing how to use your software properly. Read your software tutorials so that you won't wander down pathways from which you can't extricate yourself without rebooting.

Turning the machine off and then on again   When software freezes the machine, nothing can get through from the keyboard, including Ctrl-Alt-Del. Your only option is to turn off the machine and then turn it back on again. Some machines are equipped with a reset button. Pressing it has much the same effect as turning the machine off and then back on. On well designed computers, this button is positioned well out of the way, sometimes at the back of the machine, to prevent someone from accidentally pushing it.

Be sure to wait a few seconds between turning the switch off and then on, because the computer has enough power to keep running for a few moments after electricity is cut off. If you don't wait long enough, the machine will freeze all over again when you restart it.

17.4 Setting the system time and date

DOS always keeps track of the time and date. It uses these values to time stamp files when they are created or changed, assigning the time and date seen in directory listings. The time and date are also available for software to use as it pleases. You can find out the current time setting by entering on the DOS command line:

    TIME ⏎

DOS displays a message like:

    Current time is 11:43:12,05
    Enter new time:

You can enter a new time or, if you don't wish to, you can simply press ⏎ to keep the current time.

Although directory listings tell whether the time is a.m. or p.m., the clock is not set in this way. Rather, the hours are counted from 0 to 23, starting at midnight. Times up till noon are named in the usual way, and times thereafter have 12 added. Thus midnight is 0 hours and noon is 12 hours. 1:00 a.m. is 1 hours while 1:00 p.m. is 13 hours, 2:00 p.m. is 14 hours, and so on. 3:10 in the afternoon is 15:10 and 3:15 is 15:15.

DOS keeps the time to hundredths of a second—hardly a necessity for most people. You can omit this part of the time when you enter it, and can omit the seconds as well. When you do, entering a number like 12:42, the values for seconds and hundredths of seconds are set to 0. Note that the DOS clock is not actually accurate to hundredths of a second; what you get is an estimate.

You can find out the current date in much the same way as the time:

    DATE ⏎

Again, DOS displays a message:

    Current date is Wed 9-14-1989
    Enter new date:

and again you can optionally enter a new date, or press ⏎ to keep the current one.

Most computers are equipped with a real-time clock, including all IBM AT-style machines and PS/2 machines, as well as some PC- or XT-style clones. A real-time clock resides on a circuit board that includes a long-life battery to keep the clock going when the machine is turned off. When DOS starts up, it automatically reads the time and date from this clock.

Setting the time and date   Normally, a machine boots, reads the real-time clock to make the DOS time setting, and that's that. Even when no real-time clock is present, no request is made of you to enter the current time and date if an AUTOEXEC.BAT file (section 11.1) is present at start-up. If this file is not present, DOS prompts you for the current time and date by displaying a message like:

```
Current date is Thu 12-28-1989
Enter new date (mm-dd-yy):
```

and then:

```
Current time is 13:53:39.14
Enter new time:
```

These messages occur even when the machine has a real-time clock that sets the time automatically. If you don't want to enter a new time and date, you can just press the ⏎ key twice to skip over these steps. When you do, settings already made by the real-time clock are preserved. When no clock is present, incorrect values appear for the date and time. Use the TIME and DATE commands to enter the correct values. To set the time to 10:35 in the morning, type:

```
TIME 10:35 ⏎
```

Similarly, to set the date to July 14, 1990, enter:

```
DATE 7-14-90 ⏎
```

Microsoft Windows   In Windows, enter the Control Panel and choose the Date/Time icon. A dialog box like the one shown in figure 17.2 appears. Select any part of the time or date you wish to change and either type in a new value or click on the arrow symbols to increment or decrement the selected value. Then click on OK.

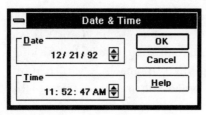

Figure 17.2

Real-time clocks   A real-time clock keeps time about as accurately as a digital watch, which is to say that it needs resetting every six months or so. PS/2 machines running under DOS 4.0 and later can use the TIME and DATE commands as shown above to set the clock. AT-style machines set the clock through the SETUP program used to configure the machine.

PC- and XT-style machines usually don't have a real-time clock built in that is automatically read at start-up. But real-time clocks may be added by inserting one on an expansion board into one of the machine's slots. Many multifunction boards include real-time clocks along with additional memory and input/output channels (serial and parallel ports). Real-time clocks introduced in this way communicate with DOS through special utility software that accompanies the board. They will have a utility program that you run to fetch the time and date from the clock and place that information in the DOS clock. And there will be another utility to set the values in the real-time clock. When this is the case, the DOS TIME and DATE commands only change the reading in the DOS clock, and not the real-time clock, so that the settings made by these commands are lost when the machine is turned off.

There is no great inconvenience associated with real-time clocks that work in this way. Simply place the name of the utility program that transfers the real-time clock reading to the DOS clock in your AUTOEXEC.BAT file. If the utility program were called SET-CLOCK.COM, you include in AUTOEXEC.BAT the line:

```
SETCLOCK
```

Once done, each time you boot the machine the utility is run and the DOS clock is set to the current time and date. You'll also need to occasionally run the utility that sets the time and date on the real-time clock, but only when the clock has drifted from the proper time.

17.5 Finding out the current DOS version

DOS has steadily evolved since the first days of IBM personal computers. Like all software, it is periodically released in a new version that incorporates new features, as well as improvements in old ones (plus bug fixes—corrections of problems and errors). Sometimes the new version represents a major overhaul; other times the changes are slight, even insignificant to most users.

The version of DOS shipped with the first IBM PCs was version 1.00, and there have been three major revisions since, resulting in DOS 2.00, 3.00, and so on. The versions released between these major revisions have versions' numbers like 2.10. In this number, the 2 is the major version number and the .10 is the minor version number. Sometimes, when the only changes are bug corrections, the version number will change in the last digit, as in 4.01 (a revision of DOS 4.00 that is identical in every way, but that has had some serious bugs corrected). In the popular press the last digit is often dropped; one speaks of DOS 3.3 or DOS 4.0.

To find out your DOS version, simply type in:

VER ⏎

on the DOS command line. The screen will show a message, such as:

```
IBM Personal Computer DOS Version 3.30
```

You may need to know the DOS version number when you have acquired new software and its installation instructions state that the software works only with a particular DOS version or later. DOS carries features that are invisible to the user but are constantly used by software. These features have also been steadily expanded. Software that uses more recently-added features simply cannot work with a DOS version that does not provide them. The addition of these features is cummulative; for example, when a program is said to require DOS 2.1, this means that it requires DOS 2.1 or any later version, such as 2.2, 3.1. or 4.0.

Remember that the functions DOS provides are divided between the main DOS file, COMMAND.COM, and the many external files that hold less-used DOS routines that don't need to be kept in memory all the time, such as BACKUP and CHKDSK. The VER command tells you the version number of COMMAND.COM alone. Usually, the files that contain the external commands must be of the same DOS version (from the same DOS diskettes) as the version of COMMAND.COM in use. Don't try to upgrade to a more recent DOS version by copying over only the newer COMMAND.COM to your boot disk. This action can leave many external files inoperative, and a flood of error messages and serious problems can result.

17.6 Rules for turning the machine on and off

Flipping the switch would seem the very simplest part of using a computer. But there are some important things to keep in mind. Every time the power is switched on, a surge of electricity passes through the machine, stressing the microchips and other components. Just like a light bulb, the computer incurs extra wear and tear each time it is powered up. By minimizing the number of times the machine is turned on and off, and by turning it on and off properly, you may stave off repairs.

Computers and their peripherals use special, rather expensive power switches. They move between their on and off states with a clear snap, thus avoiding any wavering between on and off that would increase the number of up-down surges the machine experiences. Inconveniently, there can be several power switches to deal with in a typical system: the computer itself, the video display, the printer, and perhaps an external modem or tape drive.

TIP

An easy short cut is to plug all equipment into a power strip—a bank of electrical sockets that plugs into one wall socket. Power strips usually have a switch that turns off power to all its sockets. All attached equipment can be left switched on, and then turned on and off in unison through the power strip switch. Don't do this unless the switch manufacturer specifically approves it because the switch may be of poor quality, causing extra power surges. If you want this convenience, consider buying a power control center specifically designed for computer equipment.

Another issue is whether to leave the computer running while not in use. As a general rule, try to avoid switching the machine on and off much more than once a day. Hard disk drives in particular have their lives shortened by the heating and cooling that occurs every time power is applied or removed. Most computers consume between 50 and 150 watts, which is exactly equivalent to running a light bulb of equivalent wattage. So, the electricity costs only a penny or two per hour.

On the other hand, some components, like the power supply and video tube, are under constant wear while the machine is running. This makes it wasteful to leave the machine on for whole days or weeks when it is not in use. In most cases, it is inadvisable to leave the machine on permanently.

It's usually inadvisable to turn off the machine while software is still running. Many programs perform a kind of housekeeping when you ask them to quit, and this work will go undone if the computer is just switched off. This is true of Microsoft Windows, which should always be exited properly.

In some cases, crucial information is written into files only at the time the files are closed. Files can be lost if the program is abruptly terminated by turning off the machine or by pressing Ctrl - Alt - Del (but not by exiting by Ctrl -Break, however). Similarly, you must be sure that disk drives have finished their work before shutting off power. If you've instructed a program to save a file and then terminate, be sure you've returned to the DOS prompt before reaching for the power switch. In fact, you may need to wait a few seconds even after the drives have quieted, since some kinds of disk caching software (discussed in section 21.8) may wait a few moments before writing data to disk.

Part III
Managing the System

Chapter 18

Using Windows

MINITUTORIAL:

DOS, the DOS Shell, Windows, OS/2, and Presentation Manager

DOS happens to be the first operating system IBM adopted for its personal computers, but it is by no means the only one available. There are several ways to move beyond DOS. In doing so, you can gain computing power and make your computer easier to use at the same time. Most innovations come at a price, however. They tend to soak up precious memory; they pose myriad compatibility problems with existing software; and they might even slow down your machine. This minitutorial provides an overview of the many options available today.

DOS is about as rudimentary as an operating system can be. It provides a user interface that is no more than a command line for typing in cryptic expressions. It offers little help when you make mistakes. Even editing your text is difficult. Internally, DOS is just as primitive. It reads and writes files in a simple fashion, and performs only the most fundamental screen operations. DOS is unable to manage memory in a sophisticated fashion to allow several programs to run at the same time.

There are a number of features users have been clamoring for, but which DOS is ill-equipped to provide. These features include:

■ Memory beyond 640K: As the minitutorial in Chapter 15 explains, conventional memory cannot be increased beyond 640K (or a little more in some machines) because of the way the original IBM PCs were designed. Computers with an 80286, 80386, or 80486 microprocessor can also access extended memory, but only when the microprocessor works in a special processing mode (the protected mode). DOS does not support protected mode, so software made to run under DOS cannot (usually) use extended memory. On the other hand, all PCs, including the very earliest, can employ expanded memory to access up to 32 megabytes of memory, although software must be specially designed to use it.

■ 32-bit operation: Besides the issue of memory quantity, there is the question of the speed of memory access. Until the advent of 80386 machines, all IBM PCs were 16-bit computers, meaning that the microprocessor could perform calculations and read and write memory no more than two bytes at a time. The 386 and 486 microprocessors work with 32 bits, so they can work on four bytes of data at a time, greatly accelerating some kinds of operations (however, 386SX machines perform calculations in 32 bits, but access memory in 16 bits). All microprocessors in this series are said to be backward-compatible, meaning that the advanced models can behave as if they were early models, and thus can run any software written for early models.

DOS is a 16-bit operating system, as is OS/2 (discussed below) in its first incarnation. A 32-bit operating system would work more quickly, but would be restricted to 386 and 486 machines. Many people would like to see a true 32-bit operating system evolve, but its appearance could divide the IBM PC world into two camps, each with its own software.

■ Task switching and multitasking: Many PC users like to be able to quickly move back and forth between programs, a practice called task switching. Memory-resident utility programs, such as calendars and calculators, are familiar examples in the DOS world. In true task switching, two or more programs may appear on the screen at the same time, each in its own window, with only one active at any moment.

A step beyond task switching is multitasking, in which two or more programs operate simultaneously. This feature might seem useless at first sight because the user can do only one thing at a time. But consider how you must sometimes wait for a program to finish sorting or printing a file. In a multitasking environment, the program could perform this work in the background while you resume work on, say, a word processing document. This is achieved by rapidly shifting the microprocessor back and forth between programs or tasks within a program. Much microprocessor time is wasted waiting for you to do something, and much more is lost as the microprocessor idles between your keystrokes; multitasking puts the squandered processing power to work.

■ An advanced file system: DOS organizes files in a rudimentary way. As applications have become more complex, so has the design of their files. To accomodate complex applications, programmers have had to devise extremely complicated systems of file management. An operating system could do much of this work, even to the point of offering database features —ways of storing and indexing data for quick retrieval—in a standard format for any program to use.

■ Data sharing: When several programs run at the same time, it would be nice to be able to share data between them. Text from a word processor could be transferred directly into a page-makeup program without first writing the data to a file, and then loading the file into the second program. It should be the operating system's job to provide the pathways for such data transfers. In addition, the designers of the operating system could set down guidelines for data design that programmers could follow to ensure compatability.

Beyond simple data sharing is the concept of hot links, in which data can be continuously shared between programs. When data is altered in one program, the change could be instantly reflected in others. Thus, the recalculation of a spreedsheet could automatically change a bar chart in a graphics program.

■ A graphical user interface (GUI): A user interface is the sum of the ways that you communicate with software and software communicates with you. In DOS, the user interface consists of nothing more than a command line on which you type in DOS commands and screen messages. A graphical user interface could replace the simple DOS command line with menus, icons, dialog boxes, and other devices made popular by the Apple Macintosh. A mouse could be used to make menu selections and to point to objects on the screen. The interface could provide all important operating system commands in an easy-to-use form for running programs, copying or renaming files, and so on. The interface features should also be made available to application programs so that they can work in the same way. Ideally, the programs will use windows the same way, menus the same way, dialog boxes the same way, and so on. In this sense, an interface should be a set of programming rules as much as it is a collection of software utilities.

Although these interfaces are called graphical, most of their advantages can be achieved using text screens. This is an important point, because many PCs are not fast enough to run a truly graphical environment well. Even the mouse can be eliminated from a graphical user interface, although keystroke combinations are often slower and more complicated. Many DOS shells, and many text-based application programs available today, offer quite good approximations of graphical user interfaces.

Several types of software have appeared to bring these capabilities to existing PCs:

- DOS shells: A DOS shell is a utility program that, in a sense, sits on top of DOS, replacing the DOS prompt with a system of menus, flexible directory listings, and tree diagrams. DOS shells make DOS much easier to use. They have no effect on the way programs operate, and can't expand the amount of available memory. A shell is shipped with DOS version 4.0. It is adequate but hardly among the best. (Don't upgrade DOS just for a copy of the shell; your money is better spent on one of the shells available from other sources.)

- Menu programs: Menu programs are a kind of utility software that take control when the computer is turned on. They can make it possible for someone to use a computer with little concern for how DOS works, how programs are run, and so on. When the machine starts up, a menu appears instead of the DOS command line. The menu may list basic tasks like Word Processing and Spreadsheet. You make a choice from the menu and the menu program automatically starts up the appropriate program. A menu program may help you find and load files without using directory paths. Essential DOS commands, such as COPY and ERASE, may also be set up as menu selections.

  Although the menus may be easy to use, setting them up is by no means a trivial task. Generally speaking, if you know DOS well enough to set up a menu program, you don't need menus. But even DOS experts can sometimes find menus handy for quickly starting up programs that are used often. The problem with menu programs that replace the DOS command line is that they limit your power over the machine, and ultimately your productivity. For those who understand DOS, a DOS shell is a better choice.

- Security shells: Security shells are a combined DOS shell and menu program designed to prevent unauthorized access to data. They can defeat some of the most sophisticated forms of penetration. Individual users are issued passwords associated with specific clearance levels for particular subdirectories and even individual files. A menu system limits users to particular options. You cannot break out of the menu system, even by rebooting from a DOS diskette in drive A or by pressing Ctrl-Break. The shell sees to it that software can be neither copied in or out of the machine by a diskette drive. The actions of every user can even be logged in a file, so that attempts to break through the system are made conspicuous.

■ Memory-resident program managers: This is a special genre of utility software that looks after numerous memory-resident programs (see sections 15.4 and 15.5 for background). Besides reducing or eliminating conflicts between these programs, these utilities make it possible to load many more memory-resident programs than you normally would have room for. This is done by storing the programs on disk or in extended or expanded memory. When one is needed, it is quickly moved to conventional memory where just enough space is set aside to hold the largest program that you've told the memory manager you'll want to use.

■ DOS extenders: DOS extenders play some clever tricks to continue using DOS while exploiting the ability of the 80286, 80386, and 80486 microprocessors to access megabytes of extended memory. These processors run in two modes: a real mode corresponding to normal DOS programs running in 640K, and a protected mode that opens up 16 megabytes of memory or more. DOS extenders work by running programs in the protected mode, and momentarily switching to the real mode when DOS services are called upon. The software you are running, however, must be specially prepared to do this. In addition to opening up more memory, DOS extenders can take advantage of the full power of 32-bit chips like the 80386 and 80486.

■ Operating environments: The next step beyond DOS shells are DOS operating environments, which not only make DOS easier to use, but add a host of basic features. The two best-known operating environments are Windows and DESQview. Besides offering a DOS shell-like interface, they let you load and run more than one program at once, they provide means for transferring data between programs, and they make as full use as your application programs allow of any extended or expanded memory installed in the machine. Environments tailored to the 386 or 486 microprocessor can allot 640K of memory to each of several DOS programs running simultaneously.

Although operating environments are designed to run software developed for plain DOS, they also offer facilities by which programs can be written to use various features of the environment. Thus, a Windows version of an application can provide a full Macintosh-style interface.

■ OS/2: OS/2 is IBM's successor to DOS. It was created by IBM and Microsoft, the same company that originally developed DOS. OS/2 completely replaces DOS; it is not an extension. It operates only on machines with an 80286 or later microprocessor. PC/XT-style machines, which use an 8086 or 8088 microprocessor, cannot run OS/2. This is because OS/2 runs the more advanced microprocessors in protected mode, allowing multitasking with access to megabytes of memory. Software must be specially written for OS/2 because ordinary DOS software cannot run in protected mode. However, OS/2 provides a feature called the compatability box that lets a single DOS program run along with OS/2 software. When a 32-bit version of OS/2 appears—one that will run only on 386 and 486 machines—it will be able to run any number of DOS programs at once, giving each a full 640K of memory to use.

OS/2 provides a number of sophisticated features associated with mainframe computers. In a process called virtual memory management, the computer can run more programs and use more data than can fit into available memory. The operating system detects which parts of programs and data are idle and moves them to hard disk storage, swapping them back to memory when they are required. A technique called dynamic linking allows parts of programs to be shared between applications. Also, the Extended Edition of OS/2 includes advanced database and communications capabilities that any program can be designed to use.

■ Presentation Manager: A program called the Presentation Manager accompanies OS/2 to give it a Macintosh-like user interface, including movable windows, pull-down menus, and dialog boxes.

Programs must be specially written to use these features. Some companies have developed versions of their software that work under OS/2, but that don't employ Presentation Manager features. Essentially, these programs are glorified DOS software that can multitask and that can access much more memory. In many respects, the Presentation Manager looks and acts like Microsoft Windows. Like Windows, it requires more memory than DOS, and a fast microprocessor, if it is to run efficiently. But the gains in productivity are well worth the price. As memory and processing power become ever cheaper, a gradual transition to Windows and Presentation Manager seems inevitable.

18.1 An overview of Windows

Unlike a DOS shell, Microsoft Windows is a multitasking operating environment. Several programs can be run and displayed at once. If they are properly designed for use by Windows, the programs can directly exchange information. Because it is often the case that a single program can barely run in the 640K of system memory available to DOS, it's only natural to wonder how Windows can manage to juggle so many tasks simultaneously. The answer is that Windows uses advanced memory-management techniques to swap information in and out of extended and expanded memory. Adding one or both of these two kinds of memory to your machine helps Windows go to the limit.

In many respects, Windows looks like an advanced operating system such as OS/2 or UNIX, but in fact it still works with DOS and shares certain DOS limitations. Windows is called Windows because everything that appears on the screen—applications, utilities, data files—is displayed within its own rectangular window frame. These frames may be overlapped, stacked, or temporarily reduced to icons. (An icon is a small picture that represents an object or process; for example, a picture of a file folder could represent a subdirectory, and a picture of two moving legs could mean run the program.)

You can change the size and shape of windows, and position them in ways advantageous to your work. For example, you could keep a calculator open on one side of the screen for use while working in a spreadsheet elsewhere on the screen. Many programs, such as word processors, can adjust their line length and other dimensions to correspond to the current dimensions of the window they appear in. For other programs, such as spreadsheets, the size and shape of the window determines how much data is exposed at any moment, and how much you'll need to scroll.

Windows has a complicated design, one that is similar in many respects to the DOS Shell program shipped with DOS version 4.0. However, it also has many more features and is highly customizable. Customization can make for confusion if you learn to use Windows on a machine someone else has set up to his own preferences; the screens you encounter may not always parallel the ones you find in the documentation. But the underlying structure of Windows is straightforward.

The Program Manager   When you start Windows, the Program Manager takes charge. Accordingly, a Program Manager window opens on the screen. At least five icons are displayed along the bottom edge of the window. Each icon may be expanded to become a window containing other icons. The five icons represent:

■ Windows applications: This icon expands to a window that offers a listing of application programs that have been specially written to work under Windows. You can start up the programs directly from the icons that represent them. Thus, the window acts as a kind of menu from which you can make selections without tracking down program files in a directory tree.

■ Non-Windows applications: This icon is just like the Windows Applications icon, except it applies to Non-Windows programs. It's important to understand the distinction. Windows can run most ordinary DOS programs. In some cases Windows can confine a DOS program to a window; in other cases it has only limited control over the program, and it must turn over the whole screen to it, as if the program was running under normal DOS. These are non-Windows applications.

■ Main: This icon is the gateway to most Windows features. Most of the remainder of this chapter concerns it.

■ Games: Games are just that—computer games. Windows comes with the card game Solitaire and a board game called Reversi that resembles the Japanese game Go.

■ Accessories: These are utility programs, including some that are familiar as memory-resident programs under DOS. Windows supplies many useful accessories, including a calculator, notepad, calendar, card file, painting program, and so on.

Windows works with a mouse or keyboard, either of which can perform any action. Mouse commands are usually much simpler than keyboard commands and a mouse is highly recommended. To open an icon so that it expands into a window, you simply double-click on it with a mouse (move the mouse cursor to the icon and click the left mouse button twice quickly). To open it from the keyboard, you must understand how pull-down menus work, as we'll now explain.

The menu bar Along the top edge of the window, just below its title, is a menu bar—a listing of main menu choices. When you move the mouse cursor over one of the selections and hold down the left mouse button, a menu pulls down (descends from the top of the screen) to display all available options. You then pull the mouse towards you, still holding down the button. When you do, a bar cursor makes its way down the menu list and when it arrives at the selection you want to use, you release the mouse button. The pull-down menu will disappear and the selection is carried out.

Menu selections are made from the keyboard by looking for an underlined or emphasized letter in each of the words on the menu bar and typing that letter while holding down the ⌨Alt key. There are four choices in the bar menu of the Program Manager window: File, Options, Window, and Help. You would type ⌨Alt-⌨F to pull down the File menu (as shown in figure 18.1), ⌨Alt-⌨O to pull down the Options menu, and so on. Each selection in the menu that drops down also has an underlined character. You choose these selections simply by typing that character next. It does not matter whether you release the ⌨Alt key first (if you decide not to make a choice, just press ⌨Alt one more time). Knowing this much, you can open one of the five icons by typing ⌨Alt-⌨F14 to pull down the Window menu. You'll find the five icons listed in the menu by the numbers 1 through 5. To open Main, just type ⌨F3.

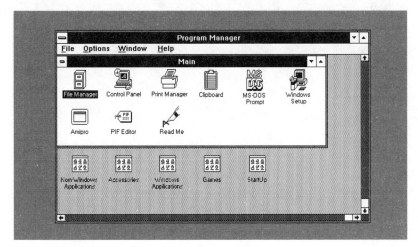

Figure 18.1

Window controls   Windows share a number of characteristics. Figure 18.2 shows the window displayed by the Notepad accessory. At the top center is the window title—in this case, Notepad. To the left of the window title is a box called the Control-menu box—a box for activating a menu that controls various characteristics of the window. Clicking the mouse on this box pulls down the control menu. Alternatively, press Alt and the spacebar to display the menu. It offers a number of selections we'll discuss in a moment.

To the right of the window title are two more boxes, one with an arrowhead pointing down, one with an arrowhead pointing up. The first is the minimize box, the second, the maximize box. Clicking the mouse in the minimize box reduces the window to an icon. Clicking on the maximize box expands the window. When you expand the window, the maximize box changes into a restore button, a symbol combining both up and down arrowheads. Clicking a mouse on the restore button returns the window to its prior size. These actions are accomplished from the keyboard by pulling down the window-control menu with Alt and the space bar and selecting Restore, Minimize, or Maximize.

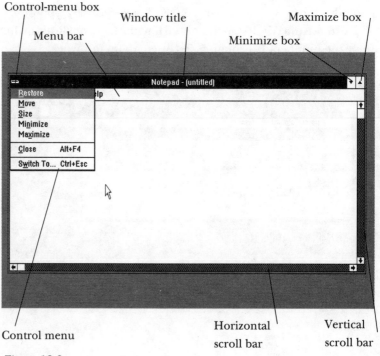

Figure 18.2

Moving and sizing windows   Two other options in the control menu are Move and Size. Selecting the first lets you reposition a window on the screen. The edges of the window will become highlighted. Use the four cursor keys to shift the window in any direction and type ⏎ when finished. You can cancel the move by pressing Esc instead. Choosing Size changes the window dimensions. The ↑ and ↓ keys move the top edge of the window, while the ← and → keys move the right edge. To extend the bottom or left edges, you must first Move the window so that the opposite edge reaches its desired position and then size it.

These actions are much easier with a mouse. To move a window, just shift the mouse cursor to the window title bar and press the left mouse button down; as you shift the mouse, the window will follow. Releasing the button sets the new window position. Resizing is also more flexible this way: Move the point of the mouse cursor to any of the window's four corners. The cursor will change into a four-arrow symbol. Holding down the mouse button, you can pull any corner to another screen position. Again, releasing the button sets the new dimensions.

Windows features   Knowing this much, you can explore many of the features Windows offers. Of chief interest are the selections offered by opening the Main icon discussed above. Its window gives six choices: File Manager, Control Panel, Print Manager, Clipboard, DOS Prompt, and Windows Setup. The File Manager is the heart of the Windows. It provides directory listings and DOS shell-like navigation around a directory tree diagram. The Control Panel lets you customize various hardware features in the machine, such as keyboard and mouse behavior. The Print Manager looks after a queue of files being output to a printer. The Clipboard is a data holding area used for transferring data between applications, or between two parts of the same application. The DOS Prompt is just that—a way to have Windows display an ordinary DOS prompt for you to type in DOS commands. Finally, Windows Setup lets you run the same set-up routines performed by the Windows installation program when Windows was first loaded onto your hard disk. Through it, you can add or change printers and can install additional application programs for automatic start-up from an icon.

Exiting Windows   One last point: to exit Windows, completely unloading it from memory, pull down the File menu and choose Exit. However, there's generally no need to leave Windows. You can get to a DOS prompt from within, and Windows largely removes itself from memory when it runs programs, automatically reloading itself when the program terminates. So you won't achieve substantial memory savings by exiting Windows, although in some cases it may be the only way to run a program that won't quite fit otherwise.

18.2 The Windows File Manager

The heart of Windows is its File Manager, which provides a tree diagram and directory listings, plus all of the commands like Copy and Rename that are familiar from DOS. To enter the File Manager, double-click on the Main icon of the Program Manager, and then on the File Manager icon that appears. If you are working without a mouse, press [Alt]-[W] to pull down the Window menu and then [4] to select Main. One of the icons shown in the Main window will be marked by a bar cursor. Use the [←] and [→] keys to move the bar cursor to the File Manager icon, then strike [←].

The File Manager window menu bar offers seven menus. They are:

■ File: This menu provides many of the most familiar DOS commands, including Copy, Delete, and Rename. Commands are used by first selecting one or more files from a directory listing. Only then do you pull down the File menu and choose an action. See section 18.3 to learn how to select files in Windows.

■ Disk: This menu contains commands for formatting diskettes, making diskette copies, and changing disk volume labels.

■ Tree: The Tree menu provides commands for expanding and contracting directory tree branches.

■ View: This menu lets you alter the criteria by which directory listings are displayed, including by file name, file type, file attributes, creation dates, and so on. This menu includes a Sort utility for sorting directory listings.

■ Options: Some miscellaneous features are contained in this menu. The most frequently used is Confirmation, which lets you decide whether Windows will display a confirmation box at critical moments. For example, when you erase a group of files, a dialog box can be made to appear and show the name of each file, asking you to confirm that the file should be erased.

■ Window: This menu is in two parts. The topmost selections let you choose how windows are displayed on the screen. Below, there appears a list of open windows, including windows that are currently minimized and appear as icons. When chosen from this menu, a window comes to the front, or expands from its icon form.

- Help: The Help menu offers a list of topics about which Windows can supply helpful information about how it works. The selections in this particular Help menu pertain only to the File Manager.

Figure 18.3 shows a typical start-up screen for the File Manager. A window with the name of the currently selected subdirectory opens on top of the File Manager window. Alternatively, the File Manager window may have the directory tree window minimized to appear as an icon. This will be the case if the window was left minimized the last time the File Manager was used. Double-click on the icon to open it, or use the keyboard or mouse to pull down the Window menu and select the window as it is listed there.

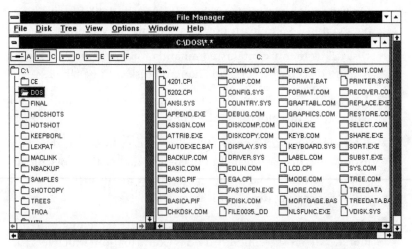

Figure 18.3

Views   While File Manager windows normally divide the screen evenly between a directly tree on the left and directory listings on the right, you can change the layout. Choose Tree Only or Directory Only from the View menu to select just one, and Tree and Directory to return to a split window. To adjust the proportion of the window devoted to each, choose Split in the Tree menu. A vertical bar will then appear and will move to the left or right in tandem with mouse motions or by pressing cursor keys. When you click the mouse or press ⏎, a new boundary will appear at the bar position.

Disk drives   From left to right along the top of every directory window is a row of symbols representing the computer's disk drives, with the current drive highlighted. Diskette drives are represented differently from hard disk drives. Moreover, there may be symbols for drives not installed. If you try to access one of these drives, Windows will display a message telling you that it cannot find the drive. You can select a different drive simply by clicking on it. To select a drive from the keyboard, presss the tab key to cycle a box-shaped cursor between the drive symbols and the tree diagram below. Once this special cursor is highlighting one of the drives, use ← or → to move it to the drive you want to make current and press ⏎. The tree diagram below will change to display the new drive. It may take a moment to assemble the new diagram as Windows scans the disk.

The tree diagram   The tree diagram is initially displayed in a collapsed state, showing only the root directory and first-level subdirectories. Whether in directory trees or file listings, directories are represented by a file folder icon. The current directory is marked by an open file folder.

To further expand the tree diagram, double-click on any of the first-level subdirectories to bring into view the second-level subdirectories it contains. Alternatively, use the tab key to move the box cursor to the directory tree, then the cursor keys to move the box cursor to the subdirectory, and then press the ⊞ key to expand the directory. Repeat the process to move farther out the tree. Double-clicking on an already opened icon closes all subdirectories beyond it, as does pressing ⊞ when the cursor has been moved to that subdirectory.

TIP

By pressing the asterisk key, all subdirectories in the branch originating from the current directory will open. To expand the entire directory tree so that all subdirectories are in view, select the root directory at the very top of the tree and press ✳. Or, as a short cut, just type Ctrl-✳ with any directory current.

Normally, you cannot readily tell which directories can be expanded to show other directories. You can look for file folder icons in the directory listings to the right, but it is inconvenient to do so. An easier approach is to choose Indicate Expandable Branches from the Tree menu. Thereafter, a ⊕ sign appears inside every directory that has contains other directories but has not been expanded, and a ⊖ sign appears after expansion and remains until the directory is collapsed.

Note that any of the above operations can also be accomplished through choices in the Tree menu, including Expand One Level, Expand Branch, Expand All, and Collapse Branch. These menu choices are the slowest way of working, and are useful only when you've forgotten how to manipulate the tree directly.

Directory listings   A directory listing appears automatically for the currently selected directory. Listings normally include only file names so that many files can be displayed at once. You can have a full DOS-like listing by choosing All File Details from the View menu. Or you can specify which elements you want listed by choosing Partial Details from the View menu and then responding to the resulting dialog box.

Subdirectories appear in listings with file folder icons, just like in directory tree diagrams. If you double-click on a file folder in a directory listing, the listing will change to the one for that file folder so that you move from parent to child directory. To move in the reverse direction, from child to parent, double-click on the arrow symbol that appears at the top of every listing.

18.3 Selecting files in Windows

As in a DOS shell, one important advantage of the Windows File Manager is that you can apply single commands to large numbers of individually selected files. Section 18.2 explains how to select individual files by mouse or keyboard. Selecting groups of files is only a little more complicated.

Selecting multiple files at random   With a mouse, just hold down the ⌈Ctrl⌉ key as you click on the desired files. Files continue to be selected even when scrolled out of view. From a keyboard, press and release ⌈⇧⌉-⌈F8⌉ to enter the multiple selection mode. The bar cursor will blink so long as you are in that mode. Move the bar cursor to a desired file and press the space bar to select it. Repeat this process as many times as you like, then exit the multiple selection mode by pressing and releasing ⌈⇧⌉-⌈F8⌉ a second time.

Selecting a sequence of files   When a directory listing presents several files in a row that you wish to select, click your mouse on the first file name, keeping the mouse button held down. Then press the ⌈⇧⌉ key and click on the last item in the sequence. The second action will cause the entire range to be highlighted. Figure 18.4 shows an example.

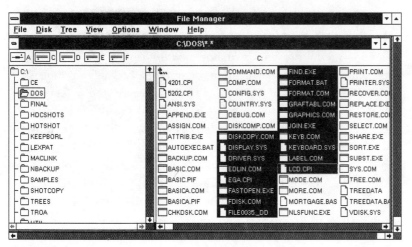

Figure 18.4

Working from a keyboard, start by moving the bar cursor to the first file. Then hold down the ⬆ key and continue moving the bar cursor with the ⬆ and ⬇ keys to select a number of files. You can use the ⬅ or ➡ keys when the directory listing shows multiple columns of files. In this case, all files from the starting point to the new cursor position are selected, with the selection wrapping around from the bottom of each column to the top of the column to the right.

Canceling a selection   When you change your mind about the files you have selected, you can cancel some or all of the selections. This can't be done as easily as selecting files, because only one file can be canceled at a time. With a mouse, hold down the Ctrl key and click on every file you wish to deselect. From the keyboard, press ⬆-F8 to enter the selection mode (the bar cursor will blink), then move the cursor to a file you want to deselt and press the space bar. Press and release ⬆-F8 a second time when you've made the selection changes you want.

Selecting multiple sequences of files   The techniques for selecting multiple individual files and multiple sequences of files may be combined. Working with a mouse, start by selecting one file or a range of files in the usual way. Then continue the process with the Ctrl key held down. To select a second range of files, click on the first file of the sequence while holding Ctrl down, then press ⬆ as well and hold it down also while clicking on the last file of the sequence.

Selecting files by global characters   Choosing Select Files in the Files menu presents a dialog box in which you can enter a specification using global file name characters. The default value is *.*, which represents all files. In this case, clicking on the Select button causes all files in a directory to be selected. You can change the specification to, say, *.TXT, in which case all files with .TXT extensions are selected in addition to all currently selected files. This command can be used multiple times to make complex selections. You also can click on the Deselect button to have files matching the specification deselected. For instance, you might first select all files and then deselect those with .BAK extensions.

18.4 Running programs in Windows

In Windows, programs are started up in two ways. You can either select the program from a directory listing and have Windows load it, or you can specify a data file belonging to the program. In the latter case, Windows automatically tracks down the program that created the file, starts the program, and then loads the file into it. Windows does this by referring to the data file's file name extension. For example, all data files with an .OL extension might be associated with an outlining program. You could specify a file with an .OL extension and Windows would locate the outline program, start it up, and load the selected file. Windows loads programs this way only when you have specially configured it to associate particular extensions with particular programs.

If you decide to use Windows this way, you need to devise extensions you'll assign to files created by your applications software. Of course, some programs automatically add a predefined extension to all files they create, and these should not be changed; you are free to devise your own system only when no extensions are added automatically.

This approach to linking data files to program files is inflexible in certain ways. If two programs use the same extension, Windows can start up the wrong program when a data file is specified. Conversely, you may want more than one application to be able to access the same data file. In the later case, you can associate the extension to one of the programs that use it; when you want some other program to access the file, start up that program directly by name and then load the file from within the program.

To associate an extension with a program, enter Windows' File Manager and choose Associate from the File menu. You'll encounter the dialog box shown in figure 18.5. In the Files with Extension box, enter the file name extension you want to associate with a program. Then select the program from the list assembled below. Selecting None from this list serves to undo an existing association. If the program is not found in the list, you can type in the program name and path. Alternatively, click on the Browse button. A dialog box will appear to let you search through directory trees for the desired program file.

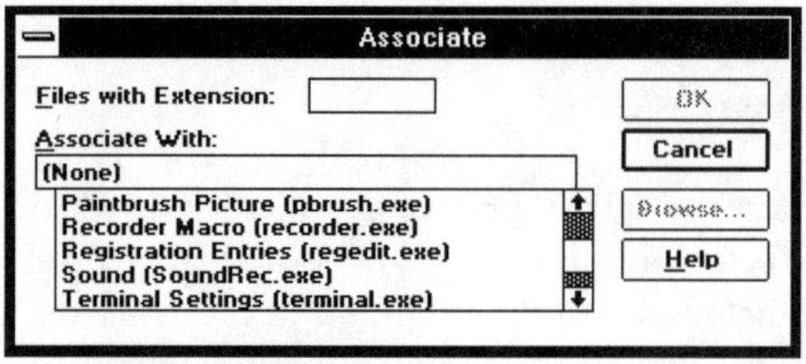

Figure 18.5

Starting programs from icons   Programs can be started directly in two ways. First, you can double-click on one of the icons displayed in the Program Manager window. Each icon refers to what is called a group in Windows—a set of program and data files that can be accessed quickly, without going through the trouble of hunting them down in the directory tree. In essence, groups are a kind of customizable menu system.

Standard groups in Windows include Windows Applications, Non-Windows Applications, Accessories, Games, and Main (the File Manager is found in the latter). When the group icon opens into a window, every file in the group is shown as an icon with a title beneath, as figure 18.6 shows. A bar cursor rests on the title of one of the icons. To start up a program from the keyboard, simply use the cursor keys to shift the bar cursor to the desired program and then strike ⏎. Working with a mouse, you need only move the mouse cursor to the program's icon and double-click.

Starting programs from the directory tree   The second way of launching programs directly is to track down the program file in the directory tree. Follow the usual methods for navigating the tree, opening directories, and selecting files. Once a program file has been selected, just press ⏎ to run it. Double-clicking a mouse on the file listing does the same thing.

Loading data files   Sometimes you'll want to load a data file as you launch a program, but haven't associated the data file with the program using a file name extension. This can also be done from groups within the Program Manager or with directory listings. If you have a mouse, drag the data file's icon onto the program file's icon. Move the mouse cursor over the data file icon and press down the left mouse button.

Then, without releasing the button, move the cursor to the program file icon. When you release the button, the program will start up and load the file. If the two icons reside in separate groups or directories, you'll need to open two windows and drag the data file icon between them.

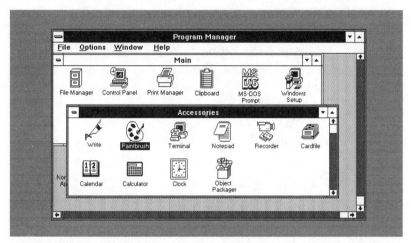

Figure 18.6

This technique works only if you use a mouse. To accomplish the same thing from the keyboard, enter the File Manager, pull down the File menu, and choose Run. You'll be shown the dialog box in figure 18.6. First type in a directory path to the program file, including the program file name. Then press the space bar to leave a gap and enter the path to the data file, naming it as well. For example:

```
C:\PROGRAMS\OUTLINE\LINES C:\BUDGET\LOSSES.OL
```

Strike ⏎ or click on the OK button to launch the program and data file.

Notice in the dialog box a check box (a small square that can be checked or unchecked with a mouse or the space bar) that lets you specify whether to run minimized. This refers to the behavior of the Program Manager window when you start up an application. When it runs minimized, the window automatically changes to an icon so that the window is removed from the screen but remains easily accessible. This option may be permanently selected by pulling down the Options menu in the File Manager to select Minimize on use. A check mark to the left of this menu item indicates that the feature is enabled. Each time you make this menu selection, the check mark toggles from on to off, or off to on.

Modifying groups   You can install whatever programs you like in the preexisting groups found in the Program Manager, or you can create new ones. To add a program to a group, pull down the File menu in the Program Manager and select New. A dialog box appears asking you to enter a Description and a Command Line. The Description is the label that will be displayed with the icon that represents the program in the group. This label does not have to match the program name. The Command Line is the program's actual name, complete with a directory path so that Windows can find it (you don't have to give a path if the subdirectory holding the program is listed by a PATH command in your AUTOEXEC.BAT file). Be aware that you also can move important data files to groups, including data files always used by programs.

To delete a program from a group, open the group window so that the program's icon is in view and select the icon. Then pull down the File menu and choose Delete. The Program Manager will display a dialog box asking you to confirm that you want the program deleted from the group. This action only removes the program from the group; the program will still be present on disk and can still be run by launching it from within the File Manager.

To move a program between groups, select the program's icon and— if you have a mouse—drag it into the icon or window of the group to which you want to transfer it. If you lack a mouse, pull down the File menu after selecting the program's icon and select Move. A dialog box will ask you to name the group the program should be transferred to.

To create a new group, pull down the File menu in the Program Manager and select New. A New Program Object dialog box will appear to ask what it is you want to do. Select Program Group and choose OK. Another dialog box will appear asking for a Description and a Group File. The Description is the label that will be used with the group icon. The Group File is the name of the file that will hold information about the group. Normally, there's no need to supply this file name; Windows will make up one on its own. After entering the Description, choose OK and the group will be created.

Finally, to delete a group, select the group icon or window and then pull down the File menu and choose Delete. A dialog box will ask you to confirm that you want the group deleted. Again, it is only the group that is deleted, not the files it contains, which can still be accessed through the File Manager.

Running multiple programs   Remember that Windows is multitasking, meaning that you can run several programs at once. Once they are running, you can move between them by clicking your mouse in the window of one program or another, or by repeatedly typing Alt-/ to cycle from window to window. When you're working in one program and want to launch another, just move to any window from which programs can be launched, whether by a Program Manager group, by a directory listing, or by a menu selection in the File Manager. Then launch the program as always.

18.5 Configuring non-Windows programs

Windows can run most applications that were not specifically designed to work with it. That is, Windows can run standard DOS programs, dubbing them Non-Windows applications. This does not mean that these programs will appear as a Windows program with standard Windows menus, dialog boxes, and the like. Rather, the program looks just as it does under DOS. When Windows runs in standard mode (see section 18.1), the program takes up the entire screen. However, if you have a 386, 486, or 586 machine and are running Windows in 386 enhanced mode , the program can be confined to a window that can be sized, moved, and reduced to an icon, just as for a Windows program.

Normally, Windows manages all resources in the machine, such as the various kinds of memory, the serial and parallel ports, and device drivers. Careful management is necessary to avoid conflicts when several programs run at once and demand the same resources. Non-Windows applications generally assume that they will be the only program running in the machine, and they have no way of telling Windows which resources they require. For this reason, Windows requires that every Non-Windows program has a Program Information File (PIF) containing information about how the program works.

The makers of many Non-Windows programs supply a PIF with the program so that it will be Windows compatible. Otherwise, you need to create a PIF for the program, and may need to modify the PIF from time to time to accomdate changing circumstances. This is done with the PIF Editor, which is started by double-clicking on the PIF Editor icon in the Main group. A window then opens to elicit information from you. The contents depend on whether you're running Windows in standard mode or 386 enhanced mode. The window shown in figure 18.7 appears in the latter case.

You are asked for the name of the program file and the title that should be displayed at the top of the window in which the program appears (the choice is yours). Optional Parameters calls for the command line parameters that you might include when starting up the program from the DOS command line. The Start-up Directory is a DOS path to the subdirectory holding files the program requires at start-up. Not all programs have such a requirement and this item is optional.

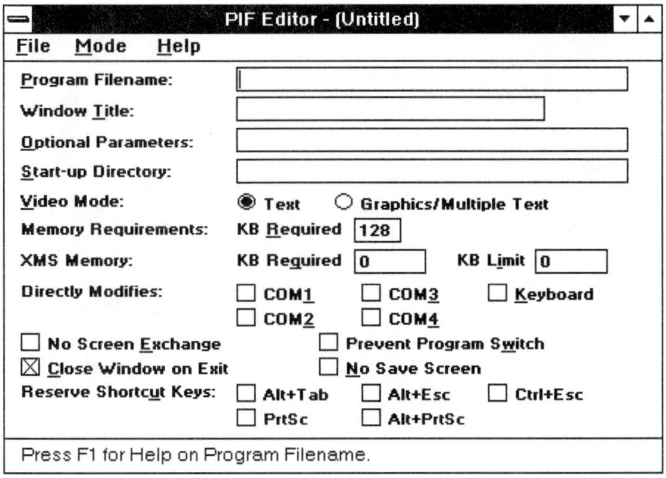

Figure 18.7

Next, you're asked to specify the amount of video memory required by the program. This is the memory in which the program writes the image projected on the screen. If the program runs in a text mode, either in color or monochrome, specify Text. On the other hand, if the program displays graphics of any kind, including text in various sizes and styles, you'll need to specify a graphics mode. In 386 enhanced mode, the options are Low Graphics for CGA graphics and High Graphics for EGA and VGA graphics. In standard mode, select Graphics/Multiple Text for any graphics mode. This option is also appropriate when a program switches back and forth between multiple text images. Select it when there are problems with the simple Text setting.

Other areas in the PIF Editor window ask you to specify the program's memory requirements, including the requirements for conventional memory (Memory Requirements), expanded memory (EMS Memory), and extended memory (XMS Memory). For each, you can specify both the number of kilobytes required and an upper limit to how much will be allocated to the program.

Finally, the PIF Editor dialog lets you set a number of switches. Choose Full Screen instead of Windows if you want the application to run exactly as from the DOS command line. And select Background or Exclusive depending on whether you want the program to multitask or not.

Chapter 19

Using Windows on Local Area Networks

- MINITUTORIAL: Network fundamentals
- Accessing network drives through Windows
- Accessing network printers through Windows
- Tips for using Windows on networks

MINITUTORIAL:
Network fundamentals

As the number of computers in business use grows, so does the need to have the computers networked. Normally, computers are networked so that several people in an organization can share the same information. Other reasons for using a local area network (LAN) include sharing peripheral equipment such as printers and communicating between computers by electronic mail. Networked computers are commonly called workstations.

Some LANs are used for access to other computers, including the mainframe computers and minicomputers that a company might have, or for access to some external service such as a public data network or an on-line information system such as CompuServe. Often, LANs that are installed for a specific reason, such as sharing printers, are soon used for many other purposes as well. For that reason, you are likely to find that LANs support several functions when you find them in your company.

No matter what purpose a LAN was originally acquired for, the most common use for LANs is usually electronic mail. Many LANs also perform closely related functions, including employee scheduling, as a part of what is now called Groupware or group productivity software. Groupware is one of the most rapidly growing areas of LAN software development. Many groupware products are well known, including Word Perfect Office, Higgins, and Office Works, to mention only three of the many that are available.

LAN users refer to their networks in a variety of ways, depending on whether they are talking about the basic type of LAN, the LAN topology (pattern of connections between machines), the LAN protocol (system of communications codes used by the LAN), or the LAN operating system. In learning how to use a LAN, you'll find that you can easily be overwhelmed by technical details. This minitutorial provides an overview of LAN technology to help you sort out what you need to know.

LAN types   Normally, a LAN is referred to as either a file-server-based LAN or as a peer-to-peer LAN. These names refer to whether the LAN operating software resides on a central computer called a file server, or whether the LAN software consists only of the collection of workstation software running on each of the computers using the LAN. While many users consider file server-based LANs to be the higher performance systems, this is really not true. Performance is influenced by many factors, but whether the LAN is server-based or peer-to-peer is not one of them.

File server-based LANs are more commonly used for businesses that must make sure that their central data store is secure, and by those who want to use software that is only available for a server-based LAN. Examples of file server-based LANs include Novell NetWare and Banyan VINES. Peer-to-peer LANs include DCA's 10Net.

Servers   Most LANs have devices attached to them called servers. These are usually special-purpose computers that are intended to perform a specific function, and whose software and hardware has been modified or optimized for that function. The most common type of server is the file server, which is present on the vast majority of all LANs. Other servers may include print servers, communications servers, database servers, and even FAX servers. Each of these machines is intended to be used by several workstations on the LAN, and are designed accordingly.

File servers   A file server is a personal computer set up specifically to manage files made available to other computers in the LAN. Normally, the file server has very large disk drives and extra memory. Most file servers run special software called a network operating system. The network operating system is designed specifically for running a network and handling operations in a multi-user environment.

Some LANs do not require a file server, but even these LANs sometimes have one. In peer-to-peer LANs, the file server is really just another workstation where most of the LAN's files are stored. On these LANs, any user can have access to anyone else's computer through the LAN. This approach can be very convenient, but it can also be very confusing if there are a large number of workstations attached to the LAN.

A file server may also be a machine with dual responsibilities, requiring it to be both a server and a workstation. This means that the file server is available for normal work as a personal computer at the same time that it is running the network. A file server used this way is called a nondedicated file server. Many LAN operating systems allow such an arrangement. It saves money because you have to buy only one machine when otherwise two would be needed. But, because the file server has two jobs to do, this approach lowers overall network performance.

In most cases, the file server appears to be just another disk drive, often appearing under the drive specifier F. Multiple servers may appear as multiple drive specifiers. In some cases, such as the Banyan LAN, several servers can be lumped together into what appears to be a single disk drive, and you won't be able to tell which specific file server you are attached to.

In addition to appearing as another disk drive, most file servers can be accessed indirectly by the use of menus. For many tasks, you may choose between using menus and typing commands on a command line. Some features may be available only through menus, or only through the command line. Most network operating systems provide special network versions of important DOS commands. Novell NetWare, for example, has an NDIR command that works just like the DOS DIR command, but which lists information for files on network disk drives. Most network operating systems also include a number of utilities that support operations that would be useful only in a networked system, such as NetWare's PCONSOLE utility, which lets you control printing on printers throughout the network, and lets you see what's being printed and where the printing is being done.

Access to a file server's files is governed by some sort of security arrangement. Every user is given a user name (often just his name, like Tom) and a password (that should be kept secret) to identify the user when the user first logs in (enters) the network from his workstation. Each user is given access to certain parts of the file server's hard disk, and not to others, in accordance with the user's job. The person in charge of the network, the system administrator, controls the network security system. Even in a peer-to-peer network, you may find that some areas of other users' disks are unavailable to you.

The reason for blocking access to certain subdirectories, or even to specific files, is so that you cannot remove or damage information important to the operation of the network, and so that you cannot read confidential information. The extent of the restrictions placed upon you varies with the type of network operating system and with the manner in which the system administrator has set things up. You may be kept from entire disks, or simply certain directories or subdirectories. You may also find that you can not erase or change the files in areas to which you do have access.

Finally, because the file server supports many users, you may occasionally be prevented from using or changing a file with which you are normally able to work. This means that the file is in use by another user, and you will have to wait until that user is finished before you can use the file. Exactly how this works depends on the network software as well as the application software you are using. Word processing files are usually limited to one user at a time. Database files, on the other hand, usually limit use of only a specific data record or group of records.

Print servers   A print server is software that may run on either a workstation or a file server to handle printing requests from workstations anywhere on the network. While file servers usually handle this function, this isn't always the most convenient way to handle printing, because file servers are not always located in the same places that you want to keep your printers. As a result, printers may be connected to workstations and may receive printing requests from elsewhere in the network.

Sometimes, the printing load on the workstation that's being used as a print server is so heavy that printing may be the workstation's only task. You may find, for example, that all of the printers assigned to an entire department are attached to one workstation that acts as the print server. Other machines in the network could access any of these printers. Since different kinds of printers could be attached, every user in the system could have a laser printer at his disposal for some jobs, a dot-matrix printer for others, and so on.

Network printing helps make printing more convenient in a number of ways. Besides giving every workstation access to a wider variety of printers, the network can manage and prioritize printing requests. The network will take a file you want to print and store it until the printer you want to use is free. This means that your computer won't be tied up during printing as it might be if the printer were attached directly to your machine. Your computer is tied up only as long as it takes to send the document to the file server.

Communications servers   Communications servers handle communications in much the same way as print servers handle printing. A workstation will have a circuit board installed that allows it to be attached to some kind of communications device. This device may be a modem (or several modems), it may be a special kind of FAX

machine, or it may even be another computer. Special network software supports communications through these devices.

Many large businesses use a type of communications server called a gateway to give their LAN access to the company mainframe computer or minicomputers. This gateway connects the LAN to the other computer's communications lines, giving the appearance that your workstation is connected directly. A similar device, called an asynchronous communications server (or asynchronous communications gateway), allows network users to use modems to connect to outside systems.

FAX servers   A FAX server is similar to the other servers, except that it manages a FAX machine. It takes a special type of FAX machine to accept data directly from a network or from a personal computer, convert it to FAX signals, and send it over a telephone line. Most FAX servers also receive FAX messages sent in from the outside world, and they include software that allows the FAX image to be displayed on a screen or printed on a printer.

Database servers   Database servers are a relatively new arrival on the network computing scene. They concentrate database operations on a personal computer that is specifically configured for this function. This normally means that the computer has a great deal of memory and large disk drives. Typically, the database server runs OS/2 or UNIX as an operating system. Application software running on the network workstations sends queries or data across the network to the database server, which in turn sends data back to the workstation in reply. Because the file server is no longer burdened with database operations, database servers improve overall network performance.

Database servers are rarely, if ever, used directly by users. Instead, they operate invisibly in the background, answering your queries and handling the competing demands of several users seeking the same information. The queries use a special database language called Structured Query Language, or SQL (pronounced sequel by computer cognoscenti) which was developed originally by IBM, and has been adopted by nearly everyone dealing with multiuser databases. Database servers are more complex than earlier versions of LAN databases, but they improve performance and data integrity to such an extent that they are one of the fastest-growing areas of local area networking.

Topologies

Topology refers to the pattern in which computers are connected to form a local area network. There are several common topologies: the star topology, bus topology, and ring topology. Associated with LAN topologies are LAN protocols (discussed below) such as ARCNET and Ethernet.

A star topology means that a number of computers are connected to a central file server or to a device called a hub. The most common LAN with a star topology is ARCNET. Another LAN with a star topology that is rapidly gaining in popularity is a form of Ethernet that uses telephone cable (called twisted pair) instead of the coaxial cable more commonly associated with Ethernet. Most LANs with a star topology are really hierarchical stars, meaning that a number of stars form the points of a larger star.

A bus topology means that the LAN consists of a single cable that runs the length of a LAN. Workstations are attached along the length of the LAN through the use of a T connector or similar device. Most Ethernet LANs use a bus topology, as do some ARCNET LANs and nearly all broadband LANs (these use cable-TV technology to transmit data). The choice between bus and star topology for Ethernet and ARCNET is frequently dictated by the design of the building in which the LAN is to be installed rather than by any operational difference between the star and bus topologies. LANs using bus topology nearly always use coaxial cable because of the distances that the signals must travel.

A ring topology is designed so that the computers in the LAN are connected in a ring with signals travelling from one computer to the next. The only LAN that uses a ring topology is IBM's Token Ring, and while it is a ring electrically, physically it is configured as a star with a hub at the center. Because it is set up as a ring electrically and as a star physically, the Token Ring cable is a special type of twisted pair that has four wires and is shielded.

LAN protocols

A LAN protocol is the system used by LAN software to allow workstations and servers to communicate without confusion. Protocols are necessary because more than one station may try to send messages on the network at the same time. Token Ring, Ethernet, and ARCNET are three examples of protocols. While LAN protocols were closely related to their topologies in the past, all that has changed. Both Ethernet and ARCNET can work on either a bus or a star topology. The

Token Ring protocol always works in a ring topology, but there are two incompatible types.

The Token Ring protocol was developed by IBM as a method of connecting devices with mainframe computers. Token Ring is also used frequently in LANs that must connect with mainframes, as well as in LANs that use the Token Ring physical star topology. Token Ring operates by passing an electronic signal, called a token, from one machine to the next, around the ring. When a workstation needs to use the LAN, it can do so only when it holds the token. The data passes around the ring until it gets to the station to which it is addressed. A Token Ring is limited to as few as 32 workstations per ring, but this can be overcome by linking several rings together.

The ARCNET protocol is Datapoint Corporation's name for a token passing protocol that can run on either a bus or a star topology. In some ways, it is similar to Token Ring, although it runs more slowly. A single ARCNET will support up to 256 devices attached to the network.

Ethernet is a LAN protocol originally developed by Xerox Corporation as a method of sending information from a mainframe computer to high-speed printers. Ethernet uses a system called carrier sense multiple access with collision detection (CSMA/CD). This means that a workstation in an Ethernet network, whether it's in the bus or star configuration, checks the network before sending data to see if some other workstation is using it. If not, it sends out a signal containing data to be transferred. If it should happen that two stations try to send data at the same time, each will wait for a random period of time and try again. A single Ethernet network will support up to 1,024 devices attached to the network. Virtually all minicomputers using UNIX and those made by Digital Equipment use Ethernet, as do LANs that connect to those computers. In addition, many LANs use Ethernet as the method of connecting multiple LANs together, even if they use some other protocol for attaching user workstations.

Groupware   There was once a time when network electronic mail was part of the LAN operating system. But this has changed and today some providers of networks do not even offer electronic mail software. Meanwhile, a number of companies, including WordPerfect, Enable, Wang Laboratories, and Data Access Corporation, have developed packages that include electronic mail, as well as electronic appointment calendars, group scheduling, resource scheduling, and a variety of productivity tools. This kind of software started out being called Group Productivity Software, but now it is known as Groupware.

All groupware packages include electronic mail, appointment calendars, and scheduling as a part of their basic suite of software. Normally, these three functions operate in close conjunction. You can send an electronic memo to another user to ask for a meeting. Or, you can look at that user's calendar and schedule a meeting yourself. The software will generate a message telling the person that you have done this. Group scheduling means that you can arrange a group meeting; the software will search for a time when everyone is free and set up the meeting automatically. This feature alone can do a lot for productivity.

There are, or course, packages devoted only to electronic mail. One of the most popular network packages available is CC:Mail, which only performs electronic mail. CC:Mail is known for its ability to support nearly every known requirement for mail, with the ability to work with a wide variety of computers, including IBM compatibles, Macintoshes, and even your company VAX. While most of the electronic mail market is being taken over by groupware, the niche for a quality product does still remain.

19.1 Accessing network drives in Windows

Windows provides a standard interface for accessing network drives. You must explicitly connect to network drives; thereafter you access them just like any other drive.

To connect to a network drive, choose Network Connections from the Disk menu. Not all networks use a command of this name; you may encounter some other name like Connect Network Drive. A dialog box opens and displays a list of all current drive connections. You can add a drive to this list by supplying certain information:

- First, you'll need to enter the path used to located the drive. This goes in the Network Path box. If you're not sure of the path, click on the Browse button. It lets you search a list of drives for the one you want. The Browse button is dimmed when this feature is not available on a network.

- Next, enter a drive letter by which the network drive will be accessed. You can type in the value or click on an arrow symbol to cycle through a list of allowed values. Make it a habit to always use the same drive letter for a particular drive.

- Finally, if the network drives requires a password for access, enter the password in the Password box.

Once this information has been entered, click on the Connect button. The File Manager will remember the connection so that later it can easily be reestablished. If you don't want the File Manager to remember the drive, hold down a Shift key when clicking on the Connect button.

In your next Windows session, you can reestablish prior network connections by again choosing Network Connections from the Disk menu, and then clicking on the Previous button. A dialog box titled Previous Network Connections appears. It displays a list of previously established network paths. Select the desired path and click on the Select button. The path will then be added to the Network Path box. Then type in a password in the Password box, if one is required, and click on the Connect button. Once all required paths have been reestablished, click on the Close button.

Sometimes you may connect to a network drive through application software. Having done so does not mean that the drive automatically appears in the File Manager. To make the drive appear, choose the Refresh command in the Window menu.

To disconnect from a network drive, again choose Network Connections from the Disk menu. The resulting dialog box will show the drive in the Current Drive Connections box. Select the drive and then click on the Disconnect button. Note that you may not be able to disconnect from network drives when running Windows in 386 enhanced mode.

19.2 Accessing network printers in Windows

Microsoft Windows is equipped to send and monitor print jobs directed to networked printers.

Connecting to a printer   Begin by choosing Network Connections from the Options menu. The Network Connections dialog box appears. Type the network name (found in your network documentation) in the Network Path box. Next, select the port to which your software will direct data (normally LPT1 or COM1, unless otherwise configured). Make this setting in the Port box by clicking on the downward-pointing arrow to scroll through a list of ports. Finally, type in a password in the Password box if your network requires one. For security, the characters you type are not displayed; rather, an asterisk appears for each. Once all this has been done, click on the Connect button. The printer is then listed in the Current Printer Connections box. Click on Close, then on OK in the Connect dialog box that appears, and then again on Close in the Printers dialog box that follows.

Some networks can remember previous printer connections so that you do not need to rename the printer path each time you want to connect. Begin by choosing Network Connections from the Options menu, as above. But in this case, choose the Previous button. A Previous Network Connections dialog box appears listing the relevant printers. You simply click on the desired printer and then on the Select button. At that point the Network Connection dialog box appears so that you can specify a port and password, as required. Then click on the Connect button and then the Close button.

Viewing printer queues   Every networked printer has its own printer queue. You can monitor work you've sent to the printer you've selected or you can view the queues of other networked printers if you want to see how busy they are.

Normally, the Print Manager will show you only your own files in a print queue. If you want to view all files in the queue, select the printer in the Print Manager window and choose Selected Net Queue from the View menu. A dialog box will then appear to display the entire queue. The dialog box may also let you operate on the queue, depending on the network. You'll need to consult your network's documentation for details.

To view the queue of some other network printer, choose Other Net Queue from the View menu. A dialog box appears, asking you to type in the path to the printer. Once specified, you can click on the View button to view the queue. You can then change the path specification to view the queues of other printers.

Disconnecting from a printer   Once you've finished printing, you can disconnect from a networked printer by choosing Network Connections from the Options menu. You'll encounter the Network Connections dialog box shown above. From the list of available printers, select the one you want to disconnect from and then click on the Disconnect button. Finally, click on the Close botton to exit the dialog box.

If you've shunted the print job through the Print Manager, you'll need to choose Exit from the Options menu if the Print Manager window is open. However, if the Print Manager is running as an icon, it will quit automatically once the print job is complete. Failure to close the Print Manager means that memory will needlessly be left allocated to it.

19.3 Tips for using Windows on networks

■ The network should be started before Windows is started. Windows will run if it is started first, but problems may ensue.

■ When using a shared copy of Windows from a network drive, always assign the same letter to that drive. This is also true of shared applications. If you initially call the drive G, then always call it G. This is because the path associated with this letter is remembered for future use. Crucial files may not be available if you change it.

■ Network printers should always be accessed through the same port. Otherwise the port configuration settings may not be correct. Section 10.3 explains how to make these settings.

■ If you have problems running Windows on a network, read the NETWORKS.WRI file found on one of the Windows distribution disks. It contains network-specific information that may be of help.

■ Be aware that some Networks will fail if you access the DOS prompt from within Windows.

■ Avoid having Print Manager spool print jobs to a network drive. Doing so greatly increases network traffic and can noticeably slow network performance. You can reduce Windows-related traffic in general by seeing to it that Windows' TEMP directory is routed to a local drive. TEMP is established by the DOS SET command in AUTOEXEC.BAT.

■ Non-Windows applications that are network-aware may have trouble running under Windows unless they are running in exclusive mode so that they do not have to share the machine with other multitasked applications. This occurs because these applications are timing-sensitive and lose data while other applications operate.

Chapter 20

Managing Files

MINITUTORIAL:
File management and mis-management

File management is the process of organizing and maintaining files so that they may be located and retrieved easily. Because DOS limits file names to eight characters plus a three-character extension, it doesn't give you much help managing files. Beyond the use of subdirectories (see the minitutorial at the beginning of Chapter 5) and global file name characters (section 1.3), there is no built in facility for categorizing or cataloging files. Moreover, few DOS commands can operate on more than one directory at a time, making it difficult to manage related files spread around a directory tree.

Recent DOS versions have made some small progress in overcoming these weaknesses (with editions like XCOPY and the DOS Shell program), but not nearly enough progress has been made to handle the myriad files that fill hard disks. To manage your files well, you must improvise your own schemes or turn to third-party software (which, in spite of numerous offerings, also falls short on some counts).

The heart of file management is the ability to find files. This can be done either by looking inside a file to see what its contents are, or by building a cataloging system external to files. The former approach is easier to implement but less reliable in its results. The latter takes much work and faithful maintenance of the system, because DOS itself will in no way help you update the system as you create new files, delete old ones, and move others around the directory tree.

DOS includes the FIND command for searching inside files. It is useful for simple jobs like scanning business letters for the name of a client. Using global file name characters, a single command can search all files in a directory, but it cannot scan the entire directory tree. A number of software utilities do a much better job. But in all cases, you are limited by the inability of such utilities to deal effectively with much more than text (word processing) files. Files created by other kinds of software, such as spreadsheet programs and databases, are formatted in a way unique to each program. Often, the information you seek will be stored in such a way that a file search utility cannot find it.

Even when a search utility can be used, it may not perform the kind of service you really need. It is one thing to be able to find every file that contains the word Napoleon, quite another to construct a listing of all files that are primarily concerned with Napoleon. Only a cataloging scheme can perform this task. Such a system requires considerable discipline, because you must update it every time you create a new file. Utility programs exist for this purpose; alternatively, you can create special catalog files of your own design and keep them on hand. The sections in this chapter explain the main strategies for building such a system.

20.1 Determining free disk space

Use the DOS CHKDSK command to find out how much room is available on a disk. Enter:

    CHKDSK C: ⏎

and, in DOS 4.0, information like the following will be displayed:

```
21299200  bytes total disk space
    2048  bytes in 1 hidden files
  186368  bytes in 80 directories
20729856  bytes in 1622 user files
   30720  bytes in bad sectors
  350208  bytes available on disk
    2048  bytes in each allocation unit
   10422  total allocation units on disk
     892  available allocation units on disk
  655360  bytes total memory
  456608  bytes free
```

The sixth line tells how many bytes of disk space are free. The number is always evenly divisible by 512 since it represents the capacity of all unallocated sectors (each sector holds 512 bytes). Don't be confused by the last two lines, which report the amount of conventional memory installed in the machine. (Conventional memory is the basic kind of memory found in all machines—most have 640 kilobytes of it. We discuss the kinds of memory in the minitutorial at the beginning of Chapter 15.)

Disk space is allocated in blocks (clusters), not one byte at a time. For this reason, you can increase the size of a file by hundreds of bytes without any change in available disk space. When the space allocated to a file has been filled, another block is allocated, and suddenly the file becomes considerably larger. The size of the blocks depends on the disk type. It is as little as 512 bytes on some diskettes, and is typically 2048 bytes on hard disks. The seventh through ninth lines displayed by CHKDSK give information about the size of the blocks by which memory is allocated (CHKDSK refers to these as allocation units). This information is not reported by CHKDSK in DOS versions prior to 4.0.

20.2 Dealing with a full hard disk

A new, freshly formatted hard disk seems like a frontier without boundaries, an expanse that can't possibly be filled. Not much later, however, little space may be left. Recent software, particularly graphics and desktop-publishing programs, tend to create very large files. And the myriad files that comprise major application programs may take up megabytes just by themselves.

The time to deal with a filing disk is when it is between 80 and 90 percent full. If you wait too long, you may encounter serious problems during crucial work, perhaps even data loss. Many programs create temporary files as they run and then erase the files before quitting so that you are never aware of their presence. For this reason, it is never safe to assume that a small amount of remaining disk space will necessarily be adequate for the job ahead.

The obvious solution to a full hard disk is to install another. Today, hard disk technology has become well standardized in the IBM world and it is not difficult to find a second drive that will run on the same controller circuitry as the first. The second drive need not be the same size as the first, nor must it be made by the same manufacturer. However, you should inquire about the suitability of the drive for your system, telling the vendor the name and model of both the drive and controller card currently installed in the machine. Note that some PS/2 models do not easily accomodate a second drive.

A second and much less costly approach is to buy a file compression utility. These utilities hook into DOS and automatically compress files when DOS writes them to disk, and uncompress them when DOS reads the files. Files are typically reduced by about a third, although in some cases an 80 percent reduction is possible. However, these utilities slow down disk access times, especially on slower machines. See section 20.3 for a detailed discussion.

Before heading out to a computer store with your checkbook, stop and think about how efficiently the space on your hard disk is used. In their daily work, most people use only a fraction of the files on their hard disks. Typically, half the space is wasted through less-than-ideal file management. It is time-consuming to clean up a disk, but doing so is probably easier than installing a new drive (not to mention paying for one). In the end, you are likely to have not just more disk space but a more efficient work environment.

We'll discuss some ways to eliminate files you never—or rarely—use.

Method 1   On diskettes, set up an archive of files that need to be available but are seldom used. Ideally, these should be files that will not be altered in the future. Business correspondence is a good example of this kind of file. Small files, in particular, tend to take up much disk space, because the space on most hard disks is allocated in 2048-byte blocks. A text file that only needs 2050 bytes takes up nearly twice that space. Large files, by comparison, waste proportionately much less space through the addition of another block.

Archives require careful planning. You need to create an indexing system, figure out how many files will fit on a diskette, label each archive diskette, make the file copies, establish a place for their safe keeping, and finally erase the original files on the hard disk. The indexing system can be maintained as a word processoressor document left on the hard disk, and a word processor's search command can be a convenient way of tracking down a particular file within the index. See section 20.7 for a complete discussion of archiving.

Method 2   Eliminate intermediate files that are based on others. For example, if you are using a page-makeup program and supplying it with text documents from a separate word processor, you may have had the word processor create a second version of the file that the page-makeup program can read. The file then exists in two forms, one used by the word processor and one used to communicate the text to the second application program. Since the second version can always be recreated if it's required, there is no reason to leave it sitting around after you have pasted it into the page-makeup program.

Method 3   Use the DOS PATH and APPEND commands (discussed in sections 8.1 and 8.2) commands to eliminate needless duplication of software. People who have not organized their hard disks well encounter problems of not being able to access programs and data files in directories other than the current directory. Rather than configure DOS properly to access the files, they'll simply duplicate the program or data in as many directories as require it. This is a terrible way of solving the problem, not only because disk space is wasted, but also because it becomes difficult to replace an old version of software with a new one when many copies exist. Generally, only one copy of each program should be on the hard disk, and that includes DOS files.

Method 4 Eliminate temporary backup files that are no longer needed. Some programs, particularly word processors, automatically make backups of your work every time you save it to disk. The backup is written in the same directory as the original, and it is usually given a .BAK extension. This kind of backup is useful while you are working on the file, since you may easily reject changes you have made and return to an earlier version. Afterwards, these files just waste disk space.

Method 5 Eliminate application software files that are never used or no longer used. First in line might be software tutorials, which are often left on a hard disk long after they have been viewed. Other super-fluous files include the many printer drivers that accompany most software. These are small programs that adapt the software to the printer you use. There may be more than a hundred such drivers residing in separate files. They should not, in fact, have ever been transferred to the hard disk. But if they have, it is time to remove all except the ones you use (the files will usually have a name resembling the name of your printer).

PITFALLS | It is very easy to become sloppy about what you are doing when erasing many files. Be careful. Don't make mass erasures when you are rushed (it is partly for this reason that you should not wait until the disk is completely full before doing your hard-disk housekeeping). A major cleanup is a good time for an overall reorganization. Set aside an afternoon for the job. Make a complete backup of the disk before starting and hang on to the backup until you are sure that everything works well. After you have finished, run any disk optimization utilities that you may have purchased (these are discussed in Chapter 21) to sort directories and reorganize disk sectors so that DOS can access files more quickly.

20.3 Compressing files

One way of conserving disk space, whether on a hard disk or a diskette, is to compress files. Any kind of file can be reduced to a more compact form through a number of techniques that capitalize on patterns and redundancies in the file. Some kinds of files are much more compressable than others. The size of simple text files can usually be cut in half, while database files can often be reduced by three-quarters. Spreadsheet files are also good candidates for compression. On the other hand, program files can hardly be compressed at all.

Data compression is performed by utility software. Usually such utilities are sold alone, rather than as part of a general utility tool kit. Most are general-purpose utilities that can be applied to any kind of file. Some are tailored to a particular product, such as Lotus 1-2-3 spreadsheet files. A number of good compression utilities are also available as public domain software (software shared by its creators free of charge).

Once files have been compressed, they are unusable until they have been decompressed. If, for example, you use the DOS TYPE command to look at a compressed text file, all you'll see is gobbledygook. There is nothing wrong with this state of affairs as long as you can trust the compression utility. Never rely upon a utility that does not come well-recommended by a computer magazine or a knowledgeable co-worker. Remember that your backups will also be in compressed form. If something goes wrong, you may never be able to get your data back.

How compression utilities work   Most compression utilities can work in both manual and automatic modes. Used manually, the utility is started from the DOS command line like any other program. You supply the name or names of files to compress or decompress; global file name characters (section 1.3) let you work on groups of related files. Some programs can compress specified files or all files in whole branches of a directory tree.

When used in automatic mode, a compression utility is loaded into memory as a memory-resident program (section 15.4) when the computer is booted. The utility links itself into the operating system and, whenever a file is read, it checks whether the file has been compressed or not; if so, it automatically decompresses the file as it is read from the disk into memory. Similarly, files are automatically compressed (or recompressed) when software writes them back to disk.

Performance considerations   File compression and decompression is time consuming. On a typical 286 computer, a 100K text file might take 10 seconds to compress. Naturally, the faster the computer, the faster the compression or decompression proceeds.

TIP

On very fast machines, a compression utility may actually improve overall performance because fewer disk sectors are required to hold one file, and thus (on average) fewer time-consuming movements of the drive's read/write heads are needed.

Whether the performance delay incurred by compression utilities is worth the savings in disk space depends on what you are using your computer for. These utilities are intended for files that are loaded entirely into memory, modified, and then written entirely back to disk. Files that are repeatedly accessed as they are used should not be compressed (it is often easy to identify this kind of file because the hard disk drive's indicator light constantly flickers when the file is in use). A good utility will allow you to specify which kinds of files are to be compressed using file name extensions. This way, you can compress files only when it's to your best advantage.

20.4 Searching for files by name

When searching for a file in a particular directory, just use the DIR command. For example:

```
DIR MYFILE.DOC ⏎
```

results in either a one-line directory listing if the file is found, or a "File not found" message. Use global file name characters (section 1.3) when you're not sure of a file's name. For example, if you know that the file name begins with the letter *M*, type:

```
DIR M*.* ⏎
```

for a listing of all files whose name begins with *M*.

Scanning a directory tree   Finding a file somewhere in a directory tree, rather than in just a single directory, is not so simple. DOS offers only an indirect method, using the ATTRIB command. This command is used to change various attributes of a file, such as whether or not it is a read-only file. The command can also find out a file's current attribute settings simply by entering ATTRIB and then the file's name:

```
ATTRIB FILENAME.EXT ⏎
```

or, using a directory path:

```
ATTRIB C:\PROJECT7\FILENAME.EXT ⏎
```

The command responds by displaying the file's name and its directory path. The file's attributes are indicated to the left of the name. (Section 4.5 explains these details, which are of no concern in this application.)

ATTRIB can be made to scan all directories beyond the specified (or current) directory in addition to searching the directory itself. This is done by ending the command with an /S switch. The whole tree is searched when the root directory is specified. Thus, you can search the entire disk for the file THATSIT.TXT by entering:

```
ATTRIB \THATSIT.TXT /S ⏎
```

The initial backslash represents the root directory; it tells DOS to search subdirectories starting from the root directory. To search for THATSIT.TXT just in the subdirectory \FELINES\CATS and all subdirectories listed in CATS and beyond, enter:

```
ATTRIB \FELINES\CATS\THATSIT.TXT /S ⏎
```

When ATTRIB finds a file, it displays a message like:

```
R     C:\FELINES\CATS\THATSIT.TXT
```

telling you that the file THATSIT.TXT is in the subdirectory C:\FELINES\CATS (and also, in this case, that the file is read-only, as shown by the *R* to the left). You can use this feature to search for groups of files by using global file name characters. For a listing of all files in a tree that end in .BAT, type:

```
ATTRIB \*.BAT /S ⏎
```

For all files named REPORT12 with any extension, enter:

```
ATTRIB \REPORT12.* /S ⏎
```

Utility software   The ATTRIB command is a clumsy way of locating files. Many utility programs let you find a file in a directory tree just by entering its name or other information. For example, the FILEFIND program in the Norton Utilities can search multiple drives using several search criteria such as file attributes and ranges of file sizes and dates. It can also search for text strings within files, a topic discussed in the next section. For file searches that are repeated many times over, theSuperFind program in the Norton Desktop for Windows lets you create and save file sets—complex specifications for groups of files— that can be activated with a click of the mouse.

The DOS 5.0 Shell   In the DOS Shell, select System File List from the View menu to display a composite listing for the entire directory tree. Then choose Display Options from the Options menu to specify global file name characters used for selecting files. Instead of *.* (for all files), type in the name of the file you seek. Then only that file will be listed, and status information at the top of the screen will report the directory in which it is found. Be sure to return the Display Options setting to *.* after you have finished searching.

Windows 3.1   In Windows, pull down the File menu and choose Search. You will be shown a dialog box like the one in figure 20.1. Type in the name of the file and click on OK (or press ⏎) to start the search. Several seconds may pass as Windows searches the entire disk. Every instance of a file of the given name is then displayed in a Search Results dialog box, which displays a complete directory path for the file.

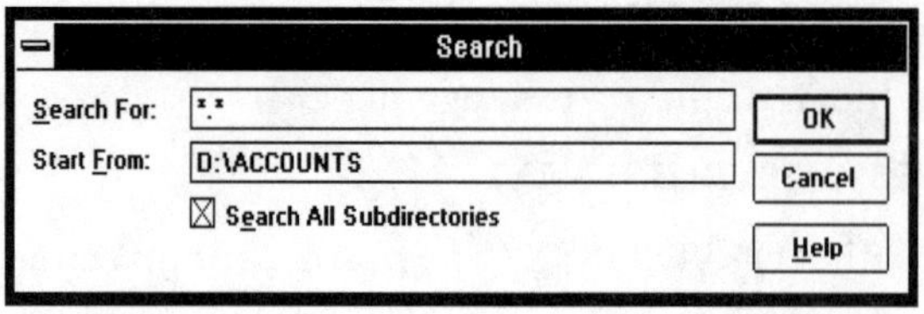

Figure 20.1

Once a file has been located, you can directly operate on its listing in the Search Results box to copy, move, delete, rename, or print the file. You can also start up programs this way, and can view information about the file using View menu commands.

The search is made on only one drive at a time. A separate Search command is required for each drive. As figure 20.1 shows, when you specify the file name you are also prompted to enter the name of the directory from which the search should begin. Only that directory and all below are searched (or only that directory if the Search All Subdirectories check box is deselected). Thus, to search an entire disk, the Start From box should name a drive's root directory using a specification like C:\. The starting directory is initially set to whichever directory is currently selected. This means that it's easier to select the starting directory in a File Manager directory tree before choosing Search than to type in the directory tree name later.

20.5 Searching for files by content

Sometimes, when you can't remember a file's name and have made no catalog to look it up in, you can find it by searching the contents of many files on a disk. A search for the word Rumplestiltskin turns up a letter to Mr. Rumplestiltskin. This approach is usually confined to text files, although more complicated data files, such as spreadsheet files, may sometimes yield results.

DOS offers a primitive facility for such searches—the FIND command. Within text files, text is usually broken up into lines of about eighty characters. The FIND command could seek the word Rumplestiltskin in a file and show each line of the file in which the expression is found. Then you'd have to load the file into your word processor to confirm that it is the one you are looking for. To search the file TALLTALE.TXT for this string, you would type:

```
FIND "Rumplestiltskin" TALLTALE.TXT ⏎
```

or, using a directory path:

```
FIND "Rumplestiltskin" C:\FABLES\TALLTALE.TXT ⏎
```

If Rumplestiltskin is found in the file, FIND might display:

```
---------- C:\FABLES\TALLTALE.TXT
Dear Mr Rumplestiltskin,
other way. Let me assure you, Mr Rumplestiltskin, that
```

You can have FIND show the relative line number of each line displayed by adding /N after the word FIND:

```
FIND /N "Rumplestiltskin" TALLTALE.TXT ⏎
```

Add /C at the same position in the command to make FIND report the total number of lines displayed (no lines are shown in this case), and /V to display only lines that do not hold Rumplestiltskin.

Restrictions FIND has a number of limitations that greatly restrict its usefulness. First, in DOS versions prior to 5.0, FIND is case-sensitive, meaning that it distinguishes between uppercase and lowercase letters in its searches. If you specify giraffe as the word to find, and the word happens to start a sentence and thus is capitalized, FIND will miss it. DOS 5.0 overcomes this limitation by introducing the /i switch to make the search case-insensitive. Thus, giraffe would match with Giraffe,

GIRAFFE, and GiRaFfe as long as this switch is included in the command.

Another problem is that FIND won't locate expressions divided between two lines of a text file. If you're looking for blue moon and blue is the last word of one line and moon is the first word of the next, FIND won't see it. FIND also sees every instance of an expression, whether or not it is a whole word. If you were to specify a search for the word cat, FIND would report instances of words like scat and catacomb.

FIND also has trouble viewing groups of files. You may specify multiple files to search by naming each on the command line:

```
FIND "Rumplestiltskin" FILE1.TXT FILE2.TXT FILE3.TXT ⏎
```

However, FIND cannot use global file name characters (explained in section 1.3) for searching large numbers of files. The command:

```
FIND "Rumplestiltskin" *.TXT ⏎
```

results in an error message rather than a search of all files in a directory with .TXT extensions. You can get around this limitation by applying the FOR keyword, which normally is used in batch files. To use *.TXT in your search, enter:

```
FOR %F IN (*.TXT) DO FIND "Rumplestiltskin" %F ⏎
```

See section 9.6 if you want to understand how this command works. However, you can use it without understanding it. Just enter the file name specification within the parentheses, and the search expression in place of Rumplestiltskin.

Utility software   Most utility packages, including the Norton Utilities and Norton Desktop for Windows, include a facility for case-insensitive text searches. More specialized utilities have been devised for researchers, lawyers, and computer programmers. These programs can perform complex searches with remarkable speed. Some even work well on non-text files. Normally these programs let you specify precise conditions for a match by using metacharacters. For instance, the expression blue^moon might match with the words blue and moon separated by any number of spaces. You can build up specifications like, Find all instances of the word King that are not followed by Kong, and which are found within 20 words of the words France or French. These utilities are not very easy to use, and most users have no need of their advanced features.

20.6　Cataloging files

With time, a hard disk can come to hold thousands of files, including hundreds of files related to application software and utility programs. It is important to keep track of files not just so you can find a particular file when you need it, but also so that you'll know what can and can't be deleted from a hard disk when it becomes crowded. Unfortunately, DOS offers almost no help in this matter, restricting you to eight-character file names with optional three-character extensions—not much room for a descriptive label. Microsoft Windows does no better, and even most DOS shells are completely deficient in this respect.

Within the confines of DOS, there are two strategies for cataloging files: through the directory tree structure, and through file-naming conventions. In directory trees, keep subdirectories small, with only related files in each. For example, if your correspondence grows to hundreds of letters, don't just dump them all in one large directory. Subdivide the files into categorized subdirectories.

Allow the names of higher-level subdirectories to partially define the content of lower-level ones. For example, a subdirectory containing documents about postal service during the French Revolution could be named something like FRREVPST (FRench REVolution PoST)—a name that, with time, would be undeciperable even by the person who created it, not to mention other people. Instead, place the subdirectory along a directory path in which the entire path defines the meaning of individual directories: \FRANCE\REVOLUTN\POSTAL.

Coding file names　File names may be coded with special characters for the purpose of cataloging them and locating them by global file name characters (section 1.3). In this technique, particular positions in file names are reserved for particular codes. For example, the file name extension may be regarded as three separate codes. The first character might represent the name of the person who created the file, with *S* for Sally, *M* for Mike, and so on. The second character could associate the file with a particular topic or project, such as *P* for plastic and *A* for aluminum. And the third character could tell the content of the file, such as *M* for memo, *L* for letter, and *R* for report. Finally, the eight-character file name would be devoted to the best-possible description of the file's contents: OVERRUN, WARNING, NEWPLAN. The result would be filenames like OVERRUN.SPL, WARNING.MAM, and NEWPLAN.SAR. You could then use global file name characters to request, for example, a listing of all reports written by Sally:

```
DIR *.S?R ←
```

One problem with this system is that many application programs require predefined extensions; they won't be able to recognize files if you replace the mandatory extension with a special coding system. In this situation, you're forced to use characters from the file name itself for codes, preferably starting from the last character and working toward the first. Unfortunately, this solution makes file names harder to read.

Perhaps a greater problem is that once you start such a system, you must maintain it. This takes discipline and care, plus forethought about how to deal with unusual situations. For example, in the scheme described above where the third character of a file's extension tells whether it is a memo, letter, or report, you'd need to keep that code in that particular position even when other codes (such as the author's name) aren't required for a particular file. Try using dashes or underscores to replace unused codes. Instead of labeling a file as a report by naming it COSTING.R, you'd have to type COSTING.--R.

Utility software   To move beyond these awkward methods for cataloging files, you'll need to turn to utility software tailored to this purpose. A handful of programs let you assign long descriptive labels, and possibly some keywords, to files. Besides viewing directory listings that include the long labels, you can ask for multidirectory searches based on the content of the labels, or based on combinations of keywords.

These facilities are introduced apart from DOS—there is no room in DOS directories to store so much extra information. Hence, such programs generate their own files on a hard disk, sometimes one in each subdirectory. Just like directory listings, these files must constantly be updated whenever a file is created, copied, or moved. For this reason, these programs often come in the form of a DOS shell that takes over common DOS commands. When you use the program to copy a file, it will see to it that its special information files are properly updated. But, if you take a vacation from the program and copy files using the DOS COPY command, the cataloging system will become confused.

Like most DOS shells, these programs remain at least partially in memory when application programs are run. They may link into DOS in a way that, when you create a new file from within an application, the utility will be activated to open a window on the screen through which it requests descriptive information and keywords for the file. This feature is invaluable, for without it you constantly must exit the program to update the information for new files (or risk forgetting to enter it later).

Ultimately, file cataloging can only be made easy through modifications to DOS. Until that day arrives, it will be up to each of us to fend for ourself, both by working cleverly with DOS and by using utility software. No scheme will be worth much, however, without considerable self-discipline.

20.7 Archiving files

You have three options when a hard disk fills. You can add another disk to the machine and cope with the problems of working in two directory trees. You can buy a file compression utility (section 20.3) to try to stave off the full-disk problem a while longer. Or you can take matters in hand and move less important files over to diskettes in a process called archiving. Archives are data files that are not required day to day—allowing them to be removed from your hard disk—but which are still important and must be available if needed. Don't confuse archives with backups. Backups keep spare copies of files that remain on your hard disk. Archived files, on the other hand, are completely removed from the disk. And while backups are just copies of files identified by their file names, proper archives are cataloged in some way so that you can easily locate files by their contents.

Building an archive index   When transferring archives from your hard disk to diskettes, you may be tempted to preserve the directory structure under which the files are organized. For example, if correspondence of a certain nature is found in the subdirectory MISSIVES, a subdirectory of that name can be created on a diskette, and the entire contents then copied to it. It's hard to set up and maintain an archive system this way. A better approach is to simply fill diskettes with files at random. Use empty diskettes and number them consecutively: 1, 2, 3, etc. When a diskette is filled with archived files, say on drive A, execute a command like this:

```
DIR A: >C:\ARCHIVES\ARCH001 ⏎
```

This example assumes that you've set up a subdirectory named ARCHIVES in the root directory of your hard disk, and that the diskette in drive A is disk 1 (001) in the series. For the next diskette, the command would be:

```
DIR A: >C:\ARCHIVES\ARCH002 ⏎
```

These commands redirect the output of directory listings from drive A to a series of files named ARCH001, ARCH002, ARCH003, and so on. Open these files one after another in your word processor. Delete the directory headings and other information so that the files are reduced to nothing more than file listings. Then annotate the listing for its content. For example:

```
ARCHIVE DISKETTE #1
#Correspondence to #Italy
MYLETTER.DOC        3405    03-12-87        12:34p
YOURLTTR.DOC        2019    09-07-89        08:44a
HISLETTR.DOC         568    12-01-90        11:01a
#Correspondence to #France
HERLETTR.DOC        5401    01-28-88        02:03p
OURLETTR.DOC        3999    11-11-90        10:30a
```

Your hard disk now has an index to each diskette. But separate indicies are not very useful, so combine them into one large file (say, ARCHIVES.LST), preferably in the order they were created. Any word processor can do this. Or use the DOS COPY command, appending a file like ARCH023 to ARCHIVES.LST by the command:

```
COPY ARCHIVES.LST+ARCH023 ⏎
```

With this index on hand, you can search for a file by loading ARCHIVES into your word processor and using its search command to find the annotations you've placed in the files. Once you encounter a reference to a desired file, look for its associated diskette number and you'll know just where to find it. One advantage of this approach is that related files may be spread across many diskettes and yet they are just as easy to find as when they have been meticulously grouped on one diskette.

Notice that there is no limitation on how much information you can enter about each file. If you're up to the job, a line-by-line explanation of each file will result in a crystal-clear catalog guaranteed to be useful years later when your memories of the files have dimmed. If you use keywords, make a habit of starting the word with a symbol such as the # sign used in the example above (#France instead of France). By doing this, your search commands can avoid extraneous appearances of the keyword.

Utility software　A number of software companies have published diskette librarians, which are intended to organize diskettes. These programs vary widely in their capabilities. Virtually all can inspect diskettes and print out directory listings on labels that may be affixed to the diskette. However, not all of these programs maintain a disk-based composite index of files that can be searched. Nor will most let you make annotations about file groupings and contents. One of these utilities might be useful for archiving, so by all means, find out what utilities the marketplace currently offers. But before buying one, be sure that it will do more than you can easily do with your word processor.

TIP

Remember that diskettes can fail, just like hard disks. Once files have been archived and erased from a hard disk, subsequent runs of your backup software will remove backups of the files from your backup diskettes (or tape). If your archives are valuable to you, make a second copy of each diskette.

- MINITUTORIAL: Optimizing hard disk performance

- DOS configuration

- The FASTOPEN command

- Defragmenting files

- File layout

- Sorting directories

- Optimizing disk interleave

- Optimizing the PATH command

- Using RAM disks

- Disk caching

MINITUTORIAL:
Optimizing hard disk performance

Generally speaking, hard disk drive performance accounts for roughly half of a computer's perceived speed. The actual influence of disk drives on overall performance depends on what software you use and how you use it. Traditionally, programs like word processors and spreadsheets, which tend to read data into memory at the start of a work session and write it out later, benefit little from fast disk drives. Databases, on the other hand, are extremely disk intensive, and a slow drive degrades performance noticeably. Recent software of all kinds tends to use a multitude of files and can make great demands on disk drives. Operating environments like Windows and DESQview can further exacerbate the problem. So, disk drive optimization—getting data to move as quickly as possible between a hard disk and the computer's memory—is an important issue. Often, just a little bit of effort can triple a drive's effective speed.

Many factors determine hard disk speed, starting with the physical characteristics of the drive itself. Most drives turn at about the same rate, but the speed at which a drive's read/write heads can shuttle between tracks varies greatly. This speed is measured as the drive's average seek time, and it typically varies from about 65 to 15 milliseconds (thousandths of a second). It is an important determinant of drive performance, but by no means the only one.

Another factor is the drive's cylinder density—the number of sectors located at a single position of the read/write heads. All hard disks actually contain at least two disks (platters) that rotate in parallel, with one read/write head for each side of each disk. The read/write heads move together so that all are at the same track on their respective disks at any given moment. High-capacity drives that have many platters hold more data at a given position of the read/write heads, since having more platters means there will be more tracks at that position. For this reason, more data can be transferred without a time-consuming head movement. The drive's electronics are also important in determining the maximum rate of data transfer between the drive and the computer's memory.

Once a drive has been purchased and installed, there is nothing you can do about its basic speed. But there is much you can do to see to it that your software can best exploit that speed and to avoid a natural tendency toward performance degradation. First, you must see to it that the drive is given an optimum interleave during formatting. Interleave is discussed both in this chapter and in section 16.2. It must be set to match the speed of your computer's microprocessor. A mismatch can cause the disk to require extra revolutions between reading disk sectors.

Most optimization techniques work at minimizing the movement of the drive's read/write heads, because this activity is glacially slow by electronic standards. The computer is essentially put on hold each time a head movement occurs. One way of minimizing head movements is to keep files defragmented. Files tend to be split into parts stored all over the disk surface, particularly on disk drives that have been heavily used and are nearly full. Reading and writing fragmented files requires much more head movement than would be required by a file packed into adjacent disk sectors. Utility software can reassemble fragmented files.

Another approach is to place particular files and subdirectories at positions on the disk where they can be found with the fewest possible movements of the disk drive's read/write heads (section 21.4). Subdirectories can be sorted so that subdirectory-to-subdirectory searches are hastened (section 21.5). And features like the DOS FASTOPEN command can keep track of frequently opened files and move the read/write heads straight to the file without looking up its location each time (section 21.2).

Even more profitable is a technique called caching (section 21.19). As programs run, they tend to repeatedly access the same data on disk drives, and so they need to access the same disk sectors again and again. Rather than write or read the same data to and from a disk over and over again, software can tuck it away in a storage area in memory and fetch it from there when it is called for. To some extent, DOS automatically works this way through its buffers. Its abilities are primitive, however, compared to those of disk-caching software, which cleverly manages which data should be kept in memory and which left on disk. Performance can triple in certain applications from this optimization measure alone.

Finally, there are ways of organizing directory trees to speed access to files. The usefulness of these kinds of optimization depends on your software. Files can be positioned for quick access by your programs (section 21.4). In some cases, critical files may be shifted to super-fast RAM disks (section 21.8). Moreover, DOS commands like PATH and APPEND, which automatically track down files, may be streamlined to avoid wasteful disk access (section 21.7).

The one hard disk optimization that no one should ignore is a proper setting for DOS buffers. Next in line is file defragmentation, which brings immediate gains to hard disks that have been in use for a long time. For those who use databases and other random access files, disk caching is another candidate for a major performance increase. The other optimizations generally tend to have less of an effect, although individual optimizations can make a big difference in certain circumstances. The better you observe how your software interacts with your hard disk drive, the better you will be able to optimize your system.

21.1 DOS configuration

Chapter 11 discusses the many ways in which DOS can be configured. The foremost concern for optimizing disk access is with setting an optimal number of file buffers. But there are many other methods, most of which can consume scarce conventional memory. The way you configure the machine can affect how fast your hard disk operates, and even how fast the microprocessor can run programs. Keep in mind the following suggestions:

Don't overallocate DOS buffers   Providing an adequate number of DOS buffers (discussed in section 11.3) is the easiest of all hard disk optimizations. Because it costs nothing, it is also the cheapest. But take care not to go overboard. The DOS buffers are not part of an intelligent disk-caching scheme (section 21.9). When too many buffers are allocated, DOS may spend, on average, more time scanning the buffers than it would require to make a direct disk access. This is particularly true of slower computers, where there tends to be less of a disparity between relative disk speed and microprocessor speed.

Don't allocate memory unnecessarily   Large amounts of memory can be used up by commands found in your CONFIG.SYS and AUTOEXEC.BAT files (section 11.1). Some commands that may be in these files, such as PRINT and GRAPHICS, take up memory even when they go unused. Similarly, memory can be wasted by loading unused or seldom-used device drivers (section 11.11) or memory-resident programs (section 15.4).

Memory shortages, when they don't make running a program impossible, tend to make it run more slowly. This is because application software may need to swap data back and forth between disk and memory since it can't keep it all in memory at once. Similarly, a program may be forced to only partially load itself into memory and then repeatedly reload other parts as they are needed. Not all programs work this way (most simply refuse to run when memory is insufficient) but this kind of software design is the wave of the future.

Allocate expanded and extended memory wisely   Many memory expansion boards may be configured to act as expanded or extended memory. Software for RAM disks (section 15.3) and disk caches (section 21.9) as well as many memory-resident utilities (section

15.4) can optionally be configured to reside primarily in expanded or extended memory. It's worth knowing that these kinds of memory generally work slower than conventional memory (the main 640K) when DOS is the operating system. In the case of expanded memory, this performance deficit results because time is wasted switching between memory ranges (see the minitutorial in Chapter 15). For extended memory, the computer's microprocessor must switch operation modes to get at the higher memory addresses and then shift back to its normal mode.

These performance deficits apply to application software as well as utilities. As a rule, utility software is less affected, and so utilities and other memory-resident programs should be placed in expanded or extended memory when possible. It makes much more sense to create a RAM disk in expanded memory and keep a program's data in conventional memory than to place the RAM disk in conventional memory and force the program to use expanded memory for data. (Strictly speaking, this is a hard disk deoptimization, since utility software that speeds up a hard disk is slightly slowed by placing it in expanded or extended memory. But the computer's overall performance is enhanced.)

21.2 The FASTOPEN command

Some of your files may be constantly opened and closed. DOS must find its way to a file each time it reopens it. This entails scanning every directory along the path to the file. First the root directory is searched for the location of the first subdirectory along the path, and then the disk's read/write heads are moved to the position(s) containing the subdirectory. It in turn is read and searched, and DOS may then continue along to more subdirectories until it finally learns the starting position of the file. The shuttling of the read/write heads back and forth can take up much time. Even on a defragmented disk (section 21.3), time is wasted loading the subdirectory files and scanning them.

With version 3.3, DOS introduced the FASTOPEN feature, a means of avoiding much of this repetitive labor. Once FASTOPEN is activated, DOS remembers the starting points of files that have been opened previously and then closed. When a file is to be opened, DOS first scans the list of recently used files to see if the desired file is mentioned. If so, it is able to move the disk's read/write heads immediately to the start of the file. If not, DOS proceeds with a normal file search starting in the root directory. Although it takes a moment to scan the list, on average much time is saved.

Since subdirectories are themselves files, DOS keeps track of all recently opened subdirectory files as well. Thus, if you were to open the file \MAMMALS\PRIMATES\GIBBONS.TXT, and subsequently wanted to open the file CHIMPS, also found in the PRIMATES subdirectory, DOS would already know the location of both the MAMMALS and PRIMATES subdirectories, and so would immediately be able to move to PRIMATES, loading it to scan for the file CHIMPS. The search of the root and MAMMALS directories would be entirely avoided, cutting the search time by two-thirds for a file that had not previously been opened at all.

FASTOPEN must be activated for each drive separately. To start up FASTOPEN for drive C, enter the command:

```
FASTOPEN C: ↵
```

Up to 34 files are tracked, including subdirectory files. You can increase this number. To track 80 files, enter:

```
FASTOPEN C:=80 ↵
```

Only one FASTOPEN command may be executed after booting (DOS displays "FASTOPEN already installed" if you try a second time), so list additional drives in the same command:

    FASTOPEN C: D: ⏎

or:

    FASTOPEN C:=80 D:=100 ⏎

Every entry takes up 35 bytes of memory, so the default value takes up roughly 1K, and 80 files would take up nearly 3K. For most people, the default value is adequate. You may specify a number lower than the default value if you wish. When, in the course of a work session, you call upon more than the given number of files, the least recently accessed files are deleted from the list and replaced by the new ones. In DOS 4.0, you may place the FASTOPEN data in expanded memory by appending an /X switch to the command:

    FASTOPEN C:=80 /X ⏎

Of course, the table of information disappears from memory when the machine is turned off, so the command must be reentered each time the machine is turned on (or rebooted by Ctrl-Alt-Del). The best policy is to put it in your AUTOEXEC.BAT file (section 11.1).

PITFALLS

Be careful of renaming subdirectories using the DOS Shell, Windows, or a utility program. FASTOPEN won't be able to take into account a new subdirectory name in paths it has recorded. Also, be careful of disk defragmenters (section 21.3), since they will relocate data on the disk without FASTOPEN knowing about it. You should reboot the machine after defragmenting a disk when FASTOPEN is active.

Don't use FASTOPEN with the JOIN, SUBST, or ASSIGN commands discussed in Chapter 8. These change the apparent structure of the drive system and directory system, and can confuse FASTOPEN. Also, when you specify the number of files to track in a FASTOPEN command, be sure that the number is at least as large as the maximum number of subdirectories, plus one, that will be held in any directory path you'll use so that

FASTOPEN can handle the worst case. Finally, note that FASTOPEN is an external DOS command held in the file FASTOPEN.EXE. This file must be on hand to use FASTOPEN, either by having it in the current directory, by loading it with a directory path, as in:

```
C:\DOS\FASTOPEN C:=80 E
```

or by accessing it through a PATH command, as explained in section 8.1.

21.3 Defragmenting files

When DOS writes files on a newly formatted disk, whether a hard disk or a diskette, it writes the files upon contiguous sectors (every disk is divided by magnetic lines into concentric rings called tracks, with each track divided into eight or more sectors). Thus, the file continues from one sector to the next, and then continues on the next adjacent track. This is the ideal situation for accessing a file, because the read/write heads that hover over the disk surface need to move very few times, perhaps only once, and the positions are close together so that mechanical motion is minimized.

As a disk fills, the layout of files becomes much less orderly. File erasures leave unused sectors at random locations across the disk surface, and these sectors are used by new files. A 50-kilobyte file copied to the disk may be scattered across many tracks, taking up a free two kilobytes here, ten kilobytes there. In addition, as data files grow, they must find free sectors into which to expand. DOS may allocate these additional sectors from any free space on the disk.

A file is said to be fragmented when it falls into this scattered state. File fragmentation hampers hard disk performance more than any other factor. In the worst case, the read/write heads may need to move a dozen times just to read a 25K data file, sometimes moving the heads across the entire width of the disk. Yet, on a hard disk, the same file could be stored so that it resides entirely at one position of the read/write heads—all of the shuttling back and forth could be eliminated.

The solution to this problem is file defragmentation, a process in which the scattered segments of a fragmented file are brought together in the proper order. Unfortunately, DOS does not offer a defragmentation feature. You must buy special utility software that is separate from DOS. Such utilities, called defragmentation utilities (or just defraggers) are widely and cheaply available. Many general-purpose utility packages contain a defragmentation utility, Speed Disk in the Norton Utilities is one.

Using a defragmenter   Most defragmentation utilities contain an analysis program that scans the disk to tell you how badly files are defragmented. Some, like Speed Disk, also let you determine the degree of fragmentation of individual files or subdirectories. This

information can be obtained in a primitive way by using the DOS
CHKDSK command, which analyzes disk directories for errors. To find
out if the file LIZARDS.DOC in the \REPTILES subdirectory is fragmented, enter:

```
CHKDSK C:\REPTILES\LIZARDS.DOC ←
```

After reporting general information about the disk, CHKDSK might
display:

```
C:\REPTILES\LIZARDS.DOC
  Contains 3 non-contiguous blocks.
```

if the file is fragmented, or:

```
All specified file(s) are contiguous
```

if not. You can check all files in a directory by using global file name
characters (section 1.3), as in:

```
CHKDSK C:\REPTILES\*.* ←
```

In this case, many fragmented files might be listed by the command.
However, the overall percentage of fragmentation (the number of
fragmentations divided by the number of clusters holding the files) is
something that you would have to laboriously calculate. Utility software
is far superior in this regard. Note that you cannot use CHKDSK to scan
an entire directory tree for this information.

It only takes a minute to have a defragmenter analyze a hard disk. On
the basis of the analysis, you can decide whether to proceed to a full-
blown defragmentation; this can take as long as an hour on a high-
capacity hard disk. To give you a taste of what this kind of software looks
like, figure 21.1 shows a map of disk usage displayed by the Speed Disk
program in The Norton Utilities, and figure 2.2 shows the disk status
report shown when you request Disk Statistics from the menu of choices
in the lower left corner of figure 21.1.

Once you request the defragmentation, there is nothing more for you
to do but wait for it to finish. Defragmentation may proceed more
quickly if you make as much memory available as possible, perhaps by
running the machine without any memory-resident programs loaded
(if your AUTOEXEC.BAT file loads these programs, temporarily alter
it and then reboot the machine). Most defragmenters can be stopped
midway with the disk only partially defragmented.

The utility will let you know when it has finished. Thereafter, disk accesses will take much less time. In some cases, performance can increase by a factor of three or more. More typically, you'll double the speed of a much-used disk. You'll need to periodically run the defragmenter again to maintain high performance, perhaps once a month just after you've made a global backup of the hard disk's files.

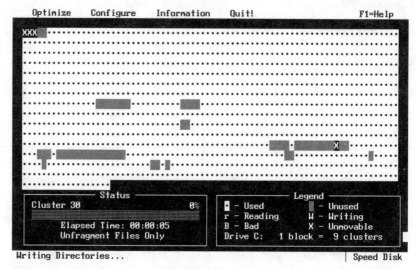

Figure 21.1

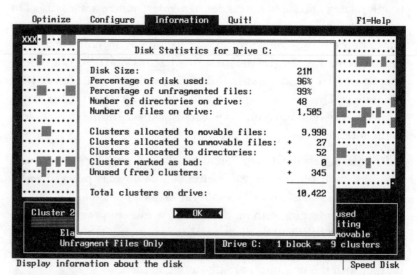

Figure 21.2

Defragmenters have become quite sophisticated and some can perform a number of other optimizations, including the relocation of important files and subdirectories. These optimizations are discussed elsewhere in this chapter (see sections 21.4 and 21.5). Defragmenters push all files toward the outer edge of the disk, filling empty sectors and leaving the inner core of the disk completely free for new files. The outer edge is filled so that the disk drive's read/write heads are kept near the disk's root directory and file allocation tables, which are constantly accessed. By removing the scattered empty sectors, new defragmentation is avoided when additional files are created or copied to the disk. But fragmentation inevitably returns, and a heavily used disk needs to be defragmented every few months if high performance is to be maintained.

PITFALLS   It is important that no other software will attempt to access the hard disk while a defragmenter is working on it. So be sure that no memory-resident programs that may access disk drives are operating in the machine at the same time. Also, remember that you should not turn off the computer while a defragmenter is running. If you want to cut its work short, use whatever command it provides for early termination.

Defragmenters are an invasive technology. They touch almost every part of the disk, including parts that only DOS was intended to manipulate. If something goes wrong during defragmentation, data may be lost and, in the worst case, everything on the disk may disappear. The best-known defragmentation utilities are well-debugged, but still you must be ready for the worst. You should make backups of everything on your disk before initiating the defragmentation.

It is unwise to use a public-domain or shareware defragmenter without a solid recommendation of its reliability. Be aware that a defragmenter can work well on one hard disk and fail on another. Be especially wary if you have a very high-capacity hard disk, because the design may be nonstandard. Check with the manufacturer about approved defragmenters.

21.4 File layout

Nothing slows a hard disk so much as unnecessary movements of the read/write heads that scan the disk surface. Excessive head motion occurs for two reasons. First, files may be fragmented (spread out over nonadjacent parts of the disk). Section 21.3 explains how this problem may be corrected. Second, related files may be poorly distributed on the disk surface. Often, software needs to access several related files. Many application programs load the same half-dozen files each time they are run. When these files are widely dispersed on the disk surface, more time must be spent finding them.

Similarly, when DOS searches for a file that is located several levels down the subdirectory tree, DOS must look into each subdirectory along the way. Since a subdirectory is itself a file, each may reside anywhere on the disk. When subdirectories are located far apart, the hard disk must shuttle its read/write heads back and forth. But, subdirectory files are usually quite small and sometimes dozens can be packed into one position on the disk so that DOS can read one after another without any head movement at all.

DOS must also constantly access the main (root) directory of a disk and the file allocation table that keeps track of where files are located. Because both are found on the outer edge of the disk, the read/write heads constantly return to this position. Insofar as often-used files can be kept close to the outer edge, head movements will be minimized and the drive will work faster. Thus, there are two goals in locating files for efficient access: placing related files on the same tracks, or on adjacent tracks, and placing frequently used files as close to the outer edge of the disk as possible.

DOS gives you no direct control over the placement of files. When a disk has been newly formatted, it lays down new files one after another, starting from the outer edge of the disk. Holes are created in this continuous series of files as individual files are erased, and newly created files (or copied files) may be placed within these holes (recent DOS versions fill the whole disk once before starting to fill in holes left by file erasures).

Because it is DOS that decides how to place files once erasures occur, it is only during the initial layout of files on a freshly formatted disk that you have any control. But at that point you have a good deal of control. Follow these steps.

Step 1 Before copying any files over to the newly formatted disk, create as much of the directory tree as you can. By doing so, all subdirectories will be packed into just a few tracks, and they will reside close to the root directory and file allocation table on the outer edge of the disk. Few movements of the read/write heads will be necessary to search for a file in the directory tree, and the movements will be quick ones. When more subdirectories are added later, there will be no way of including them with this main grouping. But the average access time for a subdirectory will be greatly reduced. (See section 21.2 concerning further optimization of file-lookup via the FASTOPEN command.)

Step 2 Copy over all DOS files and frequently used utility files (such as memory-resident programs). By doing so, these small, often-accessed programs are placed close to the outer edge of the disk next to the subdirectory files. If batch files are on hand, copy these over too.

Step 3 Copy over application program files such as your word processor or spreadsheet program.

Step 4 Copy over data files used by programs. Data files are moved last because they change in size, whereas program files do not. Nor are program files often deleted from a disk. By following this strategy, the outer edge of the disk is filled with a solid, unchanging mass of files, while the middle and inner core of the disk is left to the constantly fluctuating hodgepodge of data files.

Utility software The above four-step procedure is worthwhile when you are installing a hard disk for the first time, or reorganizing a hard disk by reformatting it and rebuilding it from backups. However, a major disk reorganization is a lot of work (and it can be dangerous if you are relying on only one set of backups, because backups can fail too). Happily, there is utility software available that can perform these optimizations for you. Almost always, the service is performed by the same programs that defragment a disk, such as the Speed Disk program in the Norton Utilities. It moves subdirectories to the outer edge of the disk and places program files nearby. Using file name extensions, particular kinds of files—all batch files, for example—can be moved toward the disk edge. You can also position particular files by name.

21.5 Sorting directories

When DOS opens a file, it begins by searching for the file's directory entry to find the file's starting point on disk. DOS scans the directory that lists the files, starting from the first entry. The file is found more quickly when it is listed near the beginning of the directory. Similarly, when the file is located several levels down a directory tree, DOS must scan each directory in turn to find the next subdirectory along the path. DOS then finds the file listing itself in the last of the subdirectories.

The files that contain subdirectories are treated like any other file in a directory listing. When they are created, they are given the first available opening in the directory, starting from the top. Thus, subdirectories may be located quite far down the directory, and time can be wasted finding them. This is particularly true when a subdirectory has become fragmented so that it occupies more than one location on the disk (section 21.3 discusses fragmentation and how to reduce it). When a subdirectory is found deep in the directory, one or more extra movements of the disk's read/write heads may be necessary to find it.

For these reasons, the most efficient organization for directories would be to have the most frequently accessed files, including subdirectory files, situated at the beginning of directories. It is especially important to have subdirectories closest to the root directory optimized in this way, because they are accessed more often than remote subdirectories. There are two ways to achieve the optimization:

Method 1   When transferring files to a newly formatted hard disk, first create as much of the directory tree as possible. In doing so, directory entries for subdirectory files will be placed at the top of each directory. Transfer frequently used program files and utilities to the disk, giving them priority in directory listings second only to the subdirectories. Next, add additional program files. Finally, transfer data files.

Of course, in the real world it is impossible to anticipate every subdirectory you will need or every program you will install. This way of optimizing directories works only when you first build up a freshly formatted disk. With time, the system will become less efficient as major additions are made to the disk's contents.

Method 2   To optimize directories on a disk that is already full of files, you will need a special utility that sorts directories, such as the DS (Directory Sort) program in the Norton Utilities. Utilities that sort directories are found in many disk utility packages. These utilities vary in the features they offer, but all perform at least two services: they move all listings of subdirectory files to the top of each directory, and they remove all empty spaces within the directory (they compact the directory). These spaces, which are invisible in directory listings, result from file erasures. They are removed because DOS wastes time scanning them as it searches through a directory.

A directory-sorting utility will usually alphabetize the files in the directory, sorting the subdirectories separately. Some will let you specify some other order, such as by size or creation date. For optimal performance, a utility should be able to specify that frequently used files be placed near the top of the directory, but this feature is not standard. The Norton DS program can work in an interactive mode in which you select individual files from a menu, or groups of files, and then move them to a desired position in the directory. Many directories—even all directories in a tree—can be sorted by a single command.

Virtually all DOS shells, including the DOS Shell program that accompanies DOS version 4.0 and later, can display a directory listing sorted in various ways, often with the subdirectory files listed together. So can the DOS SORT filter, which we discuss in section 2.3. These sortings are done on the spot when you issue a request to see the directory presented in this way. It is only the listing on the screen that is sorted, and not the directory itself. So, there is no gain in efficiency when DOS subsequently scans the directory looking for a file. Don't confuse this kind of sorting with an actual reordering of entries in disk directories.

21.6 Optimizing disk interleave

The information written on a disk, whether a hard disk or a diskette, is broken up into units called sectors. The surface of the disk is divided by magnetic lines into concentric rings called tracks, and each track is divided into so many sectors, depending on the size of the disk. As the disk spins, a device called a read/write head hovers over a track—one on each side of the disk—and reads or writes data as the appropriate sector passes beneath.

On fast computers, a read/write head and its accompanying electronics can continuously read or write one sector after another. But slower computers, including most machines built around the 80286 microprocessor, cannot move data to and from the disk drive quickly enough. Consequently, the disk drive must access every-other sector, or every third sector, or sectors farther apart still, so that time is allowed for data transfer. This separation of sectors is called a disk's interleave. A disk with 1:1 interleave writes to adjacent sectors, 2:1 to every-other sector, 3:1 to every third sector, and so on. Hard disks in IBM XT-style machines typically run with a 6:1 interleave; AT's run at 3:1 or 2:1. These values are called interleave factors.

It is important to understand that the interleave is not an inherent mechanical property of the disk (although disks operating at a 1:1 interleave need special electronics to keep up with so fast a data flow). Rather, the interleave is set when the disk is formatted. As the mini-tutorial in the beginning of Chapter 16 explains, there are two levels of formatting for any disk. In high-level formatting, DOS creates the root directory and other structures it requires to keep track of files. But first the disk requires low-level formatting in which magnetic markers are written on the disk to define tracks and sectors. Each sector along a track is given a code number, and the distribution of these code numbers determines the disk's interleave.

Determining the proper interleave   When a disk's interleave is too large, say 3:1 when it should be 2:1, time is wasted waiting for the next sector to rotate under the read/write head. A hard disk's performance may be improved by testing whether the interleave is set optimally, and changing it when it isn't. However, one must be careful not to make the interleave too small. Otherwise, a disk sector will arrive at the read/write head before the computer's electronics are ready to access it and the disk will have to make an additional full rotation before the data transfer can be made.

It is possible to change a disk's interleave by reformatting it. A low-level formatting program (described in section 16.2,) usually prompts the user for an interleave factor. But reformatting a disk entails destroying all data on it. You would need to make a global backup of all files on the disk, reformat it, and then restore the data. Unfortunately, DOS offers you no way of finding out whether the current interleave is optimal or not. Nor can a manufacturer necessarily tell you the proper interleave when you buy a disk, since the electronic properties of IBM machines vary considerably, even among machines that are nominally of the same kind and speed rating.

So, the only realistic way of optimizing a disk's interleave is to purchase one of the special utilities available for this purpose. Such programs appear in a number of disk utility packages (there is one called Calibrate in the Norton Utilities). These utilities can usually perform a variety of tests on the disk to see that it is working well mechanically. They will also test for bad sectors with much greater accuracy than DOS can. In optimizing interleave, they perform a careful analysis of the disk's behavior with several tracks set to various interleave factors. Once the analysis has been performed, the program asks you for permission to proceed, and then it goes on to change the formatting markings on the disk so that the sectors are numbered differently.

PITFALLS | Early versions of these utilities destroyed the data on the disk as they worked. But today there are several offered (including Calibrate) that can perform their magic without harming the data. Still, it is essential that you understand that these utilities are potentially danger-ous to your data. To do their work, they must delve into the deepest recesses of a disk drive's electronics. Be-cause there are a multitude of drive designs, there is always a chance of malfunction.

In addition, while changing the format markings, the utility must store in the computer's memory all data held on one or more tracks. If power goes out, the data is lost; if the data includes subdirectories, all files in the subdirectory and all subdirectories beyond it are lost. It is possible to design a utility in such a way that these dangers are lessened. But still, you should never use one of these utilities without first making a full backup of all data on the disk.

21.7 Optimizing the PATH command

The DOS PATH command causes DOS to look in directories other than the current directory when it needs to find a program file. For instance, the DOS CHKDSK command resides in its own file, CHKDSK.COM, that must be loaded when the command is used. If the file is not in the current directory, you would need to include a directory path in the command so that DOS could find it. Instead of entering:

CHKDSK ↵

you would have to go to the trouble of typing:

C:\DOS\CHKDSK ↵

PATH saves you the extra typing when the DOS subdirectory is one that has been specified in the command. If DOS fails to find the CHKDSK file in the current directory, it searches the directories listed in the PATH command in the order they are listed.

You'll find a discussion of how to use PATH in section 8.1. In itself, PATH does not optimize hard disk performance, although the command contributes substantially to the productivity of the person using the computer. However, a wrongly formulated PATH command can slow down the speed at which DOS works, and in this sense a streamlined command contributes to hard disk optimization by minimizing the average number of hard disk accesses required to find files.

Suggestions for using PATH   There are four suggestions to keep in mind, and they are simple ones:

■ Don't name subdirectories in a PATH command unless they really need to be included. Seldom accessed directories shouldn't be included.

■ Try to confine PATH lookups to subdirectories listed in the root directory. By doing so, you'll minimize the disk accesses required to find the subdirectory. Remember that long directory paths often entail extra, time-consuming motions of the disk drive's read/write heads.

■ List the most frequently accessed subdirectories first in the command. By doing so, fewer subdirectories on average will need to be searched to find a file.

■ Keep extraneous files out of subdirectories listed in a PATH command. The larger a directory, the longer a directory search takes. If a subdirectory is included just to have one file on hand, consider placing the file in its own directory. You might even want to move several programs into one subdirectory specially designed for PATH lookups.

Note that these suggestions also apply to the DOS APPEND command (explained in section 8.2), which has DOS search multiple directories for data files. You should understand that these optimizations are minor ones, for they only affect disk drive response when files are being searched for, not when files are actually being read or written. On fast computers, the performance gains will probably be imperceptible. The optimizations are less beneficial, even inconsequential, if you apply a FASTOPEN command, as explained in section 21.2.

21.8 Using RAM disks

A RAM disk, sometimes called a virtual disk, is a sort of phantom disk drive set up in memory. Instead of storing files on magnetic media (that is, on the surface of a disk), they are kept in memory chips in the computer. A RAM disk is created by utility software, usually when a computer starts up. The RAM disk is initially empty, and files are copied to it from actual disk drives. RAM disks are discussed in section 15.3.

RAM disks are important for optimized performance, since they operate much faster than physical disk drives. When a RAM disk accesses a particular sector of data, it directly calls upon the memory addresses that hold the data; the data is transferred immediately. In contrast, a sector of data in a disk drive may be far from the current position of the drive's read/write heads. The heads must be moved into position, and then the computer waits for the sector(s) containing the data to swing beneath the heads so that the heads may access the data as it passes by. Time is also spent conveying the data through the disk drive's electronics.

Strictly speaking, the addition of a RAM disk does not improve hard disk performance. But, properly used, a RAM disk can relieve a hard disk of certain repetitive chores and thereby give a virtual increase in its performance. For example, if a spelling checker file is placed on a RAM disk, an increase in efficiency results from having fast access to what is usually a very disk intensive kind of file. If a data file is constantly read at the same time as the spell check file, moving the latter to a RAM disk means that the hard disk's read/write heads will be able to remain over the data file, rather than shuttling back and forth between it and the spelling checker file. Thus, the data file also ends up being read more quickly in spite of its remaining on the hard disk.

Of course, a RAM disk may take up scarce memory. Some software loads as much data into conventional memory as there is room and then swaps data back and forth to disk as it needs it. When a RAM disk takes over part of conventional memory, it can cause software to require more swapping and, thus, more disk activity than it would otherwise, decreasing overall performance. But these days, virtually all RAM disk software can use expanded memory or extended memory (both explained in the minitutorial at the beginning of Chapter 15). This option gives you the best of both worlds.

The great danger of using RAM disks is that all data is lost if the machine loses power even momentarily. For this reason, it's seldom a good idea to entrust data files to a RAM disk. Instead, use the RAM disk for frequently accessed read-only files. These include:

■ Program files and program auxiliary files: The main .EXE or .COM file that holds a program is usually only loaded once in a work session, and so there is no point in placing it on a RAM disk. But there may be numerous associated files, including files that hold resources used by the program, such as screen fonts, and overlay files, which hold sections of the program's code.

■ Reference files: Placing the dictionaries used by spelling checkers and thesauruses on a RAM disk can make a tremendous difference in performance.

■ Temporary files: Some software, including databases, word processors, and the compilers used by computer programmers, create temporary files when they are run. These files hold information temporarily generated by the software as it processes data. The software erases the files before it quits, so you are unlikely to be aware of their fleeting existence. But software documentation will often tell you about these files, and may let you specify the drive on which they are generated. Temporary files are usually intensively used by the software, so you can eliminate much disk drive activity by transferring them to a RAM disk.

TIP

As disk caching software (discussed in the next section) has become more efficient, RAM disks have gradually lost their comparative advantage as a disk optimization technique. In many situations, it makes more sense to allocate extended or expanded memory to a cache instead of a RAM disk. This is particularly true in machines that are equipped with a lot of memory and that can maintain a large cache, since files you might otherwise keep on a RAM disk are apt to stay in the cache. Experimentation is often the only way to decide which approach is better for a particular time-critical application.

The best way of managing a RAM disk is to create it automatically at start-up by placing a command in your CONFIG.SYS or AUTO-EXEC.BAT file (section 11.1). Then use COPY commands in AUTO-EXEC.BAT to load files onto the RAM disk. See section 15.3 to learn about the RAM disk software that comes with DOS.

21.9 Disk caching

Disk caching is a way of increasing disk drive performance without changing the disk's physical characteristics. It is based on the statistically demonstrable fact that when a computer program accesses a particular piece of data, it is likely to access it again one or more times soon thereafter. Rather than repeatedly write or read the data to and from disk, the data can be kept in memory until the software has finished with it for a while.

Most software is not designed to make this optimization on its own. But the same effect can be achieved by installing disk caching software in the machine. It inserts itself between DOS and all programs running in the machine, including memory-resident programs. Programs function normally, making reads and writes to disk drives. However, the disk caching software intercepts the requests for a disk access and handles them in its own way.

The disk caching software sets aside a specified amount of memory in which to store data. When data is read from disk, the contents of one or more 512-byte disk sectors are transferred from the disk to this area and the required data is then plucked out and sent on. Often, a few moments later the same data, or the data just beside it, is required by the software, which requests that the data be read from disk. The caching software grabs the request before it gets to DOS, finds the data that it has already stored in memory, and hands it to the program. Had caching software not been present, the program would have had to wait for another time-consuming physical disk access.

Of course, when the desired data has not already been stored in memory by the caching software, a disk read will be necessary, bringing even more data into the caching software's storage area. Once the available space has filled, the caching software begins to replace older data with newly requested data. The quality of disk caching software largely depends on how intelligently it decides which data to keep and which to discard. The decision is made on the basis of both the frequency and recency of the data's use.

The opposite occurs when data is written to disk. The caching software intercepts the outgoing data and doesn't actually have DOS write it to disk until adjacent data has also been received. This is called write-behind caching, as opposed to the usual read caching discussed above.

It's dangerous to write data this way, however, since data stored in memory will be lost if the computer loses power, or if software malfunctions and hangs the machine. In deference to these threats, most disk caching software writes out data to disk shortly after it is intercepted. Recent versions of Microsoft's SMARTDrive program (discussed below) support write-behind caching, and may delay disk writes for up to five seconds. Thus, you can exit a program before the last-saved file has actually been written. To avoid calamity, the SMARTDrive blocks out Ctrl-Alt-Del until data has been written—but it can't stop you from switching off the machine.

Relative performance gains   Caching software reaps the greatest performance gains when used with random access files. These are files that software accesses a piece at a time, without reading the whole file into memory. Most database files are random access files, as are files like the dictionary files used by spelling checkers. Many other files, including word processing documents, are sequential files, which are read from beginning to end, typically just once to move them into memory. Software tends to keep an entire sequential file in memory as it is changed and then write it entirely back to disk when the file is closed. Since each disk sector used by the file is read just once and later written just once, no performance gains are made by disk caching (indeed, the extra processing introduced by caching slightly increases the access time for sequential files).

Some disk caching software responds to these differences by letting you switch caching on and off. The software works as a memory-resident program (see section 15.4), and, as such, it may be awakened by pressing a special keystroke combination (a hot key). Other options may let you set aside part of the software's data storage area for use by particular files. This feature is useful when you switch back and forth between applications; you can keep important data in memory rather than reload it each time a program is reentered. Another feature is full-track buffering, in which the caching software automatically reads all sectors from the track upon which data is accessed. There is a high probability that data from other sectors on the track will soon be required, and, for various technical reasons, an entire track can sometimes be moved to memory almost as quickly as a single sector. Keep your drive defragmented (section 21.3) if you use this feature.

Allocating memory   The most important decision you must make when running caching software is how much memory should be devoted to it. The DOS buffers established by the DOS BUFFERS command perform primitive caching, but they use a system too awkward to profitably employ more than about 20 one-sector buffers, amounting to about 10K of memory. When disk caching software runs, the program itself typically takes up about 25K, and hundreds of kilobytes of memory may be used efficiently, although 50K devoted to caching can bring impressive results, sometimes tripling the access speed of some applications.

These days, most disk cachers let you place data, and even the caching program itself, in expanded or extended memory. This approach offers the best of both worlds, increasing disk performance while at the same time increasing available system memory (the number of DOS buffers is usually reduced to only a few when disk caching software is installed). Some caching software can temporarily relinquish the expanded or extended memory when it is required for other purposes.

Using the IBMCACHE program   PS/2 machines are shipped with a disk caching programed called IBMCACHE. To install it, place the Reference Diskette in drive A and enter IBMCACHE ⏎. A menu with four choices is displayed:

```
1. Install disk cache onto drive C:
2. View disk cache settings
3. Change disk cache settings
4. Remove disk cache from drive C:
```

By selecting the first menu choice, the file IBMCACHE.SYS is copied to the root directory of drive C. In addition, the following line is added to your CONFIG.SYS file (section 11.1) to start up disk caching when the machine is booted:

```
DEVICE=\IBMCACHE.SYS 64 /NE /P4
```

This creates a 64K cache in conventional memory, using a page size of four pages (the page size is the number of disk sectors the cache program reads or writes at once). You may create a larger cache by changing the value 64. Replace the /NE switch (which stands for not extended) with an /E switch to have the cache located in extended memory. Alternatively, you may alter the cache parameters by making the appropriate selections in the menu shown above.

The MS-DOS cache program   Starting from version 4.0, MS DOS has included a disk caching program that also comes with Windows. This program is held in the file SMARTDRV.SYS or SMARTDRV.EXE. By default, the cache is created in extended memory. To prevent memory conflicts, you must first have installed the HIMEM program, which is discussed in section 15.6. To create a 512K cache in conventional memory when SMARTDRV.SYS is in the root directory, you would place the following command in your CONFIG.SYS file:

```
DEVICE=C:\DOS\HIMEM.SYS
DEVICE=C:\DOS\SMARTDRV.SYS 512
```

When no value is specified for the cache size, a default value is used that depends on available extended memory. SMARTDrive always tries to establish a cache of at least 1 megabyte.

Adding /A to the end of the command causes the cache to be created in expanded memory, or, if you have extended memory, to have your extended memory board used as expanded memory by the cache. Using /A without preceding it with a cache size causes all of expanded memory to be devoted to the cache.

Disk cachers like SMARTDrive or the caching program found in the Norton Utilities are laden with features. You can specify which drives are to be cached, the caching method, and the sizes of buffers and data blocks. It takes a bit of work to figure out the documentation so that you can fine tune a cacher. This work is most worth while when you have a much-used, disk-intensive application that keeps you waiting a lot.

Chapter 22

Backups

MINITUTORIAL:
All about backups

There are dozens of ways in which data can be destroyed. One danger is that a hard disk malfunction will destroy sectors on the disk surface. If you are especially unlucky, crucial sectors used by DOS to track files may be obliterated, and everything on the disk will be lost. In the worst case, the disk may simply stop functioning for mechanical reasons, preventing any possibility of data recovery except by a disk drive repair service. Less dramatic events can also make you lose sleep. Disk sectors can go bad (lose their ability to hold data) and format markings may fade to the point that a sector can no longer be read.

Data may also succumb to software malfunctions. Except for very simple utilities, there really is no such thing as perfect software. Even popular programs from well-known companies have been know to suddenly attack a hard disk, erasing massive amounts of data. And, of course, there are malicious computer viruses (discussed in sections 23.6 and 25.7) that attach themselves to software and travel from machine to machine. A really sinister virus may not only destroy the files on your hard disk, but infect many diskettes as well.

Another way of losing data is through mistakes on the part of those using the computer. Files can be accidentally erased and whole disks accidentally reformatted. Even experienced users blunder occasionally. For example, you might copy a file from one directory to another, only to find that you have overwritten (and thus destroyed) a different file that happened to have the same name.

Finally, you can lose data through one of the old fashioned ways: fire, theft, vandalism, and the like. It is astonishing how many people religiously insure their computer hardware against these hazards, yet make no effort to protect the data held by that hardware, even when the value of the time spent creating the data exceeds the hardware cost.

Neglect of backups For all of these reasons, you must make backups of your data frequently. To fail to do so is to ask to be included in a long and ever-growing list of people who are still kicking themselves for having lost months of work for want of a few minutes of precaution. People neglect backups because backups are essentially unproductive; it's hard to devote oneself to something that one hopes never to use. Do all you can to overcome this resistance because eventually, every disk fails.

Backups are required not just for the data on hard disks, but also for diskettes. In some ways, diskettes are less vulnerable than hard disks. They cannot suffer a head crash (explained in the Chapter 24 minitutorial), and when a diskette drive fails, a diskette can always be moved to another drive. But diskettes tend to be more susceptible to the failure of individual disk sectors. For many kinds of files, the loss of a single sector is as bad as losing the whole file.

What to back up   The point of backups is to always have at least one extra copy of all information on a disk. There are four kinds of information:

- Program files: These include many auxiliary files, some of which you may not presently use but might require some day.

- Configuration and utility files: These are sometimes created and maintained by software. If they are lost, you'll need to install and customize your software all over again. Or, configuration and utility files may be your creations, such as the CONFIG.SYS and AUTOEXEC.BAT files used for booting (section 11.1), not to mention batch files (Chapter 9) you've made for other purposes. These files can represent a good deal of labor.

- Data files: These are the files that contain your work.

- Directory tree information: A major disk crash can wipe out a directory tree. When software has been configured, and batch files designed to work within a particular tree structure, you'll need to restore the tree to its former design after a major disk crash.

Backups of program files are usually not a problem. A hard disk owner automatically has one copy of a program on his or her hard disk and one on the diskettes on which the program is distributed. Users without hard disks should be working from copies of the original diskettes, keeping the originals as backups. As software has become more complicated, installation programs (section 12.2) have come to decide which files on the distribution diskettes should be transferred to a hard disk or to other diskettes. Keep in mind that utility programs, alternate printer drivers, and other miscellaneous files might be found only on the originals. If the originals fail, you may find yourself waiting a couple of weeks for replacements from the publisher.

Data files may be grouped with configuration and utility files, because all three contain data. Whenever a file is written to by DOS, a special notation is made in the file's directory entry. This notation is called the file's archive attribute, and the attribute is said to be set when the file is changed (attributes are discussed in the minitutorial at the beginning of Chapter 4). The archive attribute is used in making backups. Backup software can check to see if the attribute is set and, if so, it makes a copy. It is assumed that backups of other, unchanged files already exist on earlier backups. Once a file has been copied, the archive attribute is switched off (reset), so that that file also will be ignored in subsequent backups unless the file has been changed again. Incidentally, it's worth noting that a file is considered changed whenever it has been written to disk. The archive attribute will be set even if you open a file and save it without having made changes.

Kinds of backups   Backup software follows two basic strategies. It may simply copy everything on a disk in what is called a global backup. Or it may copy only recently changed files (those with set archive attributes) in an incremental backup. The backups may be saved on a series of diskettes (see section 22.2) or to tape cartridges in a special kind of tape recorder made for just this purpose (section 22.3). A global backup takes more time and fills more media than an incremental backup. Theoretically, one could make just one initial global backup, and then only incremental backups thereafter. However, following a major hard disk crash, it would be extremely laborious to find the latest versions of all files from a long series of incremental backups. And so you should make periodic global backups with incremental backups between. Should you need to restore all data to a disk, the global backup would restore most files, and the incremental backups would then update new files and other files changed since the global backup was made.

In a simple backup system, whenever a global backup has been made, all prior backup media may be erased and reused. But a series of global backups is sometimes useful. Section 22.1 gives suggestions for how backups should be sequenced and scheduled.

In addition to global and incremental backups, you may wish to maintain various temporary copies of files on the same disk as the originals. These guard against damage that might occur to the files while you're working on them. For example, every few hours, you might save a copy of a report you are editing, placing the first copy in a file named REPORT.001, the next copy in REPORT.002, and so on. If later you regret deleting some material, you can reclaim it by searching the backups for it. You need nothing more than the DOS COPY command to create this kind of backup. Some software automatically keeps a second copy of each file, giving it a .BAK extension.

Backup media   Most backup software does not just transfer files from your hard disk to a diskette or tape cartridge. Instead, individual files are packed into one large file. The files are compressed to varying degrees in this process, and extra error-checking information is added to ensure that the data is internally sound in the event that it ever needs to be restored to the disk. Many programs can use these error-checking codes to recreate data even if the backup disks or tapes suffer a certain degree of damage while in storage. The system used varies by program; because it is not always standard, the backed-up data may be said to be stored in a proprietary format. It can only be retrieved by the same software that created it.

Besides copying files to diskettes or tape, backup software also records the structure of the disk's directory tree. By having this information on hand, backup software can restore a reformatted disk to exactly the way it was before a major crash occured. Or, when only a single file or group of files are lost, the backup software can scan its diskettes or tape and pluck out just the file required, even when several files on a disk have the same name.

Image backups   One way of capturing every byte of data on a hard disk is to perform an image backup. Rather than read file after file and transfer it to diskette or tape, the entire surface of the disk is read sector-by-sector, starting from the outer edge and working inward. Later, the entire content may be restored to exactly the same positions. Image backups are usually restricted to tape, but some utilities can make them on diskettes.

Image backups often can be performed more quickly then file-by-file backups, but they are inflexible. The backup software may not be able to selectively restore individual files to your hard disk, if that is what you require. And many programs cannot deal with the situation in which the hard disk has lost sectors, perhaps through a head crash (as explained in the Chapter 24 minitutorial) or through degradation of the disk surface. Having nowhere to restore certain sectors, a program may just give up and refuse to restore any data at all. Be wary of this problem if you use image backups.

Good backup software is a joy to work with. But it is important that you be aware of certain limitations and pitfalls, which are discussed in section 22.6. More than one backup should be on hand when data is critical. Remember that it can be as important where backups are kept as that they have been made. Having a dozen global backups on hand will do you no good if your system falls prey to fire, theft, or sabotage. Computer viruses are particularly insidious because they can infect backups along with originals. In this case, maintaining a long-term series of global backups may make it possible to find uninfected copies.

22.1 Scheduling backups

The frequency at which you should back up a hard disk and the kind of backups you make—global or incremental—depends on how important the data is, how much the computer is used, and whether changes to data are widespread or centered on only a few files. When many files are heavily modified in a short period, frequent global backups are called for. When work has focused on a few files, frequent incremental backups are more appropriate.

Most people recycle the same diskettes (or tape cartridge) again and again, keeping only a single global backup. One obvious danger in this approach is that, should your hard disk fail while you're making the backup, you will probably lose part of the only backup you have.

More important, you should recognize that much time may pass before it becomes evident that data has been lost or damaged. For example, faulty software could scramble scores of files that happened not to be accessed during a particular week. During the weekly global backup, the scrambled versions would then be copied over the undamaged versions on your backup diskettes. When you finally discover the problem, you would find that the backups had been destroyed too. For this reason, always keep at least two global backups. Additional backup media are inexpensive and well worth the added protection.

Backup generations Managers of business computer systems normally maintain three generations of global backups: the grandfather, father, and son. When the next global backup is made, the son becomes the father, the father the grandfather, and the former grandfather media is reused for the new son backup. Generally, a global backup is made once a week so that the state of the data two weeks before is maintained.

For added protection, a second series of three monthly global backups may be kept. Rather than actually back up a hard disk twice at the end of a month—once for the weekly backup and once for the monthly backup—you can make a weekly version, and when it retires two weeks later from being a grandfather, place it in the queue of monthly backups.

Always make a global backup immediately before embarking on a major reorganization of a hard disk. It's easy to accidentally delete needed files during a general housecleaning of the disk, when hundreds of files are erased, moved, and archived. Just as important, make a global backup before running invasive utility software that moves data around the disk surface. Defragmenters and directory sorters (sections 21.3 and 21.5) are examples of such utilities, which perform miracles in optimizing disk performance, but which can scramble your data if something goes wrong. A prior global backup keeps your data safe. The best order is:

1. Make a global backup.

2. Carry out disk housekeeping.

3. Run disk optimization utilities.

Keep the global backup for a long time until you are sure that every part of the disk is OK.

Incremental backups are interspersed among these global backups on an ad hoc basis. When important changes have been made to a few files, only a few minutes is required at the end of each day to back up the data. These backups are abandoned whenever a global backup is made.

TIP

For crucial files, consider maintaining a long series of backups in addition to normal global and incremental backups. It can sometimes be invaluable to have snap shots of a document taken at regular intervals. You can easily set things right if you find yourself regretting changes or deletions that have been made.

Backup scheduling should also provide for rotating off-site media. Depending on the importance of the data, you may want to keep at least a monthly backup out of reach of fire and similar calamities. It's as easy to neglect moving such a backup to some place far from the computer as it is to neglect backups altogether. Again, think of the value of your data and form good habits.

22.2 Making backups on diskettes

Unless you have a tape backup unit at your disposal (see section 22.5), your backups will probably be directed to diskettes. The obvious disadvantage of diskettes is their limited capacity; for large-scale back-ups, you must sit by as the backup proceeds and swap diskettes in and out of a drive. Even incremental backups can fill more than one diskette.

The COPY command   The COPY command can perform simple diskette-based backups. When your work is restricted to only a few files located in only a directory or two, COPY can do the job almost as quickly as a high-powered backup utility. The biggest problem is specifying multiple files without entering multiple COPY commands. If the file names share the same extension, global file name characters (section 1.3) are adequate. For example, the command:

```
COPY *.PRJ A: ⏎
```

copies all files with .PRJ extensions to drive A.

But say that you want to backup only some of your .PRJ files. If the same files are backed up again and again, you could write all of the necessary COPY commands into a batch file (see Chapter 9) and call the batch file each time a backup is needed. Alternatively, use individual COPY commands to back up the files to diskette once, and thereafter use the DOS REPLACE command (section 7.12) to renew the backups:

```
REPLACE *.PRJ A: ⏎
```

In this form, REPLACE copies files to drive A only when they already exist in the current directory of the diskette in that drive. Be sure to allow space for expansion of the files.

The XCOPY command   XCOPY is an extended version of COPY that can operate across multiple subdirectories. The way it transfers files to another disk is complicated; see section 7.8 for an explanation. By adding an /M switch to the command, only files that have been changed since they were last backed up are copied. This is to say that XCOPY can use the files' archive attributes (discussed in the minitutorial at the beginning of the chapter) to determine whether they should be copied or not. The attribute is turned off once the copy has been made. To back up to drive A all changed .DOC files held in the subdirectory LIZARDS on drive C, enter:

```
XCOPY C:\REPTILES\LIZARDS A: /M ⏎
```

Backup utility programs   Comprehensive backups require a program dedicated to that purpose. DOS provides the BACKUP and RESTORE programs for this purpose. They are discussed in section 22.3. These programs are adequate and reliable for simple backups, but they are slow, inflexible, and onerous to use. Their greatest disadvantage is that they cause backups to be so much work that one is discouraged from making them very often.

On the other hand, backup utilities from independent software houses offer an abundance of features. Because of tremendous competition, these programs constantly improve. Indeed, if they can be faulted, it is for becoming so complex that the user may be overwhelmed by the choices they offer.

These utilities emphasize backup speed. For most people, speed is really only important during global backups, which are not required often. The fastest utilities achieve their speed by pushing DOS to the side and directly controlling the computer's hardware. Normally, data is transferred to diskettes in two discrete steps: first, from hard disk to memory, and second, from memory to diskette. Sophisticated utilities may perform both steps at the same time, using the computer's main microprocessor to move data to memory, and the machine's direct memory access (DMA) chip to shift the data to a diskette drive.

Under some circumstances, the DMA chip can transfer data faster than the microprocessor can move it to memory from the hard disk. To keep up with the chip, the backup software transfers whole tracks of data from the hard disk at once, rather than shuttle the drive's read/write heads around looking for the pieces of individual files. Having a lot of memory available can assist this process. Some early PCs have DMA chips that are too slow; in some cases, the chip may even require replacement. Certain backup programs come with utilities that test a computer's DMA chip and adjust the backup accordingly.

Some backup programs organize backup diskettes in special ways. They may dispense with disk sectors altogether and record data in long tracks. By using the space normally left between sectors, the raw disk capacity is increased by about 15 percent. The data may also be compressed using various techniques. By feeding more data onto a single diskette, the number of diskettes that need to be swapped in and out of the machine is reduced. Some programs can alternate between two diskette drives, if present, to make the backup even faster.

A good backup program pays for itself many times over. Many programs have begun to take on the characteristics of a DOS shell, allowing you to select individual files and groups of files with a click of a mouse or a single keystroke. Figure 22.1 shows this facility in the Norton Backup program. Using a mouse or the keyboard, you can quickly select the files you want backed up. As files are backed up or restored, detailed information is displayed—as shown in figure 22.2—so you know what's going on.

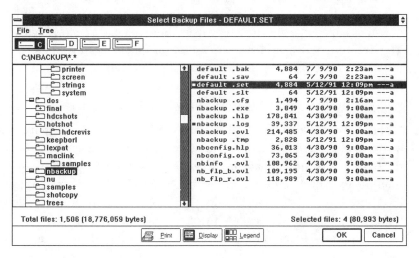

Figure 22.1

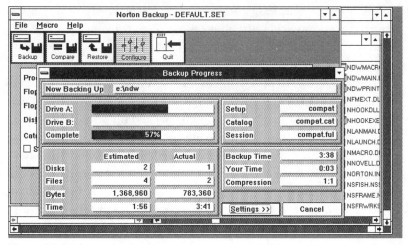

Figure 22.2

Most backup programs allow you to create a set-up file in which you may make elaborate specifications—including individual files—for a number of different kinds of backups. Thereafter, you need only select the set-up file from a customized menu and you are on your way. In the Norton Backup program, there are five basic kinds of backups to choose from, including a full global backup; a normal incremental backup; a differential backup in which all files that have been changed since the last global backup are copied, even if they have already been saved in an incremental backup; a full copy backup in which selected files are backed up (this is done without excluding them from future incremental backups); and an incremental copy backup in which only new or changed files are backed up from those that have been selected. The differential backup feature is useful for quick backups when you use the same few files each day. A full copy backup lets you transfer selected files between machines—say, between office and home— without affecting your regular backup schedule.

Perhaps most important, good backup software introduces extensive error checking and error recovery that can deal with damage on either the hard disk or on the backup diskettes themselves. Programs set up multiple lines of defense against errors. Norton Backup, for example, has three levels of data verification; it automatically rejects bad diskettes and confirms the readability of backup media; and—when the worst happens—it can often reconstruct information from damaged diskettes.

Backup utilities offer an abundance of features that make backups easier to create and easier to get at when you need them. Norton Backup provides a scheduler that can perform backups automatically when you're away from the computer (ordinarilly to a tape drive), and a memory resident utility to remind you that backups are overdue. There's also password protection to stop people from fishing confidential data off your backup media. As backups are made, you can quickly view files to see whether they should be backed up or not; this can be done without opening the applications that created the files. The program can search your hard disk for specified files so that you don't have to hunt them down before backing them up. Similarly, files can later be restored just by naming them, thus saving you the trouble of hunting through the backup catalog. Finally, the program can scan hard disks for bad sectors or corrupted files so that the backup will proceed without a hitch.

TIP

The feats performed by the most advanced backup utilities comes at a price, because all standards are left behind. Not only are the backup files unreadable by DOS, but in some cases the diskettes themselves will draw a "Nonsystem disk" error message if inserted into a drive without the backup program running. Acquire a backup program only from a reputable software house and, once you have it running, try restoring a single file to your hard disk to see that everything goes well. Don't wait until you need your backups to learn that they have never been properly made.

22.3 Using the DOS BACKUP program

The DOS BACKUP and RESTORE utilities have been constantly upgraded, but they are primitive compared to the sophisticated programs available from independent software houses. BACKUP works much like any DOS command. Your specifications are limited to what can be typed on the DOS command line. To back up only the file KEEPFILE.DOC from drive C to drive A, make the file's directory current and type:

    BACKUP KEEPFILE.DOC A: ⏎

Use global file name characters (section 1.3) to back up groups of files, such as all .DOC files:

    BACKUP *.DOC A: ⏎

Or, to back up all files in a directory, enter:

    BACKUP *.* A: ⏎

Of course, a directory path could be used in any of these specifications. For example:

    BACKUP \MAMMALS\FELINES\CHEETAHS*.* A: ⏎

would backup all files in the CHEETAHS subdirectory.

Scanning multiple directories   By appending an /S switch, BACKUP can be made to extend its activity across multiple subdirectories. It begins with the specified directory (or current directory, if none is specified), then moves on to the subdirectories listed in that directory, then to the directories listed in those directories, and so on. Thus, an entire branch of a directory tree can be backed up, or, when the starting directory is the root directory, the entire tree may be included in the backup. To back up all files in the FELINES subdirectory, and all directories beyond it, type:

    BACKUP C:\MAMMALS\FELINES*.* A: /S ⏎

To backup the entire tree on drive C:

    BACKUP C:*.* A: /S ⏎

Of course, the file specification may still be limited when many subdirectories are included. The statement:

    BACKUP C:*.BAT A: /S ⏎

would backup all batch files (files with a .BAT ending) from the directory tree of drive C, and no others.

Incremental backups   The examples shown above perform global backups in the sense that every file will be backed up, whether it has been altered or not since the last backup. To make an incremental backup, append an /M switch to limit the backups to files that have been changed. The command:

```
BACKUP C:\*.* A: /S /M ⏎
```

makes backups of all changed files on drive C, while the command:

```
BACKUP C:\*.BAT A: /S /M ⏎
```

backs up all changed .BAT files from drive C. Whether the /M switch is used or not, BACKUP always resets the archive attribute of every file it copies so that the file will be excluded from future backups in which /M is used (the archive attribute is discussed in the minitutorial at the beginning of this chapter).

Backups by time and date   Backups may also be restricted by time and date through the /T and /D switches. /D restricts backups to files of a given date or later, as in:

```
BACKUP C:\*.* A: /S /D:11-07-90 ⏎
```

The backup will include files with the date 11-07-90 or any date thereafter; unfortunately, you can't restrict the backup to a particular date. The /T switch works in the same way except that you specify a time, rather than a date.

Ordinarily, when a backup begins, all files on the target diskette are erased. There are times, however, when you'll want to keep files from prior backups, as when you chain a succession of incremental backups from diskette to diskette. You can have BACKUP append backups to others already on a diskette by adding an /A switch to the command. This example makes an incremental backup of all files on drive C with an .XYZ extension, appending them to other backups on diskettes in drive A:

```
BACKUP C:\*.XYZ A: /S /M /A ⏎
```

Disk formats   BACKUP saves data in a special format. The files may not be viewed directly, and they can only be restored to a disk using RESTORE. The backups are placed on ordinary formatted diskettes.

The diskettes needed to be preformatted in early DOS versions. In DOS 3.3 you can add an /F switch to your BACKUP command to make it format diskettes when it discovers that they are unformatted. Diskettes are automatically formatted even without an /F switch in DOS 4.0 and later.

Prior to DOS version 3.3, BACKUP copied each file into a separate file on the target diskette, inserting information at the start of the file to record the file' position in the directory tree. Finding a particular file entailed going through diskette after diskette. Each diskette had a file named BACKUPID.@@@ containing a file index. This system changed completely with DOS 3.3. On each diskette, all files have been combined in one giant file named BACKUP.xxx, where xxx is a value from 001 upward telling the diskette number. A second file on each diskette is named CONTROL.xxx (with a matching number). It keeps track of file names, directory paths, and various directory information. The volume label of each diskette is named BACKUP.xxx so that you can easily identify the diskette by entering VOL A: ↵ if it is in drive A.

Log files   This more advanced version of BACKUP can also create a log file named BACKUP.LOG in the root directory of your hard disk. The file records a backup's date and time, and provides complete information about the names and directory paths of files, and their corresponding diskette numbers. It is an ordinary text file that can be viewed by the TYPE command (see section 2.6) or by your wordprocessor. To create the file, you must append the /L switch to the command:

```
BACKUP C:\*.* A: /S /L ↵
```

This is the standard command for a global backup of your hard disk. By way of comparison, the standard expression for an incremental backup is:

```
BACKUP C:\*.* A: /S /M /L ↵
```

Restoring data to the disk   The RESTORE program works in much the same way as BACKUP. To restore every file to drive C, enter:

```
RESTORE A: C:\*.* /S ↵
```

Again, the /S switch extends the operation of the command across multiple directories, in this case working from the root directory to cover the entire tree. To restore only the files of the directory \MAMMALS\AQUATIC\WALRUS, type:

```
RESTORE A: C:\MAMMALS\AQUATIC\WALRUS\*.*  ⏎
```

Individual files may also be restored:

```
RESTORE A: C:\MAMMALS\AQUATIC\WALRUS\TUSK.TXT  ⏎
```

By consulting the log file in advance, you can have the necessary backup diskettes on hand before entering the RESTORE command. Otherwise, RESTORE will prompt you to insert one diskette after another until the data restoration is complete. Be aware that the RESTORE program from DOS versions earlier than 3.1 is not totally reliable.

TIP

BACKUP and RESTORE are dreadfully slow compared to other backup utilities. They offer no error checking whatsoever except for the standard DOS VERIFY command (section 7.13), which makes them work even more slowly. They cannot deal well with bad disk sectors. Furthermore, because the user interface is limited to a single command line, your control over backups is minimal. Considering the many hours that will be wasted coping with these deficiencies, you would do well to purchase a good backup utility and do the job right.

22.4 Making backups with XCOPY

The DOS XCOPY command works well for small-scale incremental backups. Unlike COPY, a single XCOPY command can scan multiple directories, copying some or all files from each directory. XCOPY expects to copy files between two matching directory trees (or, at least, between matching tree branches) and when it does not find a required directory on the target drive, it creates one. The command is a complicated one and, used incorrectly, it can wreak havoc by making unwanted additions to your directory tree. Be sure to read the discussion of XCOPY in section 7.8.

XCOPY can use global file name characters (section 1.3) to restrict the command to particular data files. In addition, a number of optional switches may be placed at the end of the command to extend its range across a tree, and to limit the files it transfers. Say that you have been working on data files with a .DOC ending and want to back up a day's work. The command:

        XCOPY *.DOC A: ⏎

would copy all .DOC files from the current directory of the current drive (assumed here to be hard disk drive C) to a diskette in drive A. In this instance, XCOPY works just like COPY. By appending the /S switch to the command, as in:

        XCOPY *.DOC A: /S ⏎

files are copied not from just the current directory, but also from directories listed in the current directory, directories listed in those directories, and so on. Thus, an entire tree branch is searched for .DOC files. When the current directory is the root directory, every .DOC file in the tree is copied. It's best to explicitly show the starting directory in the command:

        XCOPY \MAMMALS\DOGS*.DOC A: /S ⏎

Or, to specify the root directory:

        XCOPY *.DOC A: /S ⏎

The archive attribute   With many .DOC files on your hard drive, a diskette would fill quickly and XCOPY would grind to a halt without completing its assignment. But another switch may be added, the /M switch, to restrict XCOPY to files in which the archive attribute has been set. Recall from the minitutorial at the start of this chapter that the archive attribute is set when a file has been changed. Backup software always resets (unsets) the archive attribute of each file after it has backed it up. If your global and incremental backups are up to date, then when you run XCOPY, the only files with active archive attributes should be those that have been recently changed. Thus, the command:

```
XCOPY \*.DOC A: /S /M ⏎
```

makes copies on drive A of all .DOC files on drive C with set archive attributes. Upon doing so, the attribute is reset so that the files will not be copied the next time the same command is run.

This feature has an added benefit: files may be copied to multiple diskettes. As many files are transferred as will fit on the first floppy. Then XCOPY issues an "Insufficient disk space" error message and halts. A new diskette is inserted, and the same command is typed in again. This time, the files already copied will have their archive attributes changed, and so they are ignored. Copying begins with the file that couldn't fit the last time around. Working this way, a backup may be extended over any number of diskettes.

Applications   As mentioned above, XCOPY creates subdirectories and branches of a subdirectory tree, on the target diskettes. The result can be messy, especially when files from the same subdirectory fall on different diskettes. Good backup software handles incremental back-ups more adroitly; its indexing scheme will make it much easier to restore files when data has been lost. For this reason, you may want to restrict your use of XCOPY to making quick backups between proper incremental backups. In this case, you shouldn't alter the archive attributes. Otherwise, the backup software won't be able to find the changed files. To leave the archive attributes untouched, use the /A switch instead of the /M switch:

```
XCOPY \*.DOC A: /S /A ⏎
```

Keep in mind that using the /A switch means that all copies made by a single command must fit onto one diskette. If you must copy more files than can fit, try dividing the backup into two or more parts, using different global file name characters each time, such as .DOC files first, and then .TXT files.

22.5 Using a tape backup unit

A tape backup unit makes backups much easier by avoiding the labor of swapping diskettes in and out of the machine. These units are expensive and they are useful only for backups and archiving files. Most are installed by adding an adapter card in one of the computer's internal slots. The tape drive itself may be housed in the computer, but many are independent units that may be shared between several machines.

Because IBM did not offer its own tape backup unit at the time the technology first became popular, there is no single standard to which all units subscribe. They vary in the size of tape cartridges they use and the number of tracks written upon the tape. They also vary in the way data is formatted on the tape. Some standards format the data into blocks with elaborate error checking and recovery code, using a special format for directories. Others treat the tape as a sort of glorified diskette with a DOS-like organization of data and little error-recovery. It is all the same from the user's point of view, although some formats are considerably faster or more reliable than others, and some are better able to recover data from damaged media.

Under ideal circumstances, data is continuously transferred from hard disk to tape as quickly as the tape drive can absorb it. This phenomenon is called streaming. It is more of an ideal than a reality, because most computers cannot supply data quickly enough. The drive reacts by constantly starting and stopping, or by leaving blank gaps as the tape moves continuously.

PITFALLS | There are three points to remember when using a tape backup unit. First, be aware that tape is a fragile medium. Keep your tape cartridges out of harm's way. If there are any signs in a cartridge of flaking from the tape surface, discard the cartridge at once, because it could contaminate the tape drive's read/write heads. Also watch for scalloping (curling) of the tape edges, a sign of approaching data loss on the outer tracks. Your drive may be accompanied by a certification utility, which scans blank tapes for faults. Some drives also have retensioning utilities that run a tape from end to end to reduce stretching and to assure that the tape runs at a constant speed. Some tape formats also require a formatting utility that must be applied to new cartridges just as the DOS FORMAT program is applied to new diskettes.

Second, you should understand that tape units are special devices that must be specially installed in the machine. Installation instructions vary from machine to machine. Most drives require that a device driver (section 11.11) be loaded into memory when the computer is booted. This is done via a DEVICE statement in the CONFIG.SYS file that DOS automatically reads at start-up.

Finally, keep in mind the warnings found in the minitutorial at the start of this chapter concerning image backups. Image backups make a sector-by-sector copy of a disk's contents without regard to the placement of subdirectories and files. Most tape unit software cannot restore individual files from an image backup, and if they can, the restoration can be quite time-consuming.

More important is the inability of some software to restore an image backup to a hard disk after the drive has sustained damage to even one sector. With the sector marked as unusable, the software may be stymied when it comes time to return the data it once copied from it. In some cases it may refuse to finish restoring data, leaving you with nothing at all. Also, image backups often cannot be used to restore data to a disk of different size or dimensions, making them generally useless for transporting data. Be very sure of your software's abilities before relying upon them.

Operating a tape drive   Tape drives are shipped with customized software. Sometimes this is the only software that will work with the drive, although many drives can work with at least a few of the many diskette-oriented backup programs. The speed at which the tape unit operates often depends as much on the software design as the hardware design.

TIP

There may be one or more configuration files used by the tape unit, and these may need to be located in particular subdirectories. If your drive suddenly stops working, ask yourself whether you have somehow interferred with its installation.

To learn how to use the software is to learn how to use the drive. The best programs emulate DOS shells and allow you to make exacting specifications for a variety of backups, just like general purpose backup programs. For example, all of the features in The Norton Backup program described in section 22.2 can be directed to the many tape drives supported by the program. In addition, a number of tape-related tools are available so that you can view directory listings of tapes, format and retension tapes, erase a whole tape or only specified portions, or perform a security erase to obliterate a tape's contents.

22.6 Avoiding backup pitfalls

It is sometimes surprising how many things can go wrong with backups. Some of the pitfalls may be invisible until it is time to restore data—that is, until it is too late. It's a lot to keep in mind, but read through the list of potential calamities and remember as many as you can:

■ When a hard disk has thousands of files, months may pass before you realize that files have been corrupted or erased. During this time, bad files (or no files) may be copied on top of your good backups. You can avoid this problem by making an occasional global backup that is set aside indefinitely.

■ As mentioned elsewhere in this chapter, image backups may be unrestorable to hard disks that have had sectors damaged. Also, single files may not be restorable from an image backup.

■ Some copy-protection schemes (section 12.2) place data at particular locations on a hard disk. When data is restored to the disk, the scheme may be undone.

■ Many backup programs are incompatible with oversized hard disk partitions, whether created by DOS or by utility software (section 16.4).

■ Some backup programs cannot cope with unusual media, such as removable cartridge hard disks and super-high-capacity diskettes. Most also cannot work with hard disk drives across a network. (Backup programs that claim to work with any logical device ought to be exempt from these limitations. They work through DOS, and pay a price in lower performance for their compatability.)

■ Just because a program can successfully back up files, including the disk's directory tree, does not necessarily mean that the program can restore this data. Restore features are used much less than backup features and so they may not be as well-debugged.

■ When the computer crashes during an incremental backup, the archive attributes of files that have been copied will be changed, but not others. If you start the backup over from scratch, the previously copied files will be neglected.

■ Computers that operate at different microprocessor speeds, such as IBM AT clones that work at both 6 megahertz and 12 megahertz, may work at only one speed with some backup programs.

■ Any kind of multitasking (the process of running two programs at once) can interfere with backup programs, particularly those that use direct memory access (section 22.2). Be careful of memory-resident programs that work in the background (section 15.4) and operating environments that let you run multiple programs simultaneously (see the minitutorial in Chapter 18).

Chapter 23

Recovering Lost or Damaged Data

- MINITUTORIAL: Kinds of file damage
- Recovering damaged files
- Recovering orphaned clusters
- Repairing cross-linked files
- Recovering erased files
- Recovering data from an accidentally formatted disk
- Detecting and eradicating computer viruses

File damage means several things. In some cases, part or all of a file is obliterated; in other cases, the data held by a file may be completely intact, but the file will become inaccessible. The better you understand how files can fail, the more likely you are to be able to reclaim lost or damaged data. We'll discuss the ways you can lose files.

Damage to disk sectors   Some diskettes, and most hard disks, have a few bad sectors when they are new. The magnetic medium of the disk surface is flawed at these points, or perhaps too thin to hold a sufficiently strong magnetic field. Bad sectors are marked as off bounds to DOS when the disk is formatted. But marginally adequate sectors may not be locked off from use, and with time these sectors can fade away, taking their data with them. A non-fatal head-crash (see the minitutorial at the beginning of Chapter 24) inside the disk can also damage sectors, as can magnetic bursts resulting from power surges and other physical hazards. When DOS fails to successfully read all 512 bytes in a sector, it rejects the data entirely. An "Abort, Retry, Ignore, Fail?" message is displayed to inform you that DOS cannot continue and to ask you whether DOS should keep trying or not (some software intercepts this message and deals with the failure in its own way).

The loss of a sector holding part of a file causes two problems. First, of course, you've lost part of your data. In complex data files, the data may be essential to the file's organization (for example, it might tell the dimensions of a spreadsheet; without this information, the remaining spreadsheet data is useless). Second, the missing sector leaves software unable to read the file. Even if the remaining data is useful, you'll need to fix the file well enough that it can be read.

Damage to format markings   As a disk is formatted, magnetic markings are laid down to define the disk's sectors. The sector contents are constantly renewed as you change files and move them around. But the format markings are untouched by disk activity after the initial formatting. They can gradually fade as the years go by, especially when they rest on the same sort of flawed media that causes bad sectors. When format markings become too weak to read, the sector they define is lost as well, even though the data in the sector remains intact. Utility software can renew format markings without interferring with the adjacent data.

Damage to the file content   File damage is sometimes the fault of the software that creates it. Bugs in the software can damage the data while it is still in system memory before it is transferred to disk. Or, the software may write data into the wrong position in a random-access file. In addition, utility programs can run amuck and damage files.

Damage can also occur when a power outage occurs while a file is being saved. The prior contents of the file are partially overwritten, leaving some of the old version and some of the new. The corrupted file is often unreadable. Rebooting the machine via Ctrl-Alt-Del has the same effect as an accidental loss of power, so be careful not to reboot the machine while the disk drive is in use. There is nothing you can do about this kind of file damage except restore an earlier version of the file from a backup.

Damage by a computer virus   A computer virus is a maliciously devised program that attaches itself to programs and travels from machine to machine as software is passed around. Once in a computer, a virus can spread to infect numerous files on disk drives. When the virus becomes active, it may destroy data or cause the computer to malfunction. Special antiviral utility software can disinfect files. For more information, see sections 23.6 and 25.7.

Damage to the file's directory entry   When rebooting or a power outage interferes with a file being entirely saved, the directory entry for the file may be left indicating a file size of 0 bytes. Even though some, even all, of the file may be intact, DOS can't read the file for lack of a proper file length. Utility software can recover such files by fixing the directory entry.

Damage to the directory tree   Because subdirectories are files, they are prone to all the kinds of damage that can afflict normal files. When a subdirectory in a directory tree is lost, all files it lists are effectively lost, even though the files themselves go unscathed. Worse, subdirectories listed in the corrupted subdirectory are lost (although they, too, remain technically intact) and thus all files in a whole branch of the directory tree can disappear.

Utility software can be used to reconstruct corrupted subdirectories. Lost subdirectories have certain identifying characteristics by which they may be tracked down and recovered. Doing so makes available all the files they list, including subdirectories further downstream.

Damage to the disk's file allocation table   The sectors that contain an individual file may be dispersed across a disk's surface. The file's directory entry records the sector at which the file begins. From there, the disk's file allocation table (FAT) tracks the chain of sectors that make up the file. A FAT can sustain damage from sectors going bad, a head crash, or other kinds of physical failure. More often, the damage results when sectors of the FAT have been read into memory for manipulation. Wayward software accidentally writes into the memory positions occupied by the FAT sectors. DOS later writes the altered sectors back to the disk, unaware that they have been harmed.

When a FAT is seriously damaged, the sectors of numerous files are effectively scrambled, leaving a horrible mess that is extremely difficult to recover from. Unformat utilities, described in section 23.5, are sometimes the only way to deal with this condition. They replace the corrupted FAT with an intact copy of the FAT that was made before the damage occured.

More often, FAT damage is minor, although devastating for the one or two files involved. A chain of sectors belonging to a file may be broken, shortening the file to leave the far end of the chain unallocated to any file at all. The data in the disconnected part of the chain remains intact, but unreachable. Sectors in the disconnected chain are called orphaned clusters (a cluster is a group of sectors, usually four on a hard disk). Sometimes the damage to a FAT crosses the chains of two files such that one file ending becomes orphaned, and the other file ending comes to be shared by both files. Such files are said to be cross-linked.

Accidental erasures or formatting   Used carelessly, the DOS FORMAT and ERASE (or DEL or DELETE) commands can wipe out a single file or every file on a disk. The data in the files themselves remains intact, but the files' directory entries are lost, as is information about the files' placement on the disk. There are ways to recover data lost this way.

There is a lot you can do to recover damaged or missing files, thanks to utility programs designed for this purpose. For example, the NDD (Norton Disk Doctor) program in The Norton Utilities can completely analyze a disk for errors. It begins by checking the disk partition table and boot record, and then goes on to analyze the file allocation tables and directory tree. It looks for orphaned clusters and can optionally test all sectors. Figure 23.1 shows an information screen from Disk Doctor. You can also have Disk Doctor print out a status report for the disk.

For severe problems, especially those that involve physical damage to a disk or drive, there are companies that are experts at data recovery and do nothing else. Their services are costly, but in many cases, your data may be worth it.

Sometimes data is recoverable, but the effort required is too great to justify. Other times, the data is just plain gone. There is, however, one form of file recovery that is virtually 100% effective and that can be performed by anyone: retrieve copies of lost files from backups you have made. There is no substitute for good backups. Be careful and don't neglect backups, thinking that your file-recovery tools will unfalteringly save you in your time of need.

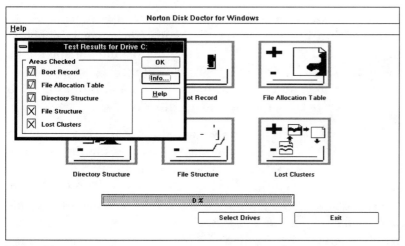

Figure 23.1

23.1 Recovering damaged files

Disk sectors may gradually become unable to hold data, either because the format markings that define a sector have faded, or because the coating on the disk surface has degraded to the point that it can no longer reliably hold information. When this happens to a disk sector that holds part of a file, the file is damaged. DOS has no way of reading the information in the damaged sector, and it displays an "Abort, Retry, Ignore, Fail?" error message when it encounters one.

By repeatedly specifying Retry, you can make DOS try again and again to read the bad sector. With luck, on one of the tries DOS will manage to pick up faint traces of the missing data and successfully move them to memory. Once the data is in memory, it should be written to a new file at once (use a new file name if the new version of the file will go into the same directory as the old one). If you happen to be in the midst of a COPY command, your problems are solved, because the new copy will be placed on a different spot on the disk than the original—hopefully on good media. But if you are loading the file into an application program, you will need to find some way of making a copy without quitting the program. Or, you can open a new file and use the software's facilities to copy the faulty file into the newly created one.

If your software won't come to your aid, you will have to return to DOS and try a DOS COPY command. The image of the file you have managed to move to memory will be lost, and once again you will probably have to go through a number of retrys as COPY attempts to read the damaged file. The success of retry sometimes depends on the temperature of the disk you're having trouble with. Particularly with hard disk drives, you may find that you'll have better luck when the machine is cold (the room is cold or the machine has just been started up) or hot (the room is hot or the drive has been running for a half hour or so).

If dozens of retrys don't save your data, you can try using a utility program that checks for faded format markings and replaces them. However, format markings may not be the problem, in which case you may have irreparably lost some data. When the data belongs to a complex data file, such as a spreadsheet file, the application software that uses the file will become completely confused when it is loaded. For all practical purposes, the loss of a sector is as bad as the loss of the entire file. In the case of simple text files, on the other hand, the remaining parts of the file can be combined into a new file and the original file reconstructed.

The RECOVER command   The DOS RECOVER command can recover files with bad sectors, as can a number of programs available as part of various disk tool kits such as The Norton Utilities. Like most DOS facilities, RECOVER appears primitive beside the utilities from independent software houses. To recover the file BADFILE.TXT, enter:

    RECOVER BADFILE.TXT ⏎

Or, if required, add a drive specifier and directory path:

    RECOVER C:\OLDFILES\BADFILE.TXT ⏎

RECOVER will set aside the bad sector and place the remainder of the original file into two separate files, marking one as FILE0001.REC and the other as FILE0002.REC. You can then recombine the two parts either by loading them into your word processor and doing it manually, or by using the COPY command (discussed in Chapter 7), as in:

    COPY FILE0001.REC+FILE0002.REC ⏎

This command appends the contents of FILE0002.REC to FILE0001.REC. When working with non-text files, add /B to the end of the first file name:

    COPY FILE0001.REC/B+FILE0002.REC ⏎

If more than one sector has been damaged, as might occur in a hard disk crash, the original file may be recovered into three or more new files.

PITFALLS | Take great care not to enter the RECOVER command without a file name, as in:

RECOVER ⏎

In this case, RECOVER operates on every file in a directory, including those that are undamaged. Each is renamed with one of the file names in the series FILE0001.REC, FILE0002.REC, and so on. If you make this mistake, you will need to look at each file to identify it so that you can change its name back. In many instances, you may have trouble figuring out what the file is. This feature is so dangerous that you may want to remove the RECOVER.COM file from your hard disk entirely and use it from a DOS system diskette. Otherwise, anyone could at any time type RECOVER ⏎ and scramble the contents of the current directory.

RECOVER can use global file name characters (section 1.3), as in:

```
RECOVER *.TXT  ⏎
```

While this kind of statement can recover many files at once, you'll be confronted with a plethora of file fragments with no knowledge of how many of the fragments are to be recombined into each of the original files. It's far better to do one file at a time. Also, be aware that each time RECOVER is used, the files it creates are named FILE0001.REC, FILE0002.REC, and so on. Files produced earlier will be overwritten. So don't repeat the command until you have cleaned up after it.

Utility software   Almost any utility program works better than RECOVER. Most will not divide the damaged file into two or more new files, and will not rename it. These programs are much better suited to mass file recoveries on a severely damaged disk. They will discard the damaged sector and insert a new sector in its place, filling it with 512 instances of one particular character so that it can be identified. In this way, the file maintains its original length, and keeps data in places where application software may be expecting to find it. Some of these programs go around DOS and directly read the disk sector using special techniques that may allow partial recovery of the damaged sector's contents.

23.2 Recovering orphaned clusters

Damage to a file allocation table (FAT) can prevent DOS from finding all parts of a file. Sectors that DOS loses track of are called orphaned clusters (a cluster is a group of sectors, usually four on a hard disk). These sectors are marked in the file allocation table as being in use, and so they are not overwritten by other files. In essence, the isolated sectors are lost, because DOS cannot find them to use them.

The DOS CHKDSK program scans a file allocation table and, among other tasks, locates and recovers orphaned clusters. The clusters are placed in one or more files. These files can be opened to recover lost data, or they can simply be erased to regain the disk space lost to the orphaned clusters. To have CHKDSK examine drive C, simply enter:

```
CHKDSK C: /F ⏎
```

Be sure to include the /F switch; otherwise DOS will merely report orphaned clusters without recovering them. CHKDSK is a DOS external command held in the file CHKDSK.COM, which must be on hand. When it finds orphaned clusters, CHKDSK displays a message like:

```
3 lost clusters found in 3 chains.
Convert lost chains to files (Y/N)?
```

If you answer Y ⏎, CHKDSK recovers the clusters and places each in its own file named FILE0001.CHK, FILE0002.CHK, and so on. The files appear in the drive's root directory, no matter the current directory. In addition, CHKDSK displays its usual report about files, directories, and disk space, and includes a statement telling the size of the recovered clusters:

```
6144 bytes in 3 recovered files
```

When you respond with N ⏎ instead, CHKDSK reports something like:

```
6144 bytes disk space would be freed
```

indicating that (in this case) 6,144 bytes of disk space are trapped in orphaned clusters and made unusable. Once finished, you can view the files with the TYPE command (section 2.6) to search for useful fragments of data. Rename those files you wish to keep, if any, and erase the remainder to free the sectors holding them so that they can be used by other files. A mass erasure can be performed by a single command:

```
ERASE FILE????.CHK ←.
```

23.3 Repairing cross-linked files

As the minitutorial at the beginning of this chapter explains, files become cross-linked when damage is done to a disk's file allocation table. The file allocation table keeps track of the chain (series) of disk sectors that hold a file. When one of the sector numbers in a chain is accidentally altered, it may be changed to that of a sector that is already occupied. So, the sector chains of two files become cross-linked. One file appears normal, but the other begins with its own sectors and then suddenly shifts to the content of the first file. The sectors that should be at the end of the damaged file are disconnected from any chain and thus are said to be orphaned.

You won't know that a file has become cross-linked until you suddenly discover this strange state of affairs. It may be immediately evident in a text file, but not in complex data files. Ordinarily, a full recovery of both files is only possible with text files. Other kinds of data are too difficult to examine and too sensitive to slight changes that inevitably occur during recovery. It's also very difficult to know that cross-linking has occured in files other than text files, because only text files are viewed directly by you when they are loaded into the software that creates them. If the text in a file suddenly changes from that of one document to that of another, you can usually track down the other file. But when the file abruptly switches from text to gobbledygook, you'll have no way of knowing which nontext file that gobbledygook belongs to.

You should take action immediately when you discover cross-linking. At the very least, you will be able to recover the file that is still complete, and you may be able to piece together the split file as well. When you first spot the damage, leave the application software immediately without saving the file. If written to disk, any changes you made to the file prior to discovering its flaws could be transferred to the file it is cross-linked to.

Utility software is available for recovering cross-linked files. Of course, every utility operates in its own way, so you'll need to read the documentation to use one. Alternatively, you can try recovering a cross-linked text file using nothing more than DOS and a word processor. We'll discuss how to do this.

Step 1   Begin by making copies of both involved files. You can place the copies in the same directory as the original by renaming them as they are copied. To rename the file OHNO.TXT to OHNOCOPY.TXT as it is copied, type:

```
COPY OHNO.TXT OHNOCOPY.TXT ⏎
```

The two copies of the files will be stored in completely different locations from the originals. One of the copies ought to be (with luck) a complete and uncorrupted file, and the other will be partly what it should be, and partly the content of the first file. Erase both originals to remove the cross-linking from the disk.

Step 2   The next task is to try to recover the missing part of the damaged file. The part that was disconnected will exist as a chain of orphaned clusters—disk sectors that are used, but not linked to any directory entry. The DOS CHKDSK program can recover orphaned clusters, as section 23.2 explains. If the damaged file resides on drive C, you would enter:

```
CHKDSK C: /F ⏎
```

and, after a few moments, CHKDSK would display a message like:

```
1 lost clusters found in 1 chains.
Convert lost chains to files (Y/N)?
```

Type Y ⏎ and the clusters are placed into a file named FILE0001.CHK residing in the disk's root directory. If more than one file is found, then more than one file is created (FILE0002.CHK, FILE0003.CHK, and so on) and you'll need to view them with the TYPE command (section 2.7) to find your missing data.

Step 3   Next, load the copy of the damaged file into your word processor and delete all the extra data at the end of the file that belonged to the file to which it was cross-linked. If the superfluous data is not text, your word processor may have trouble loading it or selecting it for deletion. You may have better luck by creating a new file and copying the good part of the file over to it, and then using the new file as the basis of your reconstruction.

Step 4   Finally, add the recovered orphaned clusters to the end of the file. One way is by opening FILE0001.CHK (or whatever) as a second document in your word processor and copying its contents over to the first. Alternatively, use the COPY command. The command:

```
COPY OHNOCOPY+FILE0001.CHK ⏎
```

appends the content of FILE0001.CHK to OHNOCOPY and still leaves FILE0001.CHK as it was. Then erase FILE0001.CHK and rename the two files that were cross-linked to their original names.

23.4 Recovering erased files

The minitutorial in Chapter 3 explains what happens when you erase a file using the DOS ERASE, DEL, or DELETE commands (the effects of the three commands are identical). In summary, the disk sectors that hold the file are not actually erased. Rather, the sectors holding the file are deallocated, freeing them for use by other files. Similarly, the directory slot that lists the file is made inactive, but directory information about the file remains intact except for the first letter of the file name.

Although a file's directory listing and disk sectors are preserved after you erase the file, both kinds of data are threatened. When another file is written into the directory, it may take over the erased file's directory slot, obliterating all information about it; or, some or all of the disk sectors used by the erased file may be incorporated into other files, destroying the sectors' prior contents.

Unerase utilities retrieve as much of an erased file as possible. When they are used immediately after the file has been deleted and before other files have been created or expanded in size, the success rate for these utilities is very high, although by no means perfect. When an unerasure is attempted long after a file has been deleted, the file often cannot be recovered.

DOS does not include an unerase utility, but many are marketed. Usually they are found in disk tool kits—collections of utilities for managing disks and data. So, when you purchase an unerase utility, you will be judging not just the features and quality of that utility itself, but also of the other parts of the tool kit. It is important that the unerase utility originate from a trustworthy software house, because a faulty unerase utility could as easily destroy data as save it.

Probability of recovery   The highest probability of recovery for older erased files occurs on hard disks that have not been long in use, that use DOS 3.0 or later, and when there has been little or no activity in the subdirectory since the file was erased. In this case, the file's former directory slot will probably be intact, as will the sectors it occupied. This is because, starting with DOS 3.0, new sectors are allocated to files starting from the outer edge of a disk and moving inward until every sector has been used once. Only afterwards are sectors that have been freed by file erasures used by other files, with DOS always allocating sectors closest to the disk's outer edge. If sector allocation is still being made from the initial pass across every disk sector, the sectors deallocated by a file erasure are sure to be untouched (provided that utility software like a defragmenter (section 21.3) has not interfered with file placements).

Attempts to unerase files fail for three reasons:

■ If the file's former directory slot has been wiped out, you may find it extremely difficult to find the beginning of the file. On hard disks, disk space is usually allocated in groups of four sectors (called clusters). A 40-megabyte hard disk holds 20,000 clusters. On a half-full disk you'd have 10,000 free clusters to inspect. That's a lot of work!

■ When the clusters that made up the file are noncontiguous— dispersed across the disk surface instead of residing in adjacent sectors along adjacent tracks—it may be prohibitively time-consuming to locate and reassemble them. Again, there may be thousands, even tens of thousands of clusters to inspect. If files of similar content have also been erased, their deallocated sectors will mingle with those of the file you want to recover. You may need a photographic memory to decide which clusters are part of a file and which are not. Files tend to be noncontiguous when they were created on (or copied to) an old disk that has many empty clusters left by erased files. Files that are repeatedly expanded also tend to be noncontiguous because between the times the file is worked on, other files take up sectors following the end of the file.

■ When clusters used by the file have been allocated to others, you can only partially recover the file. A partial recovery may be better than nothing with simple text files. In the end, some paragraphs may be missing from a document, but at least part of the work is saved. However, for complicated data files, such as database files and spreadsheet files, the software that generated the file is unlikely to be able to load the file unless it is complete. To lose one cluster is often to lose it all. This is increasingly true even of word processor documents, which may be laden with special codes to control formatting and other characteristics.

Kinds of file recovery   There is no standard design for unerase utilities. Each has its own way of doing things; some offer more features than others. Most provide two approaches to reclaiming a file: a manual method and an automatic method. The automatic method is preferred. You specify the file to be recovered and the software does the best job it can. When the results are not good enough, you may turn to the manual method in which you inspect the contents of the sectors to be included in the reconstituted file.

Automatic file recovery   The automatic method works by locating the file's erased directory entry. It learns the size of the file (which tells the number of clusters it must find) and the location on the disk of the starting cluster. Then it assembles the starting cluster and as many free clusters as it needs, taking the clusters closest to the starting cluster, moving inward toward the center of the disk (the direction in which DOS allocated clusters to a file when it was created).

When you start an unerase utility, you begin by telling it which drive and directory the erased file was located in. The utility then displays the names of all erased files for the directory slots which have not been taken over by other files. It identifies these entries by a special character written where the first letter of the file name would be kept. If the file was named ELEPHANT.TXT, the utility will find and display the name with some other character in place of the initial *E*, such as a question mark. Figure 23.2 shows a status report from the Norton UnErase program for an erased file named ?GLIB.EXE. Notice how the utility is able to judge the likelihood of a successful recovery; the chances are poor in this case because the file was erased long before recovery was attempted.

If you can find the file's listing, you select it and supply a first character for its name. Then recovery begins. If you can't find the file, and you're sure it was in the directory you specified, recovery will be more difficult since you must track down the first cluster of the file by instructing the utility to display one free cluster after another, examining each in turn. As mentioned above, that can be a tremendous amount of work. Besides, by the very fact that the file's directory entry has been taken up by another file, you confront the possibility that some of the file's sectors may have been absorbed as well.

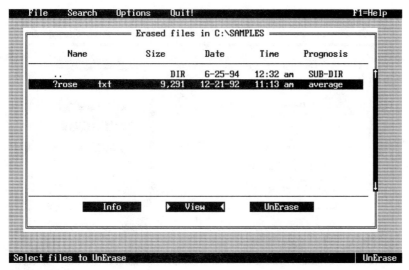

Figure 23.2

Most unerase utilities help you with this problem by offering a search facility. You specify a few words that you recall being near the start of the document and the utility examines every free disk sector to see if it can find them. If you can locate the first cluster, you may then initiate an automatic file recovery. The unerase utility will provide a way of creating a new directory entry for the file. You will need to specify a probable file length, and then may need to make adjustments to the length until the file is properly reconstituted.

Manual file recovery   An automatic recovery always generates a file of the proper name and length, but the file may have picked up clusters that did not belong to it. If the file contents are bad, you will know it right away when you try to use the file. In this case, you must continue the recovery by searching for the missing clusters manually— that is, by employing a search facility to view free clusters. A well-designed unerase utility does a good deal to help you with this process. With just a keystroke, it displays cluster after cluster and provides a way of tracking and reordering clusters that belong to the file. Figure 23.3 shows the main menu for these facilities in the Norton UnErase program.

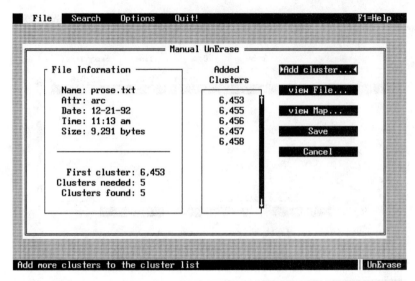

Figure 23.3

Yet, even the best designed utility makes a manual recovery risky. The problem is not just in finding a file's clusters, but also in recognizing them when they are before your eyes. Clusters belonging to text files are the easiest to discern, but it may be difficult to decide whether a given cluster belongs to the erased file, or to some other long-abandoned document. Other kinds of files are far more difficult to track and reassemble. Spreadsheet and database files contain identifying words and phrases, but much of a cluster's content is numeric data that appears as sheer gobbledygook on the screen. Some clusters may be impossible to identify, and even when all can be rounded up, it may be prohibitively difficult to arrange them in the proper order.

For these reasons, a manual recovery of an erased file is unlikely to succeed except for text files. Fortunately, files are seldom completely fragmented. Usually the clusters fall into a few blocks of contiguous sectors, and you need only locate the beginning of each block. But, still, considerable labor is required, and, if you are unlucky, the recovery may fail despite your efforts. It is far easier to make frequent backups than to struggle through this experience.

Unerasing files in DOS 5.0 Starting with version 5.0, DOS can undelete files. DOS has an inherent advantage in this matter since it has the option of modifying what happens when the ERASE, DEL, or

DELETE commands are used. It does just this by providing a way in which information about every deleted file can be set aside when the file is erased. To recover a deleted file, all DOS needs to do is consult this information to find out which clusters the file occupied. Of course, a complete recovery cannot be made when one or more of those clusters has been appropriated by other files.

DOS 5.0 does not automatically set aside information about deleted files. Instead, this is done by the MIRROR command, which we'll be discussing a little later in this chapter. MIRROR is used to set up the disk so that data can be recovered easily should the disk be accidentally reformatted. To do this, it's generally best to execute the MIRROR command everytime the machine starts up by placing the command in AUTOEXEC.BAT. DOS is made to set aside information about deleted files by adding a /T switch to this command, following it with the name of the drive it should serve. For example, the command:

```
MIRROR /TC
```

sets aside information about drive C. Multiple drives may be specified:

```
MIRROR /TC /TA
```

In the root directory of each disk specified, MIRROR sets up a file to hold information about deleted files. The file (called a delete tracking file) is named PCTRACKR.DEL. This file cannot be allowed to expand in size indefinitely, lest it ultimately take over the entire disk. So, by default, MIRROR limits the file's size. For diskettes, the file ranges from 5K (25 entries) for 360K floppies to three times this size for 1.44M diskettes. On hard disks, sizes range from 18K (101 entries) for 20M drives to 55K (303 entries) for drives holding 32M or more. You can set a different value by specifying the number of entries along with the /T switch. Just follow the switch with a dash and the number. For a 300-entry limit, you would type:

```
MIRROR /TC-300
```

When the file fills to its limit, information for new deletions replaces that of the oldest deletions.

The UNDELETE command restores a file. To restore the file \RODENTS\MICE\MICKEY.DOC, you simply enter:

```
UNDELETE C:\RODENTS\MICE\MICKEY.DOC ⏎
```

UNDELETE will search the file containing information about deletions for an entry for this file. If it doesn't find it, UNDELETE will proceed to search the directory \RODENTS\MICE for an empty directory slot that had previously been held by the file, and then will go on to do the best job it can of recovering the file. In the latter case, UNFORMAT automatically replaces the missing first character of the file with a pound sign (#).

Groups of files can be undeleted. For example, to restore all batch files in the MICE directory, you'd type:

```
UNDELETE C:\RODENTS\MICE\*.BAT ⏎
```

Or, to recover all files in the MICE directory:

```
UNDELETE C:\RODENTS\MICE ⏎
```

If you want UNDELETE to only recover files found in the tracking file, add a /DT switch at the end of the command. Conversely, to only have it undelete files not listed in the tracking file, add /DOS. To find out what files are available for recovery, enter the command:

```
UNDELETE /LIST ⏎
```

23.5 Recovering data from an accidentally formatted disk

Before considering unformat utilities, let's review how formatting works. A disk is formatted in two steps. First, in the low-level format, magnetic lines are layed down on the disk to define the tracks and sectors that hold data. Then, in the high-level format, certain disk sectors are set up for use as the root directory and for a file allocation table (FAT) that keeps track of which sectors belong to which files. Optionally, some sectors may also be set aside to hold parts of the operating system used to boot the computer. See the minitutorial in Chapter 16 for details.

The FORMAT program that accompanies DOS may be used with either diskettes or hard disks. When applied to a floppy, it performs both low-level and high-level formats. But in the case of hard disks, it only performs the high-level format, creating the disk's root directory and file allocation table, and optionally adding the boot files (again, see Chapter 16 to learn why).

While a low-level format acts on every part of the disk and destroys all data it holds, a high-level format merely writes a fresh root directory and file allocation tables, destroying the contents of those that preceeded, if any. Most sectors on the disk are untouched, and the data they hold remains intact. Since subdirectories are files, they also remain intact. Thus, when the DOS FORMAT program is accidentally applied to a hard disk, it is theoretically possible to recover the data.

Because the root directory has been erased, it appears as if everything on the disk has been obliterated by formatting. Subdirectories listed in the root directory can no longer be found and, thus, none of the sub-directories nor associated file that they, in turn, contain can be found. But the data is still there, as is information about file lengths and starting locations held in the subdirectories. However, all information about files listed in the root directory is obliterated; although the files themselves remain intact, tracking them down is made doubly difficult.

The loss of the root directory is only part of the problem. A directory listing keeps track of only the first cluster (group of sectors) used by a file. The file allocation table then takes over, tracking the file's distri-bution across the disk surface. Because a file may be fragmented, with parts of the file dispersed among parts of other files, the loss of the file allocation table through a high-level format reduces the disk to a hodge-podge of intermixed file parts.

Unformat utilities   Certain utilities are said to unformat a hard disk that has been accidentally reformatted by the DOS FORMAT program. If you happen to own The Norton Utilities, you'll find the FR (Format Recover) program for this purpose. Such a utility can do a good, but usually not perfect, job of recovering all of the disk's data when the utility has been properly installed before the accidental reformatting occurs. If the utility is brought into play after the reformatting occurs, it can still recover some of the disk's data, but perhaps not much.

PITFALLS | Unformat programs don't ordinarily work on diskettes since the DOS FORMAT command performs both a low-level and a high-level format on diskettes. The data on the disk is completely destroyed when the disk's tracks and sectors are redefined. Some software utility packages contain a special formatting program for diskettes that skips the low-level format unless it is required. The Norton Utilities provides the SFORMAT (Safe Format) program for this purpose. Since the DOS FORMAT command is an external command—one held in a file separate from the main DOS program, COM-MAND.COM—it may be replaced with such a utility. Then, when a diskette is accidentally reformatted with the utility, it may be unformatted. See section 25.6 to learn how to avoid accidental formatting altogether.

How unformat utilities work   The utility is installed on a hard disk before trouble occurs. It makes copies of the root directory and file allocation table, placing them in a large file on the disk. The copies are safe since files go untouched by an accidental reformatting. In order to set up a recoverable file, the utility moves around bits and pieces of other files until it creates a continuous stretch of disk space (if the recovery file were to be dispersed, a chicken-and-egg problem would arise of not having a file allocation table to find the parts of the file that holds the copy of the file allocation table). Then a special signature sector is placed at the start of the file.

After the disk drive has been accidentally reformatted, you start up a recovery program from a diskette. The utility searches the hard disk for the signature sector, reads the root directory and file allocation table that follows, and copies them back to the sectors from which they were erased by the FORMAT command.

Of course, the contents of the root directory and file allocation are constantly changing. Thus, the file that holds copies of them must constantly be updated. This is also done by a utility program. By executing the utility from your AUTOEXEC.BAT file, it runs automatically each time the machine is booted. For example, to use the FR program from The Norton Utilities, you place this line in your AUTOEXEC.BAT file:

```
FR /SAVE
```

Thereafter, the format data file is updated every time you boot the machine. You can run the program more frequently if you wish, but there is generally no point.

When the disk is unformatted, the root directory and file allocation table revert to the state they were in when the recovery file was last updated, not necessarily to the state they were in immediately before the FORMAT command was run. Some files on the disk probably will have been changed during the interim. When a file has been lengthened or shortened, its actual distribution on the disk will no longer accord with that given in the (recovered) file allocation table. After unformatting, the end of some files may be clipped, or have extraneous data added. Erased files may reappear, and files may become cross-linked (section 23.3). Complex files, such as spreadsheet files, may no longer be readable by the software that created them. Hence, there is a danger that your most important work will be lost despite a successful unformat.

Matters are made much worse when the unformat utility is acquired after the disk has been reformatted. In this case, the utility must act as a massive unerase program. Fortunately, subdirectories bear certain characteristics that the utility can scan the disk for. Since the root directory has been erased, the names of subdirectories listed in the root directory are lost, and so temporary names are given to them by the recovery software (in Norton Format Recover, for example, they are named DIR0000, DIR0001, and so on). With subdirectories recovered, it is possible to find the starting points of their files and to automatically recover many of the files—provided the files are not greatly fragmented. (Section 21.3 discusses file fragmentation and defragmentation. Keeping a disk defragmented increases the chances of successful file recovery.) Files that were in the root directory can be very difficult to recover, because virtually all information about the files—their names, lengths, starting locations, and distribution on the disk surface—has been wiped out during formatting.

Unformatting in DOS 5.0   Starting with version 5.0, DOS contains its own provisions for recovering from accidental formatting. Like other such utilities, it works through either a snap shot or recovery approach. As we mentioned earlier in out discussion of unerasing file, the MIRROR command creates a file named MIRROR.FIL to hold copies of the root directory and file allocation table. The file is listed in the root directory of the disk. As usual, this command should be placed in AUTOEXEC.BAT so that it is executed every time you start up the machine. To have MIRROR update the unformatting information for drive C (or to create the MIRROR.FIL file for the first time), you would type:

```
MIRROR C:
```

MIRROR normally keeps a second, older copy of the relevant information in a second file it names MIRROR.BAK. Each time MIRROR runs, it renames the format MIRROR.FIL as MIRROR.BAK. You can use either file when it's time to unformat a disk. The second file can be dispensed with by adding a /1 switch to the end of the command:

```
MIRROR C: /1
```

The UNFORMAT command is partner to MIRROR. When you enter the command:

```
UNFORMAT C: ⏎
```

UNFORMAT looks for the MIRROR.FIL file and uses it to reconstruct the disk. Before starting, it reports the time and date at which the file was last updated and gives you the option of halting the recovery if the file is too old. If you are not sure whether MIRROR.FIL ever existed, add the /J switch to the end of the command. In this case, UNFORMAT will report whether the file is present, but won't actually unformat the disk.

When no mirror file is found, or the file is too old, you can have UNFORMAT skip the file and try to recover data by scanning for subdirectories to piece together the disk as best it can. As it works, UNFORMAT reports how many subdirectories it has found. Add an /L switch to the command to make it also display the names of files it finds. Each time a fragmented file is discovered, UNFORMAT asks you whether to truncate the file so that you are left with the first part of it, or whether to delete the file altogether. Add a /P switch to the command to have the screen messages echoed to a printer.

The MIRROR command can also save partition table information. This occurs only if the command is followed by the /PARTN switch:

> `MIRROR /PARTN` ⏎

Since the partition table needs to be saved only once, this command need not be placed in AUTOEXEC.BAT so that it executes every time the machine starts up. The resulting partition table data cannot be left on the hard disk because DOS wouldn't be able to find the disk if the partition table fails. For this reason, the MIRROR command writes the files containing the partition data (PARTNSAV.FIL) to a diskette. It prompts you to insert the diskette into drive A. The UNFORMAT command restores the partition table. Just place the diskette holding the partition data in drive A and type:

> `UNFORMAT /PARTN` ⏎

Applications   In spite of their limitations, unformat utilities do have a legitimate role, even among experienced computer users. The root directory and file allocation tables can be destroyed in ways other than an inadvertent reformatting of the disk. For example, a power surge at just the wrong moment could scramble the root directory, causing you to loose contact with all of your subdirectories. Such occurences are rare, but when they occur, it's nice to have had an unformat utility quietly updating a recovery file day after day. Still, in the end, the best protection for your data is frequent, thorough backups.

23.6 Detecting and eradicating computer viruses

A computer virus is a kind of program that sneaks into your machine by hiding in software you introduce by diskette or modem. They also may enter through a local area network. At best, viruses make mischief by displaying unwanted messages on the screen; at worst, they may destroy data on your hard disk and diskettes. Viruses are one example of a genre of software created for no purpose other than vandalism. They are called viruses because in some ways they act just like biological viruses. They are small fragments of code that have no life until they invade other software. They hide themselves within healthy programs and may lie dormant for long periods until suddenly they awaken and start doing harm. And, to make things worse, they go through periods of replication in which copies of the virus spread elsewhere in the system, making it difficult to eradicate them completely.

Viruses are not to be confused with other forms of destructive software. Trojan horses are application programs that have been modified to contain damaging code. They enter a computer only by being deliberately copied to the hard disk. Trojan horses generally come alive only once, and they do not replicate themselves. Worms, on the other hand, are programs that do nothing more than replicate themselves without directly attacking data. They're found in computer networks, where they worm themselves from station to station past security measures intended to stop them. By replicating over and over, they fill memory and overwhelm the computer's main processor, bringing everything to a grinding halt.

Kinds of viruses   Some viruses are considered benign. When they awaken, it is only to display a message on the screen (one famous virus announces itself as the Cookie Monster). But malignant viruses damage data in various ways. They may erase files by damaging their directory entries, or by trashing a disk's file allocation table. With proper precautions, data may be at least partially recoverable in such situations (see section 25.7 to learn about safeguards against virus attacks). The worst viruses go further and write nonsense into every disk sector to completely obliterate your data. The only fallback is good backups.

A virus may read the system clock when it first enters the machine. It records the time and date internally and then starts counting through the period during which it will lie dormant. Whenever such viruses are activated, they check the clock to see if the time has arrived to emerge and destroy. Other viruses respond to random events within the machine and may awaken at any moment. Some have been known to gradually take their toll, first flashing messages, repeatedly crashing the machine a few days later, and finally attacking the hard disk at a later date still. The virus may replicate itself while it is dormant, infecting not just other files on your hard disk, but also files on diskettes, including your backups.

How viruses work   It is worthwhile to understand how viruses work. Usually, they will attach themselves to an application program file. Shell viruses wrap themselves around the program, leaving the original code unchanged, but making the program file longer. Intrusive viruses overwrite part of the program, leaving the program length unchanged. Usually, these viruses are tailored to attack a particular program, and so they may replace part of the program that is seldom used and unlikely to be missed.

When it hooks into a program, a virus arranges itself so that control jumps to the viral code when the program is started or a certain task is performed. Usually, the virus looks around a bit and then decides to go back to sleep, returning control to the program code and letting everything proceed normally, giving not a hint of the virus's presence. Other times, when the virus is awakened it may use the opportunity to search the hard disk for suitable places to replicate and hide. And, of course, sometimes the virus may wake up and throw a tremendous tantrum, possibly leaving your data in ruins. But the virus can do nothing until the program containing it is run.

It is for this reason that a viral infection of the operating system is especially dangerous. Parts of DOS are constantly running, not only when you are working at the DOS prompt, but also as you run any application program. If COMMAND.COM is infected, the virus may virtually be always awake. Worse, it sits at the center of control over your disk drives, allowing it to spot opportunities to send copies of itself out to diskettes.

Viruses directed toward the operating system tend to be especially well hidden. They may invade a disk's boot record or special system files used for booting. Sometimes the body of the virus is hidden in unallocated disk sectors that are then falsely marked as being bad sectors that DOS should not use. A tiny bit of code inserted somewhere in the operating system is all that is required to load the virus from these sectors into memory and start it moving. The body of a virus may also sometimes hide within data files.

Vaccine programs   In response to the viral menace, a new genre of software, called vaccine programs, has been developed. They have two functions: to detect and to remove viruses. Often, they are far better at the former. Actually, the word vaccine is not entirely appropriate. Computers have no immune system that may be bolstered, and most of these programs cannot identify and attack viruses at the moment they enter the machine or are replicated. Rather, they recognize individual viruses, or evidence of viral damage, and report the viral presence to you by providing a list of suspect files. You can prevent further spread of the infection by swiftly removing infected files. Some vaccine programs can try to sterilize your hard disk by tracking down and removing every instance of a virus.

Vaccine programs work in many ways. To be effective, they must be run frequently, usually at start-up from the computer's AUTOEXEC.BAT file (section 11.1). They'll maintain information about your program files and DOS files so that changes can be detected. The most obvious sign of infection is an alteration of a program's length, which may be checked easily and quickly. But only shell viruses can be detected this way. In-vasive viruses are found by looking for fragments of their code within the program's own code. (More and more software authors are including antiviral self-analysis within the application programs they write.) Vaccine programs also operate by closely monitoring all parts of DOS, and by surveying supposedly bad disk sectors for hidden code. They may watch out for inexplicable shrinkage of available system memory—another sign of viral proliferation. Finally, vaccine programs may watch for certain characteristic signals given off by viruses when they interfere with the operating system.

Viruses become ever more sophisticated, not by some form of natural mutation, but because the sociopaths who create them constantly release new ones. In response, vaccine programs undergo constant change. Owners of these programs must constantly upgrade to new versions to renew their protection. Updates may include code extracts from the most recently introduced viruses. An extract is used as a sort of mug shot to track down the virus in your files.

Unfortunately, recent virus designs defy identification by code extracts. As they spawn offspring, these viruses mutate by rearranging their constitutent parts into one of many thousands of possible patterns. Even worse, viruses may encrypt parts of themselves using a random key (numeric password). These strategies make it very difficult to take a snap shot of a virus, since the same virus can look very different only moments later. By most accounts, the computer virus problem will become much more serious before it gets better. Ultimately, the problem can only be solved by virus-resistant operating system design.

PITFALLS | Most of these techniques make a computer boot more slowly, since time is required to scan many files. Because the programs are normally active only at start-up, they won't detect a newly arrived viruses until the next time the machine is booted. At least one vaccine program uses an entirely different strategy. It propagates its own benign virus that links into every application program. The virus comes alive whenever the program is loaded. But, instead of causing mischief, it analyses the program to see that it is unchanged and alerts you if anything has gone wrong.

Remedies   When viruses are detected, vaccine software displays a status report naming all suspect files. It may rank their condition with terms like dangerous or fatal. While this is not the sort of news one likes to hear, a vaccine program can at least inform you of your computer's infection before the virus announces its presence in its own nasty way. Another advantage is that a vaccine program makes clear that it is a virus that is at fault when you are having hardware problems that have defied diagnosis.

Viruses can be especially hard to eradicate in networks where they can travel from computer to computer, only to return to machines that have been disinfected. Be sure to acquire a network-compatible vaccine program if this could be a problem for you. A useful feature (one found in the Norton AntiVirus program) is an automatic logging facility that tracks all warnings about viruses in a network. Without such a record, evidence of viral infection can be spread among many users, none of whom can see the whole picture.

Not all vaccine programs actually attack viruses when they find them. Some only list the corrupted files. You are expected to erase the files and replace them with backups. Unfortunately, your backups may have become contaminated too, so it's good to select a vaccine program that will try to recover files. Shell viruses, which wrap themselves around a program, can often be eliminated. But invasive viruses permanently destroy parts of a program's code, and so the program must be reinstalled from its original distribution diskettes. In any case, always back up your files before having a vaccine program try to fix them. Even infected backups may be better than no backups at all.

Other solutions   When a virus skirts every effort of vaccine programs, the only cure for the infection is to reformat your hard disk and completely rebuild it. If you have a global backup of the disk, this process shouldn't entail a good deal of labor—provided that the backups are not themselves infected. Otherwise, you will need to meticulously rebuild the disk file by file, copying programs from their original distribution diskettes. You may need to acquire new copies of these diskettes from the manufacturer because, when a virus has linked into the operating system, it may secretly transfer itself to a diskette even though files have been copied only from the diskette. So, the viral infection may appear on any diskette loaded into the computer after the virus was first introduced into the machine.

Chapter 24

Dealing with Hardware Malfunctions

- MINITUTORIAL: Hard disk crashes and other disasters

- Dealing with crashes at start-up

- Dealing with crashes during operation

- Diagnosing faulty expansion boards

- Recovering from a hard disk crash

- Repairing a damaged diskette

MINITUTORIAL:
Hard disk crashes and other disasters

In all computerdom, no term is so ill-defined as crash. The word evokes images of billowing smoke and flying sparks. But even the most serious crashes are hardly so dramatic. In the worst case, components of the machine fail, and the computer needs to be repaired. In the best case, the computer only needs to be rebooted, resulting in nothing more than the loss of the work you've just done. In between, a wide spectrum of things can go wrong.

The most notorious of all crashes is a hard disk crash. This phenomenon is called a head crash when a hard disk drive's read/write heads slam into a disk surface. Head crashes are the computer equivalent of shark attacks—they are greatly feared but don't occur all that often. Drives fail far more often for other reasons, and when a head crash does occur, most of the data can usually be recovered. This is not to say that the data on disk drives is not in substantial danger. Drives can fail in many other ways, and when they do, it is sometimes impossible to recover any data at all.

Most so-called disk crashes are not the result of a mechanical or electronic failure on the part of the drive. Rather, crucial information on the disk surface is corrupted. A drive's root directory, for example, ultimately keeps track of every subdirectory in a directory tree. If the root directory is destroyed, there is no way of getting to the subdirectories, and so the files listed in subdirectories disappear. Similarly, a disk's file allocation table is used by DOS to keep track of how individual files are dispersed across the disk's surface. When the table is corrupted, all data is essentially scrambled.

Sometimes data is obliterated by physical defects of the disk's surface. A faulty disk sector that could barely hold data when the disk was new gradually wears out until it fails; or the format markings that define disk sectors may fade until the sector can no longer be located and read; or information in disk sectors can be destroyed by software. One way this happens is that application programs may accidentally write information into the wrong point in memory. If the memory happens to hold DOS buffers (section 11.3), the damage can be transferred to the disk surface when these sectors are written out. Another source of damage is malfunctioning utility programs that operate on directories and file allocation tables.

Computers may also appear to crash when they lose their configuration information. On most machines, this information is stored in a special memory chip powered by an internal lithium battery. Sooner or later the battery fails. Other times, files used for booting may be accidentally changed or erased. Since the machine is already running, the files won't be missed until the next day when power is switched on again. It may appear that an alarming crash has occured when actually nothing more is needed than replacement of the file.

Often, people say that their computer has crashed when actually it is their software that has malfunctioned. All large programs contain programming errors. Sometimes the errors are minor and result in nothing more than a glitch on the screen. But other errors cause the software to fall into an infinite loop from which it cannot recover. When this happens, the machine hangs and must be rebooted. No harm is done to the computer but your recent work may be lost.

Memory-resident programs (section 15.4) are particularly prone to causing software crashes. DOS was not designed to have several programs loaded and running at once. Because there is no officially approved manner for using hot keys to call up dormant utility programs, all sorts of conflicts can occur between memory-resident programs. Some memory-resident programs work simultaneously in the background as you use your application programs. These are especially mischievous because they can sometimes cause the application software to malfunction.

The most insidious of all crashes are those that occur sporadically. A computer may repeatedly fail for no apparent reason and need to be rebooted. Sporadic failures are usually caused by software, but they also may occur from overheating, particularly in a hard disk drive. It's difficult enough to diagnose the cause of a crash that has a clear-cut origin. Diagnosing sporadic crashes requires the patience of a saint and the insight of Sherlock Holmes.

It is important that you know enough about crashes that you can decide whether or not the machine has physically failed. Repair shops are flooded with machines that are in perfectly good condition but which have suffered some slight damage to information used for configuration or booting. Even if you can't fix the problem yourself, much time and money can be saved by seeking the right kind of help from the start.

One way of finding out what may be wrong with a machine is to run diagnostic software. IBM ATs are shipped with a diagnostic diskette that also holds the system configuration program. In addition, an Advanced Diagnostics disk is available separately. The Advanced Diagnostics are included with all PS/2 machines. Just start up the computer with the Reference Diskette and press Ctrl-Alt when you see the main menu. Independent software houses also offer a variety of diagnostic software.

24.1 Dealing with crashes at start-up

When a computer won't start up properly, even though it has in the past, it's usually possible to narrow down the source of the problem in a few minutes. The initial difficulty is in deciding whether the machine is having trouble booting (generally indicating a software problem) or whether the hardware has fallen into disrepair. Work through the following steps.

Step 1   Did the machine actually start up when you flipped its power switch? In most machines, you'll hear a fan if so. Otherwise, check the wall socket, power strip, or surge protector the machine is connected to. If there is no fan noise in a machine that uses a fan, yet you're sure the computer is plugged in properly, take it in for repairs. Even if the only problem is a malfunctioning fan, you'll need to have it fixed immediately since overheating could damage other parts of the machine.

Step 2   Indicator lights on the keyboard and front panel of the machine should flash when you first turn on the computer. Then the machine settles into its Power-On Self Test (POST). The test may take as much as a minute on old, slower machines. Various circuits are tested, including all memory chips. When a fault is found, the speaker will emit an unusual, repetitive beep or squeal, and a code number will be displayed on the screen, sometimes with a message of a few words. Usually, there is nothing to do but write down the code number (which will be meaningful to a technician) and take the computer in for repairs. Code numbers beginning with 01 indicate a problem on the system board, 02 refers to memory, 03 to the keyboard, 06 to disk drives, 07 to a math coprocessor, 09 through 12 to serial and parallel ports, and 04, 05, 24, 25, and some other values to video adapters. You may also encounter the messages "PARITY CHECK 1" and "PARITY CHECK 2," which refer, respectively, to memory errors on the system board or in an expansion slot. When PS/2 machines display these numbers, they add a few words about what part of the machine is malfunctioning.

Step 3   An error message may indicate that the computer's internal battery has failed. Except for PCs configured by internal dip switches, configuration data is held in special CMOS memory powered by a lithium battery. You'll need to replace the battery when it goes bad and rerun the machine's configuration program. If the configuration program can be started up when the machine won't operate otherwise, there's probably a problem in CMOS memory.

Step 4   If the machine passes the Power-On Self Test, it moves on to booting. It begins by trying to boot from diskette drive A and, failing that, it tries drive C. To boot from A, place a bootable diskette in the drive and close the drive door. To boot from C, leave the door to drive A open while booting goes on. From experience, you'll know the sound of a diskette drive or a hard disk drive as it successfully boots the computer. When the boot fails, the drive makes noise for only a fraction of a second and then an error message appears.

On PC XT and AT machines that have the BASIC programming language built in, the control screen for the language may come up when DOS fails to boot, as shown in figure 24.1. When this screen appears, you know that the computer is having trouble booting. You don't know if the disk drives are working properly, because BASIC is stored on chips inside the machine and is not loaded from disk. Check again that everything is set up properly for booting. In this situation, PS/2 machines display a diagram of a computer that prompts you to press F1 when the boot drive is ready.

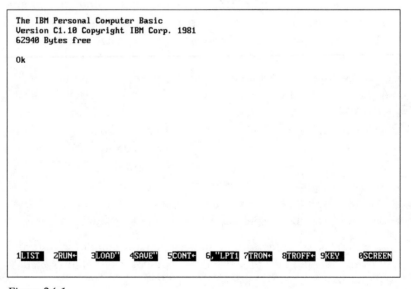

Figure 24.1

Step 5   If it sounds like the computer is booting properly, but nothing is appearing on the screen, you probably have a video problem. Start by seeing to it that the brightness and contrast controls on the video display are set so that something should be visible. If your monitor is independently powered, be sure it has been switched on. Then check if the cable connecting the monitor to the back of the computer is secure. It should fit tightly into its socket. If nothing still appears on the screen, either the video circuitry or the monitor may have gone bad. Borrowing a monitor from another machine can quickly narrow down the search for the culprit. Note that the computer's Power-On Self Test will beep the computer's speaker in an unusual way if it senses problems in the video circuitry. However, the computer has no way of finding out whether the monitor is working properly.

Step 6   When a message is displayed telling you that booting has failed, it may be that either the boot disk or the boot disk drive is the culprit. Find the original diskettes on which DOS was shipped and place the one marked for booting in drive A. Restart the machine by turning it off, waiting a few seconds, and then turning it back on. If the machine boots correctly and you initially tried booting from drive A, make yourself a new boot diskette and restart the machine. If, however, you initially tried to boot from drive C and failed, you have more serious problems to contend with.

Step 7   When the problem is a boot failure on drive C, any of several factors could be at fault. First, you need to figure out whether the drive is working at all. After booting from drive A, type C: ⏎ to move to drive C. If directory listings appear normally, the drive is probably fine and the problem is in booting. You may have encountered a "Bad boot record" error message in this case. Somehow, some of the boot information deposited during high-level formatting (see the minitutorial at the beginning of Chapter 16) has been trashed. You'll need to acquire a disk repair program like the Norton Disk Doctor that can analyze and repair the damage. Until then, you can boot from drive A and use the computer as usual.

Step 8   If, after booting from drive A and typing C: ⏎, you encounter an "Invalid Drive Specification" message, or DOS simply refuses to move to C, you have a more difficult diagnosis before you. One possibility is that the drive is no longer properly configured. Even if the computer's internal battery (discussed in Step 3) is all right, it's a good idea to run the machine's configuration program. Perhaps software has somehow tampered with the configuration data, or perhaps an error occured within configuration memory. If this sort of thing is the problem, simply running the configuration program will probably restore the drive.

Another possibility is that your hard disk may use special partitioning software, such as SpeedStor. These utilities were developed before DOS provided ways of handling drives larger than 32 megabytes (see the discussion in section 16.4). They can be used, for example, to make a 40-megabyte drive appear as two 20-megabyte drives named C and D. Such software works through a device driver loaded during booting from the boot disk's CONFIG.SYS file. If this driver has inadvertently been removed from the disk, or the mention of it removed from CONFIG.SYS, the drive will not be linked to DOS and will appear to malfunction.

Finally, the problem may be in the hard disk's Master Boot Record. In this case, it's likely you will encounter a "Bad Drive Specifier" error message at start-up. The Master Boot Record resides in the very first sector on the disk. It tells the machine where to look on the disk for the beginning of the DOS partition—that is, for the part of the disk used by DOS. The entire disk is used by DOS in most machines, but a lookup in the Master Boot Record is still required.

Two things can go wrong here. First, the Master Boot Record may be corrupted. Start up the FDISK program, described in section 16.3, and select F4 from the main menu to view disk parameters. If it issues an error message, possibly "No partitions defined," the Master Boot Record needs fixing and you'll require special utility software to do it. Don't use FDISK to repartition the disk to restore the damaged record, because it will destroy the root directory and file allocation tables, effectively annihilating all data.

On the other hand, FDISK may report that everything is well with the disk, but that the DOS partition is not currently selected as the active partition. The information displayed will include a category headed Active Partition. The partition labeled DOS should have an *A* (for active) next to it. If instead it is *N* (for not active), you've found the problem. Press Esc to return to the main menu, select Change active partition, and then type the number of the DOS partition when FDISK requests your input. The machine should be all right after you quit FDISK and reboot.

Step 9   If you successfully get past booting, the DOS prompt appears on the screen, and then the machine freezes, it may be that software loaded by your CONFIG.SYS or AUTOEXEC.BAT files is malfunctioning. Temporarily modify or disable these files (renaming them makes DOS ignore them) to see if the machine can function after nothing more than a simple boot. If it does, reintroduce the contents of the files one line after another until the culprit appears (temporarily placing a few 'x's before unwanted lines in the files causes the lines to be cast aside as errors during booting). This kind of problem should not arise if the machine has worked before. But any changes that were made in these files the last time the machine was used are highly suspect. Keep an eye out for conflicts between memory-resident programs (section 15.4).

Step 10   If none of the above suggestings has done any good, the problem may reside in one of the circuit boards inside the machine. You'll need to strip the machine down to its bare bones. The discussion in section 24.3 tells you how to go about this procedure.

If you're still stymied after all of these investigations, there's not much choice but to take the machine in for repairs. If at all possible, try to borrow equipment from another computer to test individual components. Knowing that certain equipment—the video monitor, for instance—is working properly saves you the trouble and expense of taking it in for possible repair. Be wary, however, of moving a suspect disk controller to another machine, because it could trash the data on more disks if it is malfunctioning. Be sure to make a list of every item inside the machine when you take it in for repairs, and have the repair service acknowledge the list before you leave the equipment behind.

24.2 Dealing with crashes during operation

A computer can function properly for hours and suddenly freeze (or hang or crash). Generally, you can tell the machine has frozen because no keystroke or movement of the mouse has any effect. When things really go wrong, the screen can be reduced to a fireworks display that won't harm the equipment but may rattle your nervous system. Usually, typing `Ctrl`-Break won't take you back to the DOS prompt when the machine freezes. You will need to reboot. But even typing `Ctrl`-`Alt`-`Del` may not do the job. In that case, turn the machine off, wait a few seconds, and then turn it back on.

Computers usually hang because of a software malfunction. Indeed, the culprit may be a malfunction of the software user. Particularly with badly crafted software, it's possible to go down a pathway that you can't get out of. The program waits for a command from you that you don't know, and it won't respond to anything else. Of course, this situation does not amount to a computer malfunction, but nonetheless it can cost you the work you've done.

Software bugs   More typically, a software bug sends the program into an infinite loop. The program never looks back to see if anything has been typed in (or moused in), and so the machine appears to have frozen. Sometimes you will be able to break out of this situation with `Ctrl`-Break, but usually rebooting is necessary. Occasionally, a program will go on a rampage and trash the data in vast areas of memory. Even `Ctrl`-`Alt`-`Del` may not be able to help you in this case.

Most software bugs are associated with a particular part of a program. With experience, you'll learn if certain functions are untrustworthy and will avoid them when you can. Get in the habit of constantly writing your data out to disk when working in parts of a program that have caused you trouble in the past. If a bug repeatedly hangs your machine, call the technical support staff of the software manufacturer and ask them about it. They may have a corrected version of the software ready to send out. Many companies only advertise new versions of their programs when they have added substantial new features. You may need to call them to learn about bug fix versions.

Memory-resident programs   Memory-resident programs (section 15.4) are another culprit in sporadic crashes. This is particularly true of those that work in the background, such as print spoolers (section 14.5) or communication programs (Chapter 13). These access an internal timer that automatically activates them 17 times a second. All sorts of trouble can occur during these brief awakenings. Even ordinary memory-resident programs can cause mischief when they are out of view. They may make a change in the computer's memory that lies waiting to trip up some other piece of software. These sorts of crashes are highly idiosyncratic; they are often impossible to reproduce, making it all the harder to track down the offender. See the discussion in section 15.5 to learn about how to minimize conflicts between memory-resident programs.

Computer viruses   Another possible cause of sporadic crashes are computer viruses, which are discussed in sections 23.6 and 25.7. A virus is a rogue program that sneaks into your system by hooking itself onto other programs copied to your hard disk or a diskette. It hides, multiplies, and then makes its appearance, sometimes conspicuously by a screen message. But a virus may cause trouble without announcing itself. If you fail in your attempts to track down the source of periodic crashes, it may be worth investing in a virus detection program.

Hardware problems   Finally, sporadic hardware failure may be causing your troubles. Overheating is frequently the problem. It arises from using the computer in a hot environment, overloading it with too many add-in boards, or defeating the built-in ventilation system. Typically, the hard disk becomes too hot, its parts expand differentially, and the drive is temporarily thrown out of alignment. When the machine hangs from overheating, rebooting it (or turning it off and on) will not get it running again. You will need to wait a while for the computer to cool down. This is a serious problem that ages your equipment prematurely. Worse, it can threaten the data on your hard disk. Read section 25.1 to learn how to avoid this problem.

24.3 Diagnosing faulty expansion boards

The mechanical parts of a computer—the disk drives and printer mechanism—are more likely to fail than the electronic components. But electronic failures also occur. When they do, it is useful to be able to isolate the faulty circuitry so that it may be sent out for repair without shipping the entire computer.

The general strategy for locating haywire circuitry is to strip the computer down to its basics, remove all nonessential peripherals, and then build the system back up piece by piece until the faulty component is reintroduced and crashes the machine, thereby identifying itself as the culprit. To do this, you will need to remove boards from the computer's expansion slots. This process can become tedious, since you need to repeatedly reconfigure the machine. Read all of this section before beginning.

Removing expansion boards   Begin by opening up the machine. Desktop machines open on top using a number of designs. Some tops are loosened by pressing two buttons and hinging it upward. Others must be unscrewed at back and slid forward. Older IBM machines use this system, and require that you lift the lid upward once it has been pulled forward as far as it will go (the reverse motion is required to put the top back on). Be careful as you slide the computer case not to catch it on cables inside the machine.

Once inside, you'll typically see from three to eight long sockets—the slots—some with expansion boards installed and (usually) others free. Each board is fastened at the back end of the machine. To remove a board, unfasten it and gently, but firmly, rock it back and forth, pulling as you do so. To insert a board, do just the opposite. Never force it.

Circuit boards, whether those in slots or those built into the machine, are highly susceptible to damage by static electricity. Never wear clothes that accumulate static when probing inside a computer, and try to avoid charged environments, such as offices with thick carpets. Be especially careful about picking up video monitors. A video screen is full of static when a monitor is turned on and the static lingers afterward. If you pick up a monitor, holding the screen against you, you will become strongly charged. These rules also apply when working with connectors at the back of the machine. It's possible to zap your computer without ever opening the case by touching exposed pins on a rear socket (touching the computer case is harmless because its paint is an insulator). One way of removing static from your body is to touch a faucet or pipe just before reaching into the computer. This works because a building's plumbing can absorb large amounts of static and convey it directly into the earth.

Hazards   Unplug the computer when working inside it. You'll see a box several inches square toward the back of older PCs, or an oblong box along one side of PS/2 machines. This is the power supply, and it will probably bear a warning about shock hazard. The warning means that you must not open up the power supply itself (the inside of a power supply may be dangerous even when the computer is turned off). You can safely touch the power supply box, and indeed should do so just before touching any other part of the computer so that static will be conveyed away from your body.

When you remove circuit boards from the machine, try to touch them only by their edges. Put them down on surfaces that are not prone to static buildup, such as paper or wood. If a circuit board is going into storage, choose a storage container that is static-resistant, like cardboard. Do not wrap the board in a material that is prone to cling (some styrofoam-type materials store up lots of static electricity) and do not use an electrical conductor like aluminum foil. It's best to keep the board's original packaging for storage.

One other warning: never work inside the computer when it is turned on. You are very likely to damage a board if you insert it or remove it while the machine is on. With bad luck, doing so can result in damage to other boards and even to the computer's main circuit board. Even if you're only going to change switches inside the machine, turn it off first. (Usually the settings of the miniature switches found inside computers are read only once, at the time the hardware initializes at start-up. So you would need to reboot in any case after resetting switches).

Stripping down the machine   To strip a machine down to its basic circuitry, begin by identifying each board and noting the slot in which it was installed. Some machines have slot sockets of two different lengths, and some have slots that can only accept half-length boards. (PS/2 machines require that a video expansion board be placed in a particular slot.) Later you will want to match boards with slots they can fit into. Usually, however, all slots are the same, and any board can go into any slot. It's still worth noting the initial positions of the boards, however, since they may be positioned for optimal cabling to disk drives or for connections at the back of the machine.

The procedures for disconnecting disk drives vary considerably. There is no need to disconnect disk drive cables on most pre-PS/2 machines. Just pull each disk controller card from its slot and place it on a nonconducting surface, such as a book placed on one corner of the machine. This circuitry may be built into the computer's main circuit board on PS/2 computers and some PC/AT-style clones, so the drive cables must be disconnected. Every drive also receives a cable from the machine's power supply. These may be left connected. Diskette drives won't operate in this case; a hard disk will still start up when the machine is turned on, but it is effectively dormant.

In early IBM machines, one slot holds a video adapter that runs the video display. Another holds a diskette controller card that is linked to the diskette drives. A third card, the hard disk controller, is similarly cabled to the hard disk drive. IBM AT-style machines combine the floppy and hard disk controllers onto one card. Various clone manufacturers have built disk controller circuitry into the machine's main circuit board (the motherboard), freeing up a slot or two. Some IBM PS/2-style machines share this strategy, and have gone further by integrating the video circuitry into the main circuit board. Observation will tell you how your machine is designed. To find the disk controller circuitry, look to see where the disk drives are connected. In some designs, the drive may directly plug into the computer's motherboard without any cables at all.

Testing the video system   Once the computer has been stripped down as much as possible, turn your attention to diagnosing the video system. Machines vary in their behavior when they are unable to boot DOS from a disk drive, but all will write something on the screen. IBM-made PCs, XTs, and ATs present the opening screen of the BASIC interpreter, a programming language that is built into IBM machines (see figure 24.1). PS/2 machines display an image of a computer. Or the machine may display some kind of error message. What matters is that you will know that the video system is working properly if an intelligible message is displayed.

When nothing at all appears on the screen, make sure the monitor is properly connected and that its brightness and contrast controls are turned up. If so, there is a good chance that the problem is in your video system, although the system unit could still be the culprit. When a video problem is diagnosed, the best way to tell whether it is the video circuitry or the monitor that is malfunctioning is to borrow a monitor from another machine and make a comparison.

Testing the disk drives   With both the screen and system unit appearing to work properly, turn off the machine and proceed to the next step, which is to reintroduce the diskette drive(s). If your machine uses a separate disk controller card for diskettes and you've left the drives cabled, all you need to do is plug the card back into its former slot. If you have a hard disk sharing the same controller card, carefully disconnect the hard disk cables from the card. Before doing this, note the orientation of the connectors so that you can later reconnect them without reversing them. Then place a reliable boot diskette in drive A and turn on the machine. If it won't boot properly, a screen message will probably tell you the problem is in the drive. If the machine hangs instead, the drive controller circuitry is probably at fault.

TIP

You can't test diskette drives just by switching the cables between drives A and B and trying to boot from B. There is something called a terminator resistor that must be put between the drives before attempting this. Since the resistor varies in both appearance and position from drive to drive, you'd best leave this sort of thing to a repair technician.

After successfully booting from a diskette, turn off the machine and proceed to reconnecting your hard disk drive, if you have one. Again, reconnect all hard disk drives at the same time, and observe the same cabling (hard disks have terminator resistors also). Then start up the machine and see what happens, still booting from drive A. Once booted, move to drive C by entering C: ⏎ and try for a directory listing. A successful directory listing tells you that the hard disk drive and its electronics are also working properly. As with a diskette drive, you'll probably see an error message if the drive is faulty, and nothing at all when the controller card is bad.

Testing remaining expansion cards

Finally, if the machine, video, and disk drives all appear to be working, you'll need to add any remaining cards to the machine, one by one, turning the power off each time before inserting the next. For some steps—particularly the addition of system memory—you will need to run the machine's configuration software when you start up again (or reconfigure the system's dip switches on PC/XT-style machines).

This entire process of rebuilding the machine can be quite time-consuming, particularly when the system must be reconfigured again and again. Sometimes, the machine will miraculously begin to work after having been taken apart and reassembled. This occurs when a bad connection existed somewhere, either in the slots or at cable ends. Occasionally, corrosion develops on the connectors pushed into the slots; it sometimes can be corrected by gently rocking the card back and forth (always with power off). Even rarer is an unseated chip—an integrated circuit that has popped part of the way out of its socket. This occurs most commonly in printers, where vibrations take their toll over months and years. Keeping an eye out for these problems may save you a lot of trouble and an unnecessary trip to a repair shop.

24.4 Recovering from a hard disk crash

Hard disks often have problems, but they seldom crash. In a true hard disk crash, the disk drive's read/write heads slam into the surface of the disks that they normally float slightly above. In the earliest hard disk drives, long before microcomputers appeared, a drive's innards could actually be torn apart by this kind of head crash. But these days, a head crash may occur with little or no permanent damage. A few kilobytes of data may be lost and perhaps a few sectors will be permanently disabled. Still, in the worst case, particles of the disk's coating may contaminate the read/write heads, or be scattered about to cause further crashes, and the drive is effectively destroyed.

For every instance of a fatal head crash, many more drives cease to work because of sudden failures of an electronic component. Drives also fail because the bearings upon which they rotate wear down and the platters begin to wobble. Indeed, some drives fail because curious owners open them up to look inside! The greatest cause of hard disk crashes, however, is damage to the information recorded on the drive, rather than damage to the drive itself.

Symptoms   A computer usually can work with a crashed disk drive running. You won't be able to boot from the drive, of course. But you can boot from a diskette in drive A and then attempt to shift to drive C by typing C: ⏎. If the drive has crashed, you'll encounter an "Invalid Drive Specification" message, or the DOS prompt will simply refuse to change to C>. If the C> prompt does appear, but no files appear in the root directory and the directory tree is gone, the problem is not a disk crash. Instead, someone has reformatted the disk, or has run the FDISK program and in doing so has wiped out the root directory and file allocation tables. See section 23.5 to learn what to do in this situation.

There are several possible causes when the C> prompt will not appear at all. It may be that for various reasons the drive is no longer configured properly for DOS to access it. Or the information in the Master Boot Record—a special sector on the outer edge of the drive—may be corrupted. In this case, DOS cannot find the DOS partition, which is the part of the drive that DOS uses. When DOS can't find its own partition, as far as it is concerned the drive simply does not exist. The steps to diagnosing these problems are explained in step 8 in section 24.1.

Physically damaged drives   When it is known that the drive is still properly configured, and when the FDISK program fails to find the disk (as section 16.3 explains), the drive is probably damaged physically. Perhaps the drive failed after the computer was jolted and you've suspected physical damage from the start. Don't give up hope. Sometimes a drive can be coaxed to come back to life for a little while longer—long enough to copy data from it that has not been backed up.

Begin by preparing an adequate number of blank diskettes so that you will be ready to make backups when the drive revives. Turn off the machine and open the case. Then disconnect the cables leading to the drive. Loosen the screws (or whatever) holding the drive in place and remove it from the machine. Then position a book or some other nonconducting platform on the corner of the machine and place the drive on of top it. Reconnect the cables, then restart the machine. Booting from drive A, try to move over to C again and again as you tilt the drive to different orientations, sometimes tapping it lightly. Grasp the drive by its sides—avoid touching the electronics. If the C> prompt does magically appear, be ready to copy the most important files to drive A at once. The drive could disappear again at any moment. You may achieve no results at all from this effort, but it's worth a try. If the drive's failure is electronic rather than mechanical, you'll have wasted your time.

Sporadic drive failures   Be aware that hard disk drives can temporarily fail when they overheat. Just turning the computer off for a half-hour to an hour may bring it back. The drive malfunctions because some parts expand more than others as the temperature rises, throwing the drive out of alignment. Overheating occurs when the machine has been improperly located, when its ventilation system has been undermined, or when it has been overloaded with heat-producing expansion boards. See section 25.1 for a discussion of these problems.

Just because the computer can recover from overheating does not mean that you should ignore the problem. High temperatures will cause your drive and the entire computer to wear out more quickly. You should consider your data to be in danger when overheating has occured even once. Deal with the problem immediately. Don't wait until a transient problem turns into a full-blown hard disk crash.

Repair services   Even when your drive has suffered a physical failure and your attempts to bring it back to life have failed, do not despair. Remember that even after a serious head crash, very little of the disk surface, and thus very little of your data, may be harmed. Specialty repair services for damaged drives are available in some cities. Because electronic failure is more common than mechanical failure, drives can usually be fixed without opening them. When worse comes to worst, the inside of the drive can be cleaned and damaged parts replaced. Some repair services have a dust-free clean room for this purpose. Be aware, however, that spare parts may be unavailable for older drives.

A drive is tested after it has been repaired. Thorough testing requires that every disk sector be written upon and then read. To do so would destroy the drive's data, of course. And so repair services ask you to specify whether data is to be preserved or not. They will give less of a guarantee on their work when testing must be curtailed.

PITFALLS | Do not let the recovery techniques explained here lull you into a false sense of security. Some hard disk crashes do result in an irrevocable loss of all data. This is particularly true when sectors on the drive's outermost tracks are damaged. Your only protection against this eventuality is frequent, comprehensive backups.

24.5 Repairing a damaged diskette

When the worst happens and a diskette goes bad with no backup on hand, there may still be a chance of recovering some of the data. DOS will display the message:

```
General Failure error reading drive A
Abort, Retry, Ignore, Fail?
```

DOS is telling you that it has been instructing the drive to read or write data, and the drive has been sending back an error message. Here are some strategies for dealing with this situation:

Faulty drive alignment   First, be sure that it is the diskette that has gone bad. The problem could be with the diskette drive, which may be able to read some diskettes, but not all. This occurs because diskette drives gradually go out of alignment. Usually it takes years to happen on machines equipped with a hard disk, since the diskette drives are rarely used. But it can happen to a drive of any age. If the drive is going out of alignment, a significant percentage of your other diskettes will be unreadable too.

Next, think about the history of the diskette. Was it formatted on the same disk drive? If not, it may be that the drive that formatted it is out of alignment. If you can, test other disks formatted on that drive. (Formatting is the crucial factor here, because formatting determines the exact placement of tracks and sectors on the disk surface).

Another question to ask: Is the diskette a 360K floppy formatted on a 1.2-megabyte 5 ½-inch drive? Disks produced by these drives are not always compatible with other drives. Indeed, it is possible to format a 360K diskette on a 1.2-megabyte drive, write data on it with a 360K drive, and then have neither kind of drive be able to read it (the problem has since been corrected, but many old 1.2-megabyte drives of this kind remain in service).

When a drive fails to read or write data, DOS keeps trying many times and only then issues the "Abort, Retry, Ignore, Fail?" message. It's worth a few minutes to try pressing ⓡ (for retry) two or three dozen times. Each time you do so, DOS will go back and try to read the disk 30 times.

If success still eludes you, remove the disk from the drive, shake it a bit, then put it back in and start over.

You have cause to be discouraged if the disk still can't be read. But, before taking the more drastic measures prescribed in the rest of this section, take the disk to other computers, if you can, and try again and again to have it read. Have a fresh diskette on hand (or an empty hard disk subdirectory) to which you can COPY files from the disk if it momentarily comes alive. Copy the most valued files first, because you may not get through them all before the disk error condition crops up again. Don't use the DOS DISKCOPY command, since it would almost certainly run into trouble and fail to complete the copy, leaving you with nothing.

Damaged data   When all attempts at getting DOS to read the disk have failed, you may take some solace in the knowledge that most of the data on the disk, perhaps all, is still intact. Possibly, one of the sectors holding the disk's root directory or file allocation table has been damaged. While DOS can proceed no further in reading the disk when these are destroyed, various utility software usually can.

Unfortunately, the information in the root directory or file allocation table is essential for tracking down files (see section 23.5). Depending on their design, utility programs deal with this obstacle in one of two ways. First, they may give you the means of editing directories and file allocation tables. This is highly technical work even for computer programmers. If you have no prior technical experience, you are very likely to make matters worse rather than better. It's best to seek professional help if this is your only option.

Second, the utility software may let you scan the disk to view the contents of each sector. For some kinds of files, particularly text files, you can identify the sectors holding your desperately needed data and have the utility reassemble them into a file on another disk. Some unerase programs (discussed in section 23.4) have this capability. Numeric data is usually much less easily recovered in this way, however. A spreadsheet file, for example, is often coded in such a way that you won't recognize your data and won't be able to specify the order in which it should be reassembled. Recovering part of such a file is usually no better than recovering nothing at all, because the software that created it probably won't be able to reread the file.

Physically damaged diskettes   Sometimes a diskette is damaged when a cup of coffee is spilled or a sandwich obeys Murphy's Law. Once the foreign material slips under the envelope surface, the diskette becomes impossible to clean. When this happens with a 5 ½-inch floppy, the data can sometimes be recovered by carefully slitting open one side of its envelope and removing the flimsy disk inside. Taking great care not to crease the disk, gently clean it with mild soap and water, rinsing it thoroughly (don't use cleaning chemicals). Rub the disk with a fine cloth; avoid materials that leave fibers behind. Then let the disk dry.

Next, slit open a new or unwanted diskette, remove and discard its disk, and insert the cleaned disk with great care. This part is much easier said than done, for inside the outer envelope is a second, cloth-like envelope that lubricates the disk's movements, and it must be kept perfectly flat. Then place the floppy in a disk drive and see if DOS can read it. If so, immediately perform a DISKCOPY (see section 7.12) to yet another diskette. The data has been recovered. The final action is the one that should have been taken in the first place to avoid all this trouble: make a backup.

Chapter 25

Preventing Computer Disasters

- MINITUTORIAL: Protecting your computer and data
- Suggestions for computer placement
- Suggestions for handling diskettes
- Avoiding hard disk crashes
- Avoiding file damage
- Avoiding accidental file erasures
- Avoiding accidental disk formatting
- Preventing infection by computer viruses

MINITUTORIAL: Protecting your computer and data

The longer you use a computer, the greater your investment in it and the more you have to protect. The computer hardware is the most obvious part of the investment, but data quickly comes to have a higher value because of the tremendous time spent creating it. Also, keep in mind that many days of labor may be invested in constructing a directory tree, writing batch files, installing and configuring software, and so on. There are four kinds of protection:

■ Hardware setup: Computer equipment is prone to damage from both physical and electrical shocks, as well as static electricity, internal heat, vibrations, and other assaults. Keeping some precautions in mind during installation and setup can avert expensive mishaps.

■ Hardware maintenance: There is not much to do in the way of hardware maintenance on your PC, but there are some tips for operating your machine that will prolong its life. Utility software can keep an eye on your disk drives to see that they are working properly and can warn you when problems are on the horizon.

■ Software setup: Software is more likely to damage data than is faulty hardware. By adopting safe procedures for handling potentially hazardous commands, such as ERASE or FORMAT, you can lessen the chances of disasters. Utility software can also be brought into play to protect data and to help in its recovery when things go wrong. Besides the recommendations found here, read section 5.1 to learn how to manage a disk's directory tree well. You will further protect your data by doing so, since disorganization leads to mistakes, and mistakes destroy as much data as hardware and software malfunctions combined.

■ File maintenance: Backups are at the heart of file maintenance, and they are so important that a whole chapter in this book is devoted to them (Chapter 22). Other procedures require regular attention. There are some time-tested suggestions to follow to avoid bringing computer viruses into your machine, and software and files should be well organized to avoid confusion between versions and the mistakes that may result from that confusion.

It takes little effort to form the habits and carry out the procedures needed to protect your system and data. But it does require some effort. Most computer users take no precautions at all (many never make a single backup!) and most pay heavily again and again for their neglect.

25.1 Suggestions for computer placement

Comfort and aesthetics are usually the factors that determine where a computer is installed. But there are a number of key technical points that should also be considered to ensure a long life for the machine.

One concern is shocks and vibrations, which are bad for computer disk drives. A sudden jolt can send a hard disk drive's read/write heads careening onto the disk surface, potentially destroying the drive and the data it holds. Diskette drives are also subject to failure. Although they cannot suffer a head crash, they may gradually go out of alignment, requiring a costly repair. Vibrations—particularly constant vibrations—exacerbate this problem. Keep these suggestions in mind to avoid unnecessary vibrations:

- Never place an impact printer on the same surface as the computer. Printers such as dot-matrix printers and daisy wheel printers send out considerable vibrations, especially when the print head swings back to the start of a line. If a printer must be placed on the same surface as the computer, put as many layers of padding beneath as are required to dampen the vibrations.

- Never drop objects on the surface on which the computer rests. Place that heavy dictionary on the desk, don't toss it. Teach others to do the same.

- Be very careful when setting up a computer on the floor. A system unit can be installed sideways, and some companies sell inexpensive plastic stands for this purpose. This approach conveniently gets the computer out of the way, but it may leave the computer in the path of foot traffic and mobile furniture. One solid jolt and the hard disk can be destroyed. (Be aware, also, that many hard disk drives are not designed to operate on their sides. The bearings that support the drive platters may age prematurely. Only the manufacturer can tell you if its safe to operate a disk drive this way.)

Heat is the other great enemy of computers. All electronic components age more quickly when operated in a hot environment. The same applies to mechanical devices like disk drives. Sporadic hard disk malfunctions are usually attributed to heat; often they will go away if the operating temperature is lowered. To avoid heat build up, keep the following in mind:

- Don't block the computer's fan. It needs a clear flow of cool air. Similarly, don't locate the system unit in an enclosed space such that the temperature of the surrounding air rises significantly.

- Keep the computer away from the vents of a room's heating system. Don't locate the machine so that it's back is to the wall near where a floor duct releases heat. The hot air will be taken in by the computer's fan, undermining its cooling system.

- If the room in which the computer is installed is particularly hot, keep the machine out of direct sunlight.

- When the computer must operate in a hot environment, consider replacing its cooling fan with a more powerful one. Such fans are available for quick do-it-yourself installation. (The companies that make them also make a point of making quieter fans that come with most PCs.)

- When you remove an expansion card from the machine, replace the metal strip (or whatever) that closes the space in the back of the machine where the card protrudes. Leaving open spaces allows cooling air to escape instead of completing its path through the computer. Several open spaces can seriously undermine the machine's cooling system. It's easy to lose track of the metal strips; make it a habit to keep all such paraphernalia in one place.

Finally, it's important to note that all computers come with three-prong plugs. The third prong is a ground—a means for unwanted electricity to escape when something goes wrong. If you're using a machine in an old building that has only two-prong wall sockets, you should not defeat the third prong by placing a two-prong adapter between the plug and the socket so that the computer operates without a ground. Such adapters usually continue the third prong as a loose end-wire that serves as a ground when connected to the screw at the center of the wall socket plate. Using the computer without a ground increases the risk of expensive electrical damage to its components (damage not covered by many insurance policies). Note that the use of a surge protector will not alleviate this danger if the surge protector itself is run with its ground disconnected.

25.2 Suggestions for handling diskettes

One hears much about hard disk crashes, but too little about diskette failure, which happens more frequently. No disk holds its information indefinitely. Sooner or later magnetic markings fade—whether it is data within sectors or the magnetic lines (laid down by formatting) that define the disk sectors. Diskettes can also lose their data through mishandling. Here are some rules for protecting them:

■ Keep diskettes away from extreme heat. Don't leave them in direct sunlight. You should be aware that, like any physical object, diskettes change dimensions slightly when they become very hot or very cold. Because information is packed on them tightly and precisely, the slight difference in size can make the disk temporarily unreadable. There may be occasions when you need to let a diskette sit for a few minutes before using it. Similarly, you should not format a diskette when it is especially hot or cold, since the format markings may change enough to make the disk error-prone.

■ Never place heavy objects, like books, on top of diskettes. By doing so, you may crease the disk or abrade its surface. This is not as great a problem with 3 ½-inch diskettes in rigid plastic packages; however, 5 ¼-inch floppy diskettes are easily damaged.

■ When labeling a diskette, make a habit of writing on the label before affixing it to the diskette (again, 3 ½-inch diskettes are much less vulnerable in this regard). Once a label is affixed, it should only be written upon with a felt-tip pen. Ball point pens and pencils can easily damage the disk's surface. When removing a label, hold the diskette by just the tip of one corner so that you're not pressing on the round disk within the square sleeve, and then pull at the label in the opposite direction. Try to go out of your way to make sure you don't pinch the disk surface.

■ Avoid exposure to dust and cigarette smoke. Foreign particles may not only damage the disk surface, but also can rub off on a diskette drive's read/write heads. Always replace 5 ¼-inch diskettes in their sleeves after removing them from a drive. If they're left lying on a desktop, they may be forgotten and will collect dust at the opening where the disk shows through. (Incidentally, you should know that cigarette smoke can damage hard disks too; they may appear to be completely sealed off from the outside world, but, in fact, they are not.)

■ Keep diskettes away from magnets and any object that produces a strong magnetic field. We are surrounded by magnetic devices, like the bells in telephones and ballasts in fluorescent lights. However, research has shown diskettes to be resistant to damage by most forces other than the direct application of a magnet. But magnets are not uncommon in offices. Occasionally, tools like scissors or screwdrivers become magnetized. And magnets are also sometimes used to hold paper in place, as on some typing stands. Make a careful survey of the objects around your computer, including tools that may occasionally be used to service the computer.

■ Never do anything to physically modify or mutilate a diskette. For example, even though the round diskette does not reach to the corners of the square envelope that contains it, it is a grave error to staple something to it in that area. You should also avoid placing anything else with a floppy diskette in the sheath that accompanies it. It might be tempting to keep a 3-by-5 card beside a diskette to catalog its contents, but the card itself may produce paper dust and can damage the disk surface.

25.3 Avoiding hard disk crashes

How you treat your hard disk will affect how long it lasts. These suggestions will help you maximize a hard disk's lifespan:

■ Avoid turning the machine on and off excessively. Just like an automobile, a hard disk undergoes thermal stress when it is started up, and this ages the drive. Hard disk manufacturers may recommend that you leave your computer on always. However, other computer components age more quickly when the machine is never turned off. A good compromise is to avoid turning the computer on and off more than once a day.

■ Don't locate the computer where it is easily jarred. This is especially true for machines that stand on their side next to a desk, where they may be kicked or struck by chairs. Ask people who will be around the computer to treat it with respect.

■ Don't place an impact printer, like a dot-matrix or daisy wheel printer, on the same surface as the computer. These printers will send constant vibrations to the disk drives as they run, making a hard disk more susceptible to head crashes and other mechanical malfunctions (printer-generated vibrations also tend to throw diskette drives out of alignment).

■ Don't place a computer on its side unless you are certain that the hard disk is manufactured to work in this position. Many hard disks are not, and the bearings that support the hard disk platters may wear out prematurely. Sometimes the disk drive documentation will warn you against running a drive sideways; otherwise, you'll need to call the manufacturer to find out.

■ Keep your hard disk defragmented (as explained in section 21.3). By doing so, fewer movements of the disk's read/write heads are required on average to read or write a file, thus saving wear and tear. Any other optimization of hard disk performance will similarly prolong the drive's life. See Chapter 21 to learn about the measures you can take.

■ Don't smoke around a hard disk. The disk drive may appear to be completely sealed, but in fact there is a minute valve through which air can pass. Very small smoke particles can pass through this valve. Although they may seem minuscule, some of the particles are wider than the distance between the drive's read/write heads and the surface of the disk. When a particle becomes lodged on the disk surface, it can cause a head crash, or can contaminate the heads so that they malfunction.

■ Be sure that the computer is adequately ventilated. High operating temperatures reduce a disk drive's life. When you remove a board from one of the machine's slots, be sure to replace the insert at the back of the machine where the board is exposed (the machine is less cool when there are openings in back). Keep the computer away from heating vents. Something is wrong if a drive is too hot to touch comfortably when the machine is opened after hours of operation. You may need to replace the machine's cooling fan with a more powerful one.

■ Consider installing one of the special hard disk monitoring utilities that have come on the market in recent years. This kind of utility inspects your hard disk every time the machine is booted. It keeps a record of the disk's characteristics and detects discrepancies that may indicate future problems. The utility detects weak format markings and automatically repairs them. Similarly, it senses that the magnetic media within a particular disk sector is no longer holding data well, moves the data elsewhere, and then places the sector off bounds for further use. The utility may even be able to detect large-scale mechanical problems, such as disk wobble.

■ Before moving the computer, make sure that the hard disk is parked. This means that the read/write heads have been positioned so that no damage can be done to the disk if it is jolted. Most newer drives automatically park their heads when the computer is turned off. But older drives may require that you run a program called SHIPDISK just before switching off the machine. Look for the program on diskettes shipped with the drive or the computer. If you can't find a head-parking program, you probably don't need one.

Finally, remember that, no matter how well it's cared for, any hard disk can fail at any time. Try to make frequent and complete backups of all your important data.

25.4 Avoiding file damage

Files are the end product of most computing. They may represent months, even years, of labor. In some cases, an entire enterprise might fail because of the loss of a single file. Yet the majority of computer users make inadequate efforts to protect their files. The best protection for files are frequent, comprehensive backups. But there are also simple measures you can take to stop original files from being damaged in the first place.

Many computer users are under the impression that a head crash in their hard disk is the greatest threat to their files. In a head crash, one or more of the disk's read/write heads slam into the surface of the disk, obliterating data and, in some cases, irreparably damaging the drive. Head crashes are actually much rarer that other kinds of hard disk malfunctions, such as the failure of a disk drive's electronic components.

The greatest physical threats to your data have more subtle origins. Rather than suddenly disappear, data can slowly fade away. One cause is a gradual weakening of the markings that define disk sectors. These are placed on the disk during low-level formatting (see Chapter 16). Because these markings are never renewed (unlike the contents of the disk sectors) they may slowly fade away. Data may also be lost as a drive's mechanics degrade to cause misalignment between the read/write heads and disk surfaces.

The discussion in section 25.3 explains how to avoid hard disk malfunctions. But, having taken the proper measures, you should not be under the impression that your data is perfectly secure. Even greater dangers are posed by software malfunctions, user accidents, and, to a lesser degree, computer viruses. Your concern should focus on these hazards.

Disruptions of file operations   Whenever a program writes data to a file, that file is in a sense momentarily destroyed. If anything happens to disrupt the data transfer, such as a power outage, the file will be left incomplete. In some cases, DOS will consider the file to have a length of zero bytes and won't be able to access it again, even though its data might remain on the disk. Often, even when a file remains intact and has suffered only partial damage, the harm is enough to make the entire file unusable, since some kinds of files must be in perfect condition for their software to be able to use them.

TIP

Rule 1 for avoiding this kind of file damage is to never reboot the computer while a disk drive's indicator light is on (that is, while the indicator light blinks on and off on a hard disk drive, or when it is on at all on a diskette drive).

Utility software   Utility software is very powerful, but it can be hazardous if used without care. File defragmenters (section 21.3) are potentially dangerous, as are any utilities that alter a disk's directories or directory tree, including those that sort directories and prune directory trees. When you select such utilities, make sure they come from a well-established software house. And be sure that your entire disk is backed up before running them. Well-designed utilities will avoid damaging data when power is disrupted as they run. But even when software claims this ability, never reboot to stop a utility midcourse.

Computer viruses   Computer viruses are the final danger to your files. They are particularly insidious since they can hide for long periods before showing themselves, and during that time contaminated files may replace earlier backups. See the discussion in section 25.7 to learn how to avoid infections.

25.5 Avoiding accidental file erasures

A single misstep can cost you hours, days, even months of work through accidental file erasures. If you keep good backups of your data you will be protected against the worst, but recent work may still be lost. The best way of avoiding accidental file erasures is to always approach the DOS ERASE (or DELETE or DEL) commands with great care, especially when you perform mass file erasures using global file name characters (section 1.3). Don't type an ERASE command nonchalantly. Read it over carefully before pressing the ⏎ key. If you are not sure, make files read-only. Read-only files are just that: files that can be read by software, but not written to. Many files, such as program files, are never changed and so can be protected in this way. So can archived data files, like old business letters that are kept on hand for reference, but that will never be modified. Once read-only status is assigned to a file, the file cannot be erased by the DOS DEL, DELETE, or ERASE commands. You need to undo the read-only status to delete the file.

A file is made read-only by using the ATTRIB command, which is explained in detail in section 4.5. Since it's easy to forget how DOS commands work, you can make a batch file that simplifies the task. Create a simple text file named READONLY.BAT and place the following line in it:

```
ATTRIB +R %1
```

Then, to make a file named MYFILE.TXT read only, you need only enter:

```
READONLY MYFILE.TXT ⏎
```

or, adding a directory path:

```
READONLY \LEVEL1\LEVEL2\MYFILE.TXT ⏎
```

The ATTRIB command can as easily undo read-only status, returning a file to normal modifiable (and erasable) form. Again, it's convenient to use a batch file, naming it NORMAL.BAT, and placing in it the single line:

```
ATTRIB -R %1
```

Then enter:

```
NORMAL MYFILE.TXT ⏎
```

to return MYFILE.TXT to normal form. Use a PATH command (section 8.1) to make these batch files available no matter the current directory.

TIP

Utility software that replaces the DOS DEL and ERASE commands with different ones that work to protect your files is available. Instead of erasing a file, these programs move it into a special holding directory, a sort of file graveyard. If you later regret having erased the file, you can retrieve it from this directory. Of course, a hard disk would soon fill with unwanted files. So the utilities maintain only as many erased files as can fit into the disk space you specify for this purpose. When the space is exceeded, older deleted files are physically erased from the disk to make room for more.

Unerase utilities   When the worst happens and a crucial file has been erased, you can try to retrieve it with an unerase utility like the UnErase program in the Norton Utilities. These utilities, which are discussed in section 23.4, are quite reliable when files are recovered shortly after they have been erased, but less so when hours or days have passed. You can substantially increase the chances of a complete recovery by frequently defragmenting your hard disk (see section 21.3). This is a process in which the parts of a file are packed into continuous disk space, making it much easier for unerase software to piece files back together. However, the defragmenter must be run before a file has been accidentally erased. Running a defragmenter after a file has been deleted may make the file much harder to recover.

25.6 Avoiding accidental disk formatting

Good habits, and a well-organized hard disk, make it virtually impossible to accidentally reformat a disk. Unlike the DOS DEL, DELETE, and ERASE commands, which erase files, FORMAT is kept in a separate file apart from the main DOS program COMMAND.COM. Because FORMAT is seldom required, it may be removed from the computer altogether or hidden away so that it cannot be used accidentally.

There are only two reasons to use the FORMAT program: to format a new hard disk or diskette and to reformat an old hard disk or diskette. There are various reasons why one might want to reformat a disk. It can be a good way of achieving a global erasure of files, especially if you wish to guard against someone's using an unerase utility to reclaim deleted files on diskettes (but not on hard disks). Or, when you want to completely rebuild a hard disk's directory tree, it is much easier to reformat the disk than to delete every subdirectory individually. Still, reformatting is seldom necessary.

Rather, FORMAT is nearly always used with new disks. A hard disk can be formatted in minutes and thereafter should function properly for years. It is usually because someone is trying to format a new diskette that hard disks are accidentally reformatted.

TIP

One way to avoid accidental formatting is to replace the DOS FORMAT program with one that is safer to use. For example, the SFORMAT (Safe Format) program in The Norton Utilities lets you avoid complicated FORMAT commands by displaying the screen shown in figure 25.1. This way, there's no confusion about which disk will be formatted and how it will be formatted. SFORMAT formats diskettes the same way hard disks are normally formatted—it erases the root directory and file allocation tables, but doesn't actually erase data. If somehow you do accidentally reformat a diskette using this option, the diskette's data can be recovered using other Norton Utilities. For added protection, SFORMAT can be password protected.

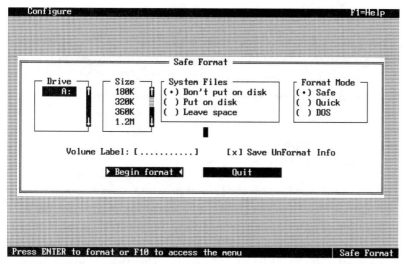

```
 Configure                                              F1=Help


                      ═══ Safe Format ═══
    ┌─ Drive ─┐ ┌─ Size ─┐ ┌─ System Files ──────┐ ┌─ Format Mode ─┐
    │   A:    │ │ 180K  ▓│ │ (•) Don't put on disk│ │ (•) Safe      │
    │         │ │ 320K  ▓│ │ ( ) Put on disk      │ │ ( ) Quick     │
    │         │ │ 360K  ▓│ │ ( ) Leave space      │ │ ( ) DOS       │
    │         │ │ 1.2M  ▓│ └──────────────────────┘ └───────────────┘
    └─────────┘ └────────┘        ▐

        Volume Label: [..........]     [x] Save UnFormat Info
              ▶ Begin format ◀              Quit



 Press ENTER to format or F10 to access the menu      │ Safe Format
```

Figure 25.1

When only DOS is available, the danger of accidental formatting is
readily averted by following these suggestions:

■ When you purchase a box of new diskettes, format them all at the
same time. After finishing with the first, FORMAT will ask you
whether you want to do another. So you can avoid repeatedly
entering another FORMAT command. By formatting ten diskettes at once, you automatically cut the odds of disaster by 90
percent because you will be entering the command 90 percent
fewer times.

■ Don't leave the FORMAT program (the file FORMAT.COM) on
the machine's hard disk if anyone will be using the machine who
might make a serious mistake. In work places, delete FOR-
MAT.COM from all copies of the DOS diskette except those in the
keeping of the person managing the computers. Let that person
format new diskettes.

■ If you do want FORMAT.COM to stay on the machine's hard disk,
but still wish to limit access to it, place it in a directory other than
the one where all other DOS files are kept. As section 5.1 explains,
the DOS directory normally should be named in a PATH command so that any DOS file is on hand no matter the current

directory. But the FORMAT.COM file could be buried deep in another directory so that it can't be used casually.

■ To stop the FORMAT command from being targeted upon the hard disk, rename it, say, to XFORMAT.COM. Then create a batch file named FORMAT.BAT that contains the line:

XFORMAT A:

When you type:

FORMAT [←]

the batch file invokes the format program, directing it automatically to diskette drive A (as usual, the program prompts the user to insert a new diskettes in drive A before it starts formatting). Again, you may use a PATH command to keep both the batch file and the XFORMAT.COM file on-line. Users who type in a dangerous command like FORMAT C: E will still have the command directed toward drive A.

25.7 Preventing infection by computer viruses

You can greatly reduce the chances of infection by a computer virus if you follow some simple suggestions (see section 23.6 to learn how viruses work). There are four lines of defense:

- Prevent viruses from entering your machine in the first place.

- If a virus does manage to enter, detect it immediately and remove damaged files before the infection can spread.

- When the virus has become widespread, remove it by rebuilding your hard disk, or by running a utility program that can (hopefully) remove the virus.

- Adopt practices that protect your floppy diskettes, and especially your backup diskettes or tape, from infection. Doing so ensures that you'll be able to replace damaged files.

Complete protection from viruses can be difficult because—although it's highly unlikely—viruses may even enter your system through commercially distributed software. The only way to be absolutely sure of avoiding infection is by refusing to introduce any new software to a currently virus-free machine. This restriction is hardly acceptable to most users. But there are many techniques for reducing the chances of infection.

Viruses enter a system through modems, through networks, or through diskettes. There is virtually nothing you as an individual user can do about viruses travelling through networks. It is up to the network administration to take the necessary precautions. To prevent infection by modem and diskette, follow these suggestions:

- Install virus detection software that automatically keeps an eye on your hard disk. These vaccine programs, which are discussed in section 23.6, analyze your files to create an index of signatures describing characteristics of each. They periodically reanalyze the files and compare them with their signatures to look for changes—that is, for a viral infection. They'll also look out for inexplicable losses of disk sectors or memory that viruses might occupy. Most are activated by a call from AUTOEXEC.BAT (section 11.1) whenever you boot the machine.

■ Try to acquire public domain software from user group meetings instead of by downloading it from a bulletin board or having it passed to you by diskette from a friend's machine. The diskettes sold at nominal cost during user group meetings usually have been checked for viruses before duplication. Of course, there is no guarantee that a virus has not evaded the best efforts of those in charge.

■ When you do acquire freeware or shareware programs, run a virus detection program on them before copying them to your hard disk. Be aware that a virus can make its way from a diskette to your hard disk without your actually transferring files from the diskette.

■ Don't use pirated software. Even when the copy comes from the original purchaser of the software, it may be contaminated by that person's machine, perhaps by a virus that has not yet made itself apparent (remember, viruses can hide for months before they become active).

■ Keep informed about viruses. Watch for articles in the computer press and read the latest gossip on computer bulletin boards. Computer viruses tend to pass through the computer world as epidemics, much like biological viruses. It's useful to know which viruses are particularly virulent, how they circulate, what they attack, their symptoms, and how they may be detected.

■ Keep track of who you share files with and when the transfer occurred. When you discover an infection on your system, warn others. You may be well repaid for keeping in touch with others, even if it is you who spreads a virus, because the virus may become active on the recipient's machine before it does on yours, giving you advance warning.

■ On machines used by many people, acquire a security shell to prevent unauthorized copying of files onto the hard disk, or running of programs from a diskette drive. A good shell can prevent unauthorized modem access as well.

■ If you work in an office that has many computers, and you wish to use or evaluate many programs, consider quarantining one machine for this purpose. Allow no diskettes to travel between it and other machines, and take extra care with backups. The machine may still be used for other purposes, but restrict it to tasks for which a graceful recovery can be made should a massive viral infection occur.

■ To guard against the very worst outcome of a viral invasion—complete infection of your backups as well as your hard disk files—periodically make a global backup that will be kept indefinitely.

Glossary

8086　　A microprocessor chip similar to the 8088 microprocessor used in IBM PCs, XTs, and compatibles. It accesses memory two bytes at a time, as compared to one byte at a time in an 8088 chip.

8088　　The microprocessor chip used in IBM PCs, XTs, and compatibles. The 8088 is a 16-bit chip, meaning that it performs its calculations two bytes at a time, but accesses memory one byte at a time.

80286　　The microprocessor chip used in IBM ATs and some PS/2 models. It is a 16-bit chip, which means that it processes data two bytes at a time; it also accesses memory two bytes at a time.

80386　　The microprocessor chip used in the IBM PS/2 model 80 and other advanced machines, including many AT-style clones. The 80386 is a 32-bit chip, meaning that it accesses memory and performs calculations four bytes at a time. The 80386 chip is fast becoming the industry standard.

80386 SX　　A less-expensive version of the 80386 microprocessor. It differs from the 80386 chip chiefly in that it accesses memory only two bytes at a time, although it still processes data four bytes at a time.

80486　　The most recent microprocessor chip, used only in the fastest machines. Like the 80386 chip, it is a 32-bit microprocessor, accessing memory and performing calculations four bytes at a time.

8514/A　　An advanced, high-resolution video adapter originally designed for PS/2 computers.

*　　A global file name character representing any number of file name characters. In the DOS command, COPY AB*.TXT A: ⏎, the asterisk matches any number of characters following AB; thus, the files ABCDE.TXT, ABWXYZ.TXT, and AB.TXT would all be copied.

?　　A global file name character replacing a single character in a file name. In the DOS command, COPY AB?DEFGH.TXT A: ⏎, the question mark matches any character in the third position in the file name. The files ABCDEFGH.TXT, ABXDEFGH.TXT, and AB3DE-FGH.TXT would all be copied.

accelerator board   An expansion board that substitutes a faster microprocessor in place of the one that comes with the machine.

active directory   The directory to which DOS directs its activities when no other directory is specified in DOS commands.

adapter   See *expansion board.*

Alt   A keyboard shift key that is used in combination with alphabet keys and function keys to create additional keystrokes. Most software uses combinations of the Ctrl key and alphabet keys to send commands to software, but Alt key combinations are also used when a large number of commands are available.

APPEND   A DOS command that configures DOS to automatically search for data files (and sometimes program files) in specified directories when the files do not appear in the current directory.

application program   Software that processes data—word processors, data bases, spreadsheet programs, accounting packages, and so on. Application programs contrast with utility programs, such as file unerase programs or file backup programs, which are used to manage the computer rather than to attain some final purpose.

archive attribute   A file attribute that, when set, indicates that a file has been changed and should be copied when backup software is next run. The backup software turns off the attribute after it makes the backup. DOS turns the attribute back on if the file is changed again.

archiving   The storage of seldom-accessed data on diskettes or magnetic tape. Archiving makes space available on a hard disk for new data.

ASCII character   A character taken from the ASCII character set, which includes all alphabetic characters, numerals and punctuation marks, and special characters that have meaning only to the computer. Each character has its own code number, from 0 to 127. (ASCII stands for American Standard Code for Information Interchange).

ASCII file   See *text file.*

ASSIGN   A DOS command that assigns a different drive specifier to a disk drive.

ATTRIB   A DOS command that reads and sets file attributes (that is, it makes changes in a file's attribute byte).

attribute   See *file attribute.*

attribute byte   A byte of information that is held in the directory entry of every file. The byte keeps track of various file attributes, such as whether the file is read-only, whether it has been changed since it was last backed up, and so on.

AUTOEXEC.BAT   A file automatically read by DOS when the machine is switched on. It may contain any number of DOS commands which are automatically executed at start-up. The file is optional, and DOS proceeds with standard booting when it does not find this file at start-up.

automatic head parking   The automatic movement of a hard disk's read/write heads to a landing strip when the machine is turned off. Once positioned this way, the heads cannot damage the disk's surface if the machine is jolted.

average seek time   The average time, measured in milliseconds, required for a disk drive's read/write heads to move from one track to another across the disk surface. A measure of disk drive performance.

background backup   A backup of the files on a hard disk that proceeds automatically in the background (invisibly) while the computer is used for other purposes.

background printing   The process of sending output to a printer in the background while using the computer for some other task.

backup program   Software that scans a hard disk for altered or new data files and makes copies of them on diskettes or tape cartridges.

backups   Extra copies of data files made for safe keeping.

bad sector   A disk sector that cannot reliably hold data because of a flaw on the disk surface or damaged format markings.

bad track table   A label affixed to the casing of a hard disk drive indicating tracks that are flawed and cannot hold data. The information is entered into the low-level formatting program before it formats the disk.

.BAT   A file name extension given to batch files. When a file with a .BAT extension is entered on the DOS command line as if it were a program to run, DOS recognizes the extension and proceeds to execute each line of the file as if it were a DOS command.

batch file   A file containing a series of DOS commands that are executed in sequence when the file is run as if it were a program. All batch files have a .BAT file name extension.

baud rate   A measure of data transmission speed used for modems and networks. The baud rate is used in the same sense as the bits-per-second rate.

bit   One of the eight on/off settings that constitute a byte of data. Sometimes a bit will act as an indicator flag. For example, every file has in its directory entry a byte in which particular bits are set to on or off depending on whether the file is read-only, hidden, and so on.

bits-per-second rate   The rate at which a device, such as a modem, communicates with the computer. As a rule of thumb, the bits-per-second rate divided by ten tells roughly how many bytes per second are transmitted.

BIOS   The Basic Input-Output System. Part of the computer's operating system that is built into the machine, rather than read from a disk drive at start-up.

board   See *expansion board.*

booting   The process of starting up the machine. It means to pull up by the boot straps, and consists of a series of operations in which the computer reads in the main operating system file COMMAND.COM from drive A or drive C, and then reads the contents of the CONFIG.SYS and AUTOEXEC.BAT files to configure the machine, load device drivers, and carry out predefined DOS commands.

boot record   A disk sector filled with information used to boot the computer. It is created when the disk is formatted.

boot security   The ability of security software to circumvent a break-in made by restarting the computer with a boot diskette in drive A (thus preventing the security software on drive C from automatically loading).

Break   See *Ctrl-Break.*

buffer   A temporary holding area in memory for data. See also *DOS buffers.*

bug   A fault in software or hardware that causes it to malfunction.

bus   The system of circuitry that ties together different parts of the computer, including the expansion slots.

byte   The basic unit of computer memory. One byte holds one character of data (one letter of the alphabet).

caching   A process in which frequently accessed data is kept on hand, rather than constantly being from the place where it is stored. See also *disk caching.*

Caps Lock   A keyboard key that shifts the alphabet keys to uppercase, just like the caps lock key on a typewritter.

card   See *expansion board.*

central processing unit   The microprocessor chip that does most of the work in a computer (CPU).

CGA   See *Color Graphics Adapter.*

check box   Check boxes are small squares drawn inside the dialog boxes that some software uses to communicate with the user. When a check box is checked (contains an X), the feature associated with the box (such as print page numbers) is enabled. The box is checked and unchecked through a mouse or the keyboard.

CHDIR   A DOS command that changes the current directory, that is, the directory to which DOS directs its operations by default when no directory is expressly named in a DOS command.

child directory   A subdirectory within a directory. In \PLANTS\ TREES\WILLOWS, TREES is a child directory of PLANTS, and WILLOWS is a child directory of TREES.

chip   See *integrated circuit.*

CHKDSK   A DOS utility that looks for errors on disks. It detects errors in directories and in the allocation of disk space, but does not sense imperfections on the disk surface or failing format markings.

clicking   In using a mouse, one is said to click the mouse on an object appearing on the screen when one moves the mouse cursor over that object and then presses and releases a mouse button.

clock speed   See *processor speed.*

cluster   The basic unit of allocation of disk space. A cluster is a collection of contiguous disk sectors, usually four sectors on hard disks, often one or two on diskettes. When DOS needs more disk space for a file, it takes it one cluster at a time, not one sector at a time.

Color Graphics Adapter   The earliest IBM graphics video adapter. It can display no more than 16 colors at once, operating in low resolution, or 2 colors in medium resolution.

.COM   A file name extension that appears only on program files.

command   A series of words or symbols typed in at the DOS prompt to tell DOS what to do next (such as to load a program, copy a file, etc.).

COMMAND.COM   The main DOS program. It is loaded automatically when the machine starts up. COMMAND.COM normally remains in memory the entire time the machine is in operation. Sometimes part is overwritten by applications programs, and this transient part of COMMAND.COM must be reloaded from disk when the an application terminates.

command line   The area to the right of the DOS prompt where you type in commands to tell DOS what to do next.

command line parameter   A word, number, or symbol typed in a DOS command to specify how the command should work. For example, many DOS commands require parameters to specify which file a command should operate on. In the expression COPY MYFILE.TXT A:, the COPY command has two parameters, the first of which names the file that is to be copied (MYFILE.TXT), and the second of which indicates the destination of the copy, in this case drive A.

communications   The process of sending data between two computers.

compression   See *file compression.*

conditional test   A situation in which if a condition is met (for example, there has been an error) one set of instructions are followed, whereas if the condition has not been met (there has not been an error) a different set of instructions are followed.

CONFIG.SYS   A file automatically read by DOS when the computer is booted. It contains information for configuring the computer, such as the names of device drivers to load, the number of DOS buffers to create, and so on. The file is optional.

configuration   The process of tailoring hardware or software so that it operates properly with all other hardware and software that is being used at the same time.

configuration file   A file that holds information that hardware or software uses to configure itself when it starts up.

console   The combination of keyboard and screen.

controller card   See *disk controller card.*

control code   A code typed at the keyboard to send a command to software running in the computer. Control codes often use the Ctrl key. For example, Ctrl-O might mean open a file.

conventional memory   Memory used by DOS, consisting of up to 640K (kilobytes). All machines have conventional memory, and so it is often referred to simply as memory.

copy protection   A system for discouraging software piracy by making it impossible to copy a program. Most copy-protection schemes work by specially modifying the diskettes on which the software is distributed, or by modifying a hard disk when the copy-protected software is installed.

coprocessor   An integrated circuit chip that works in tandem with the computer's main microprocessor. The best known coprocessors are math coprocessors, which perform certain kinds of mathematical calculations more quickly, and with greater accuracy, than the microprocessor can.

CPU   See *central processing unit.*

CPU speed   See *processor speed.*

crash   Any malfunction that brings work to a halt. A hard disk crash or head crash may entail physical damage to a disk drive. A system crash, on the other hand, usually is caused by a software malfunction, and it can ordinarily be remedied by rebooting the machine.

cross-linked files   Two files that have been crossed, such that both share the final portion of one of the files. This problem is caused by an error in the file allocation table of the disk holding the files.

Ctrl   A keyboard key used in combination with other keys, mostly A through Z, to send commands to software.

Ctrl-Break   The keystroke combination of the Ctrl and Break keys that can be used to break out of a program and return to DOS if you run into trouble and cannot exit a program normally.

current directory   The directory to which DOS directs its activities when no directory is specified in DOS commands. For example, when the current directory is C:\DOS, the command DIR ⏎ would give a directory listing for the DOS directory on drive C, whereas the command DIR C:\UTIL ⏎ would list a directory other than the current directory—the UTIL directory. The current directory is set through the CHDIR command.

current drive   The drive to which DOS directs its activities when no other drive is specified in DOS commands. When the DOS prompt is A>, drive A is the current drive. In this case, the command DIR ⏎ would give a directory listing for drive A since no drive is specified in the command (for example, DIR B: ⏎, which would give the directory of drive B).

cursor   A pointer on the screen. In text modes, the cursor is usually a blinking underline character, or a blinking box. In graphics modes, it may be an arrow, a vertical bar, or some other symbol. The cursor marks the position in the data shown on the screen that will next be affected by your actions. For example, characters you type on the keyboard normally appear on the screen at the current cursor position. The cursor is moved to another position with the keyboard cursor keys or a mouse.

cylinder   Hard disk drives have multiple platters, with parallel concentric tracks on each side. A read/write head is associated with each side of each platter, all heads moving in parallel. The group of all tracks at a given head position forms a cylinder. The concept is useful because all sectors in a cylinder can be read or written to without moving the read/write heads; the more sectors in a cylinder, the more potentially efficient the disk drive.

cylinder density   The number of sectors in a cylinder on a hard disk drive. That is, the number of sectors that can be read without moving the drive's read/write heads.

data decryption   See *data encryption.*

data encryption   The transformation of data into a form that can't be read without a password. Both encryption and decryption (the restoration of encrypted data to its original form) are performed by special software.

data file   A file containing data (as opposed to a program file, which contains code). All files that are not program files are actually data files. Usually, the term data file refers to files that you create for your own purposes (such as a letter or spreadsheet), rather than data files the program creates for its own purposes (such as a configuration file the program uses to store data by which it configures itself).

data transfer rate   The rate at which data is transferred between a disk drive and system memory.

deallocated cluster   A cluster of disk space that was once occupied by a file but is now free.

DEBUG   A DOS program used to examine what is happening in the computer's microprocessor or memory. DEBUG can also modify files, and so it is sometimes used for repairing software.

decryption   See *data encryption.*

default directory   The directory in a directory tree to which DOS directs its actions by default unless some other directory is specified. When a disk has no directory tree, its root directory (the only directory it has) is the default directory.

default drive   The disk drive to which DOS directs its actions when no other drive is specifically named by means of a drive specifier (such as A:). The DOS prompt normally indicates the default drive; when it is A>, drive A is the default drive. In this case, the command DIR r causes DOS to give a directory listing from drive A, since no other drive has been indicated in the command. On the other hand, the command DIR B: r would give a directory listing from drive B even while drive A remains the default drive.

defragmentation   See *file defragmentation*.

defragmenter   Utility software for defragmenting files. See *file defragmentation*.

Del   A keyboard key whose function varies from program to program. Del stands for delete, and usually it removes the character under which the cursor rests (the backspace key, on the other hand, removes the character preceeding the one marked by the cursor).

device   An electronic, and possibly mechanical, device that is connected to the computer and interacts with it. Printers, plotters, modems, mice, scanners, and disk drives are all devices. Nonstandard devices require the installation of a device driver for DOS to be able to communicate with them.

DEVICE   A DOS command (placed in the CONFIG.SYS file) that makes DOS load a device driver into memory when the machine is booted.

device driver   A memory-resident program that lets the computer control a device, like a plotter or expanded memory board. Device drivers are loaded into memory by DOS DEVICE commands.

dialog box   A small window opened on the screen by software to convey messages about what is happening in the software, or to ask you for information the software needs to do its work. For example, when you print a document, a dialog box may open to ask how to set page margins, page numbering, and so on. Similarly, if an error occurs during printing, a dialog box may open to tell you about it.

dip switch   A miniature switch found on circuit boards that is used to configure hardware.

direct memory access (DMA)   Electronic circuitry that transfers data between computer memory and a peripheral, such as a disk drive, without passing the data through the microprocessor chip. DMA allows computers to operate more quickly.

directory   A collection of information about a group of files on a disk. Directories tell the names of the files, their sizes, and the times and dates they were created or last modified. Directories also keep track of each file's starting location on the disk.

directory listing   The display of information about some or all files in a directory.

directory path   The sequence of directories that leads from the root directory in a directory tree to a particular subdirectory. For example, the directory path \MAMMALS\AQUATIC\DOLPHINS tells that the DOLPHINS subdirectory is listed in the AQUATIC subdirectory, which is listed in the MAMMALS subdirectory, which is listed in the root directory (the initial backslash stands for the root directory). The complete directory path to a file named FLIPPER in the DOLPHINS subdirectory would be \MAMMALS\AQUATIC\DOL-PHINS\FLIPPER.TXT. A directory path may also include a leading drive specifier , such as C:. When the directory tree is located on drive C:, the complete path would be C:\MAMMALS\AQUATIC\DOLPHINS\ FLIPPER.

directory tree   A hierarchy of directories that begins with a root directory that contains a number of level 1 subdirectories, each of which may contain level 2 subdirectories, and so on.

disk caching   A process in which recently accessed or frequently accessed disk sectors are kept in memory so that they can be quickly retrieved when software requires them again. The apparent speed of a hard disk can be tripled by this measure.

disk controller   Electronics that mediate the transfer of data between disk drives and the computer's memory.

disk read   The act of reading one or more sectors of data from a disk.

disk drive   A unit that reads and writes data stored on a disk.

disk sector   See *sector*.

disk write   The act of writing one or more sectors of data to a disk.

diskette   A removable disk contained in either a floppy 5 ¼ sleeve or a 3 ½ rigid casing.

distribution diskettes   The original diskettes upon which software is sold.

DMA   See *direct memory access*.

DMA channel   Circuitry that allows data to travel directly between disk drives and memory, without passing through the computer's microprocessor. A computer may have several DMA channels.

DOS   Disk Operating System. The basic software required to run and manage the computer. The main DOS program, COMMAND.COM, is loaded into the computer's memory at start-up and remains there throughout operation.

DOS buffers   Small holding areas in system memory through which data passes on its way to and from disk drives.

DOS command line   The line on the screen at which a DOS prompt (such as A> or C>) appears. It is called a command line because it is the place where DOS commands are typed in.

DOS error message   A message displayed by DOS when an error has occured while trying to execute a DOS command. Occasionally a DOS error message appears when application software has tried to use DOS and run into trouble.

DOS path   See *directory path*.

DOS prompt   The symbol DOS writes on the screen to indicate that it is waiting for a command. The normal DOS prompt tells the current drive: A>, B>, C> and so on. The DOS PROMPT command can alter the form of the prompt.

DOS shell   A program that extends the capabilities of DOS and makes it easier to use.

download   To transfer files into your computer by modem.

drive   See *disk drive.*

drive geometry   The specifications that define a disk drive's capacity: the number of platters it holds, the number of tracks on each side of each platter, and the number of sectors in each track.

drive specifier   A symbol used in DOS commands to tell which disk drive an operation should be directed to. For example, the symbols A:, B:, and C: are all drive specifiers.

EDLIN   A primitive text editor provided by DOS for making batch files and configuration files.

EGA   See *Enhanced Graphics Adapter.*

EMS   The extended memory specification. See *extended memory.*

encryption   See *data encryption.*

Enhanced Graphics Adapter   A video adapter that includes the capability of the Monochrome Display Adapter and the Color Graphics Adapter, and adds several advanced modes that use up to 64 colors.

End   A keyboard key situated on the numeric keypad that often is used to scroll a document to its end.

environment   A list of information about the computer's configuration that is maintained by DOS and made available to all programs. The SET command can add information to the environment and its current contents can be viewed by typing SET ⏎.

errorlevel code   A code transmitted to DOS when a program terminates. It tells whether the program was able to do its work successfully. Batch files can intercept errorlevel codes and use them to decide what to do next.

error message   A message displayed by DOS or a program to inform you that you have done something wrong, or that something has gone wrong with the computer hardware, the software in operation, or the data with which the software is working. The DOS manual includes a listing of error messages, as does the documentation accompanying many programs.

Esc   See *escape key.*

escape key   A keyboard key usually used to escape from or cancel a situation. For example, if you start to enter a command but change your mind, striking ' may cancel the command. Similarly, Esc is often used to move from a submenu back to the menu in which it was listed.

escape sequence   A sequence of characters that forms a command for controlling a printer, modem, or other device. The sequence begins with an escape character (ASCII character 27).

.EXE   A file name extension that appears only on program files.

expanded memory   A way of adding additional memory to any kind of IBM microcomputer by installing a specially designed memory board. Software must be tailored to use this kind of memory.

expansion board   A circuit board that may be inserted in one of the computer's empty slots. Expansion boards are used to add memory, input/output ports, modems, and many other kinds of hardware.

expansion slot   An oblong socket inside a computer. A circuit board can be plugged into an expansion slot to expand the machine's capabilities. Most computers have several slots.

extended boot record   A boot record that begins each volume of an extended DOS partition. The machine uses these records for identifying and managing the partitions, not for actual booting.

extended memory   Memory beyond the one megabyte that can be accessed by all IBM PCs. PC ATs and PS/2s can have extended memory; PC XTs cannot. Most software running under DOS cannot use extended memory.

extended partition   In DOS 3.3, a hard disk may have two partitions that serve DOS—an ordinary, bootable partition (called the primary partition) and an extended partition, which may contain any number of volumes of up to 32 megabytes each.

extension   See *file name extension*.

external command   A DOS command that is performed by software held in a file separate from the main COMMAND.COM program that is kept in memory at all times. An external command can't be used unless the required file is in the current directory, or is accessed by a directory path or a PATH command.

FASTOPEN　A DOS command that initiates a time-saving feature in which DOS keeps track of the placement of files it has already opened once.

FAT　See *file allocation table.*

FCB　See *file control block.*

FCBS　A seldom-used DOS command that increases the number of file control blocks available to programs.

FDISK　The standard DOS utility for partitioning hard disks.

file　A collection of information given an identifying name and stored on disk. A file may hold pages of text, the numbers in a spreadsheet, the instructions that form a program like a word processor, and many other kinds of information as well.

file allocation table　A table of numbers kept on every diskette or hard disk to keep track of the contents of each disk sector. Chains of numbers in this table report the sequences of sectors that make up individual files.

file attribute　One of several markings kept in the directory entry of every file to defines special characteristics of the file, such as that it is a read-only file.

file compression　The reduction of files to a smaller size so that they will take up less disk space. File compression utilities may link into DOS to automatically compress files as they are written and automatically uncompress them as they are read.

file control block　A small block of memory initialized by DOS when it opens a file. File control blocks are now obsolete and are only found in old PC software.

file defragmentation　A process in which utility software rearranges the placement of files on disk. A file that is dispersed over the disk surface takes longer to read or write, since the disk drive's read/write heads must make more motions to reach the file's sectors. Defragmentation software rearranges the sectors into consecutive sectors in adjacent tracks.

file locking   In networks, the temporary denial of access to a file to anyone other than the person currently working on it. Locking prevents people from undoing each other's work.

file name   A word of from one to eight characters assigned to a file when it is created. A file name extension of up to three characters may optionally be appended to the file name, with a period separating them (as in MYFILE.TXT).

file name extension   A tag added to the end of a file name, and separated from the file name by a period. For example, .TXT is the extension in MYFILE.TXT. Extensions are used to classify files. Some extensions always have the same meaning. For example, the extensions .EXE and .COM indicate program files (files containing software), and .BAT indicates a batch file. Other extensions are defined by application software, or by the person who creates the file. Thus a word processor might always append .DOC to a file name, or a user might assign .DOC to files to mark them as documents.

file recovery   Techniques for repairing and reassembling files that have been damaged by failures in hardware (such as bad disk sectors) or in software (such as files that have become fused with others).

file server   A computer that runs under special software to serve shared files to workstatioms in on a local area network.

filter   A program through which the output of some DOS commands are altered. For example, the SORT filter sorts the output of commands like DIR.

FIND   A DOS command that searches files for a specified line of text.

fixed disk   Another name for a hard disk. See *hard disk drive*.

floppy disk   See *diskette*.

formatting   For disks, formatting is the process of writing magnetic lines on the disk surface to define tracks and sectors, and the installation of structures used by DOS to keep track of files, such as the root directory and the file allocation table. Formatting may optionally add files to the disk that allow the disk to be used for booting the computer.

formatted capacity   A disk's capacity in bytes after it has been formatted. The formatted capacity is usually several percent less than its unformatted capacity because disk space is lost between sectors.

form feed   On computer printers, a form feed causes the page last printed upon to be forwarded (or ejected), and a new page to be aligned at top of form. Most printers have a form feed switch. Normally, it operates only when the printer is off-line (deselected).

fragmentation   The dispersal of disk sectors belonging to one file to nonadjacent positions on a disk. Fragmented files take longer to read and write because more motions of the disk drive's read/write heads are required.

freeware   Software that is shared with others free of change.

full track buffering   A kind of disk caching in which an entire disk track is read whenever only part of it is required. Statistically, other sectors from the track are likely to be required next, and so they will already be in memory, thus avoiding redundant mechanical activity. Full track buffering may be handled either by specially designed hardware, or by disk caching software. It is most efficient on very fast hard disks.

function key   One of ten or more keys found on any IBM-style keyboard, number F1 , F2 , F3 , and so on. Software may assign special uses to each key so that, for example, striking F6 causes a program to open a new file. Additional functions may be made available by combinations with the ⇧ and Alt keys, such as ⇧-F4 or ⇧-F4 . Every program uses the keys in its own way.

global backup   A backup of every file on a hard disk, whether it has been changed since the last backup or not.

global file name characters   Two special characters—the asterisk (*) and question mark (?)—that may be inserted in file names within DOS commands to designate a group of files.

graphical user interface   A way of presenting information on the screen in which a program is operated by a system of icons, pull-down menus, windows, and dialog boxes. Graphical user interfaces work best with, and sometimes require, a mouse.

graphics mode   See *video mode*.

GUI   See *graphical user interface*.

hard disk   See *hard disk drive*.

hard disk crash   Any mechanical failure of a hard disk drive. The term crash comes from head crash, in which the disk drive's read/write heads slam into the disk surface, destroying data and perhaps themselves. Most hard disk disasters result not from a mechanical crash, but from damage to DOS structures that keep track of data, including directories and file allocation tables.

hard disk drive   A disk drive that uses multiple, nonremovable platters turning nonstop at high speed to store much more data than can fit on a diskette, and to access the data more quickly.

hard error   An error that occurs because of a continuing hardware failure. Compare to soft error.

hardware configuration   The job of setting up hardware so that it can work with DOS and software without conflicting with other hardware. Hardware configuration is performed by setting switches on the hardware, by running special configuration software, and by installing device driver software to control the hardware.

hardware installation   The process of physically inserting, connecting, or cabling hardware to the computer.

head   See *read/write head*.

head crash   A kind of hard disk failure in which the drive's read/write heads slam into the disk surface. Usually data is destroyed, a problem that, at best, may be confined to only a file or two, and at worst may wreck directories and other DOS structures so that massive amounts of data are made inaccessible.

head seek   The motion of a disk drive's read/write heads from one disk track to another.

Hercules Graphics Card   A non-IBM video standard—much supported by business software—that provides black-and-white text and black-and-white medium-resolution graphics. Video adapters that follow this standard are often called monographics adapters.

hexadecimal number   A number counted in base 16, a system that uses the letters A through F as well as the numerals 0 through 9. The numbers are counted 0, 1, 2, 3, 4, 5, 6, 7, 8, 9, A, B, C, D, E, F, 10, 11, and so on. These numbers are sometimes employed in configuring memory expansion cards.

HGC   See *Hercules Graphics Card.*

hidden attribute   A file attribute that, when set, causes a file to be omitted from directory listings.

hidden file   A file for which the hidden attribute is set, such that it is omitted from directory listings. DOS leaves two hidden files in the root directory of every disk. Others may be created by software, although generally they are not.

high-level format   The part of disk formatting in which structures required by DOS are written on the disk, including the boot record, root directory, and file allocation tables.

Home   A keyboard key situated on the numeric keypad that often is used to scroll a document to its beginning.

hot key   A keystroke combination that brings a memory-resident program into action.

IBMBIO.COM and **IBMDOS.COM**   Two files kept in the root directory of every boot disk that DOS requires to start up the computer. These are hidden files not shown in a directory listing.

icon   A graphic symbol displayed on a computer's screen to represent data or actions upon data. For example, the symbol of a page with writing on it could represent a file, while arrows on the symbol could mean reformat the file. Typically, a mouse is clicked on the icon to access data or operate on it.

incremental backup   A backup of all files that have been changed since the last backup was made.

Ins   A keyboard key that generally is used to toggle back and forth between insertion mode and overwrite mode when entering text or data into software. In insertion mode, each incoming character is inserted between the character under which the cursor lies and the one before. In overwrite mode, the incoming character replaces the character above the cursor.

installation   The process of physically moving and connecting hardware or software to a computer. Hardware installation consists of inserting expansion boards into slots and connecting cables. Software installation usually entails copying files to a hard disk. In addition, configuration may be required to tailor the hardware or software to your system.

installation program   A utility program, shipped with many application programs, that transfers files from the distribution diskettes to a hard disk in your machine. It may also help you configure the software at the same time so that it matches your printer, video display, and so on. The program is usually named INSTALL and is started up by typing INSTALL ⏎.

integrated circuit   An electronic component containing many thousands of miniturized circuits. Often called a chip.

interface card   An expansion board that connects a computer to an external device, such as a modem, plotter, or local area network.

interleave   In disk formatting, the interleave is the numbering of sectors on a track so that the next sector arrives at the read/write heads just as the computer is ready to access it.

interleave factor   The number of sectors that pass beneath a disk drive's read/write heads before the next numbered sector arrives. For example, when the interleave factor is 3:1, a sector is read, two pass by, and then the next is read.

internal command   A DOS command that resides in the main COMMAND.COM file that is always in memory, such that the command is always available for your use.

interrupt   A brief interruption of the computer's activity so that an urgent task can be performed. For example, a modem may interrupt the computer every time it receives a character of data from a telephone line, requesting that the character be stored in the computer's memory. Interrupts constantly occur in a computer, but happen so quickly that they generally go unnoticed by the user.

interrupt vector　A computer may use up to 256 interrupts, and, loosely speaking, the number of each interrupt, from 0 to 255, is the interrupt vector. (The vector is actually a memory address associated with this number). When configuring hardware, you may be called upon to specify an unused interrupt vector that the hardware can employ to interrupt the machine.

JOIN　A DOS command that can link a directory on one drive into a directory tree on another drive.

jumper　A primitive kind of switch found on the surface of some expansion boards. The jumper is a tiny box that connects pins protruding from the board. You may need to change jumpers to configure a board to your system.

K　See *kilobyte*.

keyboard macro　A sequence of keystrokes that is recorded and then associated with a single keystroke, such that the whole sequence is sent to the computer when the single keystroke is typed.

keyboard macro file　A file holding a set of keyboard macro assignments. Loading a different file customizes the keyboard layout for a different purpose.

key disk　A diskette that must reside in a diskette drive for a program to run, even if the program is installed on a hard disk. Key disks are sometimes shipped with copy-protected software.

kilobyte　1,024 bytes. The prefix kilo means one thousand, so this term is an approximation. If you have ten kilobytes of disk space available (10K), you have 10,240 bytes, not 10,000).

LAN　See *local area network*.

label　In a batch file, a word that marks a position in the file. Labels begin with a colon, as in :BEGIN or :END. GOTO statements in the file can cause control to jump to the point in the file marked by the label.

landing strip　A track on a hard disk, usually the innermost, to which the drive's read/write heads are retracted when the machine is turned off. No data is recorded on this track.

level 1 subdirectory   A subdirectory immediately above the root directory of a directory tree and thus one that is listed in the root directory. Level 1 subdirectories hold level 2 subdirectories in turn, and so on.

line feed   The turn of a printer platen (roller) by the height of one printed line.

listing   See *directory listing.*

loading   The process of moving data from disk to system memory. A program is loaded into memory and then run. Similarly, data is loaded from disk into memory when a file is loaded.

local area network   A system in which two or more microcomputers are linked together to share files and peripherals such as printers.

logical drive   A disk drive regarded from the point of view of a DOS prompt. A single hard disk may be partitioned into two or more logical drives named C>, D>, and so on. Conversely, special software can combine the space on two physical hard disk drives so that they appear as one logical drive.

low-level formatting   Formatting that lays down markings on a blank disk surface to define disk sectors. The root directory and other structures are created by high-level formatting.

M   See *megabyte.*

main group   In the DOS 4.0 SHELL, the main group is the group of programs and subgroups that appears on the screen when you first start up the shell. It is the main menu to the shell.

master boot record   A sector of data used during booting by hard disks. It contains essential information about the disk and tells the starting location of the various partitions.

math coprocessor   An integrated circuit chip that works in tandem with the computer's main microprocessor to perform certain kinds of mathematical calculations much more quickly.

MCGA   See *Multicolor Graphics Array.*

MDA   See *Monochrome Display Adapter.*

mean time between failure   A manufacturer's specification telling the average time a device will run before it breaks down and requires repair. MTBF is usually measured in thousands or tens of thousands of hours.

MHz   See *megahertz*.

megabyte   One million bytes.

megaHertz   A million cycles per second. A 12-megaHertz computer uses an internal electronic clock that pulses twelve million times a second. The pulse sets the tempo at which the microprocessor and other components operate.

memory   A holding area in which the computer keeps programs and data when they are in use. Memory is not to be confused with disk storage. The computer cannot use information while it is stored on disks. It must transfer it to memory (that is, to memory chips inside the machine), work with it, and then write it back to disk.

memory allocation   The process of deciding which programs will be used, and how they will be used, so that they can all fit into memory at once. Besides application programs, memory can hold device drivers, memory-resident programs, and operating environments like a DOS shell. Some of these programs, such as RAM disks and disk caching programs, can take up large amounts of memory to hold data. Besides deciding which programs to load, you may also need to decide in which kind of memory a program is to reside: conventional, extended, or expanded.

memory-resident program   A program that stays in memory after it terminates. When started up, most memory-resident programs display a message saying that they have been loaded and then they quit immediately. Thereafter, the program can usually be awakened by pressing a special key combination (the hot key). These pop-up programs include a wide variety of calendars, calculators, notepads, and other utilities. Memory-resident programs are also known as TSRs, or terminate-and-stay-resident programs.

menu   A list of software commands or options from which you may make a selection, either by typing a keystroke combination associated with an option, or by clicking on the option with a mouse. Menus save you the trouble of memorizing the commands.

menu bar   A menu whose options are displayed (usually) along the top line of the screen. Each menu selection opens downward into a vertical submenu called a pull-down menu. A pull-down menu is activated by clicking a mouse over a menu bar selection, or by entering a code from the keyboard—often the first letter of the menu selection's name.

menu program   Utility software that makes a computer easier to use by letting you run programs and use basic DOS commands simply by making menu selections.

MicroChannel   The bus design (the system used to interconnect expansion boards with the computer's main circuitry) employed in most PS/2 machines. The MicroChannel bus has potential performance advantages over earlier designs.

microprocessor   The main integrated circuit chip that does most of the computer's work. A number of microprocessor models operate in IBM PCs, including the 8086, 8088, 80286, 80386, and 80486. A microprocessor is also called a central processing unit or CPU.

millisecond   One-thousandth of a second.

modem   A device that lets you hook your computer up to a telephone line to communicate data. Internal modems are an expansion board residing in one of the machine's slots. External modems are housed in a separate case outside the computer and connect to a serial port at the back of the machine.

monitor   See *video monitor.*

Monochrome Display Adapter   An early, text-only video system that has no color capability.

monographics adapter   See *Hercules Graphics Card.*

MORE   A word used in some DOS commands, such as DIR and TYPE, to cause the command to display only a screenful of information at a time, waiting until you strike a key before showing the next.

motherboard   The computer's main circuit board. Usually the motherboard has a number of slots into which expansion boards may be inserted.

mouse   A palm-sized box connected to the computer that, when moved across a desk top, causes the screen cursor to move in a similar direction. A mouse has one or more buttons that can be pushed (clicked) to execute commands. For example, the cursor may be moved over a menu selection and a mouse button clicked to make the selection.

mouse driver   Software that interprets the motions of a mouse and communicates the information to programs. A mouse driver is a kind of device driver that is loaded into memory when the machine starts up.

ms   A millisecond—one thousandth of a second.

MTBF   See *mean time between failure.*

Multicolor Graphics Array   The video standard used in model 25 and 30 PS/2 computers. It resembles the VGA standard used in other PS/2 machines, but lacks the VGA's most advanced modes.

multifunction board   An expansion board that provides more than one service, such as adding both additional memory and additional ports to a machine.

multisync monitor   A kind of video monitor that can work with a variety of video adapters in spite of their varying technical characteristics.

multitasking   A system in which two or more programs can run at the same time in a computer. The computer switches back and forth between the programs many times a second, creating the illusion that each is completely in charge of the machine. Multitasking allows a user to perform several tasks at once, or, in multiuser systems, allows several people to use the same computer at once.

multiuser system   A computer system in which multiple keyboards and video displays are connected to one machine. All users may work in the same program at once, or the machine may use multitasking to allow individual users to run different programs at the same time.

network   See *local area network.*

numeric keypad   The part of a keyboard in which the number keys are arranged in a square for rapid data entry. In most software, it doesn't matter whether you enter a number through the numeric keypad or by one of the number keys along the top row of the keyboard.

NumLock   A keyboard key that toggles the numeric keypad between two modes. In one mode, the keypad is used for entering numbers; in the other, it is used for moving the cursor or scrolling.

off-hours backup   A backup that is performed automatically while the computer is not in use. A tape backup unit is normally required.

off-line   Not ready to receive data. This term is usually associated with printers and modems.

on-line   Ready to receive data. The term usually refers to printers and modems.

on-line service   A commercial service that provides data and entertainment across phone lines. Computers use modems to communicate with on-line services.

operating environment   An extention to DOS, such as Windows or DesqView, that makes DOS easier to use, allows you to run several programs at once, and makes more memory available. Programs specially written to work with particular operating environments may take on features of the environment, including a graphical user interface and the ability to transfer data directly to other programs.

operating system   The basic software that runs the machine, such as DOS or OS/2. A primitive part of the operating system called the BIOS is built into the machine. Part of the operating system is always kept in memory. Other parts are utility programs that are loaded as they are needed.

orphaned clusters   A cluster (group of disk sectors) that has been accidentally cut off from the file it was associated with. The disk's file allocation table (the mechanism by which a disk tracks files from cluster to cluster) considers the cluster to still be in use, and so the disk space cannot be allocated to another file.

OS/2   An advanced operating system intended to replace DOS, at least in powerful PCs. Unlike DOS, OS/2 can run several programs at once. It offers a number of advanced features, including a graphical user interface called the Presentation Manager.

overlay   Part of a program that is kept on disk until it is required; it is then read into memory on top of some other part of the program (which may itself later be read back into memory at the same place). In this way, scarce memory is conserved by having a program share one section of memory between several parts of the program.

overlay file   A file that contains a program overlay. Overlay files must be in reach of the program that uses them or the program will not be able to operate properly.

overrun   A kind of data loss. Overruns occur during data communication when data arrives more quickly than the receiving electronics or software can process it.

overwrite   To write new data on top of older data, destroying the older data.

parallel port   An electrical circuit, and electrical socket, through which a computer is connected to various devices, especially printers. Parallel ports are called parallel because they send a byte of data in parallel, eight bits at a time across eight separate lines. Compare this to a serial port in which a byte of data is sent one bit at a time across a single line (such as a telephone line).

parameter   A word, number, or symbol that is typed after a command to further specify how the command should function. For example, many DOS commands require parameters to specify which file a command should operate on. In the expression COPY MYFILE.TXT A:, the COPY command has two parameters, the first of which names the file that is to be copied (MYFILE.TXT), and the second of which indicates the destination of the copy, in this case drive A.

parent directory   The directory that holds another directory. In \PLANTS\TREES\WILLOWS, TREES is a parent directory of WILLOWS, PLANTS is a parent directory of TREES, and the root directory is the parent directory of PLANTS.

parity bit   In serial communications, a parity bit may be added to the end of every byte of data that is transmitted. When the byte arrives at the receiving station, the parity bit is tested to see if an error was introduced into the data as it was transmitted.

partition   A section of a hard disk's total capacity that is accessed under a single drive specifier. For example, a hard disk may be divided into three partitions named C, D, and E. Some partitions may be devoted to operating systems other than DOS and cannot be accessed by DOS.

partitioning   The process of dividing a hard disk's capacity into partitions. Partitioning is performed by the DOS FDISK program after low-level formatting and before high-level formatting.

partition table   A table kept in a hard disk's boot record that keeps track of how many partitions the disk has and where each begins.

PATH   A DOS command that configures DOS to automatically search for a program file in specified directories when the file is not found in the current directory.

peer-to-peer LAN   A local area network in which there is no central controlling computer.

PgDn   A keyboard key that causes displayed text to scroll upward by one screenful.

PgUp   A keyboard key that causes displayed text to scroll downward by one screenful.

physical drive   A term used in opposition to logical drive. A single hard disk may be partitioned into two or more logical drives named C, D, and so on. Conversely, special software can combine the space on two physical hard disk drives so that they appear as one logical drive, C.

platter   Hard disks have multiple disks turning in parallel. Each disk is referred to as a platter.

plotter   A kind of printer that uses pens to make technical drawings.

port   A point of connection between a computer and other electrical devices, such as printers, modems, mice, scientific instruments, and so on. A port is an electrical circuit that presents a socket, usually at the back of the machine, to which a device is connected. There are a number of different kinds of ports, including serial ports, parallel ports, mouse ports, and game ports, some of which may be built into the computer, and some added through expansion boards.

port address   A number used by software to access a peripheral device, such as a disk drive or printer. Port addresses range from 0 to 65535. Occasionally hardware must be configured so that it uses port addresses that do not conflict with those used by other hardware. These software ports are not to be confused with hardware ports, such as serial ports or parallel ports, which are addressed by DOS using names like LPT1 or COM1.

POST   See *Power-On Self Test.*

Power-On Self Test   Built-in software that the computer runs when it is turned on to test that the machine is functioning properly.

primary partition   In DOS 3.3, a hard disk may have two partitions that serve DOS—a primary partition, which is an ordinary, bootable partition, and an extended partition, which may contain any number of volumes of up to 32 megabytes each.

print server   Software used in local area networks that manages requests for document printing from all users. Usually, a print server can send a print job to any printer in the network, no matter which computer the printer is connected to.

printer port   A serial port or parallel port through which a printer is connected to a computer.

processor   See *central processing unit.*

processor speed   The speed, measured in megaHertz (MHz— millions of cycles per second), that a microprocessor performs its simplest instructions. Every cycle is referred to as a clock. Complicated instructions, such as multiplications, may take many clocks, so there is no simple correlation between processor speed and the number of instructions a processor can perform per second.

prompt   See *DOS prompt.*

PROMPT   A DOS command that changes the form and content of the DOS prompt.

PS/2   Personal System/2. One of IBM's second generation of personal computers, featuring built-in video systems and ports. Most PS/2 machines use a Micro Channel bus, which allows more advanced communications and control between the computer and expansion boards placed in its slots. These PS/2 machines cannot share expansion boards with non-PS/2 computers.

Presentation Manager   The graphical, icon- and window-based software interface offered with the OS/2 operating system. Programs must be specially designed to operate in the Presentation Manager.

processor speed   The speed at which a computer's microprocessor runs, measured in millions of cycles per second, or megaHertz (MHz).

program file   A file that holds a program, whether an application program like a word processor, a utility program, or DOS files like COMMAND.COM. Generally speaking, program files have .EXE or .COM file name extensions. However, auxiliary files containing other parts of the program may have different extensions and you must take care that they are in reach of the main program file.

protocol   A standardized system of codes or signals. Hardware or software that adheres to a particular protocol can communicate or share data with other hardware or software that uses the protocol.

PrtSc   A feature built into any IBM microcomputer that lets you print out the current contents of the display by typing `Prt Sc` (`⇧`-`Prt Sc`). You must install the GRAPHICS program to print out a graphics display in this way. `Ctrl`-`Prt Sc` toggles the computer into a state in which everything typed at the DOS prompt is printed out along with DOS messages.

pull-down menu   A kind of menu that descends from the top of the screen to reveal its selections. This name is given because these menus work most quickly when pulled down by a mouse.

RAM   See *random-access memory*.

RAM disk   A phantom disk drive for which a section of memory is set aside to hold data, just as if it were a number of disk sectors. To DOS, a RAM disk looks like, and functions like, an actual disk drive. RAM disks are also called virtual disks.

random-access file   A data file in which all data elements are the same length. Software can calculate the location of any element and read it directly, without tracing it from the start of the file. Compare this organization to that of sequential files in which data elements have different lengths, with special characters between them. To find a particular element, software must read through each element in sequence from the beginning of the file.

random-access memory (RAM)   A computer's electronic memory in which it stores programs and data. The three basic kinds of memory used by software—conventional memory, extended memory, and expanded memory—are all random-access memory. Random-access memory loses the information it holds when the computer is turned off. Compare it to read-only memory, which permanently holds special software, such as parts of the computer's operating system.

read-only attribute   A marking in a file's directory entry that makes it a read-only file.

read-only file   A file that can be read, but not written to, and thus not changed. In DOS, read-only files also cannot be deleted, although they can be renamed.

read-only memory (ROM)   Memory that already has information written in it—information that is not erased when the computer is turned off. ROM chips built into the machine hold important parts of the operating system.

read operation   In disk drives, the act of reading one or more sectors of data from a disk.

read/write head   In disk drives, the armature that moves across the disk surface to read or write data. Most disks have a read/write head on each side. The heads move between disk tracks. Data is read as the sectors along the tracks rotate beneath the heads.

real-time clock   A battery-powered clock that keeps the time and data in a computer even when the machine is turned off. A real-time clock is different from the system clock, which is a timer created by operating system software, one that exists only when the machine is turned on.

ring topology   The organization of all computers in a local area network into a ring. Messages are passed from one machine to another in the ring, with all messages moving in the same direction.

record   In files, a record is one instance of a collection of related data. Database files typically contain many records, each holding, for example, the name, age, and height of an individual. All records in a file are the same length so that the computer can calculate the position of any record in a file and access the record directly.

record locking   An operating system facility used in networked computers. When one computer accesses a particular record in a database file, all other computers are barred from accessing the record until the first computer relinquishes it. This feature prevents two or more computers from trying to change the same data at the same moment.

RECOVER   A DOS command that recovers the fragments of a damaged file.

RMDIR   A DOS command that removes a subdirectory from a directory tree. There is also an abbreviated form of the command, RD.

root directory   A disk's main directory. All disks have a root directory, even disks that do not have a directory tree. What some call the directory on a diskette is the same thing as the root directory. Root directories have a fixed size, so they can hold only so many files. The size varies by disk type.

ROM   See *read-only memory.*

ROM BIOS   See *BIOS.*

scroll bar   In graphical user interfaces, a scroll bar is a bar placed along the edge of a window. The contents of the window are scrolled by using a mouse to click on the bar itself or buttons within the bar.

ScrollLock   A keyboard key that may toggle the scroll-lock feature on and off. When off, the cursor keys cause the display to scroll up and down; when on, scrolling is locked so that the cursor keys cause the cursor to move instead. Most software does not employ this system and the key is seldom used.

sector A tiny area on the surface of a disk that normally holds 512 bytes of data. Every sector is surrounded by markings laid down during formatting. These give the sector an identifying address and other information that enables the disk drive to read and write the data. The 512-byte sector size is a convention used on all IBM microcomputers; in special circumstances small or larger sectors may be employed.

security shell Special software that restricts the access of computer users to particular directories or files, particular programs, and particular DOS commands. A security shell inserts itself between DOS and the computer user. Using a system of passwords and authorizations, it intercepts all incoming commands, evaluates them, and restricts user access accordingly.

seek time See *average seek time.*

serial communications The process of sending or receiving data through a serial port (usually through a modem and telephone line) to a remote station, such as an on-line data service.

serial port An electrical circuit, and electrical socket, through which a computer is connected to various devices, especially modems. Serial ports are called serial because they transmit a byte of data as a series of eight bits across a single line, such as a telephone line. Compare this to a parallel port in which a byte of data is sent in parallel, eight bits at a time across eight separate lines.

sequential file A data file in which variable-length data elements are laid end to end with demarcating characters between. To find a particular element, software must read through each element in sequence from the beginning of the file. Compare this organization to that of random-access files, in which all data elements have the same length, and so software can calculate the location of a particular element. Text files are the most common kind of sequential file.

shareware Software that is distributed by passing it from user to user. Those who elect to use the program are encouraged to contact the developer and pay a small user's fee. In exchange, the developer usually provides full documentation and upgrade notices.

shell See *DOS shell.*

SHIPDISK   A short utility program shipped with many hard disks (usually on an accompanying diskette). When run, it parks the disk drive's read/write heads over an area of the disk that goes unused. Should a severe jolt slam the heads into the disk surface, no data is lost. The program should always be run before relocating the computer. Most recently made disks do not require a SHIPDISK program, however, since they automatically park their heads when the machine is turned off.

slot   See *expansion slot.*

soft error   An error occuring in disk drives or other computer hardware that is not attributable to permanent hardware damage, and thus is not likely to happen again soon. Soft errors may occur because of power surges, cosmic rays, vibrations, and other physical factors.

software installation   Generally, the transfer of program files from the diskettes they are distributed upon to a hard disk. Subdirectories of a particular name in a particular directory tree position may need to be created to receive the files. Often an INSTALL program accompanies the software to perform this task. For machines lacking a hard disk, software installation may consist of combining required files from several distribution diskettes onto one diskette used to load the program.

SORT   A DOS filter that can sort the lines of a file. It may be applied to directory listings.

source disk   In a COPY or DISKCOPY operation, the source disk is the disk from which files are copied.

spooling   The process of sending output to a printer in the background while using the computer for some other task.

stack   A place in the computer's memory where the microprocessor can momentarily store information.

star architecture   A network architecture that consists of a central control computer with all other computers in the network connected directly to it.

start bit   In serial communications, just before a byte of data is transmitted, one or more start bits are broadcast to notify the receiving computer that a byte is about to be sent.

starting cluster   The first cluster (group of disk sectors) occupied by a file on a hard disk or diskette. Every file's starting cluster is recorded in its directory entry. The file allocation table keeps track of the remaining clusters belonging to the file.

stop bit   In serial communications, one or more stop bits are broadcast after each byte of data has been transmitted to flag that the transmission is complete.

string   A sequence of characters.

structure   A collection of data organized in a particular way for software to use it.

subdirectory   A directory listed in another directory. DOS maintains subdirectories as variable-length files.

subdirectory file   A file that holds a subdirectory. Unlike a disk's root directory, which is always located in the same place on a disk and has a fixed size, subdirectories may be positioned anywhere on a disk, just like files, and may be any length.

Super VGA   An unofficial extension of the VGA video standard. It allows the simultaneous display of 256 colors in high resolution.

switch   A symbol appended to a DOS command to make it act in a special way. In DOS, all switches consist of a slash character followed by a letter. For example, the format of directory listings is changed when the /W switch is appended to a DIR command.

Sys Req   A keyboard key that may be used in networked computers to call up central control software.

system attribute   A file attribute that marks a file as belonging to the operating system.

system clock   A clock maintained by the computer's operating system. The clock is set automatically by the computer's real-time clock if it has one, or else when the user enters the time at start-up. Because the clock is implemented by software, it does not operate when the computer is turned off.

system crash   A general failure of the computer's operation. Usually the machine freezes and refuses to respond to input from keyboard or mouse. System crashes mostly result from software bugs rather than hardware problems.

system file   A file that is part of the computer's operating system.

tape backup unit   A special kind of tape recorder used for backing up data from a hard disk.

target disk   The disk to which data is transferred from a source disk.

text editor   A simple word processor.

text file   A file that holds nothing but text. A true text file contains no formatting codes or other specialized information, thus allowing it to be read by many kinds of software. These files are also called ASCII files.

text modem   See *video mode.*

token ring network   A kind of ring network in which an electronic token is passed between workstations. The token determines which machine is given access to the network at any moment.

track   A ring of disk sectors on a hard disk or diskette. Both sides of a disk are formatted into scores of concentric tracks, each divided into (typically) 9 to 15 sectors.

trackball   A device that takes the place of a mouse. Unlike a mouse, which moves across the desk surface, a trackball is stationary. It presents a billiard ball-sized sphere which is pushed in any direction to make a corresponding shift in the cursor's position on the screen.

tree   See *directory tree.*

tree diagram   A diagram of a disk's directory tree. Tree diagrams are displayed by DOS shells and other utility software.

typematic rate   The rate at which the keyboard repeatedly enters a character when that character's key is held down.

TSR   Stands for terminate and stay resident. See *memory-resident program.*

unerase program   A program that attempts to recover one or more accidentally erased files. Such programs are not infallible, and they are often useless for recovering files erased long before the program is applied.

unformat program   A program that attempts to recover as much data as possible after a disk has been inadvertently reformatted. These programs work best when they are installed on the disk before the accidental reformatting takes place.

uninterrupted power supply   An electrical device connected between the computer and the wall socket. It sees to it that the computer continues to receive power when a power outage occurs.

upload   To transmit files to a central computer. For example, a data file you wish to share with others could be uploaded through a modem to an on-line service.

utility program   Software used to manage the computer and the data it stores, such as backup programs, DOS shells, data compression and encryption software, and so on. Utility programs contrast with application programs (such as word processors and data bases) which perform the basic functions for which the computer is acquired.

vaccine program   Utility software that detects the presence of computer viruses. In some cases it may be able to remove the virus.

VDISK   A RAM-disk program that accompanies DOS.

VGA   See *Video Graphics Array*.

video adapter   A circuit board that fits into one of the computer's slots to run the video monitor. Video adapter follow video standards, such as CGA or EGA to determine a computers graphics and color capability.

Video Graphics Array   The video system built into most PS/2 machines. It includes most capabilities of the earlier EGA video standard, and adds some advanced modes that can display up to 256 colors at once.

video mode   A mode—usually one of several offered by a video adapter—that sets the way the video display operates. Video modes affect the screen resolution and the number of colors that may be shown at once. There are two basic kinds of modes, graphics modes and text modes. Graphics modes can display text, but text modes cannot display graphics (however, they can assemble special graphic characters into primitive figures). The screen is generally drawn more quickly in text modes.

video monitor   The video display tube and its casing and controls.

video system   A computer's video circuitry and video display. In combination, they determine what video modes the machine is capable of using.

virtual disk   See *RAM disk*.

virtual memory   A technique used by some operating systems, including OS/2 but not DOS, in which it appears that more software and data is loaded into memory than there is memory available. This is done by constantly swapping parts of programs and data between memory and disk storage.

virus   A maliciously devised program that attaches itself to programs and travels from machine to machine as software is passed around. Once in a computer, a virus can spread to infect numerous files on hard disks and diskettes. It may lie dormant for months before becoming active, whereupon it may destroy massive quantities of data.

voltage regulator   An electronic device that monitors the flow of electricity on its way to the computer from a wall socket. It keeps fluctuating voltage perfectly constant.

volume   Everything contained on a disk. Hard disks, however, may be partitioned to hold two or more volumes, each with its own drive specifier, own directory tree, and so on.

volume label   An electronic label that may be added to a disk. It may be up to eleven characters long and is kept in the disk's root directory. Volume labels are useful for finding out which diskette currently resides in a diskette drive. It is added to the disk during formatting, and is displayed at the top of directory listings or by the VOL command.

wild-card characters   Another name given to global file name characters.

window   A rectangular area of the screen devoted to a particular purpose. Many windows may be displayed at once with, for example, a calculator in one, a directory listing in another, and a spreadsheet in a third. Windows may overlap in some software, and you can adjust their sizes.

Windows   An operating environment that extends the capabilities of DOS by allowing several programs to be run at once, and by making more memory available to programs. Windows also provides a graphical user interface that makes DOS commands easier to use. Programs specially crafted to work with windows can use all features of this interface, including icons, pull-down menus, multiple windows, and dialog boxes.

worm   Maliciously devised software that spreads through a computer network, continuously replicating itself until the network is overwhelmed and stops functioning.

write operation   In disk drives, the act of writing one or more sectors of data to a disk.

XCOPY   An advanced version of the DOS COPY command that can copy groups of files from multiple subdirectories. It also can select files on the basis of their time, date, or archive attributes.

Index

C

D

E

Q

R

T

X

```
              BOOKS-A-MILLION
          2601 NW 13TH STREET

       GAINESVILLE    FL   32601
       STORE #0397   REGISTER #  2
       1 04 1566860121         29.95
        LESS DISCOUNT    5%     1.50-
          SUB TOTAL    :        28.45
          CLUB DIS  10 %:        2.85-
       SUB TOTAL       :        25.60
       SALES TAX  6.00%:         1.54
       CLUB MEMBERSHIP :         5.00
       TOTAL           :        32.14
       AMOUNT TENDERED :        32.14
       CHANGE DUE      :
        4  VISA              78
        16:01:52     12/16/93  WC

     ACCT NO:  4820895068855405
     EXP DATE:  0294   TR TYPE:  05
     AMOUNT:    32.14   APPROVAL 482340-016
              CUSTOMER COPY

         THANK YOU FOR SHOPPING
      AT BOOKS-A-MILLION -- GAINESVILLE
             904-376-6623
     ---------- THANKS A MILLION ! ----------
     YOUR CLUB MEMBERSHIP SAVED YOU     $3.02
```